MEMORY IN MIND AND CULTURE

This text introduces students, scholars, and interested educated readers to the issues of human memory broadly considered, encompassing individual memory, collective remembering by societies, and the construction of history. The book is organized around several major questions: How do memories construct our past? How do we build shared collective memories? How does memory shape history? This volume presents a special perspective, emphasizing the role of memory processes in the construction of self-identity, of shared cultural norms and concepts, and of historical awareness. Although the results are fairly new and the techniques suitably modern, the vision itself is of course related to the work of such precursors as Frederic Bartlett and Aleksandr Luria, who in very different ways represent the starting point of a serious psychology of human culture.

Pascal Boyer is Henry Luce Professor of Individual and Collective Memory, departments of psychology and anthropology, at Washington University in St. Louis. He studied philosophy and anthropology at the universities of Paris and Cambridge, where he did his graduate work with Professor Jack Goody, on memory constraints on the transmission of oral literature. He has done anthropological fieldwork in Cameroon on the transmission of the Fang oral epics and on Fang traditional religion. Since then, he has worked mostly on the experimental study of cognitive capacities underlying cultural transmission. After teaching in Cambridge, San Diego, Lyon, and Santa Barbara, Boyer moved to his present position at the departments of anthropology and psychology at Washington University, St. Louis.

James V. Wertsch is Professor in Arts and Sciences at Washington University in St. Louis. After finishing his Ph.D. at the University of Chicago in 1975, Wertsch was a postdoctoral Fellow in Moscow at the USSR Academy of Sciences and Moscow State University. His research is concerned with language, thought, and culture, with a special focus on collective memory and national identity. Wertsch is the author of more than two hundred publications appearing in a dozen languages. These include the volumes *Voices of the Mind* (1991), *Mind as Action* (1998), and *Voices of Collective Remembering* (2002).

Memory in Mind and Culture

Edited by

Pascal Boyer
Washington University

James V. Wertsch
Washington University

 CAMBRIDGE
UNIVERSITY PRESS

CAMBRIDGE UNIVERSITY PRESS
Cambridge, New York, Melbourne, Madrid, Cape Town, Singapore, São Paulo, Delhi

Cambridge University Press
32 Avenue of the Americas, New York, NY 10013-2473, USA

www.cambridge.org
Information on this title: www.cambridge.org/9780521758925

First published 2009

Printed in the United States of America

A catalog record for this publication is available from the British Library.

Library of Congress Cataloging in Publication data
Memory in mind and culture / edited by Pascal Boyer, James V. Wertsch.
p.   cm.
Includes bibliographical references and index.
ISBN 978-0-521-76078-2 (hardback) – ISBN 978-0-521-75892-5 (pbk.)
1. Memory – Social aspects.   2. Collective memory.   3. Recollection (Psychology)
4. Cognition and culture.   5. Oral tradition.   I. Boyer, Pascal.
II. Wertsch, James V.   III. Title.
BF378.S65M475   2009
153.1′2–dc22   2009007297

ISBN 978-0-521-76078-2 hardback
ISBN 978-0-521-75892-5 paperback

CONTENTS

CONTRIBUTORS

DORTHE BERNTSEN Department of Psychology, University of Aarhus, Aarhus, Denmark

CRAIG W. BLATZ Deptarment of Psychology, University of Waterloo, Waterloo, ON, Canada

DAVID W. BLIGHT Department of History, Yale University, New Haven, CT

ANNETTE BOHN Department of Psychology, University of Aarhus, Nobelparken, Aarhus C, Denmark

PASCAL BOYER Departments of Psychology and Anthropology, Washington University, St. Louis, MO

ANDREW C. BUTLER Department of Psychology, Washington University, St. Louis, MO

MARTIN A. CONWAY Institute of Psychological Sciences, University of Leeds, Leeds, Great Britain

AMY L. GONZALES Department of Communication, Cornell University, Ithaca, NY

ANGELA H. GUTCHESS Department of Psychology, Brandeis University, Waltham, MA

LARRY JACOBY Department of Psychology, Washington University, St. Louis, MO

ELIZABETH A. KENSINGER Department of Psychology, Boston College, Chestnut Hill, MA

ALAN J. LAMBERT Department of Psychology, Washington University, St. Louis, MO

JAMES W. PENNEBAKER Department of Psychology, University of Texas, Austin, TX

HENRY L. ROEDIGER III Department of Psychology, Washington University, St. Louis, MO

CHAD ROGERS Department of Psychology, Washington University, St. Louis, MO

MICHAEL ROSS Department of Psychology, University of Waterloo, Waterloo, ON, Canada

DAVID C. RUBIN Department of Psychology, Duke University, Durham, NC

DANIEL L. SCHACTER Department of Psychology, Harvard University, Cambridge, MA

LAURA NESSE SCHERER Department of Psychology, Washington University, St. Louis, MO

JAMES V. WERTSCH Department of Anthropology, Washington University, St. Louis, MO

HELEN L. WILLIAMS Institute of Psychological Sciences, University of Leeds, Leeds, Great Britain

JAY WINTER Department of History, Yale University, New Haven, CT

FRANKLIN M. ZAROMB Department of Psychology, Washington University, St. Louis, MO

PART I

IN MIND, CULTURE, AND HISTORY:
A SPECIAL PERSPECTIVE

Why this particular collection? There is a tide in the affairs of memory, which we thought we should take at the flood. The study of memory in cognitive psychology – one of the most venerable traditions of the discipline – has grown by leaps and bounds in the last twenty years, providing us with new tools and models, from the neural foundations of recollection to the creation and maintenance of autobiographical and historical memories (as well as many other things in between). In the same period, historians have thrown themselves with great abandon into the study of official and private memories, of celebrations and monuments, and of the invention and use of traditions. Even anthropologists have, to some extent, overcome their belief in culture as a *deus ex machina* or prime mover, and are beginning to describe it as the aggregation of myriad operations of remembrance and forgetting. Since these developments happened in isolation, as guaranteed by the cordons of academic specialization, it was time to understand how they all relate to each other.

Mere juxtaposition would be of little interest, as the lowliest search engine can do precisely that – juxtapose results, if nothing else – and especially as these are exciting times for anyone interested in memory as a psychological process fundamental to history and culture. As we report in the following chapters, in a whole variety of domains it makes little sense to think of memory as "individual" (for psychologists) or "cultural" (for historians and anthropologists), as the most fascinating phenomena occur in the individual creation of cultural and historical representations. To understand those phenomena, one should not be "interdisciplinary," if that means concocting a witches' brew of disparate results. Rather, one should ignore disciplines altogether and forge ahead, as many of our contributors are doing with blithe eagerness and thorough opportunism, using whatever tools and techniques will best further their particular interests.

So this volume presents a *special* perspective, emphasizing the role of memory processes in the construction of self-identity, of shared cultural norms and concepts, and of historical awareness. Although the results are fairly new and the techniques suitably modern, the vision itself is, of course, related to the work of precursors such as Frederic Bartlett and Alexandr Romanovich Luria, who in very different ways represent the starting point of a serious psychology of human culture.

A perspective is not a doctrine, nor should it be. This volume does not offer a definitive and synthetic view of human memory's contribution to culture and history, because that is neither possible nor desirable in the current state of our knowledge. But a perspective is what one needs as a guiding principle in the exploration of a vast literature. That is how the present volume was intended, and we hope that it will be used as a scholarly but reader- and student-friendly introduction to the domain of memory processes and their cultural effects.

1

What Are Memories For? Functions of Recall in Cognition and Culture

PASCAL BOYER

What is memory for? The easy and spontaneous answer is that "memory is for storing information about the past," "memory helps us preserve past events," and variations on that theme. But what is the point of *that*? Why should any organism have that kind of a capacity? What good is it? Surprisingly, this is not a topic that has received much attention from specialists of memory. There are, of course, many models and accounts of memory in psychology, but they generally focus on the internal workings of the organ, as it were, rather than its function in relation to the rest of human behavior. So it makes sense to ask, what does memory actually do? If we follow an organism around and try to understand its behavior, can we say that some of that behavior is influenced by memory? When? How? Perhaps, as we form a better idea of what memory does, we will be able to make more informed guesses about what memory is for and how it came to be.

MEMORY IS FOR THE PRESENT – SO WHY MEMORIES?

Obviously, we have memory because of evolution, because of the kinds of organisms we are, as a consequence of our evolutionary history. Now the past does not affect an organism, except through its consequences for present circumstances. So if we consider memory as a biological function, we are led to consider that memory is certainly not about the past but about present and future behavior. Memory has a biological function to the extent that it serves to organize current behavior.

Why would efficient behavior require any connection to the past? To answer this question, it helps to step back from what we know of memory and consider cognitive design in terms of biological engineering. Behavior should be appropriate, given the relevant features of the environment. Storing information about the past may be of use to organisms that (a) live in environments stable enough that past situations carry information about present ones; and (b) cannot directly grasp, through perceptual processes, all the relevant features of their present environment. If all a paramecium needs is information about the salinity gradient of its environment, then it needs perception but not memory, both because salinity can be directly sensed and because the environment is constantly changing. We and most other animals are more complex organisms, depending on richer information about our environments, and the relative stability of these environments means that the past carries potential information about the present.

This makes good evolutionary sense of some of our memory systems. Psychologists generally distinguish between semantic, episodic, and procedural memory stores. Having *semantic* memory, in the usual sense of stable, declarative, and accessible knowledge of the environment, allows us to extract relevant information about current situations from past state of affairs. Whatever is stable across time is in our semantic memory. In the same way, various forms of *procedural* memory (skills, expectations, priming) have a straightforward biological function. They provide fast, appropriate responses modeled by past encounters – frequent and distant in the case of skills, unique and recent in the case of priming.

In this scheme of things, it is more difficult to explain why any organisms should have *episodic* memories, or what we most commonly refer to as simply "memories" – information about unique, specific situations that they encountered in the past. What is the point of that? The answer may seem straightforward enough – we recall the past so we can learn from it – but the existence of semantic and procedural forms of memory shows that episodic memories are not really of much help. The different forms of learning observed in natural organisms, from operant and classical conditioning, to associations, to more complex forms of information-processing, all reflect the influence of past situations on present cognition – but not via memories of particular episodes. If anything, it would seem that organisms learn about the past mostly to the extent that they can extract from past situations what is *not* unique about them, and what will be relevant in the future. So why do we have this interesting, and to human minds extraordinarily important, capacity to store unique episodes?

EPISODIC MEMORY AND TIME TRAVEL

Episodic memory was originally defined as knowledge of the "what, when, where" of a scene, as opposed to information that could be extracted from either a single or multiple situations without reference to these individual situations (Tulving, 1983). The technical distinction between "episodic" and "semantic" stores captured (but also modified) a familiar if not altogether precise assumption that there is a difference between "memories" in the ordinary sense on the one hand and knowledge or skills on the other.

However, this definition in terms of what-where-when soon proved less than satisfactory. It turns out that we often have information about what-where-when for situations that we did not actually experience; conversely, many autobiographical memories lack at least some of that information. Temporal markers in particular are known to be rather poor cues in autobiographical memory (Brewer, 1988; Robinson, 1976; Wagenaar, 1986). More important, the early definition of episodic memory did not capture one of its essential features, at least in humans, namely, our capacity to *reexperience* past situations. As episodic memory often consists of imaginatively revisiting the original scene; it can be described as "mental time-travel" (Suddendorf & Corballis, 1997; Tulving, 2001).

The terms "what-where-when memory" and "mental time-travel" (henceforth WWW and MTT) correspond to distinct phenomena, accessing information about a great many unique details of past experiences on the one hand and constructing a simulation of the affective as well as sensory-perceptual experience itself on the other.

Imagery and affective tenor are essential to the specific phenomenology of recollection and trigger a powerful indication that the scene really occurred as mnemonic reconstruction depicts it, that is, it is what psychologists call a "remember," and not just a "know" memory (Roediger, Wheeler, & Rajaram, 1993; Tulving, 1985). The assumption may be misleading, as we know from research on memory illusions, but is nonetheless almost inescapable. If the memory of it feels like reliving the scene, then we think we really experienced *that* scene (Johnson & Raye, 1981; Ross, Buehler, & Karr, 1998).

AUTOBIOGRAPHICAL MEMORY FROM PHENOMENOLOGICAL RECORDS

Conway and colleagues proposed a synthetic model to summarize the connections between knowledge of self-related facts and episodic recollection (Conway, 2001; Conway & Pleydell-Pearce, 2000). Self-memory knowledge consists of a hierarchy of representations, including at the topmost level a version of one's *life-story*, a general narrative that combines several, lower-level *lifetime periods*. These correspond to such extended periods as "when I was at school" or "when we lived in Italy." Each of these periods is characterized by a set of relevant *general events*, for example, "taking the school bus," "show and tell," or "having my morning *cappuccino.*" The general event representations are themselves linked to episodic memories proper, that is, records of short specific experiences that Conway calls *phenomenological records.*

Phenomenological records have the following properties: (1) They retain summary records of *sensory-perceptual-conceptual-affective* processing derived from working memory; (2) they represent *short time slices*, typically limited to the contents of consciousness as one specific goal was being pursued; (3) these contents are represented roughly in *order of occurrence*; (4) the records are only retained in a durable form if they become *linked to knowledge* of one's own life (autobiographical facts); (5) they are recollectively *experienced* when accessed; (6) they provide *specificity* to representations of general autobiographical events; (7) their *neural correlates* may be separate from other autobiographical knowledge networks (Conway & Pleydell-Pearce, 2000). The combination of semantic memory and phenomenological records would suggest that "memories" of one's own experience come in a great variety of shapes, from the most specific – the raw record of experience, as it were – to the most abstract – the association of a mere fragment of experience with a lot of knowledge (Schacter et al., this volume).

This capacity for autobiographical memory is served by a variety of orchestrated but distinct cognitive systems. Rubin (2006), for instance, notes that recollection certainly involves modality-specific stores – memory for specific visual, auditory, and linguistic information – as well as a capacity for visual imagery (Watson & Rubin, 1996). Beyond these external sources of information, three specific capacities in particular are engaged in autobiographical recall: (1) *self-reflection* – an ability to have thoughts about one's own experiences as meta-representations (so experienced past is an experience but not a hallucination); (2) a sense of *personal agency and ownership,* which connects current thoughts and intentions to a unified self; (3) an ability to represent a *continuous self* enduring through time (Klein, German, Cosmides, & Gabriel, 2004). Impairment of any of these capacities results in dramatically altered autobiographical memory. For instance, autistic patients whose meta-representational abilities are impaired have poor autobiographical memories. The same goes for those schizophrenic patients with a disrupted sense of ownership (e.g., delusions of thought-control) (Elvevåg, Kerbs, Malley, Seeley, & Goldberg, 2003). Autobiographical memory is also poor in subjects like young children whose sense of enduring temporality is rudimentary (Klein et al., 2004).

To sum up, having episodic memories consists of constructing a plausible, seemingly veridical though vicarious form of experience from the faint cloth of records of consciousness, within the frames supplied by knowledge of one's past. The result is an imaginative engagement with the past – but what are the effects of such engagement?

MEMORIES FOR THE SELF

One main answer, from the psychological literature, is that memories constitute the self (Rubin, 1996) – a representation of distinctive personhood through particular facts "owned" by the person (Klein, 2001). This is actually a classical philosophical assumption found, for instance, in John Locke's statement that a human being is a person only to the extent that they can relate to their own, distinctive past (Locke, [1697]1975). This would imply that very young children, who seem to lack integrated autobiographical memory, are not full selves in this sense; and that amnesic patients have lost one of the essential components of the self.

The empirical evidence, however broadly consistent with this view, also gives it a particular twist, in that the capacities that support selfhood are in fact necessary for autobiographical memory. Recall of both facts and episodes from one's personal past are essential to one particular component of the self, what Ulric Neisser called a "narrative" self (Neisser, 1993), in contrast to other components, for instance, the sense of ownership of one's bodies and actions, the "ecological" self that is impaired in alien-hand or other control delusions (Boyer, Robbins, & Jack, 2005; Frith, 2005). Also, recall of phenomenal experience is useless if it is not integrated in self-knowledge (Conway & Pleydell-Pearce, 2000). This is manifest in both the development and impairments of episodic memory.

Contrary to the simple assumption that having a past directly creates a self, the developmental literature suggests that having a sense of self is a precondition for entertaining episodic memories as autobiographical. Even though we as adults can remember few, if any, episodes before the age of five, there is considerable evidence that children from the age of two maintain a considerable store of episodic memories (see, for instance, Fivush, 1997). These memories, however, are not strictly speaking *autobiographical*, as (a) they are not associated with a clear sense of distinctive personal experience (young children may represent the event as something that happened, not necessarily as something that happened to *them*) and (b) the episodes are not integrated in a causal story that would lead to one's present experience, as they are in adults (Nelson, 1988). Nelson and colleagues' systematic studies of spontaneous and cued recall show that distinct aspects of self-representation come online at different stages of development, and each of these stages is characterized by a different way of representing one's own past experience (Nelson, 2003; Nelson & Fivush, 2004). A distinction between actually experienced and imagined events predates a sense that recalled experiences are located in the past. This is true of one's own, unique past, and one's access to that past is also unique (Nelson & Fivush, 2004). Early episodic recall in children lacks the certainty that makes memory seemingly real – in psychological terms, a developed capacity for reality monitoring (Sluzenski, Newcombe, & Ottinger, 2004), a point vividly illustrated by this dialogue between father and daughter in Shakespeare's *The Tempest*:

PROSPERO

[…] Canst thou remember
A time before we came unto this cell?
I do not think thou canst, for then thou wast not
Out three years old.

MIRANDA

Certainly, sir, I can. […]
'Tis far off
And rather like a dream than an assurance
That my remembrance warrants.

Indeed, one of the components that selfhood creates is the "assurance" that memory "warrants," that the facts are indeed records of own experience rather than of dreams or fantasies. This dependence of autobiographical memories on self-representations is certainly relevant to the familiar phenomenon of childhood amnesia, a failure to retrieve all but a few of the episodes encoded before age four or five (Rubin, 2000).

Autobiographical memories, then, depend on what Conway, (1996) called a "self-system" of current goals and semantic knowledge of the self. This is clear not just in the developmental facts reviewed so far but in cultural differences as well. People in different places construe the connections between self and others in slightly different ways. They also retrieve autobiographical memories that support these implicit assumptions about selfhood. For instance, the U.S. versus East Asia difference in terms of "independent" versus "interdependent" ways of construing the self (Markus & Kitayama, 1991) is correlated with important differences in the age of first memories (later by about six months in Asia) as well as their content (more generic, with more characters, in Asia) (Ji, Schwarz, & Nisbett, 2000; Leichtman, Wang, & Pillemer, 2003; Wang & Conway, 2004). The differences in both self-image and memory may be mediated by early, culturally variable practices of child-adult dialogue about own experience (Wang, 2001). Even in terms of large-scale narrative, it would seem that autobiographical memory is driven by normative considerations, among them by a sense of what the normal cultural "life-script" is, what events punctuate it, in what order and with what results (Berntsen & Rubin, 2004; Berntsen & Bohn, this volume).

As far as impairment is concerned, here too the evidence would point to a major revision of the Lockean picture. We may expect that losing access to one's past is, in some real sense, losing access to one's self or at least to a major component of it. However, apart from exceedingly rare cases of fugue states with complete and durable retrograde amnesia, this is not what the clinical evidence suggests. On the contrary, patients do know that they have a past, and that it is connected to their personal identity. They also have access to some summary description of their own personality traits, before and after their accident (Klein, Cosmides, & Costabile, 2003; Klein, Cosmides, Costabile, & Mei, 2002a). Contrary to the classical picture, the loss of most episodic memories, even accompanied by anterograde amnesia (failure to form new memories), does not quite result in the complete loss of identity – see the famous cases of patients HM (Corkin, 2002) and KC (Rosenbaum et al., 2005). This, too, would support the notion that a large part of the sense of self, including the narrative self, is maintained by *semantic* knowledge of the past, as a frame within which recalled episodes are intelligible and provide an intuition of reality (Conway, 1996; Williams & Conway, this volume).

MEMORIES FOR SOCIAL GROUPS

What do shared memories do for social groups? Here too we find that empirical evidence to some extent challenges a common and seemingly innocuous assumption – that memories sustain a distinctive *identity*, which is what social groups need, maintain, and transmit to further generations. This is one of the main themes in what David Blight called the "memory boom" (this volume), the renewed interest of historians, anthropologists, and the general public in the collective construction of a common past. Increasingly, historians have focused on the development of memories for historical events, in the many ways in which the past is constructed, retrieved, or distorted as part of various identity projects (see, for instance, Blight, 2002, on the American Civil War) and in particular on the ways in which people associate particular places with particular visions of the historical past (see Nora,

1984, 1986; Winter, 1995, this volume). This interest in memory as an active, goal-driven process among social groups reminds one of a similar view of individual memory originally proposed by Bartlett (1932).

There is, of course, a lot of evidence for an interest-driven appropriation of the past (see, for instance, Blatz & Ross, this volume). Also, we know that ethnic or national groups are "imagined communities" as well as real ones, normative as well as descriptive (Anderson, 1983), and that nationalism creates nations rather than the other way around. That is, the specific form of the modern nation, with a common language and polity and the (often largely spurious) claim of common descent and cultural norms, owes a lot to the need to create a viable state with a common administration and educational system (Gellner, 1983). Indeed, the period of strongest emphasis on the creation of *national* states in the nineteenth century was also that of unprecedented and deliberate *invention* of "ancestral" national traditions (Hobsbawm & Ranger, 1983). A great deal of ingenuity went into the transformation of various folktales, historical memories, and cultural norms into "ethically constitutive stories," narratives that provide national histories with emotional and moral impact (Smith, 2003a). The instrumentalist vision seems to follow naturally from all this.

There is danger, though, that phrasing collective remembering in terms of constructive memory may lead to a simplistic, instrumentalist vision of shared historical narratives. Following this, people, and especially people in groups, simply adhere to the most convenient, identity-boosting, or morally satisfactory view of the historical past that is available. Indeed, collective remembering is not *just* the outcome of deliberate construction (Wertsch, this volume). The ways in which particular episodes become part of shared histories are far from simple. As Pennebaker and colleagues demonstrated on a variety of events and social contexts, the appropriation of an event requires complex *individual* processes whereby people locate historical events in relation to their own life stories (Pennebaker, Páez, & Rimé, 1997, this volume). Also, the ways people think of themselves as parts of groups is strongly constrained by individual cognition, in particular by people's essentialist assumptions about communities. Tacit assumptions about ethnicity are often derived from spontaneous, early-developed (and largely false) assumptions about living kinds. Young children, like most adults, assume that all members of an animal species possess some non-apparent, inherited, and causally efficacious "essence." Cats are what they are – and what makes them different from dogs – because they inherited some essential "catness" that makes them grow and behave the way they do (Hirschfeld & Gelman, 1999). There are many signs that this biological essentialism is activated in the representation of ethnic and "racial" groups (Gil-White, 2001; Rothbart & Taylor, 1990). The transfer of assumptions is only partial – people generally do not assume that members of distinct ethnic groups could not mate, or that their innards are different – but biological essentialism explains why claims to ethnic commonality are so easily "naturalized" and combined with claims of common descent. This also explains why even modern nationalism worked best in places where people, *pace* Gellner, already had some essentialist notion of their ethnicity before they tried to turn it into a nation (Smith, 1987).

COLLECTIVE PAST AND INDIVIDUAL COALITIONS

Precisely because memory is constructive, a causal account of social identities should include – indeed, give pride of place to – individual processes of representation of the past. This is a far cry from the ordinary, spontaneously antipsychological assumptions of both cultural anthropology and history. For a long time, cultural anthropologists and some historians have followed the recommendations of Emile Durkheim and other founders of modern sociology to ignore human psychology altogether and treat cultural facts, for example, American race concepts or Melanesian cargo cults, only at the level of the group (see, for instance, Durkheim, 1947; Hertz, 1960). The work of Maurice Halbwachs, to some extent, extended the Durkheimian vision to the problem of how memory contributes to the transmission of culture (Halbwachs, 1925; Halbwachs & Coser, 1992). Halbwachs's work is familiar to anthropologists and historians mainly because of the notion of "collective memory." This is generally taken to mean that societies or other human groups, just like individuals, do maintain memories, that is, encode events in particular ways and retrieve them to serve particular goals. It is not entirely clear, however, whether Halbwachs saw this as more than a convenient metaphor to describe the way people in groups construct a shared representation of their past (Wertsch, 2002, this volume). Although he insisted that the notion of "collective memory" was not metaphorical (see, e.g., chapter 5 of Halbwachs, 1925), his own usage was precisely just that. Also, Halbwachs often described the particular ways in which *individual* memories combined to create the illusion of a shared, unique memory, a phenomenon very close to what modern authors would describe in less misleading terms as *distributed* memory (Hutchins, 1995).

In most debates about the constitution of a collective past, it generally has been assumed that *groups* were the agents – that social groups did collectively choose and fashion some image of the relevant past. But, as Rogers

Brubaker pointed out, that is precisely what we should question (Brubaker, 2004). The notion that groups are agents is a claim that we should analyze and explain – not one that we should take as the straightforward expression of a fact of the matter, even less as a sound analytical principle. Once we have discarded Durkheim's illusions and Halbwachs's metaphors, we are faced again with the difficult questions, why people in groups cooperate in such a way as to create a common identity, and why specific memories should play an important role in that process.

Most evolutionary anthropologists and psychologists would answer the first question in terms of human "groupishness," a disposition for creating social categories in which different agents can be placed, and interacting on the basis of these categorical affiliations. This disposition is very familiar to all social psychologists, ever since the first experiments on "minimal groups" (Asch, 1955; Tajfel, 1970) in which people spontaneously created within-group solidarity and intergroup caution on the flimsiest possible basis, for example, having been randomly assigned different color labels by an experimenter. Is there a deep, evolutionary background to this phenomenon? Some models of early human social evolution lay great stress on the formation of "communities of norms," within which there was a high degree of solidarity, conformity, and punishment of defectors (Gintis, 2000; Richerson & Boyd, 2006). Other models, in contrast, emphasize the fluidity of social groups among early modern humans (Cosmides & Tooby, 1992). The question of the evolutionary origins of human cooperation and coordination, which are unique even among primates, is by no means solved in either type of model. But both imply that in situations of uncertain cooperation with nongenetically related strangers, humans needed a whole suite of specific cognitive dispositions: for reciprocal altruism (Trivers, 1971), for maintaining coalitions (Kurzban & Leary, 2001; Kurzban, Tooby, & Cosmides, 2001), for the identification of reliable, trustworthy partners (Bacharach & Gambetta, 2001; Kuran, 1998), for the detection of cheaters (Cosmides & Tooby, 1992), and for signaling one's own willingness to contribute to common goods (Frank, 1988).

Given this psychological background, why are historical memories particularly important? The best place to start is with the contrast between collective remembering and scholarly history as presented and explained by Wertsch (this volume). The differences – in terms, for instance, of goal-driven, morally laden narratives versus method-driven, supposedly dispassionate scholarship – are salient to us mostly because we are school-educated *and* participate in national identities. But note that an interest in archiving the past preceded the development of the specific *metier* of modern historians. Indeed, the practice of chronicling the past – that is, storing memories following a particular method rather than a specific purpose – may be found, to some degree, in most societies with important social stratification and social inequality (Brown, 1988). It would be unfortunate to think that historiography as a practice only appeared with a Western interest in history (Goody, 2006). So the contrast is not so much between modern scholarly history and collective remembering as between chronicles and arguments.

As Wertsch points out, adherence to a specific version of the historical past is often a highly antagonistic phenomenon (this volume). Memories of the rape of Nanking may well owe some of their modern salience for Chinese people to the stubborn and quasi-official Japanese denial of the atrocities (Buruma & Yoshida, 2006). In a converse and perverse way, Holocaust deniers draw some of their animus and energy from the fact that the Nazi camps are extensively remembered and commemorated (Vidal-Naquet, 1992). This would suggest that the "contested past" matters precisely because it is contested. Shared narratives of the historical past are all the better when they are such that others, and especially *identified* others, could not possibly endorse them. This applies well, for instance, to the national theme of Russia as the victim of periodic, unprovoked, and treacherous attacks from foreigners, a claim that seems almost calculated to be unpalatable for the Swedes, Frenchmen, Poles, and assorted Asian nations that figure in Russian collective remembering (Wertsch, this volume). This would suggest that the construction of a collective past is perhaps a modern by-product of our coalitional psychology. What is modern about it, in contrast to the narratives of small-scale oral cultures, is a focus on actual events that engaged more than one ethnic group. What is coalitional is the emotional attraction of narratives that would offend the other participants.

MEMORY AS A TOOL?

Let me return to the question of adaptive function. So far, I have emphasized some of the effects of constructing memories, in both individuals (the materials of a stable self) and groups (emotionally laden identity). In both domains, I argued that we can only understand the effects of memories if we focus on cognitive capacities and dispositions *other* than memory itself – the development of self-representations in the first case and coalitional psychology in the other. If episodic recall and time-travel have all these effects, what is their original function in cognitive evolution? Since this is, in the state of our knowledge, a rather speculative question, let me review some serious candidates and evaluate to what extent they fit the picture of memory as a part of imagination.

Memory and Foresight

One hypothesis is that episodic memory is of crucial importance in thinking about future contingencies. Indeed, this is the main function ascribed to "mental time-travel" in Tulving's account (Tulving, 1999, 2001). The engagement of episodic recall in the service of foresight is also predicted on the basis of functional and comparative evidence (D'Argembeau & Van der Linden, 2006). From an evolutionary standpoint, Suddendorf and Corballis argued that mental time-travel, like other memory systems, is not so much about the past as about current decision making (Suddendorf & Corballis, 1997, 2007). In this perspective, episodic recall evolved as a precious way of providing relevant information to organisms faced with complex choices. In particular, a store of accessible past situations, together with most of their experiential material, would provide organisms with a range of examples against which to compare present situations and select the most beneficial course of action. This would suggest that MTT is a recent adaptation, connected with the sudden increase in cognitive flexibility that accompanied the transition to modern *Homo sapiens* (Mithen, 2002, 2007). This is consistent with the connection between MTT and other capacities such as language, meta-representation, and controlled imagination. Indeed, Suddendorf and Corballis (2007) have recently argued that mental time-travel and foresight – imaginative construction of possible outcomes of present situations – evolved as a unique capacity, and that memory evolved as a guide to the construction of specific possible futures.

Case-Based Reasoning and Inferential Scope

As some evolutionarily minded authors have argued, the complexity of many situations of interaction creates a computational bottleneck, such that it becomes difficult to create appropriate behavioral responses on the hoof (Boyer & Barrett, 2005). For instance, typical social interaction in a small group implies computing the different agendas, relative positions, and differential access to knowledge of n participants as well as $n!$ social relations, a cognitively intensive task that would preempt quick and appropriate responses (Malle, 2004). In contrast, an organism equipped with a store of preconstrued, similar situations (recalled, imagined, or anticipated) may be able to bypass this computational bottleneck by directly accessing precomputed responses to those counterfactual scenarios (Boyer, 2007). From a different perspective, in a general survey of memory systems (Klein, Cosmides, Tooby, & Chance, 2002b) and an application to memories of self and others' personalities (Klein, Cosmides, Tooby, & Chance, 2001), Klein and colleagues suggested that episodes may help constrain inferences from summary (or more generally, semantic) information.

Social and Epistemic Vigilance

Unsurprisingly, many specific cognitive adaptations stem from the extreme complexity of social interaction in humans, relative to other primates. Any population in which most people tend to cooperate is a heaven-sent gift to cheaters and defectors. This opportunity for the evolution of free-riders is a constant threat on the stability of cooperation. So it would make great sense to store episodes of social interaction in great detail as a means to form impressions about the reliability of other agents (Cosmides & Tooby, 2000). Crucially, our impressions of others should be revisable, given their subsequent behaviors. Such revision is efficient if we can revisit past episodes and give new meaning to details that were of no consequence at the time – a routine occurrence in human memory (Hoffrage, Hertwig, & Gigerenzer, 2000). Also, other people may put us at risk by propagating false information, on the basis of which it would be unwise to act (Sperber, 2006). Gauging the reliability of different sources of information is routine business for humans (Bergstrom, Moehlmann, & Boyer, 2006; Koenig, Clément, & Harris, 2004) and in most cases requires revisiting a series of past statements made by different persons, which in turn requires detailed episodic records.

These functional aspects of episodic memory are probably part of a proper evolutionary account of the capacity – indeed, there is no reason to think that they are mutually exclusive. For now, they must remain largely speculative. This is not because all evolutionary accounts are confined to speculation. They are not, once one bothers to consider their implications in some detail and derive from them some testable predictions (Ketelaar & Ellis, 2000). That particular work remains to be done, as far as memory functions are concerned.

However, the functions listed here may not be sufficient to explain the phenomenology of episodic recall. As Conway, Rubin, and their colleagues have emphasized, one crucial aspect of recollection is its affective component and imagery – the possibility of experiencing (at least part of) the emotional impact as well as the details of the revisited scene (Conway &

Pleydell-Pearce, 2000; Rubin, Schrauf, & Greenberg, 2003). This is a constant feature of autobiographical memory and certainly a crucial difference between "what-where-when" recall on the one hand and "mental time-travel" on the other. That memory brings back the affective flavor of particular scenes is not altogether easy to explain in terms of the functional accounts described earlier. That is, all that is required to limit our inferences, to keep an eye on possible cheating and misinformation, to create a catalogue of social situations, is to maintain an extensive database of details about what happened to whom, when, and where. But it does not seem to require how past situations felt like and to reexperience their emotional impact.

BEYOND MEMORY: THE ADAPTIVENESS OF IMAGINATION

What is the point of having affective memories? The question may become more tractable if we keep in mind that memory is only part of a range of distinctly human cognitive capacities, having to do with *representation of what is not actually the case.* One important feature of human cognition, which on the face of it is rather puzzling, is that many of our thoughts are about objects and situations that just do not exist. That is, a great deal of thinking is about what might happen if such and such were the case (even though it is not the case), what would have happened if things had turned out differently (but they did not), what will happen once something particular occurs (but it hasn't occurred yet), and what conditions once obtained (but are no longer the case). Also, many of our thoughts and feelings are about people who are not physically present with us; indeed, some are dead or unborn. Finally, all human beings spend a great deal of time having thoughts and feelings about imaginary beings, from the characters of films and novels to the monsters of our childhood or the fantasies of adult life. In other words, a great deal of mental activity is about what just ain't so.

This is puzzling, or rather it should be puzzling. Why spend so much of our cognitive resources on situations and objects that are just not real? This seems doubly costly. First, some of our cognitive resources are diverted from more useful purposes. As you watch Shakespeare's play and empathize with Othello's rage or Desdemona's plight, you are not acquiring information about people with whom you will actually interact. Second, a mind that is full of representations of imaginary situations may be in danger of mistaking them for the real thing. It would seem really maladaptive to assume that real bears are as approachable as Baloo in Kipling's *The Jungle Book.*

Talking about the many ways in which the mind disconnects from reality has not been, and still isn't, at the forefront of psychologists' attention. Very few experimental psychologists or neuroscience specialists focus on domains such as pretence, counterfactuals, and our enjoyment of imaginary worlds. This is, of course, unfortunate, given that the capacity is so crucial to human cognition.

It may seem that our fondness for imaginary stuff is just a strange and perhaps inevitable *by-product* of having a complicated mind. Computer viruses get a system to run pointless or dangerous tasks instead of doing useful work, so perhaps fiction, fantasies, and hypotheses are viruses of the mind. But the virus comparison does not do justice to the fact that our imagination capacity is, in many circumstances, highly functional. To see how that can be the case, consider our thoughts about people. We often think about people who are not around. Memories of what people did or said, as well as expectations, fears, and hopes of what they may do, are a constant theme of trains of thought and ruminations (and also the quintessential subject matter of social gossip). It may be a special feature of the human mind that we can create such representations and, more importantly, run social inferences about them. It is certainly a central capacity of human thinking; it appears early, and it is universal and distinctive of normal human minds.

There is some evidence that imaginary practice supports actual performance. For instance, many children have imaginary friends with whom they entertain stable and complex relationships as well as, in some cases, sustained conversations (Taylor, 1999). Children who do have such companions seem to develop social skills earlier. Contrary to widespread anxiety among parents, a relationship with an imaginary person does not make you oblivious of real ones but even more skilled in interacting with them (Taylor, 1999). This also may explain the universal human penchant for stories and the universal capacity to follow and enjoy fiction (Zunshine, 2006).

It makes good sense to consider memory as a member of this impressive suite of tools for representing nonexistent states of affairs. True, memory is at least in principle about what really happened, but, as I said earlier, that does not matter to present fitness. From the evolutionary standpoint, it is quite untrue, *pace* T. S. Eliot, that:

> Time present and time past
> Are both perhaps present in time future
> (*Four Quartets:* "Burnt Norton")

On the contrary, past is of no moment, and memory should be seen as one of the forms of imagination. As Hobbes put it, "Imagination and memory are but one thing, which for diverse considerations hath diverse names" (*Leviathan*, II-1). The notion is central to classical theories of memory as imagination of the past and foresight as memory for future events. It receives some support from recent neuroimaging studies showing that imagining future circumstances modulates activation of the same cortical networks as remembering past episodes (Addis, Wong, & Schacter, 2007; Schacter, Addis, & Buckner, 2007). For instance, imagining future schema-driven events such as birthdays seems to recruit similar neural resources as episodic recall of past ones (particularly visuospatial imagery). There are also differences, notably engagement of regions associated with motor imagery in the future event conditions. Both future and past imagery are neurally distinct from counterfactual scenarios, such as imagining another person in similar circumstances (Szpunar, Watson, & McDermott, 2007).

MEMORIES AS CONSTRAINTS?

Imagination is generally construed as a form of liberation, a process whereby the mind breaks its shackles and can envisage situations and issues far beyond its evolutionary heritage (Mithen, 1996). Similar arguments have been applied to episodic recall, inasmuch as it makes the modern mind better equipped to foresee possible occurrences in an uncertain future (Suddendorf & Corballis, 2007; Tulving, 1999). Terms such as "fluidity" or "flexibility" generally convey this idea. From an evolutionary standpoint, the notion is slightly puzzling (Boyer, 2000, 2007). A more "flexible" mind is not necessarily better at any particular problem, so that the selective pressure for this kind of development seems minimal. More importantly, imagination and memory actually are as *constraining* as they are *liberating*, and that fact may be crucial to their evolution.

As I noted earlier, humans are special in that they engage in nonopportunistic or other-regarding behaviors, in which they benefit others without a direct return in terms of one's own fitness. These behaviors have long been a mystery to economists. However, a wealth of data from experimental economics had shown that other-regarding dispositions are general and stable (McCabe & Smith, 2001), and that they organize even supposedly rational markets (Smith, 2003b). Economic theory now includes various types of models for the stability of such cooperation norms (Bowles, 2003; Gintis, 2000). Modern humans developed complex social systems because of a suite of prosocial dispositions and capacities. In this as in other domains, evolution created motivational proxies for adaptive fitness. People do not engage in prosocial behaviors because they judge those to be ultimately adaptive or even potentially beneficial – indeed, the benefits of cooperation often take a long time to become apparent. People cooperate because of intuitive, often emotion-based, preferences for prosocial behavior (Fessler, 2001; Gintis, 2000).

This is important because prosocial dispositions are in general on a collision course with our motivational systems. One of the major hurdles for cooperation is that its benefits are in the future and the sacrifices that it entails are (in general) to be made right away. Conversely, failing to cooperate may bring about negative outcomes, but (in general) that will happen in the future. One of the most general psychological principles is that later counts for less than now; in other words, people, like all other animals, engage in *time-discounting* (Rachlin, 2006). The value of future rewards is always downplayed, as it should be. Future rewards impinge on fitness only if they do occur. So their role in guiding behavior should be modulated by the probability of their occurrence, which diminishes as they recede into the future (Ainslie, 1975; Loewenstein & Elster, 1992; Loewenstein & Read, 2003).

So what could motivate us toward prosocial behaviors, in which we often need to prefer larger-later rewards (e.g., the establishment of good cooperation relations, a good reputation, a network of grateful friends) to smaller-sooner ones (e.g., cheating and pilfering when possible, being less than altogether generous)? Punishment and rewards are no complete solution, as they, too, will occur in the future and are therefore time-discounted. Some economists have suggested that *emotions* may play that motivational role (Frank, 2001). To the extent that prosocial plans make us feel good (and antisocial ones make us feel bad) *right now*, they may provide rewards that compensate the discount curve and make us choose larger-later, virtuous rewards against smaller-sooner, opportunistic ones. In that sense, emotions such as shame, pride, and guilt may constitute commitment devices that force us to be more prosocial than purely rational, opportunistic agents (Fessler, 2001).

This argument could also apply to affective recall. Episodic memory does activate emotional neurocognitive circuitry (Damasio et al., 2000). Moreover, this affective coloring of recollection is only partly driven by executive processes. The experience of involuntary, unpleasant, or undesired memories is a common one. Finally, an increasing body of evidence shows the crucial contribution of emotion to decision making (Ursu & Carter, 2005). In particular, emotions connected to episodes constitute self-persuasion devices (Albarracín, 2002), especially when there is no clear way to explain away the emotion, and when it comes from one's own experience (Albarracín & Kumkale, 2003).

Memories and fantasies can play the role of a brake on impulsiveness and a boost on prosocial patience only to the extent that they are fairly accurate versions of what we did and what we will experience. They make us feel, right now, all the consequences of our actions, by way of emotional rewards. This means that memory for affect should not be revisable. Indeed, despite a large literature focusing on memory distortions (see the survey in Roediger, 1996), it is remarkable that people seem rather accurate in their evaluation of past emotions. In a series of naturalistic studies, Levine and colleagues only found evidence for very limited distortion in a small minority of subjects (Levine, 1997; Levine & Bluck, 2004). Memory for emotions, then, does not align with our current goals. This is especially striking in the common phenomenon of rumination, the unwanted but persistent activation of thoughts concerning an unpleasant past situation (Wèanke & Schmid, 1996). Rumination is triggered by awareness that one failed to reach a specific goal. It becomes worse if the goal was more important to the subject; it stops if the subject finds an alternative way to reach the goal or discards it altogether (Martin & Tesser, 2006; Teasdale & Green, 2004).

So imagination and memories may well be functionally adaptive – not because they liberate us from down-to-earth, here-and-now cognition but, on the contrary, because they constrain our planning and decision making in efficient ways.

CONCLUSION: THE LONG MARCH TO FUNCTIONAL ACCOUNTS

So far, I have mostly discussed memories rather than memory. If there is one general lesson from the extraordinary development of our knowledge of brains and memory systems, it is that it makes little sense to talk about a general faculty of memory. Memory systems are diverse. It follows that functional accounts should be diverse too. Interestingly, very few psychologists have ventured to consider properties of memory systems in functional terms, with notable exceptions (see Anderson & Milson, 1989; Anderson & Schooler, 2000; Klein et al., 2002b; Nairne, Thompson, & Pandeirada, 2007; Tulving, 2001).

Why are functional models so few and far between? One reason is that it is not always clear how a functional account would differ from an account of what a cognitive system actually does. But there is a crucial difference. Consider, for instance, the capacities to read and write, which serve a specific communicational function. They are supported by two other cognitive capacities (shape recognition and speech perception) that serve other, distinct functions. Our literacy capacities are derivative; they ride piggyback on functional cognitive systems that would exist, literacy or not. The only principled way to distinguish function from accidental capability is in terms of adaptive function, seeing different cognitive capacities as features of organisms that evolved under the pressure of natural selection (Cosmides & Tooby, 1994; Nairne et al., 2007). To the extent that complex design supports an increase in an organism's fitness (relative to close, equally possible designs) and is influenced by genetic inheritance, it can be described as a functional adaptation (Williams, 1966). Obviously, any such account should be evaluated against the hypothesis that the capacity has no specific, and therefore no adaptive, function, and that it is a direct by-product of other, properly functional features (Buss, Haselton, Shackelford, Bleske, & Wakefield, 1998).

In the past fifty years or so, our knowledge of how memories impinge on the individual and collective lives of humans has increased enormously, as a result of ever finer-grained behavioral protocols, neuroimaging techniques, and neuropsychological case studies, as well as the consideration of cultural transmission and acquisition and the construction of a shared past. All of this makes it possible to generate precise, predictive functional models for varieties of memory-systems in terms of cognitive adaptations. It may be time to go back to the evidence and test the implications of these various functional models, to understand why we have memories.

REFERENCES

Addis, D. R., Wong, A. T., & Schacter, D. L. (2007). Remembering the past and imagining the future: Common and distinct neural substrates during event construction and elaboration. *Neuropsychologia, 45*(7), 1363–1377.

Ainslie, G. (1975). Specious reward: A behavioral theory of impulsiveness and impulse control. *Psychological Bulletin, 82*(4), 463–496.

Albarracín, D. U. (2002). Cognition in persuasion: An analysis of information processing in response to persuasive communications. In M. P. Zanna (Ed.), *Advances in experimental social psychology* (Vol. 34, pp. 61–130). San Diego, CA: Academic Press, Inc.

Albarracín, D. U., & Kumkale, G. T. (2003). Affect as information in persuasion: A model of affect identification and discounting. *Journal of Personality and Social Psychology, 84*(3), 453–469.

Anderson, B. R. (1983). *Imagined communities: Reflections on the origin and spread of nationalism*. London: Verso.

Anderson, J. R., & Milson, R. (1989). Human memory: An adaptive perspective. *Psychological Review, 96*(4), 703–719.

Anderson, J.R., & Schooler, L.J. (2000). The adaptive nature of memory. In E. Tulving & F.I.M. Craik (Eds.), *The Oxford handbook of memory* (pp. 557–570). New York, NY: Oxford University Press.

Asch, S.E. (1955). Opinions and social pressure. *Scientific American, 193*(5), 31–35.

Bacharach, M., & Gambetta, D. (2001). Trust in signs. In K.S. Cook (Ed.), *Trust in society* (pp. 148–184). Series on Trust, vol. 2. New York: Russell Sage Foundation.

Bartlett, F.C. (1932). *Remembering. A study in experimental and social psychology.* Cambridge: Cambridge University Press.

Bergstrom, B., Moehlmann, B., & Boyer, P. (2006). Extending the testimony problem: Evaluating the truth, scope, and source of cultural information. *Child Development, 77*(3), 531–538.

Berntsen, D., & Rubin, D.C. (2004). Cultural life scripts structure recall from autobiographical memory. *Memory & Cognition, 32*(3), 427–442.

Blight, D.W. (2002). *Race and reunion: The Civil War in American memory.* Cambridge, MA; London: Harvard University Press.

Bowles, S. (2003). *Microeconomics: Behavior, institutions, and evolution.* New York, Princeton, NJ, Oxford: Russell Sage Foundation & Princeton University Press.

Boyer, P. (2000). Evolution of a modern mind and origins of culture: Religious concepts as a limiting-case. In P. Carruthers & A. Chamberlain (Eds.), *Evolution and the human mind: Modularity, language and meta-cognition* (pp. 93–112). Cambridge: Cambridge University Press.

(2007). Specialised inference engines as precursors of creative imagination. In I. Roth (Ed.), *Imaginative minds* (pp. 239–258). London: British Academy.

Boyer, P., & Barrett, H.C. (2005). Evolved intuitive ontology. In D. Buss (Ed.), *Handbook of evolutionary psychology* (pp. 96–118). New York: John Wiley.

Boyer, P., Robbins, P., & Jack, A.I. (2005). Varieties of self-systems worth having. *Consciousness and Cognition: An International Journal The Brain and Its Self, 14*(4), 647–660.

Brewer, W.F. (1988). Memory for randomly sampled autobiographical events. In U. Neisser & E. Winograd (Eds.), *Remembering reconsidered: Ecological and traditional approaches to the study of memory* (pp. 21–90). New York, NY: Cambridge University Press.

Brown, D.E. (1988). *Hierarchy, history, and human nature: The social origins of historical consciousness.* Tucson: University of Arizona Press.

Brubaker, R. (2004). *Ethnicity without groups.* Cambridge, MA: Harvard University Press.

Buruma, I., & Yoshida, T. (2006). The making of the "Rape of Nanking": History and memory in Japan, China, and the United States. *The New York review of books, 53*(14), 5.

Buss, D.M., Haselton, M.G., Shackelford, T.K., Bleske, A.L., & Wakefield, J.C. (1998). Adaptations, exaptations, and spandrels. *American Psychologist, 53*(5), 533–548.

Conway, M.A. (1996). Autobiographical knowledge and autobiographical memories. In D. Rubin (Ed.), *Remembering our past. Studies in Autobiographical Memory* (pp. 67–93). Cambridge/New York: Cambridge University Press.

(2001). Phenomenological records and the self-memory system. In C. Hoerl & T. McCormack (Eds.), *Time and memory: Issues in philosophy and psychology* (pp. 235–256). Oxford; New York: Clarendon Press; Oxford University Press.

Conway, M. A., & Pleydell-Pearce, C. W. (2000). The construction of autobiographical memories in the self-memory system. *Psychological Review, 107*(2), 261–288.

Corkin, S. (2002). What's new with the amnesic patient H.M.? *Nature Reviews. Neuroscience, 3*(2), 153–160.

Cosmides, L., & Tooby, J. (1992). Cognitive adaptations for social exchange. In J. H. Barkow, L. Cosmides & J. Tooby (Eds.), *The adapted mind: Evolutionary psychology and the generation of culture* (pp. 163–228). New York, NY: Oxford University Press.

(1994). Beyond intuition and instinct blindness: Toward an evolutionarily rigorous cognitive science. *Cognition, 50*(1–3), 41–77.

(2000). Consider the source: The evolution of adaptations for decoupling and metarepresentation. In D. Sperber (Ed.), *Metarepresentations: A multidisciplinary perspective* (pp. 53–115). New York: Oxford University Press.

D'Argembeau, A., & Van der Linden, M. (2006). Individual differences in the phenomenology of mental time travel: The effect of vivid visual imagery and emotion regulation strategies. *Consciousness and Cognition: An International Journal, 15*(2), 342–350.

Damasio, A. R., Grabowski, T. J., Bechara, A., Damasio, H., Ponto, L. L. B., Parvizi, J., et al. (2000). Subcortical and cortical brain activity during the feeling of self-generated emotions. *Nature Neuroscience, 3*(10), 1049–1056.

Durkheim, E. (1947). *The elementary forms of the religious life.* New York: Collier Books.

Elvevåg, B., Kerbs, K. M., Malley, J. D., Seeley, E., & Goldberg, T. E. (2003). Autobiographical memory in schizophrenia: An examination of the distribution of memories. *Neuropsychology, 17*(3), 402–409.

Fessler, D. M. T. (2001). Emotions and cost-benefit assessment: The role of shame and self-esteem in risk taking. In G. Gigerenzer & R. Selten (Eds.), *Bounded rationality: The adaptive toolbox* (pp. 191–214): Cambridge, MA, 2001, xv, 377.

Fivush, R. (1997). Event memory in early childhood. In N. Cowan (Ed.), *The development of memory in childhood* (pp. 139–161). Hove, England: Psychology Press/Erlbaum (UK) Taylor & Francis.

Frank, R. H. (1988). *Passions within reason. The strategic role of the emotions.* New York: Norton.

(2001). Cooperation through emotional commitment. In R. M. Nesse (Ed.), *Evolution and the Capacity for Commitment* (pp. 57–76). New York: Russell Sage Foundation.

Frith, C. (2005). The self in action: Lessons from delusions of control. *Consciousness and Cognition, 14*(4), 752–770.

Gellner, E. (1983). *Nations and nationalism.* Oxford, England: Blackwell.

Gil-White, F. (2001). Are ethnic groups 'species' to the human brain? Essentialism in our cognition of some social categories. *Current Anthropology, 42*, 515–554.

Gintis, H. (2000). Strong reciprocity and human sociality. *Journal of theoretical biology, 206*(2), 169–179.

Goody, J. (2006). *Theft of history*. Cambridge: Cambridge University Press.

Halbwachs, M. (1925). *Les cadres sociaux de la mémoire*. Paris: Librairie Alcan.

Halbwachs, M., & Coser, L. A. (1992). *On collective memory*. Chicago: University of Chicago Press.

Hertz, R. (1960). *A Contribution to the Study of the Collective Representation of Death*. London: Cohen & West.

Hirschfeld, L. A., & Gelman, S. A. (1999). How biological is essentialism? In S. Atran & M. D. (Eds.), *Folk-Biology*. Cambridge, MA: The M.I.T. Press.

Hobsbawm, E. J., & Ranger, T. O. (1983). *The invention of tradition*. Cambridge Cambridgeshire: New York.

Hoffrage, U., Hertwig, R., & Gigerenzer, G. (2000). Hindsight bias: A by-product of knowledge updating? *Journal of Experimental Psychology: Learning, Memory, & Cognition, 26*(3), 566–581.

Hutchins, E. (1995). How a cockpit remembers its speeds. *Cognitive Science, 19*(3), 265–288.

Ji, L.-J., Schwarz, N., & Nisbett, R. E. (2000). Culture, autobiographical memory, and behavioral frequency reports: Measurement issues in cross-cultural studies. *Personality & Social Psychology Bulletin, 26*(5), 585–593.

Johnson, M. K., & Raye, C. L. (1981). Reality monitoring. *Psychological Review, 88*(1), 67–85.

Ketelaar, T., & Ellis, B. J. (2000). Are evolutionary explanations unfalsifiable? Evolutionary psychology and the Lakatosian philosophy of science. *Psychological Inquiry, 11*(1), 1–21.

Klein, S. B. (2001). A self to remember: A cognitive neuropsychological perspective on how self creates memory and memory creates self. In C. Sedikides & M. B. Brewer (Eds.), *Individual self, relational self, collective self* (pp. 25–46). Philadelphia, PA: Psychology Press/Taylor & Francis.

Klein, S. B., Cosmides, L., & Costabile, K. A. (2003). Preserved knowledge of self in a case of Alzheimer's Dementia. *Social Cognition, 21*(2), 157–165.

Klein, S. B., Cosmides, L., Costabile, K. A., & Mei, L. (2002a). Is there something special about the self? A neuropsychological case study. *Journal of Research in Personality, 36*(5), 490–506.

Klein, S. B., Cosmides, L., Tooby, J., & Chance, S. (2001). Priming exceptions: A test of the scope hypothesis in naturalistic trait judgments. *Social Cognition, 19*(4), 443–468.

(2002b). Decisions and the evolution of memory: Multiple systems, multiple functions. *Psychological Review, 109*(2), 306–329.

Klein, S. B., German, T. P., Cosmides, L., & Gabriel, R. (2004). A theory of autobiographical memory: Necessary components and disorders resulting from their loss. *Social Cognition, 22*(5), 460–490.

Koenig, M. A., Clément, F., & Harris, P. L. (2004). Trust in testimony: Children's use of true and false statements. *Psychological Science, 15*(10), 694–698.

Kuran, T. (1998). Ethnic norms and their transformation through reputational cascades. *Journal of Legal Studies, 27*(2), 623–659.

Kurzban, R., & Leary, M. R. (2001). Evolutionary origins of stigmatization: The functions of social exclusion. *Psychological Bulletin, 127*(2), 187–208.

Kurzban, R., Tooby, J., & Cosmides, L. (2001). Can race be erased? Coalitional computation and social categorization. *Proceedings of the National Academy of Sciences of the United States of America, 98*(26), 15387–15392.

Leichtman, M. D., Wang, Q., & Pillemer, D. B. (2003). Cultural variations in interdependence and autobiographical memory: Lessons from Korea, China, India, and the United States. In R. Fivush & C. A. Haden (Eds.), *Autobiographical memory and the construction of a narrative self: Developmental and cultural perspectives.* Mahwah, NJ: Lawrence Erlbaum Associates Publishers.

Levine, L. J. (1997). Reconstructing memory for emotions. *Journal of Experimental Psychology: General, 126*(2), 165–177.

Levine, L. J., & Bluck, S. (Eds.). (2004). *How emotions fade: Valence, appraisals, and the emotional impact of remembered events.* Hauppauge, NY: Nova Science Publishers.

Locke, J. ([1697]1975). *An essay concerning human understanding* [ed. by Nidditch, P. H.]. London: Oxford University Press.

Loewenstein, G., & Elster, J. (1992). *Choice over time.* New York: Russell Sage Foundation.

Loewenstein, G., & Read, D. (Eds.). (2003). *Time and decision: Economic and psychological perspectives on intertemporal choice*: New York, NY; Russell Sage Foundation.

Malle, B. F. (2004). *How the mind explains behavior: Folk explanations, meaning, and social interaction.* Cambridge, MA: MIT Press.

Markus, H. R., & Kitayama, S. (1991). Culture and the self: Implications for cognition, emotion, and motivation. *Psychological Review, 98*(2), 224–253.

Martin, L. L., & Tesser, A. (2006). Extending the goal progress theory of rumination: Goal reevaluation and growth. In L. J. Sanna & E. C. Chang (Eds.), *Judgments over time: The interplay of thoughts, feelings, and behaviors* (pp. 145–162). New York, NY: Oxford University Press.

McCabe, K. A., & Smith, V. L. (2001). Goodwill Accounting and the process of exchange. In G. Gigerenzer & R. Selten (Eds.), *Bounded rationality: The adaptive toolbox* (pp. 319–340). Cambridge, MA: The MIT Press.

Mithen, S. (2002). Human evolution and the cognitive basis of science. In P. Carruthers, S. Stich & M. Siegal (Eds.), *The cognitive basis of science.* New York, NY: Cambridge University Press.

Mithen, S. J. (1996). *The prehistory of the mind.* London: Thames & Hudson.

(2007). Key changes in the evolution of human psychology. In S. W. Gangestad & J. A. Simpson (Eds.), *The evolution of mind: Fundamental questions and controversies.* New York, NY: Guilford Press.

Nairne, J. S., Thompson, S. R., & Pandeirada, J. N. S. (2007). Adaptive memory: Survival processing enhances retention. *Journal of Experimental Psychology: Learning, Memory, and Cognition, 33*(2), 263–273.

Neisser, U. (1993). The self perceived. In U. Neisser (Ed.), *The perceived self: Ecological and interpersonal sources of self-knowledge* (pp. 3–21). New York, NY: Cambridge University Press.

Nelson, K. (1988). The ontogeny of memory for real events. In U. Neisser & E. Winograd (Eds.), *Remembering reconsidered: Ecological and traditional approaches to the study of memory* (pp. 244–276). New York, NY: Cambridge University Press.

Nelson, K. (2003). Narrative and self, myth and memory: Emergence of the cultural self. In R. Fivush & C. A. Haden (Eds.), *Autobiographical memory and the construction of a narrative self* (pp. 1–28). Mahwah, NJ: Lawrence Erlbaum Associates Publishers.

Nelson, K., & Fivush, R. (2004). The emergence of autobiographical memory: A social cultural developmental theory. *Psychological Review, 111*(2), 486–511.

Nora, P. (1984). *Les Lieux de mémoire. I, La République.* Paris: Gallimard.

(1986). *Les Lieux de mémoire. II, La Nation.* Paris: Gallimard.

Pennebaker, J. W., Páez, D., & Rimé, B. (1997). *Collective memory of political events: Social psychological perspectives.* Mahwah, NJ: Lawrence Erlbaum Associates.

Rachlin, H. (2006). Notes on discounting. *Journal of the Experimental Analysis of Behavior, 85*(3), 425–435.

Richerson, P. J., & Boyd, R. (2006). *Not by genes alone: How culture transformed human evolution.* Chicago, IL. Bristol: University of Chicago Press; University Presses Marketing distributor.

Robinson, J. A. (1976). Sampling autobiographical memory. *Cognitive Psychology, 8*(4), 578–595.

Roediger, H. L., III, Wheeler, M. A., & Rajaram, S. (1993). Remembering, knowing, and reconstructing the past. In L. M. Douglas (Ed.), *The psychology of learning and motivation. Advances in research and theory* (Vol. 30, pp. 97–134): Academic Press, Inc, San Diego, CA.

(1996). Memory illusions. *Journal of Memory and Language, 35,* 76–100.

Rosenbaum, R. S., Köhler, S., Schacter, D. L., Moscovitch, M., Westmacott, R., Black, S. E., et al. (2005). The case of K.C.: Contributions of a memory-impaired person to memory theory. *Neuropsychologia, 43*(7), 989–1021.

Ross, M., Buehler, R., & Karr, J. W. (1998). Assessing the accuracy of conflicting autobiographical memories. *Memory & Cognition, 26*(6), 1233–1244.

Rothbart, M., & Taylor, M. (1990). Category labels and social reality: Do we view social categories as natural kinds? In K. F. G. Semin (Ed.), *Language and social cognition.* London: Sage Publications.

Rubin, D. C. (1996). *Remembering our past: Studies in autobiographical memory.* Cambridge; New York: Cambridge University Press.

(2000). The distribution of early childhood memories. *Memory, 8*(4), 265–269.

(2006). The basic-systems model of episodic memory. *Perspectives on Psychological Science, 1*(4), 277–311.

Rubin, D. C., Schrauf, R. W., & Greenberg, D. L. (2003). Belief and recollection of autobiographical memories. *Memory & Cognition, 31*(6), 887–901.

Schacter, D. L., Addis, D. R., & Buckner, R. L. (2007). Remembering the past to imagine the future: The prospective brain. *Nature reviews. Neuroscience, 8*(9), 657–661.

Sluzenski, J., Newcombe, N., & Ottinger, W. (2004). Changes in reality monitoring and episodic memory in early childhood. *Developmental Science, 7*(2), 225–245.

Smith, A. D. (1987). *The ethnic origins of nations.* Oxford, UK; New York, NY: B. Blackwell.

Smith, R. M. (2003a). *Stories of peoplehood: The politics and morals of political membership.* Cambridge; New York: Cambridge University Press.

Smith, V. L. (2003b). Constructivist and Ecological Rationality in Economics. *American Economic Review, 93*(3), 465–508.

Sperber, D. (Ed.). (2006). *An evolutionary perspective on testimony and argumentation*. Mahwah, NJ: Lawrence Erlbaum Associates Publishers.

Suddendorf, T., & Busby, J. (2003). Mental time travel in animals? *Trends in Cognitive Sciences, 7*(9), 391–396.

Suddendorf, T., & Corballis, M. C. (1997). Mental time travel and the evolution of the human mind. *Genetic, Social, & General Psychology Monographs, 123*(2), 133–167.

(2007). The evolution of foresight: What is mental time travel, and is it unique to humans? *The Behavioral and brain sciences, 30*(3), 299–313.

Szpunar, K. K., Watson, J. M., & McDermott, K. B. (2007). Neural substrates of envisioning the future. *PNAS Proceedings of the National Academy of Sciences of the United States of America, 104*(2), 642–647.

Tajfel, H. (1970). Experiments in inter-group discrimination. *Scientific American, 223*, 96–102.

Taylor, M. (1999). *Imaginary companions and the children who create them*. New York: Oxford University Press.

Teasdale, J. D., & Green, H. A. C. (2004). Ruminative self-focus and autobiographical memory. *Personality & Individual Differences, 36*(8), 1933–1943.

Trivers, R. L. (1971). The evolution of reciprocal altruism. *Quarterly Review of Biology, 46*, 35–57.

Tulving, E. (1983). *Elements of episodic memory*. Oxford: Oxford University Press.

(1985). Memory and consciousness. *Canadian Psychologist, 26*, 1–12.

(1999). On the uniqueness of episodic memory. In L.-G. Nilsson & H. J. Markowitsch (Eds.), *Cognitive neuroscience of memory* (pp. 11–42). Ashland, OH: US Publishers.

(2001). Origin of autonoesis in episodic memory. In H. L. I. Roediger & J. Nairne (Eds.), *The nature of remembering: Essays in honor of Robert G. Crowder* (pp. 17–34). Washington, DC: American Psychological Association.

Ursu, S., & Carter, C. S. (2005). Outcome representations, counterfactual comparisons and the human orbitofrontal cortex: Implications for neuroimaging studies of decision-making. *Cognitive Brain Research, 23*(1), 51–60.

Vidal-Naquet, P. (1992). *Assassins of memory: Essays on the denial of the Holocaust*. New York: Columbia University Press.

Wagenaar, W. A. (1986). My memory: A study of autobiographical memory over six years. *Cognitive Psychology, 18*(2), 225–252.

Wang, Q. (2001). "Did you have fun?" American and Chinese mother-child conversations about shared emotional experiences. *Cognitive Development, 16*(2), 693–715.

Wang, Q., & Conway, M. A. (2004). The stories we keep: Autobiographical memory in American and Chinese middle-aged adults. *Journal of Personality, 72*(5), 911–938.

Watson, M. E., & Rubin, D. C. (1996). Spatial imagery preserves temporal order. *Memory, 4*(5), 515–534.

Weanke, M., & Schmid, J. (Eds.). (1996). *Rumination: When all else fails*. Hillsdale, NJ, England: Lawrence Erlbaum Associates, Inc.

Wertsch, J. V. (2002). *Voices of collective remembering*. New York: Cambridge University Press.

Williams, G. C. (1966). *Adaptation and natural selection. A critique of some current evolutionary thought.* Princeton, NJ: Princeton University Press.

Winter, J. M. (1995). *Sites of memory, sites of mourning:* The Great War in European cultural history. Cambridge; New York: Cambridge University Press.

Zunshine, L. (2006). *Why we read fiction: Theory of mind and the novel.* Columbus: Ohio State University Press.

PART II

HOW DO MEMORIES CONSTRUCT OUR PAST?

Ever since Bartlett, psychologists have insisted that memories are *constructed*, that they should not be seen as simple and passive preservation of experiential information (Bartlett, 1932). Mental representations are not the direct outcome of physical stimuli that impinge on our sense organs; they are an interpretation of those stimuli in terms of particular concepts of objects in the world around us. In the same way, memory requires an elaboration of information about the past, including traces of experience, within meaningful schemata. Fine, but what does that mean in practice? One thing that it does *not* mean is that memories are by nature inaccurate, produced at will by the subject or by some goal-driven mechanism. Accuracy and elaboration are orthogonal dimensions, so that more elaboration does not mean that memories are not faithful to experience. Memories are constrained but also created by schemata – but how does that actually occur? That is the central question addressed by most experimental research on memory – so that giving a proper answer to the question, How are memories constructed? should take us through an exhaustive tour of memory research.

The best starting point is with the most salient and obvious kind of memories, namely autobiographical memories, information about our own past. For a long time, this domain of personal memory of experience used to be a rather marginal field in the scientific study of memory. This may seem odd. But autobiographical memory is extremely difficult to study in a way that reconciles the opposite requirements of experimental control and ecological validity. We need control in the form of precise and constant methods as well as identical stimuli for all subjects, to convince ourselves that our findings result from the factors we manipulated in our experiments. We need ecological validity, that is, some assurance that our protocols reflect processes that do occur in the actual use of memory. But autobiographical memories, by their nature, were created by "stimuli" – the subjects' own experiences – that cannot be replicated, and that the experimenter can never fully reconstitute. This once led Ulric Neisser to state as a "law" of psychology that if an aspect of memory is interesting and crucial to the use of memory, then it is probably not studied by psychologists (Neisser & Winograd, 1995). Yet a whole suite of ingenious techniques have allowed psychologists to bridge the gap between overly controlled (and contrived) experiments and ecologically sound (but anecdotal) studies of memory. Some of these are explained in the chapters that follow, ranging from diary studies to laboratory experiments to neuro-imaging.

Autobiographical memories are an essential component of the self. Locke already suggested that losing personal memories amount to losing one's identity. This seems intuitively obvious, which is why amnesia (and recovery from amnesia) has provided the right dramatic stuff for a great many plays and films. Amnesic patients seems to be literally in search of their lost selves.

But why should memories be so fundamental to identity? Note that in retrograde amnesia, when patients have no access to their past, they still retain a fair amount of knowledge about themselves. Even without remembered events, in many cases they still know the essential facts and even seem to have a fairly accurate picture of their own personalities (Klein, Cosmides, Costabile, & Mei, 2002).

So there is a paradox here. When someone remembers the plot of the play, but not the color of the actress's hat, or when they recall the gist of a newspaper article, but not the type font in which it was printed, we see that as an ordinary and indeed desirable effect of memory – the function of which is to extract the meaningful and general information from the wealth of experienced detail. But for memories of the self, we think on the contrary that losing the details of experience is tantamount to losing the whole thing, as it were.

A crucial point is that memories are related to goals – to the hierarchy of current goals that **Martin Conway** describes as the "working self" (this volume). In Conway's synthetic model of autobiographical memory, a person's self representation is organized around current goals (Conway & Pleydell-Pearce, 2000). The raw material of memories consists of records of perceptual experience in the pursuit of particular goals – but these records only make sense against semantic knowledge of one's past. In this chapter, Conway expands on the notion of constructive retrieval, describing the interplay between current goals and memory records in creating the remembering experience. Because memories depend on the current "working self," each individual possesses, not just an autobiographical memory but a set of memory networks, each of them relevant to particular aspects of current goals.

Organization into a coherent life-narrative is a crucial component of autobiographical recall. At the highest level of generality, people see their lives in terms of a coherent trajectory and perspective, but not all epochs of one's lifetime are created equal. Most writers had noted, and psychologists have confirmed, that people over the age of 30 tend to have more memories for the period between 15 and 25 than for other ages. This "bump" in the reminiscence curve does not change with age, so that even at 80 people still seem to have many more accessible memories of their youth than of any other period, excluding the months just prior to testing (Jansari & Parkin, 1996). Why is that the case? Our wistful reminiscence of those salad days does not seem to support any obvious function. But as **Dorthe Berntsen** and colleagues have shown, this privilege of youthful recollections should be understood as a way of connecting our self narrative to shared cultural models of a person's development, what she calls "cultural life-scripts" (this volume). These are idealized, simplified representations of a person's normal course through the major life events, childhood, marriage, work, parenthood, etc. Now detailed studies of life scripts show that people in a community tend to agree to a surprising degree on the timing and order of these major events, as well as their specific features and their causal connections. Our "reminiscence bump" consists to a large degree of positively valued events, situations in which we accomplished some of the goals included in our life script. In this sense, memories of youth are intrinsically normative – they tell us not just what happened but also to what extent it reflected what should have happened.

We do not just *know* what happened to us, even in great detail – we can also *recollect* it, that is, experience it with perceptual imagery (the sounds and sights of the original scene) and often with emotional engagement as well (Roediger, Wheeler, & Rajaram, 1993). The fact that we can recollect as well as know a past scene, is for us clear evidence that it really did happen (Hyman, Gilstrap, Decker, & Wilkinson, 1998). This is why autobiographical episodic memory can be called a form of "mental time-travel" (Tulving, 2001), the function of which is still mysterious (see Boyer, this volume). Since so much in the power of memory depends on the capacity for *detailed* recall, it makes sense to wonder, what processes support specific recall – as opposed to gist – and what conditions favor it. In this volume, **Dan Schacter** and his colleagues survey behavioral and neuroimaging experiments that shed light on the structures involved in creating specific memories. Psychologists commonly distinguish between implicit and explicit processes – the former being special in that they occur without the subject's deliberation or even beyond conscious access (Roediger, 1990).

A standard example is priming, whereby a previous experience (e.g., seeing the picture of an apple) makes further performance easier or quicker (e.g., completing the word "_ _ P L E"). Although priming is easy to produce, its explanation is far from simple – but it is also crucial, as the phenomenon gives us access to the way memory works. Priming reveals what kinds of mental representations and processes are activated, such that they could transfer to the further test (Roediger, Weldon, & Challis, 1989; Schacter, this volume) and therefore how memories are constructed on the hoof, as it were. In the course of investigating specificity in memory, Schacter and his colleagues also take us back to the domain of self-representation – as the richest and most specific information domain accessible to memory.

REFERENCES

Bartlett, F. C. (1932). Remembering. A Study in Experimental and Social Psychology. Cambridge: Cambridge University Press.

Conway, M. A., & Pleydell-Pearce, C. W. (2000). The construction of autobiographical memories in the self-memory system. Psychological Review, *107*(2), 261–288.

Hyman, I. E., Jr., Gilstrap, L. L., Decker, K., & Wilkinson, C. (1998). Manipulating remember and know judgements of autobiographical memories: An investigation of false memory creation. Applied Cognitive Psychology, *12*(4), 371–386.

Jansari, A., & Parkin, A. J. (1996). Things that go bump in your life explaining the reminiscence bump in autobiographical memory. Psychology and Aging, *11*(1), 85–91.

Klein, S. B., Cosmides, L., Costabile, K. A., & Mei, L. (2002). Is there something special about the self? A neuropsychological case study. Journal of Research in Personality, *36*(5), 490–506.

Neisser, U., & Winograd, E. (1995). Remembering reconsidered : ecological and traditional approaches to the study of memory. Cambridge England ; New York: Cambridge University Press.

Roediger, H. L., III. (1990). Implicit memory: Retention without remembering. American Psychologist, *45*(9), 1043–1056.

Roediger, H. L., III, Weldon, M. S., & Challis, B. H. (1989). Between implicit and explicit measures of retention: A processing account. In H. L. I. Roediger & F. I. M. Craik (Eds.), Varieties of memory and consciousness: Essays in honor of Endel Tulving. Hillsdale, NJ: Erlbaum.

Roediger, H. L., III, Wheeler, M. A., & Rajaram, S. (1993). Remembering, knowing, and reconstructing the past. In L. M. Douglas (Ed.), The psychology of learning and motivation. Advances in research and theory, Vol. 30. (pp. 97–134): Academic Press, Inc, San Diego, CA.

Tulving, E. (2001). Origin of autonoesis in episodic memory. In H. L. I. Roediger & J. Nairne (Eds.), The nature of remembering: Essays in honor of Robert G. Crowder. (pp. 17–34). Washington, DC: American Psychological Association.

2

Networks of Autobiographical Memories

HELEN L. WILLIAMS & MARTIN A. CONWAY

An individual's *autobiographical memory* is made up of their *episodic memory*, memory for specific episodes of their lives, and their conceptual, generic, and schematic knowledge of their personal history: their *autobiographical knowledge*. In a typical act of remembering, these two types are brought together and a specific memory from one's life is recalled. These autobiographical memories are the content of the self. They locate us in sociohistorical time, they locate us in our societies and in our social groups, they define the self. In important ways, autobiographical memories allow the self to develop and at the same time they constrain what we can become. In this chapter we outline a little of what is known about the representation of autobiographical memories in the mind and how they are constructed in consciousness. With this in mind, we then turn to the function that autobiographical memories have in defining the self by making certain networks of memories that ground the self in making a specific experienced reality highly accessible.

AN INTRODUCTION TO AUTOBIOGRAPHICAL
MEMORY RESEARCH

Although the formal scientific study of memory has been in existence for at least a century, since the early work of scientists such as Ebbinghaus (1885/1964), Galton (1883), and Ribot (1882), the study of autobiographical memory was neglected during much of this period as a result of the complexities associated with this type of recall. In his experimental studies, Herman Ebbinghaus tested the learning, forgetting, and relearning of relatively meaningless items, such as short lists of constant-vowel-constant (CVC) letter strings. Through these studies, Ebbinghaus was able, in precise terms, to communicate to others a great variety of aspects of memory for the first time, such as the forgetting curve. In addition to carrying out experimental studies using simple to-be-remembered materials, Ebbinghaus also attempted the study of memory for meaningful materials such as passages of prose and poetry. However, he found that memory for such materials could be influenced by too many extraneous factors that lay beyond the experimenter's control. He came to the conclusion that the study of materials over which the experimenter had powerful control, such as CVC strings, was preferential for the advancement of the scientific study of memory. This shift, from philosophical speculation to rigorous scientific methodologies, enabled researchers to communicate about their research findings and facilitated development of new research areas and approaches to memory research (Ohta, 2006). The preference for rigorous testing methods in the study of memory and the use of to-be-remembered materials selected and controlled by the experimenter led to autobiographical memories being excluded from this research domain for almost an entire century. This is because autobiographical memories are formed outside the laboratory in an individual's everyday life and their formation is in no way under the control of the experimenter.

One contemporary of Ebbinghaus did, however, attempt to study autobiographical memories in a systematic way at the end of the ninteenth century. Sir Francis Galton (1883) was interested in how many memories an individual has and developed a technique that one hundred years later became known as the *cue word* technique. In this procedure, Galton revealed words to himself, one at a time. He then noted the thoughts that passed through his mind. He repeated this procedure for his long list of words on several separate occasions. One of Galton's most interesting findings from this repeated testing was that many of the thoughts that came to mind when he presented himself with the words were (autobiographical) memories and that these memories often included an aspect of visual imagery. A related finding that disappointed Galton was that he did not seem to possess endless variety in his thoughts or memories, as he found that he often recalled the same thoughts/memories on subsequent occasions of testing. In response to this finding, he concluded that we probably have far fewer memories than we imagine we have. It is likely, however, that Galton underestimated the extent and variety of his autobiographical memories. One clear problem with the methodology that he employed is that once having recalled a memory to a cue-word, that memory is likely to have become associated with the cue-word. Therefore, it was much more likely to be recalled during subsequent testing. Despite this issue, the cue-word method remains a particularly useful technique and is still used in contemporary studies of autobiographical memory (Conway & Williams, 2008).

In addition to the texts produced by Ebbinghaus and Galton near the turn of the twentieth century, the French psychologist Theodore Ribot also studied memory at this time. His 1882 text provided psychology with one of the first theories of autobiographical memory as well as providing detailed descriptions of case studies of memory distortions and malfunction following brain injury. Other late-nineteenth-century memory researchers studied autobiographical memory (see Conway, 1990 and 2004, for reviews); however, behaviorism came to dominate psychology.

As behaviorism is based on the argument that all psychological theory should be built on that which is observable, memories became much more difficult to study. Memories cannot be directly observed, as they are internal mental states. They only can be inferred by how they influence a person's behavior, that is how they influence what an individual is able to recall in an experiment in which the conditions of encoding, retention, and retrieval are highly controlled. This type of approach became known as *verbal learning* and it dominated memory research for decades; in many respects, it still does. During this period, one researcher, Sir Fredrick Bartlett (1932), took a different standpoint on memory research. His approach holds central the concept of a *schema* (defined as a general representation of similar experiences, narrative, and cultural conventions), and social interactions and culture are also viewed as playing important roles in remembering. Detailed memories of specific experiences, what we now call episodic memories, were of little interest to Bartlett, however, and because of this his work did not reinvigorate the study of autobiographical memory.

It was not until the 1970s that the study of autobiographical memory reemerged after one hundred years of silence (Cohen, 1989), and interest from the research community accelerated from the 1980s to the present day. Until the 1970s, autobiographical memory was studied almost exclusively from a psychoanalytic or clinical orientation. The aim of such study was only diagnostic or therapeutic. There were two central factors that led to reinterest in this important aspect of memory in the 1970s. The first was the growth of *neuropsychology* as a distinct research area and within it research into malfunctions of human memory following brain damage. After traumatic injury to the brain, one remarkable finding is that virtually all impairments to memory experienced by patients include some disruption to autobiographical memory. The second factor, *cognitive science*, was becoming interested in how to model and represent stories and memories. Two important papers, by Robinson (1976) and Crovitz and Shiffman (1974), employed a cue word method similar to Galton's to investigate differences between memories. This research demonstrated an effective way in which autobiographical memory could be studied under laboratory conditions. In addition to this, papers such as Brown and Kulik's (1977) survey of *flash-bulb memories*, and the highly significant volume edited by Neisser (1982), *Memory Observed*, which reprinted many earlier papers on autobiographical memory and other areas of memory that at that time were suffering from neglect, all helped rejuvenate autobiographical memory as a research area. These were also some of the first papers that began to show the links between autobiographical memory networks (AMNs) and culture; this interplay will be discussed in detail later. It is interesting to note that this rejuvenation employed similar methods and became interested in the same areas that, since the work of Galton, Ribot, and others, had been forgotten: studying one's own memory, investigating malfunctions and distortions of memories, and surveying memories. In the last thirty-five years, psychologists interested in memory have primarily adopted a cognitive approach and seek to interpret autobiographical memory within the theoretical framework of mainstream memory research. This undertaking has been fraught with difficulty because of the great quantity and variability of the data. It is a daunting task to try to discover the general principles that govern the encoding, storage, and retrieval of personal experiences accumulated over their lifetimes by different individuals with different personal histories. Nevertheless, some progress has been made, and in the current chapter we aim to present a broad review of how cognitive psychology has come to understand the interplay that exists between memory, self, and culture within an individual's networks of autobiographical memories. First, we briefly discuss the manner in which autobiographical memories are constructed within AMNs and, second, we turn our attention to how these networks are influenced by, and in turn have influence over, the self.

MEMORY NETWORKS

Autobiographical Memory Networks consist of multiple cross-coded memories. Individual autobiographical memories may be indexed by several networks; and this is a form of "overdetermination," as described by Freud (1938). For example, recalling a specific episodic memory of meeting a girlfriend for the first time could be cued through discussion of that girlfriend, discussion of girlfriends in general, discussion of the town in which you met, or discussion of the particular bar in that town where you were working on the night that you met her. Each network of autobiographical memories will have areas of

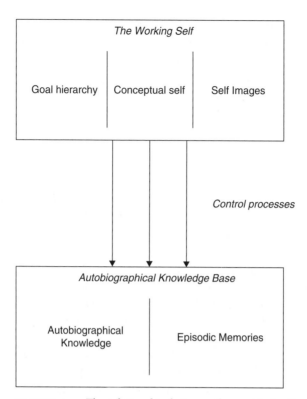

FIGURE 2.1. The relationship between the working self and the autobiographical knowledge base.

crossover with other networks. Some networks are *neural,* whereas others will extend beyond the neural and are *self* networks. Within these networks, memories are networked by their relation to a person's sense of self – more precisely, the particular version of the person's *working self,* which was active when that memory was formed. As *selves* only exist in social groups, self-networks are networks that extend beyond the neural. The *working self* and the *autobiographical knowledge base* are two significant concepts introduced to the area of memory in the last decade. They form the basis of the Self-Memory System (SMS) as proposed by Conway and Pleydell-Pearce (2000), a complex neural system that mediates autobiographical remembering (also see Conway [2005, 2007] for further explanation). The relationship between the working self and the autobiographical knowledge base is shown in Figure 2.1.

The working self functions to maintain coherence among current goals. It coordinates, manages, and prioritizes goals by modulating the construction of specific memories, determining which memories are accessible and inaccessible, and which current events are encoded and consolidated into memory (see Conway & Pleydell-Pearce [2000] and Conway [2005, 2007] for further explanation of the SMS and its components). The highly complex goal-subgoal hierarchy is hypothesized as being part of the working memory system (Baddeley, 1986, 2000), and its purpose is to regulate behavior by reducing conflict between desired goals and the current state (Conway, 2005; Conway & Pleydell-Pearce, 2000).

CONSTRUCTING A MEMORY

The construction of autobiographical memories in the SMS is based on the premise that autobiographical memories are transitory dynamic mental constructions generated from the underlying knowledge base. It is through the working self that preexisting knowledge is accessed from the autobiographical knowledge base in long-term memory and specific memories are constructed. The autobiographical knowledge base contains two distinct types of representation: *autobiographical knowledge* and *episodic memories.* Autobiographical knowledge is organized in partonomic hierarchical knowledge structures (Barsalou, 1988; Burt, Kemp, & Conway, 2003; Conway, 1996; Conway & Bekerian, 1987; & Lancaster & Barsalou, 1997), which range from highly abstract and conceptual knowledge, for example, one's "life story" (see Bluck [2003]; Bluck & Habermas [2001]; and Pillemer [1998] for more on the concept of a life story), to conceptual knowledge that is event-specific and experience-near. At a highly conceptual level lie a person's *self-images,* which divide the individual into different selves, as discussed earlier. These various self-images may have differential links to particular AMNs as they relate to a particular lifetime period, the goals that were prioritized within that lifetime period, and the episodic memories that provide evidence of goal-related progress within that lifetime period (Conway, 2005; Conway & Pleydell-Pearce, 2000). Highly accessible memories and knowledge from across the life span are thought to provide a more or less coherent story of the individual and their achievements; however, knowledge about goals that were abandoned or which the individual failed to achieve also may remain highly accessible in the memory network, as they provide directive or instructive information (Bluck, 2003; Pillemer, 1998) or provide a confirmatory context for the achievement of other goals, for example, "I wasn't a success at college and I left to earn money" (see Csikszentmihalkyi & Beattie, 1979). Memories of knowledge or experiences that contradict or undermine central facets of the working self may, however, be assigned low levels of accessibility or may be actively inhibited (Conway, 2005; Conway & Pleydell-Pearce, 2000).

So within AMNs, how is a specific episodic memory constructed? When a part of the autobiographical knowledge base is activated by a cue, this knowledge becomes available to evaluative control processes. Search can either be terminated or a new search cycle can be activated from the results of the previous search. When searching for a specific memory – for example, concerning whether you paid a bill yesterday – when you retrieve the memory of putting the bill in the mailbox your memory search may terminate. However, the result of this search may initiate another search, for example, for memories concerning what other bills you have received recently. This iterative model of memory construction called search-evaluate-elaborate (originally proposed by Norman & Bobrow [1979]; developed further by Williams & Santos-Williams [1980], Conway & Pleydell-Pearce [2000], and Burgess & Shallice [1996]), or generative retrieval, can be contrasted with direct retrieval, although the two are intimately linked, as will be explained later in this chapter. Generative retrieval involves iterative retrieval cycles of elaboration and verification. These cycles are linked to central control process and modulated by supervisory executive processes, most probably located in networks in the frontal cortex. In any memory construction situation, a crucial component is an analysis of what are the demands of the task.

It is assumed that the analysis of a task or the demands a task places on a rememberer are conducted largely by nonconscious processes. The aim of these processes is to specify the context in which the memory is to be retrieved. This is especially important because, for any given memory, there will be a wide range of information available that potentially could be brought to mind. However, not all of this information will be relevant to a particular task and some of it may be antithetical. To give a rather trivial but nonetheless important example, if one recalls where one parked ones car yesterday while trying to recall where one parked one's car today, then that might block the attempt to locate the car in the present. It is clearly important that the task demands are fulfilled or satisfied by the knowledge that is brought to mind. It is the purpose of nonconscious processes that analyze task demands to set the criteria that have to be met by the retrieval of information from long-term memory.

The resulting mental model of these task demands determines the criteria against which the accessed knowledge will be evaluated. Verification criteria will vary with the task demands, and the types of memories constructed will be determined by different sets of criteria on different occasions. For example, recalling memories with intimate others, ruminating over the past, constructing memories in order to make strategic self-disclosures in a social interaction, and even recalling specific memories at the request of an experimenter entail the generation of criteria that fit the goals of the self in each context. For example, in a social situation in which you are required to offer advice to a close friend, the goals of your current self in this situation presumably will be along the lines of being caring and supportive and the task demands will be for you to offer helpful advice. In this situation, you may need to draw on memories of being in similar advice-giving situations – what you said in those past situations, how that advice was received, and so on, as well as memories of being in a similar dilemma to the one about which your friend wishes to get advice. The memories you retrieve have to meet the criteria set by the goals of the current self, which are related to what are deemed to be the demands of the task. The verification criteria that evolve may have facilitative effects so that when any knowledge accessed in the knowledge base corresponds within some preset tolerance to the criteria, then that knowledge immediately enters into current control-processing sequences. By contrast, verification criteria may, as we have seen, have a very different purpose, namely, the inhibition of irrelevant knowledge and inhibition of access to knowledge that is prohibited by self-goals (i.e., knowledge that would result in unacceptable increases in self-discrepancies; see Conway & Pleydell-Pearce [2000] for a fuller description of this).

Within an AMN, an elaborated cue or memory description is thought to activate pathways through the knowledge base, and this activation is channeled by the indexes of the knowledge structures. As knowledge is activated, it becomes available to control processes and to the retrieval model, where it is continuously monitored and evaluated. By rapidly generating new memory descriptions and entering these into the knowledge base, a pattern of activation can be shaped that matches the criteria set down by the retrieval model. As soon as this pattern of activation is established, a memory has been constructed. Thus, by this view, a specific autobiographical memory is a pattern of activation across the indexes of the autobiographical memory knowledge base conjoined with the retrieval model used to shape that pattern.

In contrast to generative retrieval, direct retrieval does not involve any iterative search processes, although the close relationship between the two processes is shown by the fact that the endpoint in generative retrieval, when the sought-for information or memory is retrieved, is a form of direct retrieval. The most well-known account of an experience of direct retrieval comes from Proust's (1925/1981) account of how the taste of a madeline cake dipped in warm tea suddenly brought to mind a whole section of his life he had previously thought lost to recollective experience (also see Salaman [1970] for many other examples from literature, and Berntsen [1996], and see Chu and Downes [2002] for experimental evidence relating to this). Such experiences of recall from distant autobiographical experiences, however, are rare in everyday life, and direct retrieval is most evident in cases of post-traumatic stress disorder (PTSD) or for very recent experiences. In PTSD, direct retrieval manifests itself in the form of intrusive highly detailed memories often triggered by specific cues. Examples from PTSD case studies (see Ehlers et al. [2002] for case study examples, some of which are briefly discussed in Conway [2005]) illustrate that this direct retrieval is a form of the encoding specificity principle (Tulving & Thomson, 1983), that is, the idea that during retrieval some item of knowledge in the search set must correspond to an item of knowledge in the sought-for-knowledge in long-term memory. Within the SMS approach, instances of direct retrieval should be most frequent in recent memory because the objects, actions, feelings, and thoughts occurring in the recent past (perhaps twenty-four hours or less) are closely associated with current highly active and accessible goals. As these working self-goals continue to be processed, then it would seem inevitable that, by encoding specificity alone, knowledge would be processed, forming an effective cue to recent episodic memories; direct retrieval would then occur. Little is known about how the current environment, internal and external, drives direct retrieval in daily life, and this is an area that awaits investigation (but see Schank [1982] for some interesting examples). It is perhaps one of the strengths of the SMS approach that these questions concerning aspects of memory in everyday life come into a clearer perspective. Without an appreciation of the complexity of the process of appropriately creating memories in the mind, largely by nonconscious means, and then acting on the conscious outputs of the processes, that is, a memory, we cannot come to have a broader appreciation of the complexity and beauty of human remembering. The SMS approach tends to explore a model of the complexity of human remembering at the same time as relating it to the goals of the individual and the social group in which the individual exists. This latter aspect of the model is currently being worked on and it is our intention to try to link individual memories into collective memories more generally.

AUTOBIOGRAPHICAL MEMORY NETWORKS

The array of networks that link autobiographical memories together is infinite and can be idiosyncratic, but a number of overarching themes exist. Below the level of the life story where networks of memories may be formed around different self-images, conceptual lifetime periods also modulate the accessibility and inaccessibility of autobiographical knowledge and episodic memories. Lifetime periods contain representations of locations, people, activities, feelings, and goals common to the period they represent. Some examples of lifetime periods are *when I worked in Birmingham,* or *when I lived on Grimthorpe Place.* The networks of memories associated with these two lifetime periods may overlap, that is, if I lived on Grimthorpe Place while working in Birmingham. However, one period also may provide access to memories to which the other period does not have access as the overarching life themes: *work* and *home,* to which these periods relate, are different. Lifetime periods have been found to contain evaluative knowledge, negative and positive, of progress in goal attainment (Beike & Landoll, 2000), and lifetime periods may play an important role in the life story. Lifetime periods may be particularly appropriate for the generation of themes within a life story because of the goal-evaluative information they contain. For example, a lifetime period such as *when I was at graduate school* will consist of representations of people, locations, activities, feelings, and goals common to the period, but also will contain some general evaluative reflections on the period, that is, this was a particularly anxious time for me, living on my own was difficult, I was lonely, I found the work very difficult, and so on (see Cantor & Kihlstrom, 1985). Research has found that these types of evaluative themes related to the self also can be consistent across individuals for particular lifetime periods (Conway & Holmes, 2004), and will be discussed later in this chapter.

The life story, the themes within it, and lifetime periods are part of the conceptual self where they represent a summary account of the self and its history and where they can be used to initiate and focus searches of the networks of information held in the autobiographical knowledge base (Conway, 2005). Conversely, general events are more clearly part of the knowledge base itself and have an important role in organizing personal knowledge. They are a form of AMN. General events can refer to a variety of autobiographical knowledge structures such as single events, for example, the day we went to see the Statue of Liberty; repeated events, for example, work meetings; and extended events, for example, our holiday in Australia (Barsalou, 1988). Networks of general events can be structured in several different ways. For example, they can resemble "mini-histories" organized around detailed and sometimes vivid episodic memories of goal attainment in developing skills, knowledge, and personal relationships (Robinson, 1992). Networks of autobiographical memories also may exist on the basis of the memories' emotional similarity (e.g., McAdams, Reynolds, Lewis,

Patten, & Bowman, 2001) or can be organized around experiences of particular significance for the self (see Pillemer [1998], Singer & Salovey [1993], and Singer [2005] for detailed discussion on this). It is to this network we now turn.

THE SELF FUNCTION OF AUTOBIOGRAPHICAL MEMORY

Three functions of autobiographical memory are commonly discussed in the literature: a directive function, a social function, and a self function. The directive function of autobiographical memory involves using memories of past events to guide and shape current and future behavior as an aid to problem solving and as a means for predicting future behavior (Baddeley, 1987). Knowing how to conduct yourself in social and professional situations or how to deal with practical problems such as changing a fuse or booking a vacation on the Internet can be performed because we remember how it worked out last time a similar experience occurred. This directive advice can then be passed on to others, eliciting the social function of autobiographical memory. Many conversations involve the sharing of personal memories. This facilitates social interaction and friendships advance by the exchange of personal narratives. Social bonding and intimacy can be heightened through reminiscing with someone who was present at the original event (Fivush, Haden & Reese, 1996; Bluck, 2003) or through discussion of autobiographical memories with someone who was not there when the event originally took place. This also can be a means of pooling experiences, of giving and receiving sympathy and understanding, and of "placing ourselves" in a given context and culture (see also Williams, Conway, & Cohen, 2007). To be in coherence with the appropriate context and culture, the self function of memory takes over. Central aspects of the self are conceptualized as working with memory in an interdependent system in which memories can be altered, distorted, and fabricated in order that beliefs and knowledge about the self may be confirmed and supported by specific autobiographical memories (Conway, 2005). The importance of memories to the concept of the self is highlighted by patients who have experienced loss of memory through trauma or disease. Because these patients cannot recall their own personal history, in a very real sense they lose their sense of self (Williams et al., 2007). Autobiographical memories are intimately related to the self. They are important for interpretation of one's past selves, current self, and possible future selves (Conway, 2005). Bluck and colleagues recently explored the three functions of memory by asking participants to what extent they thought about their life experiences in certain situations. They found that the social function was deemed to actually reflect two different functions: developing relationships and nurturing relationships. The self function was found to be narrower than previously thought, solely reflecting the idea of self-continuity across the life span, but the directive function appeared to include making sense of the past so as to have a coherent view of the self with which to direct future behavior and thus was broader than originally conceptualized (Bluck, Alea, Habermas, & Rubin, 2005).

The connection between the self and memory is perhaps most obvious from the literature on "self-defining" memories that are proposed to contain critical knowledge of progress on the attainment of long-term goals (Singer, 2005; Singer & Salovey, 1993). For example, both alumnae and students have been found to be able to recall very detailed vivid memories of exchanges with professors and other teachers that they perceived as having significantly influenced their own academic careers (Pillemer, Picariello, Law, & Reichman, 1996). Self-defining memories are characterized by affective intensity, vividness, rehearsal, and links to other memories (Singer, 2005; Singer & Salovey, 1993). The central node of an AMN may well be the self-defining memory related to that particular self. In times of crisis or uncertainty, self-defining memories been proposed as being a landmark that can remind an individual of his/her identity (Blagov & Singer, 2004).

One area that has received particular attention from researchers is the development of the self in late adolescence. In general, one of the main existential problems that faces the adolescent is how to integrate an emerging self with larger social groups, culture, and society generally (Erikson, 1950, 1997), or the problem of the formation of a generation identity (Conway, 1997; Mannheim, 1952). Investigating this, Thorne (1995) found that the content of memories freely recalled across the life span by twenty-year-olds conformed to what she termed "developmental truths." Memories from childhood tended to refer to situations in which the child wanted help, approval, and love, usually from parents, whereas memories from late adolescence and early adulthood very frequently referred to events in which the rememberer wanted reciprocal love, was assertive, or helped another. In further studies in which young adults have been asked how they had made meaning out of peer- and parent-relationship experiences – how they had gained insight or learned lessons from these events that were now self-defining memories – experiences involving conflict were found to be most strongly associated with both gaining insight and learning lessons and often were accompanied by insight relating to issues such as beginning to understand one's own independence or a greater need for self-sufficiency (McLean & Thorne, 2003; Thorne, McLean & Lawrence, 2004).

In examining students' memories related to community service experiences, studies also have found that the more personal growth students attributed to these memories, the more likely these students were to place an overall emphasis on "generative" goal pursuits in their lives (Singer, King, Green, & Barr, 2002; see also de St. Aubin & McAdams, 1995). The relationship between the initial event, memories of those events, and the lessons and insights that have come forth as a result, links one's past to one's present, giving an individual the capacity to monitor the coherence of their psychological self-identity via this network of autobiographical memories and autobiographical knowledge. Memories of adolescence are often of events in which identity formation is preeminent, either at the group or societal level or in individual personal relationships. Such memories clearly relate to the pursuance of important goals that mark the emergence of an independent self-system in late adolescence. Assuming that the goals that preoccupy the individual at this point do not change in kind, then the memories that ground them in remembered reality should remain highly accessible across the life span. This is, indeed, exactly what a broad range of research has found.

Recently, Conway and Holmes (2004) asked older adults to freely recall events from each decade of their lives and then content-analyzed these memories on the basis of the psychosocial stages of life as proposed by Erikson (1950, 1997). In Erikson's theory of development, an individual is confronted with different psychosocial problems during different lifetime periods. In childhood, these problems are concerned with trust and mistrust. In adolescence, problems are centered on identity-identity confusion. In adulthood, the issue is intimacy versus isolation. Middle age is associated with generativity versus stagnation, and old age is concerned with integrity versus despair. In the study by Conway and Holmes, the most memorable or most easily accessible events recalled by older adults from each decade of their lives were found to be those memories that were related to the psychosocial concern associated with that lifetime period (Conway & Holmes, 2004). As shown in Figure 2.2, those memories classified as being strongly related to a particular psychosocial stage tended to predominate at the point in the life span when the stage would have been dominant. This is not an all-or-none effect but, rather, one of degree, as at any given psychosocial stage memories relating to a variety of psychosocial themes are present. The network of memories associated with each decade of life was found to be indexed in part by the appropriate psychosocial concern. This, and other findings from Conway and Holmes (2004), suggests that (self) networks of memories of events that were once of high relevance to the self remain

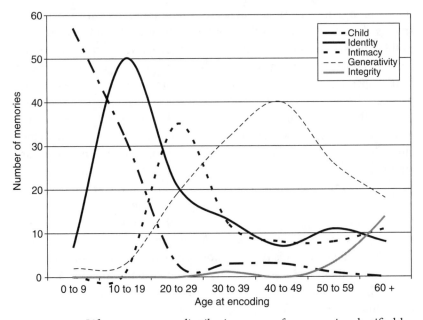

FIGURE 2.2. Life span memory distribution curves for memories classified by psychosocial theme (redrawn from data presented in Conway and Holmes, 2004, Experiment 1).

in a state of high accessibility and are among the first memories to come to mind when a period in the past is freely sampled.

CHILDHOOD AMNESIA AND THE REMINISCENCE BUMP

The development of the self in childhood and late adolescence/early adulthood is reflected in the *life span retrieval curve*, which is a distribution of memories frequently observed when older adults (about thirty-five years and older) recall autobiographical memories in free recall or in a variety of cued recall conditions (e.g., Franklin & Holding [1977]; Fitzgerald & Lawrence [1984]; Rubin, Wetzler, & Nebes [1986]; Rubin, Rahhal, & Poon [1998]). Memories are plotted in terms of age at encoding of the remembered experiences and the resulting life span retrieval curve typically takes a form similar to that shown in Figure 2.3 (this is an idealized representation).

As Figure 2.3 shows, the life span retrieval curve consists of three components: the period of childhood amnesia (from birth to approximately five years of age), the period of the reminiscence bump (from ten to thirty years), and the period of recency (from the present declining back to the period

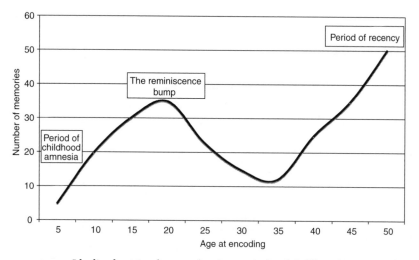

FIGURE 2.3. Idealized retrieval curve showing periods of childhood amnesia, the reminiscence bump, and the peak in recent memories typically recalled by older adults in free- or cued-recall autobiographical memory studies.

of the reminiscence bump). *Childhood amnesia* (originally called *infantile amnesia* by Freud [1905/1953]) refers to the phenomenon that people are typically unable to recall autobiographical events from the earliest years of life. The pattern of the life span retrieval curve is extremely robust and has been observed in many studies, to such an extent that it has become one of the most reliable phenomena of contemporary memory research (Conway & Rubin, 1993). This reliability is remarkably striking and a recent study examining life span memory retrieval curves from participants in China, Japan, England, Bangladesh, and the United States found very similar periods of childhood amnesia and reminiscence bump across these cultures (Conway, Wang, Hanyu, & Haque, 2005). Figure 2.4 shows the life span curves for each of these countries. Note that participants were asked to free recall memories from their life and additionally were instructed not to recall events from the previous year (to eliminate the recency portion of the curve). It can be seen in Figure 2.4 that there were striking periods of childhood amnesia and the reminiscence bump across countries and that these were statistically reliable. This further suggests a certain universality to the two phenomena of childhood amnesia and the reminiscence bump.

There are many theoretical explanations of the period of childhood amnesia (see Pillemer & White, 1989; Peterson, 2002; and Wang, 2003), but most flounder on the fact that children who are younger than five years

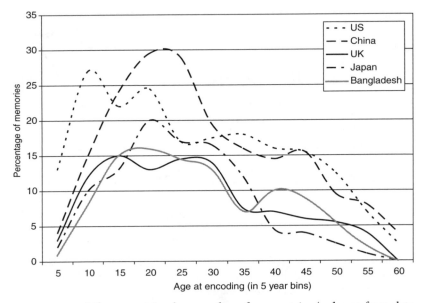

FIGURE 2.4. Life span retrieval curves from five countries (redrawn from data presented in Conway et al., 2005).

old have a wide range of specific and detailed autobiographical memories (Bauer, 1997; Fivush et al. 1996). Explanations that postulate childhood amnesia to be related to general developmental changes in intellect, language, emotion, and so on fail simply because apparently normal autobiographical memories were in fact accessible when the individual was in the period of childhood amnesia. It seems unlikely that an increase in general functioning would make unavailable already accessible memories. From the SMS perspective, this period in infancy and early childhood is seen as reflecting changes in the goals of the working self. The goals of the maturing, seven-plus-year-old child, are very different from those of the child younger than five years old. Because of this, these networks of early memories become progressively less accessible as we age.

There are, too, many explanations of the reminiscence bump (see Conway, 2005, for a review). Some explanations emphasize the novelty of experiences occurring during this period, some suggest that perhaps memory functions more efficiently during this period, others focus on affect, vividness, and distinctiveness. But none of these have received unequivocal support, and for each there are findings that they cannot explain. For example, less than 20 percent of memories from the reminiscence bump have been found to be of first-time experiences (Fitzgerald, 1988). Instead, what is clearly central to memories from this time is that they have an enduring and important relation to the self that persists long after the experiences are past. Memories from the reminiscence bump tend to be self-defining; they ground the self in a network of important moments from a period when a stable and persisting self finally emerged from the long period of development through infancy, childhood, adolescence, and into young adulthood.

AUTOBIOGRAPHICAL MEMORIES, THE SELF, AND SOCIETY

Self-defining memories are typically memories of highly personal experiences that are unique to or idiosyncratic of the individual. There are, however, other self-defining memories that in a sense are more public than private, which can form nodal points of a memory network that extends into culture and society. These memories were originally termed *flashbulb memories* (Brown & Kulik, 1977, 1982), and they generally refer to memories for learning of surprising, shocking, or consequential items of public (national and international) news. For example, how many adults in the United States or the United Kingdom do not have a memory of where they were, who they were with, or what they were doing when they found out that the World Trade Center (WTC) had been attacked by terrorists on September 11, 2001? This special type of witness memory is the detailed recollection that people often have of the occasion when they first heard about some very surprising, dramatic, important, and emotionally arousing event. Other events for which people's flashbulb memories have been studied are hearing the news that President John F. Kennedy had been shot, that Pearl Harbor had been bombed, that man had successfully landed on the moon, or that Princess Diana had been killed in a car crash. Flashbulb memories are memories of the "reception event" – the encoding of the circumstances in which the person first received the news rather than the event itself. This encoding typically includes the place, who was present at the time, what activities were going on, the affect occasioned by the event, and the source of the news. They also have a "live quality" (Brown & Kulik, 1982) and tend to include seemingly irrelevant and trivial details. Once encoded, flashbulb memories appear to be long-lasting and remain unchanged over time. However, considerable controversy exists concerning whether so-called flashbulb memories are different from other memories of events that are highly distinctive and personally significant.

Some researchers argue that a special neural mechanism exists that is triggered by high levels of emotion, surprise, and consequentiality (Brown & Kulik, 1982). However, other researchers challenge this and argue in favor of a reconstructive theory, in which flashbulb memories are the same as memories for other experiences but are preserved by frequent rehearsal and retelling after the event, rather than special processes activated during the initial experience (Neisser, 1982; McCloskey, Wible, & Cohen, 1988). This account posits that flashbulb memories are not necessarily true or accurate because they are the product of successive reconstructions. Much of the debate has centered on whether flashbulb memories can be shown to be unusually accurate; however, Neisser has suggested that the primary importance of flashbulb memories relates to their associations with society and culture and that they function as "benchmarks" in one's personal history. They mark a point where the individual can state with authority "I was there!" (Neisser, 1982) and as such are part of a self network of memories that locate us in specific epochs of sociohistorical time. As for ordinary autobiographical memories, sharing of flashbulb memories allows individuals to bond over a common theme in their self-networks, increasing intimacy and understanding of the event(s) in question.

The importance of cultural context to flashbulb memory recall was highlighted in a number of studies in a special issue of the journal *Applied Cognitive Psychology* in 2003. In one study, British participants demonstrated few differences in the phenomenological characteristics of their memories relating to learning about the WTC attacks and their memories for the death of Princess Diana, although for the WTC attacks level of detail in memory descriptions declined over time. By contrast, for Italian participants memories of September 11 were much more detailed than memories of learning about the death of Diana (Kvavilashvili, Mirani, Schlagman & Kornbrot, 2003). This fits with earlier findings that indicated that whereas 86 percent of British participants' memories for the resignation of Margaret Thatcher as prime minister could be deemed to have flashbulb memory quality, only 29 percent of non-British participants had flashbulb memories of this event (Cohen, Conway, & Maylor, 1994). Utilizing a new methodology, a recent study carried out in Denmark found a similarly powerful role for social identity in the recall of long-lasting personal memories (Berntsen & Thomsen, 2005). This study compared memory accuracy for the reception of important news by comparing memory reports against objective records and a baseline obtained from participants who were too young to have experienced the original event – the invasion, and subsequent liberation, of

Denmark in World War II. In this study, older adults' memories for details of learning the news of these momentous events (e.g., weather, time, day of the week) were found to be generally accurate, with 55 percent of answers being correctly answered. Accuracy was higher, however, among participants who reported ties to the Danish resistance movement; the descriptions provided by these participants had higher clarity than those of individuals who reported no ties to a specific, and important, group within the society. The number of intrusive memories stemming from the time of the German occupation also was found to correlate positively with the degree to which the individual regarded the time of the occupation as central to their life story and identity, illustrating how the influence have self-concepts over both voluntary and involuntary memory retrieval can be pervasive and long-lasting.

Societal or generational identities are both reflected in the flashbulb memory data collected as part of the *BBC Radio 4 Memory Survey*, an online survey of over twelve thousand memories collected from the general public. Table 2.1 displays preliminary data on the percentage of flashbulb memories ($n = 1656$) reported by each age group for all events for which at least 10 percent of one age group reported having a flashbulb memory for that event. Effects of culture and age at encoding are clearly evident. For example, the eleven-to-fifteen age group is the only age group for which over 10 percent of the memories reported were of the London underground and bus bombings that occurred on July 7, 2005. Although this event occurred most recently, it was not mentioned by the majority of participants. The attacks on the WTC on 9/11 were recalled most frequently ($n = 377$), followed by the death of Princess Diana ($n = 289$) and the assassination of JFK ($n = 277$). This reflects cultural biases, as 85.9 percent of memories were provided by people in the United Kingdom. It fits with the data concerning the quality of memories of the death of Diana held by British and Italian samples mentioned earlier. It also concurs with data on the reminiscence bump as a greater percentage of participants reported having a flashbulb memory for an event if it occurred when they were between the ages of ten and thirty, although events such as the moon landing and the assassination of JFK also were recalled by people who were less than ten years old at the time of the event. This probably reflects the significance of these events on a worldwide level. These types of flashbulb events help define generation identities; they place individual selves within a sociocultual context that is distinct from the cultural and social contexts experienced by those generations who precede and follow. Our final comment on flashbulb memory highlights the way in which a relationship to

TABLE 2.1. *Percentage of flashbulb memories referring to each public event by age group of participant (excluding events for which fewer than 10 percent reported a memory)[1].*

Age range	11-15	16-20	21-25	26-30	31-35	36-40	41-45	46-50	51-55	56-60	61-65	66-70	71-75	76-80
N	58	89	146	162	140	155	131	149	176	195	130	51	34	23
London bombings	13.8													
September 11	44.8	58.4	54.1	38.9	32.9	24.5	15.3	13.4						
Death of Princess Diana	10.3	22.5	24.7	29.6	33.6	27.7	15.3	14.8	11.4					
Moon landing							10.7							
Death of John Lennon							11.5							
Assassination of JFK								19.5	35.8	47.7	44.6	31.4	23.5	
Death of King George VI											10.0	11.8	11.8	13.0
World War II												17.6	29.4	47.8
TOTAL PERCENTAGE ACCOUNTED FOR[2]	68.9	80.9	78.8	68.5	66.5	52.2	52.8	47.7	47.2	47.7	54.6	60.8	64.7	60.8

[1] Events were excluded if they were not mentioned by at least 10 percent of any age group. For those events included, figures are only reported for percentages over 10 percent.

[2] The remainder of events were either unable to be classified, referred to personal instead of public events, or were mentioned by fewer than 10 percent of participants.

social context at the time of the terrorist attack can even be considered important at the time of a news event:

> I was on holiday in Italy with my boyfriend. We were at Lake Como, staying in a simple tourist guest room above a cafe with a view over the lake. I remember the promenade and the side street exactly, even though I have forgotten the name of the town. We slept badly because the local youths met up below our window on their scooters. There was no TV, so we were oblivious to the news as it broke. We only found out second-hand when my boyfriend phoned his elderly mother. It was a phone-card conversation, so he only got snippets of information. I stood nearby wondering what was so important. When he told me, the idea seemed preposterous. I remember exactly where I was standing. It was evening, but not dark. I remember reflecting on how we had spent that day in complete oblivion, simply enjoying our holiday. In retrospect it felt almost like we had cheated and failed to engage in the collective concern and dismay ...
> *Flashbulb memory of learning of the WTC attacks on September 11, 2001, from female, aged thirty-five, BBC Memory data.*

The findings discussed here reflect the influence that wider contexts such as social identity and culture have over encoding and retrieval of memories. In line with this, researchers have recently begun to focus on the function that remembering serves with regard to coherence of goals, beliefs, self-identities, and memory for personal events within a cultural context.

CULTURAL INFLUENCES ON THE SELF-MEMORY RELATIONSHIP

Traditionally, Asian societies place emphasis on social rules, group harmony, interconnectedness, solidarity, and personal humility. This emphasis fosters the development of a more *interdependently oriented* sense of self. The members of these societies tend to view themselves as part of a hierarchical social network of kinship. In contrast, in Western cultures societal emphasis is on being *independently oriented* and such societies promote the development and expression of individual autonomy, self-expression, and personal capability (e.g., Wang & Conway, 2006). These cultural differences in how the self is conceptualized have led to research into the interactions among culture, the self, and autobiographical memory. This bridge between the cognitive study of memory and research stemming from other disciplines such as sociology and anthropology is what makes this network of autobiographical memories, those that intertwine the individual in their culture and time, extremely interesting for a much wider audience than just psychologists. Cross-cultural variations in autobiographical memory have been observed by a number of authors (e.g., Pillemer, 1998; Röttger-Rössler, 1993; Weintraub, 1978; and Han, Leichtman, & Wang, 1998). Wang (2001) studied the interactions among culture, self-concepts, and autobiographical memories by asking American and Chinese college students to recall their first memory from childhood, rate it on a number of measures (e.g., rehearsal of this memory), and then complete 10 "*I am ...*" statements. These statements were coded as either being *private self-descriptions,* for example, "I am friendly, conscientious, intelligent"; *collective self-descriptions,* for example, "I am a brother, a footballer, a Protestant"; or *public self-descriptions,* for example, "I am in love with my girlfriend." The earliest memories provided by the Chinese sample came from an average age of four years, whereas the Americans' earliest childhood memories were found to come from approximately six months earlier. Chinese participants' memories were more centered on collective activities, routines, and emotionally neutral events, whereas Americans tended to write emotionally elaborate, self-focused memories referring to specific one-off events. This finding was also replicated by Wang and Conway (2004). Americans' memory descriptions were also longer than those written by the Chinese participants. Also, in the *I am* statements, American participants were found to emphasize individual attributes to a greater extent than the Chinese participants, who tended to describe themselves more in terms of social roles. However, across both cultures, participants who used more positive and self-focused terms also were found to provide more specific and self-focused memories. These results highlight the dynamic and reciprocal nature of the relationship between individual and cultural influences on the construction and retrieval of autobiographical memories.

Traditional cultural influences on patterns of AMNs also may be changing over time as a result of the impact of other cultures. As shown in Figure 2.4, Conway, Wang, and colleagues observed very similar periods of childhood amnesia and reminiscence bump across five cultures (Conway et al., 2005). However, these authors had expected to find a later reminiscence bump in Asian participants, as in some Asian societies adulthood is not considered to start until the age of about thirty, when a stable social network is formed. The authors suggested that one of the reasons that they may not have found the expected later reminiscence bump in Asian participants could be a result of the increased Westernization of Asian cultures over the last fifty years. Increased Westernization may have led to changes in cultural norms concerning the timing of movement into adolescence and adulthood. An alternate explanation could be that there is universality in memory retrieval curves, as in all cultures neurodevelopmental changes occur in the frontal lobes throughout childhood and into adolescence.

Networks of memories around different themes also have been found to differ across cultures (Wang, 2006). For earliest childhood memories cued by the words *self, mother, family, friend,* and *surrounding,* memory for *mother* was found to come from the youngest age (American = 3.8 years, Taiwanese = 5.4 years), and memory for *surroundings* came from about the same age, suggesting early development of knowledge about the physical environment. Earliest memory for *self* came from approximately six to eight months later. Memory for *friend* was the latest memory retrieved in both cultures (American = 5 years, Taiwanese = 6.33 years), which supports previous findings that the social self in relation to friendships develops in the late preschool years. This indicates that networks of memories linked to the social self, and particularly the self in relation to mother, are able to be formed before memories relating to the self as an individual. Across conditions, European Americans' earliest memories were again found to be from a younger age than were Taiwanese memories, and European Americans tended to recall more specific events and focus on individual roles and autonomy than did Taiwanese participants.

The interactions that occur between mother and child and their influence on autobiographical memory styles have been studied both within and between cultures, and it has been found that Western mothers talk about the past in more elaborate and emotional ways than mothers from Eastern cultures (Leichtman, Wang, & Pillemer, 2003). In conversations with their children, mothers from Western cultures focus on the child's own abilities and emotions. When discussing past events, they also provide rich and embellished information about the events being discussed and elaborate and augment children's responses. Conversely, Eastern mothers tend to place the child in a more collective setting, minimize emotions such as anger that may divide the child from the group, and instead highlight moral emotions and lessons. Eastern mothers also have been found to not use embellishment in conversations with their children, instead just repeating questions to try to elicit more information about the event being discussed (Wang & Brockmeier, 2002). These styles of reminiscing have been termed "high-elaborative" and "low-elaborative," respectively, and have been shown to influence the elaborative style adopted by the child and the amount of detail elicited in memory sharing conversations. Simple sharing of past experiences between mother and child thus perpetuates cultural styles of memory content, memory retrieval, which in turn will have influence over the types of associations, and themes that link memories together in individual's AMNs.

A further aspect of cognition that can influence retrieval of memories from different networks is language. In a study of middle-aged immigrants who had fled from Poland to Denmark thirty years previously, when asked to recall memories to word cues (of which half were given in Danish and half in Polish), participants judged memories of events that had taken place in Poland as being retrieved from memory in Polish, whereas events that occurred after immigration were retrieved in Danish (Larsen, Schrauf, Fromholt, & Rubin, 2002). Participants who had immigrated at a younger age (average age twenty-four years) also reported experiencing more inner speech behaviors in Danish than those who had immigrated later late in their lives (average thirty-four years). This indicates that those in the first group were thinking in Danish. These results suggest that some element of autobiographical memory encoding takes into account language, or at least some linguistic elements feature in encoding specificity and subsequent retrieval. This implies that memories encoded in one language are stored in separate AMNs from memories encoded in another language and that the links or overlaps between these networks are either weak or limited.

The way in which we talk about our memories may not always reflect what we remember about our memories, however. Wang and Ross (2005) studied earliest childhood memories in Caucasian and Asian Americans and found that priming of private self-concepts (e.g., I am clever) or collective self-concepts (e.g., I am a Christian) before recall influenced the focus of memories retrieved (privately focused or collectively focused) and the number of social interactions reported in memories. However, the effects of culture were found to be stronger and to have separate influence over memory content. These findings indicate that the cognitive frame activated at the time of retrieval was not the only influence over recall and that encoding of representations in memory is also critical. This relates to changes in the goals of the working self, as discussed earlier. As time passes between encoding and retrieval, changes in the goals of the working self may influence the attention paid to different aspects of a representation in memory or reinterpretation of the event information. Therefore, when recounting a memory to different people at different points in time, the narrative that we provide may differ greatly (Wang & Ross, 2005).

CONCLUSIONS: MEMORY SELF NETWORKS

In this chapter, we have argued for a concept that we call *self networks*. A critically important component of these networks is networks of specific autobiographical memories that ground the self in a remembered reality.

One important self network represents, in highly accessible form, the emerging self in late adolescence and early adulthood. This network is undoubtedly of enduring significance for the self and central in defining who we are and, importantly, who we can become. Another network of memories links the self into society and history; this network consists of flashbulb memories – vivid memories of learning of highly consequential items of public news. These two self networks may then be interlinked in an overriding memory network as the most easily accessible memories both from one's own personal experiences and from one's flashbulb memories relating to public events date from the period of the reminiscence bump, between the ages of fifteen and twenty-five (see Figures 2.3 and 2.4, and Table 2.1). Perhaps then, both our personal identity and our cultural or generational identity are formed at this time and endure over the life span.

REFERENCES

Baddeley, A. D. (1986). *Working memory*. Oxford: Clarendon Press.
   (1987). But what the hell is it for? In M. M. Gruneberg, P. E. Morris, & R. N. Sykes (Eds.), *Practical aspects of memory: Current research and issues* (pp. 3–18). Chichester: Wiley.
   (2000). The episodic buffer: A new component of working memory? *Trends in Cognitive Science, 4*, 417–423.
Barsalou, L. W. (1988). The content and organization of autobiographical memories. In U. Neisser & E. Winograd (Eds.), *Remembering reconsidered* (pp. 193–243). Cambridge: Cambridge University Press.
Bartlett, F. C. (1932). *Remembering: A study in experimental and social psychology*. Cambridge: Cambridge University Press.
Bauer, P. (1997). Development of memory in early childhood. In N. Cowan (Ed.), *The development of memory in childhood* (pp. 83–112). Sussex: Psychology Press.
Beike, D. R., & Landoll, S. L. (2000). Striving for a consistent life story: Cognitive reactions to autobiographical memories. *Social Cognition, 18*, 292–318.
Berntsen, D. (1996). Involuntary autobiographical memories. *Applied Cognitive Psychology, 10*, 435–454.
Berntsen, D., & Thomsen, D. K. (2005). Personal memories for remote historical events: Accuracy and clarity of flashbulb memories related to World War II. *Journal of Experimental Psychology: General, 134*, 242–57.
Blagov, P. S., & Singer, J. A. (2004). Four dimensions of self-defining memories (specificity, meaning, content, and affect) and their relationships to self-restraint, distress, and repressive defensiveness. *Journal of Personality, 72*, 481–511.
Bluck, S. (2003). Autobiographical memory: Exploring its functions in everyday life. *Memory, 11*, 113–123.
Bluck, S., Alea, N., Habermas, T., & Rubin, D. C. (2005). A tale of three functions: The self-reported uses of autobiographical memory. *Social Cognition, 23*, 91–117.

Bluck, S., & Habermas, T. (2001). The life story schema. *Motivation and Emotion*, 24, 121–147.

Brown, R., & Kulik, J. (1977). Flashbulb memories. *Cognition*, 5, 73–99.

(1982). Flashbulb memory. In U. Neisser (Ed.), *Memory observed: Remembering in natural contexts*. San Francisco, CA: W.H. Freeman.

Burgess, P. W., & Shallice, T. (1996). Confabulation and the control of recollection. *Memory*, 4, 359–411.

Burt, C. D. B., Kemp, S., & Conway, M. A. (2003). Themes, events, & episodes in autobiographical memory. *Memory & Cognition*, 31, 317–325.

Cantor, N., & Kihlstrom, J. F. (1985). Social intelligence: The cognitive basis of personality. In P. Shaver (Ed.), *Self, situations, and social behavior. Review of personality and social psychology* (pp. 15–34). Beverly Hills: Sage.

Chu, S., & Downes, J. J. (2002). Proust nose best: Odors are better cues of autobiographical memory. *Memory & Cognition*, 30, 511–518.

Cohen, G. (1989). *Memory in the Real World* (1st ed.). Erlbaum.

Cohen, G., Conway, M. A., & Maylor, E. (1994). Flashbulb memory in older adults. *Psychology and Aging*, 9, 454–463.

Conway, M. A. (1990). *Autobiographical memory: An introduction*. Buckingham: Open University Press.

(1996). Autobiographical memories and autobiographical knowledge. In D. C. Rubin (Ed.), *Remembering Our Past: Studies in Autobiographical Memory* (pp. 67–93). Cambridge: Cambridge University Press.

(1997). *Recovered memories and false memories*. Oxford: Oxford University Press.

(2004). Autobiographical memory and the self. In J. H. Byrne, H. Eichenbaum, H. Roediger III, & R. F. Thompson (Eds.), *Learning and Memory* (2nd ed.) Michigan: Macmillan Reference USA, and imprint of The Gale Group.

(2005). Memory and the self. *Journal of Memory and Language*, 53, 594–628.

(2007). *Autobiographical memory*. Oxford: Oxford University Press. In preparation.

Conway, M. A., & Williams, H. L. (2008). The nature of autobiographical memory. In J. H. Byrne (Ed.), *Learning and Memory: A Comprehensive Reference*, (pp. 893–909). Oxford: Elsevier Ltd.

Conway, M. A., & Bekerian, D. A. (1987). Organization in autobiographical memory. *Memory & Cognition*, 15, 119–132.

Conway, M. A., & Holmes, A. (2004). Psychosocial stages and the accessibility of autobiographical memories across the life cycle. *Journal of Personality*, 72, 461–480.

Conway, M. A., & Pleydell-Pearce, C. W. (2000). The construction of autobiographical memories in the self memory system. *Psychological Review*, 107, 261–288.

Conway, M. A., & Rubin, D. C. (1993). The structure of autobiographical memory. In A. E. Collins, S. E. Gathercole, M. A. Conway, & P. E. M. Morris (Eds.), *Theories of memory* (pp. 103–137). Hove, Sussex: Lawrence Erlbaum Associates.

Conway, M. A., Wang, Q., Hanyu, K., & Haque, S. (2005). A cross-cultural investigation of autobiographical memory – On the universality and cultural variation of the reminiscence bump. *Journal of Cross-cultural Psychology*, 36, 739–749.

Crovitz, H. F., & Schiffman, H. (1974). Frequency of episodic memories as a function of their age. *Bulletin of the Psychonomic Society*, 4, 517–518.

Csikszentmihalkyi, M., & Beattie, O. V. (1979). Life themes: A theoretical and empirical exploration of their origins and effects. *Journal of Humanistic Psychology, 19*, 45–63.

de St. Aubin, E., & McAdams, D. P. (1995). The relations of generative concern and generative action to personality traits, satisfaction/happiness with life, and ego development. *Journal of Adult Development, 2*, 99–112.

Ebbinghaus, H. (1885/1964). *Memory: A contribution to experimental psychology.* (H. A. Ruger & C. E. Bussenius, Trans.). New York: Dover Publications.

Ehlers, A., Hackmann, A., Steil, R., Clohessy, S., Wenninger, K., & Winter, H. (2002). The nature of intrusive memories after trauma: The warning signal hypothesis. *Behaviour Research and Therapy, 40*, 995–1002.

Erikson, E. H. (1950). *Childhood and society.* New York: W.W. Norton & Company. (1997). *The life cycle completed.* New York: W.W. Norton & Company.

Fitzgerald, J. M. (1988). Vivid memories and the reminiscence phenomenon: The role of a self narrative. *Human Development, 31*, 261–273.

Fitzgerald, J. M., & Lawrence, R. (1984). Autobiographical memory across the lifespan. *Journal of Gerontology, 39*, 692–698.

Fivush, R., Hayden, C., & Reese, E. (1996). Remembering, recounting, and reminiscing: The development of memory in a social context. In D. Rubin (Ed.), *Remembering our past: Studies in autobiographical memory* (pp. 341–359). Cambridge: Cambridge University Press.

Franklin, H. C., & Holding, D. H. (1977). Personal memories at different ages. *Quarterly Journal of Experimental Psychology, 29*, 527–532.

Freud, S. (1905/1953). Childhood and concealing memories/infantile sexuality. In A. A. Brill (Ed.), *The basic writings of Sigmund Freud* (pp. 62–68/580–585). New York: The Modern Library.

Freud, S. (1938). Interpretation of dreams. In A. A. Brill (Trans. and Ed.), *The basic writings of Sigmund Freud* (pp. 181–549). New York: Modern Library-Random House.

Galton, F. (1883). *Inquiries into human faculty and its development* (1st ed.). London: Macmillan and Co.

Han, J. J., Leichtman, M. D., & Wang, Q. (1998). Autobiographical memory in Korean, Chinese, and American children. *Developmental Psychology, 34*, 701–713.

Kvavilashvili, L., Mirani, J., Schlagman, S., & Kornbrot, D. E. (2003). Comparing flashbulb memories of September 11 and the death of Princess Diana: Effects of time delays and nationality. *Applied Cognitive Psychology, 17*, 1017–1031.

Lancaster, J. S., & Barsalou, L. W. (1997). Multiple organisations of events in memory. *Memory, 5*, 569–599.

Larsen, S. F., Schrauf, R. W., Fromholt, P., & Rubin, D. C. (2002). Inner speech and bilingual autobiographical memory: A Polish-Danish cross-cultural study. *Memory, 10*, 45–54.

Leichtman, M., Wang, Q., & Pillemer, D. P. (2003). In R. Fivush & C. A. Haden (Eds.), *Autobiographical memory and the construction of a narrative self: Developmental and cultural perspectives* (pp. 73–98). Mahwah, NJ: Erlbaum.

Mannheim, K. (1952). The problem of generations. In K. Mannheim (Ed.), *Essays on the sociology of knowledge* (pp. 276–321). London: Routledge & Keegan Paul Ltd.

McAdams, D. P., Reynolds, J., Lewis, M., Patten, A. H., & Bowman, P. J. (2001). When bad things turn good and good things turn bad: Sequences of redemption and contamination in life narrative and their relation to psychosocial adaptation in midlife adults and in students. *Personality and Social Psychology Bulletin, 27,* 474–485.

McCloskey, M., Wible, C. G., & Cohen, N. J. (1988). Is there a special flashbulb mechanism? *Journal of Experimental Psychology: General, 117,* 171–181.

McLean, K. C., & Thorne, A. (2003). Late adolescents' self-defining memories about relationships. *Developmental Psychology, 39,* 635–45.

Neisser, U. (1982) (pp. 43–48). Snapshots or benchmarks? In U. Neisser (Ed.), *Memory observed: Remembering in natural contexts* (pp. 43–48). San Francisco, CA: Freeman.

Norman, D. A., & Bobrow, D. G. (1979). Descriptions an intermediate stage in memory retrieval. *Cognitive Psychology, 11,* 107–123.

Ohta, N. (2006). Introduction: Harmony between principle-seeking and problem-solving research. In L.-G. Nilsson and Ohta (Eds.), *Memory and society: Psychological perspectives* (pp. 1–4). Hove, UK, and New York: Psychology Press.

Peterson, C. (2002). Children's long-term memory for autobiographical events. *Developmental Review, 22,* 370–402.

Pillemer, D. B. (1998). *Momentous events, vivid memories.* Cambridge, MA: Harvard University Press.

Pillemer, D. B., Picariello, M. L., Law, A. B., & Reichman, J. S. (1996). Memories of college: The importance of specific educational episodes. In D. C. Rubin (Ed.), *Remembering our past: Studies in autobiographical memory* (pp. 318–337). New York: Cambridge University Press.

Pillemer, D. B., & White, S. H. (1989). Childhood events recalled by children and adults. *Advances in Child Development and Behavior, 21,* 297–340.

Proust, M. (1925/1981). *Remembrance of things past: The fugitive* (C. K. Scott-Moncrieff, T. Kilmartin, & A. Mayor, Trans.). New York: Random House.

Ribot, T. (1882). *Diseases of memory: An essay in the positive psychology* (W. H. Smith, Trans.). New York: D. Appleton.

Robinson, J. A. (1976). Sampling autobiographical memory. *Cognitive Psychology, 8,* 578–595.

(1992). First experience memories: Contexts and function in personal histories. In M. A. Conway, D. C. Rubin, H. Spinnler, & W. Wagenaar (Eds.), *Theoretical perspectives on autobiographical memory* (pp. 223–239). Dordrecht, The Netherlands: Kluwer Academic Publishers.

Röttger-Rössler, B. (1993). Autobiography in question: On self presentation and life description in an Indonesian society. *Anthropos, 88,* 365–373.

Rubin, D. C., Rahhal, T. A., & Poon, L. W. (1998). Things learned in early adulthood are remembered best. *Memory & Cognition, 26,* 3–19.

Rubin, D. C., Wetzler, S. E., & Nebes, R. D. (1986). Autobiographical memory across the life span. In D. C. Rubin (Ed.), *Autobiographical memory* (pp. 202–221). Cambridge: Cambridge University Press.

Salaman, E. (1970). *A collection of moments: A study of involuntary memories.* London: Longman.

Schank, R. C. (1982). *Dynamic memory.* Cambridge: Cambridge University Press.

Singer, J. A. (2005). *Memories that matter: Using self-defining memories to under-stand and change your life.* Oakland, CA: New Harbinger.

Singer, J. A., King, L. A., Green, M. C., & Barr, S. C. (2002). Personal identity and civic responsibility: "Rising to the occasion" narratives and generativity in community action interns. *Journal of Social Issues, 58,* 535–556.

Singer, J. A., & Salovey, A. P. (1993). *The remembered self.* New York: The Free Press.

Thorne, A. (1995). Developmental truths in memories of childhood and adolescence. *Journal of Personality, 63,* 138–163.

Thorne, A., McLean, K. C., & Lawrence, A. M. (2004). When remembering is not enough: Reflecting on self-defining memories in late adolescence. *Journal of Personality, 72,* 513–542.

Tulving, E., & Thomson, D. M. (1973). Encoding specificity and retrieval processes in episodic memory. *Psychological Review, 80,* 353–373.

Wang, Q. (2001). Cultural effects on adults' earliest childhood recollection and self-description: Implications for the relation between memory and the self. *Journal of Personality and Social Psychology, 81,* 220–233.

(2003). Infantile amnesia reconsidered: A cross-cultural analysis. *Memory, 11,* 65–80.

(2006). Earliest recollections of self and others in European American and Taiwanese young adults. *Psychological Science, 17,* 708–714.

Wang, Q., & Brockmeier, J. (2002). Autobiographical remembering as cultural practice: Understanding the interplay between memory, self and culture. *Culture & Psychology, 8,* 45–64.

Wang, Q., & Conway, M. A. (2004). The stories we keep: Autobiographical memory in American and Chinese middle-aged adults (pp. 9–27). *Journal of Personality, 72,* 911–938.

(2006). Autobiographical memory, self, and culture. In L.-G. Nilsson and Ohta (Eds.), *Memory and Society: Psychological Perspectives* (pp. 9–27). Hove, UK, and New York: Psychology Press.

Wang, Q., & Ross, M. (2005). What we remember and what we tell: The effects of culture and self-priming on memory representations and narratives. *Memory, 13,*(6), 594–606.

Weintraub, K. J. (1978). *The value of the individual: Self and circumstance in autobiography.* Chicago: University of Chicago Press.

Williams, D. M., & Santos-Williams, S. M. (1980). A method for exploring retrieval processes using verbal protocols. *Attention and Performance, VIII.* Hillsdale, NJ: Lawrence Erlbaum Associates.

Williams, H. L., Conway, M. A., & Cohen, G. (2007). Memories for personal events. In G. Cohen & M. A. Conway, *Memory in the Real World* (3rd ed.). Hove: Psychology Press.

3

Cultural Life Scripts and Individual Life Stories

DORTHE BERNTSEN & ANNETTE BOHN

Imagine that you are to tell your life story to a new friend, whom you have just met and who therefore does not know anything about your past. It is a friend with whom you are absolutely confident and with whom you can be completely honest. You want to tell him or her about the events from your own personal life that you think are most central to your life story. Which events would you include?

There are probably many candidates, but some events are more likely to spring to mind than others. If you are like most people, you would be unlikely to include, for example, the day you read your first book, when you learned to write your own name, once your wallet was stolen, once you had a toothache and a root canal treatment, or the first time that you went on a plane trip. You would be more likely to tell your new friend about having siblings, beginning school, the first time you fell in love, some major achievement in sports or academics, when you left home, and when you graduated. You might also include your first job, marriage, the birth of your children or grandchildren, and so forth, if you are old enough to have experienced such events.

How are these events selected over others? You may say that they are selected because they are important, much more important than learning to read a book. But then what do we mean by importance here? Was it not important to you as a child finally to be able to read a book or even learn to tie your own shoes? And how is it that different people come up with some of the same important events to be included in their life stories? Are all lives highly similar, or is something else going on? In this chapter, we will argue that the content of our life stories is constrained by cultural norms that influence what we think of as important and as less important from the perspective of telling a life story. Such collective norms are called life scripts – defined as culturally shared expectations about the order and timing of life events in a prototypical life course (Berntsen & Rubin, 2002, 2004; Rubin & Berntsen, 2003). This chapter deals with culturally shared life scripts, their relevance for individual life stories, and how life scripts and life stories develop in childhood.

THE THEORETICAL BACKGROUND

In a modern Western society, the individual is commonly described as released from the cultural constraints that dominated people's lives at earlier times (Ziehe & Stubenrauch, 1982). In a feudal society, the individual had very little freedom regarding where to live, what to do for a living, whom to marry, when to have children, and so forth. In a contemporary Western society, the individual to a much larger extent decides independently what kind of life he or she would like to live. Individuals are no longer born with a predestined life; instead, we all have to "get a life," according to this view. Life stories are often depicted as a process through which the individual attempts to maintain a sense of identity and continuity through the construal of personal meaning with very few stable cultural norms for guidance (e.g., Giddens, 1991). Consistent with this view, psychological theories of autobiographical memory generally have focused on the level of the individual and minimized the impact of culture and tradition on the content and structure of autobiographical memory (see Berntsen & Rubin, 2004, for a review). That is, theories of autobiographical memory usually assume that the central structures for the organization of autobiographical memory originate in the life course of the individual and not in the way this life course is normatively described by the culture to which the individual belongs. For example, in the self memory system (SMS) account by Conway and Pleydell-Pearce (2000) the goal structure of the self is assumed to determine the accessibility of autobiographical memories. Examining autobiographical memory and personal life stories in relation to culturally shared life scripts is a movement away from a narrowed focus on the individual.

What Is a Life Script?

Although the modern individual has many more options regarding his or her personal life than an individual in a so-called traditional society, the idea of a normative biography still exists in most people's mind, even though their own lives may to some extent deviate from it. Not everything can happen at any time in life. Pregnancy at age 15 would probably be considered "too early" by most people in our culture, and graduating at age 50 would be "too late." Such culturally sanctioned age norms are well documented by research in anthropology and sociology. As Neugarten, Moore, and Lowe pointed out: "There exists what may be called a prescriptive timetable for the ordering of major life events: a time in the life span when men and women are expected to marry, a time to raise children, a time to retire" (1965, p. 711). People are aware of these age norms as well as their own timing in relation to them.

A life script is a mental representation of culturally expected life events and their age norms. It combines the idea of culturally sanctioned age norms as studied in anthropology and sociology with the concept of script, as this notion was developed by Schank and Abelson (1977) in cognitive psychology. A script is a general knowledge structure that organizes the way that we think about a recurrent everyday event, such as eating in a restaurant or traveling by airplane. A person who has a script for airplane trips knows that he or she is supposed to do certain things in a fixed order. The person is supposed to check in, get a boarding pass, go through security, go to the gate, board the plane, and so on. It is not possible to reverse the order of these mini-events. Described in more abstract terms, a script is a series of events that unfold in a specific order, with each event enabling the events that follow, together composing a stereotypical episode (Schank, 1982, 1999; Schank & Abelson, 1977). Scripts are collectively shared knowledge that enables us to communicate about and orient ourselves in recurrent, complex situations. In the same way, a life script represents a series of life events that take place in a specific order, and it represents a prototypical life course within a certain culture (Berntsen & Rubin, 2004; Rubin & Berntsen, 2003). It influences how we communicate and think about our life and how we plan our future. Just as you are supposed to have a boarding pass before you can proceed to the gate, you are supposed to have graduated before you can get your first real job, and (at least in some cultures) you are supposed to marry before you have your first child. Both the script as introduced by Schank and Abelson (1977) and the life script as described by Berntsen and Rubin (2004) are cognitive representations of socially sanctioned rules of behavior.

The Content of Life Scripts

The following summary is based on Berntsen and Rubin (2004). The contents of life scripts are culturally important transitional events and their expected timing and sequencing. Culturally important transitional events are events that mark a culturally approved transition from one social role to another, such as from unmarried to married or from having no children to becoming a parent. Some events may be highly personally significant without fulfilling these criteria (e.g., having a serious accident or winning in the lottery). Such events would not be part of a life script and would have no age norms. More culturally important transitional events are expected to happen in young adulthood than in any other period of life. This is the reason why life scripts may help to explain a dominance of autobiographical memories from this period of life relative to the surrounding ages, a point on which we will elaborate later.

Because life scripts deal with socially sanctioned rules of behavior, life script events that happen "on time" are usually considered positive (Luborsky, 1993; Rubin & Berntsen, 2003). They typically are celebrated socially, whereas events that conflict with the life script (e.g., dropping out of school instead of graduating) and transitional events that are "off-time" (e.g., pregnancy in adolescence) often are seen as stressful and socially stigmatizing (Neugarten & Hagestad, 1976). The life script therefore represents an idealized life story. Whereas a restaurant script may be said to represent an averaged version of many recurrent visits to restaurants (Abelson, 1981), the life script does not depict an average life, because an average life would have to include many events that are common but not culturally expected (e.g., losing one's job). Because we only live once, the life script is not learned from personal actions in recurrent contexts, in contrast to the event script introduced by Schank and Abelson (1977). Instead, the life script is handed down from older generations, from stories, and from observations of the behavior of other, typically older, people within the same culture (see Berntsen & Rubin, 2004, for more details). Later in this chapter we discuss how life scripts develop in childhood.

How Life Scripts May Structure Recall from Autobiographical Memory

According to most accounts, voluntary recall from autobiographical memory is a cyclic process that begins with a search description providing a rough specification of what kind of memory to look for. Retrieval failures lead to a readjustment of the search description, followed by additional retrieval attempts, until – eventually – the person comes up with a satisfactory result (e.g., Conway & Pleydell-Pearce, 2000). Faced with the question that we asked in the beginning of this chapter, a person would have to generate a search description for memories that he or she might include in his or her life story. Such a search description would most likely be generated at least partly on the basis of the life script. If no specific time slot in a life script is allocated to a certain type of event, these events will not benefit from a life script that supports and structures retrieval. Thus, these events should be underrepresented as compared to events that do. This is one important way in which life scripts may structure our life stories. In addition to structuring retrieval, life scripts may influence encoding and retention by providing more cultural importance and opportunities for rehearsal to events that fit the script (e.g., social celebrations) compared to events that do not, thus increasing the accessibility of the former (see Berntsen & Rubin, 2004, for more detailed discussion).

Although life scripts help to structure individual life narratives, the two concepts are theoretically and empirically distinct. A life script is a culturally shared part of our semantic knowledge, whereas a life story is personal, as it belongs to a specific individual and is part of one's autobiographical knowledge. A life script is measured by a request for events in a stereotypical life within a given culture. A life story is measured by asking an individual to tell the story about his or her life (Berntsen & Rubin, 2002, 2004; Rubin & Berntsen, 2003).

Studying Life Scripts and Autobiographical Memory in Adults

Although several autobiographical memory researcher have mentioned the importance of culturally expected events for autobiographical memory (e.g., Bluck & Habermas, 2000; Cohen & Faulkner, 1988; Fitzgerald, 1988; Robinson, 1992; Robinson & Taylor, 1998), systematic empirical research clarifying the specific content of such norms and their cognitive structures only began when Berntsen and Rubin (2002) stumbled on a surprising finding. Many previous studies had shown that people over the age of 40 recall more memories from age 15 to 30 than from the surrounding periods. This so-called reminiscence bump was discovered by Rubin, Wetzler, and Nebes (1986) in a reanalysis of data from several studies on word-cued memories, and it has been replicated numerous times (see Rubin, 2002, for a review). Surprisingly, when Berntsen and Rubin (2002) asked a large sample of Danes how old they were during their most important, their happiest, their saddest, and their most traumatic memory, they found no bump for the saddest and most traumatic memories, whereas there was a clear bump in the 20s for the most important and happiest memories for respondents over the age of 40 (see Figure 3.1). The absence of a bump for memories of negative events was replicated by Rubin and Berntsen (2003, Study 1), who asked another representative sample of Danes how old they were when they had

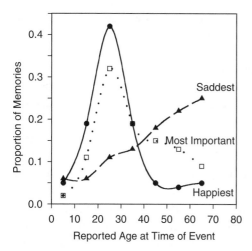

FIGURE 3.1. The distribution of the saddest, happiest and most important memories for participants in their sixties, reproduced from Rubin and Berntsen (2003, figure 1).

felt most afraid, most proud, most jealous, most in love, and most angry. Respondents were also asked when they had experienced their most important event and whether this event had been positive or negative. Again, there was a bump for positive but not negative memories.

Could these findings simply reflect that life is better in young adulthood than at any other time? This explanation could be ruled out by the fact that a similar dissociation between positive and negative memories is not found when recall is triggered by word cues (Rubin & Schulkind, 1997). However, many other explanations were possible – in fact, far too many explanations. Berntsen and Rubin (2002, table 2) listed eight different explanations that were able to account for the absence of the bump for negative memories. One that seemed most parsimonious was based on the idea of life scripts favoring events from young adulthood and favoring positive events over negative events. To examine this idea, Rubin and Berntsen (2003, Study 2) asked Danish psychology students to think about a fictitious average 70-year-old and estimate this person's age during each of a series of emotionally charged events. The events were the same as those used in Rubin and Berntsen (2003, Study 1). The crucial difference between the two studies was that the students in Study 2 did not base their age estimates of the events on their own memories but on their expectations as to when different emotional events were likely to occur in a prototypical life course. In support of the life script account, they came up with roughly the same life distributions for the emotional events as the memories had shown in Study 1. Again, a bump in young adulthood was seen for positive but not for negative events. Moreover, the students agreed more on the age estimates for positive events and had more confidence in their age estimates for the positive events than the negative events. Indeed, this was what one would expect if the age estimates for the positive events but not the negative events were governed by a culturally shared life script.

One limitation of Rubin and Berntsen's (2003) second study was that the participants did not generate the events themselves. Therefore, Berntsen and Rubin (2004) asked 103 Danish psychology students to generate the seven most important events that they imagined were highly likely to take place in a prototypical infant's life. They were asked to write down these seven events in the same order as they came to mind and to give each event a short title that specified its content. When the participant had recorded seven events, he or she turned to the next page in the booklet and rated the importance, real-life prevalence (i.e., how many out of 100 people would experience this event), and emotional content for each of the seven events. The participants also estimated at which age in an average person's life this event was most likely to take place. Based on the notion of life scripts as a shared cognitive structure that favors positive events over negative events and that favors events from young adulthood relative to other events from other periods, Berntsen and Rubin (2004) predicted the following: (1) a high overlap among the events generated by the participants; (2) a dominance of events rated positive; (3) more agreement across participants for the estimated ages for positive events relative to negative events; and (4) that the majority of positive events would be estimated to occur between ages 15 and 30 (i.e., the period for the bump), whereas the life-span distribution of negative events should be relatively flat or show a slow increase (see Berntsen & Rubin, 2004, for the full list of predictions).

The participants recorded, all together, 721 events. However, consistent with the first prediction, these events were highly overlapping. When classified independently by two judges, 36 different categories emerged (see Table 3.1).

These categories were predominantly positive, consistent with prediction 2. Also, when looking at the standard deviations for the age estimates for the negative events as compared to the positive events (see Table 3.1), the negative events show much more variability, consistent with prediction 3. The frequencies (i.e., number of records) were not predicted by ratings of real life prevalence. However, consistent with prediction 4, frequency was predicted by (positive) valence and whether the event was estimated to take place in the period of the bump. This latter point is illustrated much more clearly by Figure 3.2, which shows the distribution of age estimates for positive, negative, and neutral life script events.In a follow-up, Rubin, Berntsen, and Hutson (2009) asked Danish psychology students and American

TABLE 3.1. *Events mentioned more than three times and their sum of records, estimated life-prevalence, importance, age at event, and emotion, reproduced from Berntsen and Rubin (2004; table 3).*

Event	Records	Prevalence		Importance		Age at event		Emotion	
	Sum	(0 to 100)		(1 to 7)		(years)		(−3 to 3)	
		M	SD	M	SD	M	SD	M	SD
Having children	93	79.91	12.32	6.70	0.66	28.08	2.45	2.58	0.87
Marriage	77	81.27	13.33	6.17	0.94	26.90	3.11	2.52	0.77
Begin school	68	99.34	1.17	5.69	1.04	6.13	0.42	1.24	1.03
College etc.	56	84.20	11.30	5.67	0.88	22.05	3.86	1.30	0.97
Fall in love	52	94.80	8.82	6.06	1.35	16.33	5.26	2.44	0.89
Others' death	32	97.81	4.69	6.41	0.76	34.35	17.32	−2.56	0.98
Retirement	31	89.97	14.44	5.55	1.06	65.10	2.36	−0.06	0.81
Leave home	26	98.50	2.16	6.12	0.95	19.42	0.95	1.12	0.91
Parents' death	24	97.04	3.64	6.29	0.81	49.09	11.51	−2.46	1.25
First job	22	90.36	7.24	5.41	1.10	25.64	3.06	1.00	0.87
Begin daycare	17	91.88	9.34	5.00	0.94	2.82	1.67	0.29	0.92
Own death	12	100.00	0.00	6.50	1.73	72.42	23.24	−0.92	1.24
Divorce	12	60.42	19.12	5.92	0.90	39.45	8.65	−2.00	1.04
Siblings	12	66.67	16.28	5.75	0.87	3.42	0.90	0.58	1.38
First friend	11	98.64	1.75	6.64	0.92	4.78	2.22	2.91	0.30
Go to school	11	95.73	11.89	6.36	0.67	8.56	4.36	1.18	1.33
Puberty	11	99.55	0.69	6.36	0.92	13.18	1.17	−0.18	0.60

(continued)

69

TABLE 3.1. *(continued)*

Event	Records	Prevalence		Importance		Age at event		Emotion	
		(0 to 100)		(1 to 7)		(years)		(−3 to 3)	
Grandchildren	11	71.64	14.75	5.91	1.22	54.22	5.04	2.73	0.47
Long trip	10	67.50	21.89	5.20	1.32	21.33	2.45	1.30	1.57
Begin walking	9	98.89	0.33	6.67	0.71	1.33	0.50	2.11	1.05
Serious disease	9	69.89	19.34	6.67	0.50	50.63	17.20	−1.33	1.94
Major achievement	8	75.63	13.21	5.38	0.74	25.63	7.82	2.00	1.07
Settle on Career	7	77.00	27.07	5.29	1.89	26.67	2.58	0.71	0.95
First sex	7	98.43	1.51	5.71	1.11	16.00	1.41	1.50	1.05
Partner's death	6	69.50	24.79	6.80	0.45	75.00	4.47	−3.00	0.00
Begin talking	6	98.67	0.52	7.00	0.00	2.20	0.45	2.17	0.75
Confirmation	6	75.00	11.83	4.33	1.63	13.67	0.52	2.33	0.82
Enter adulthood	6	94.00	7.87	6.67	0.52	19.40	6.39	1.17	1.72
Having peers	5	72.00	21.68	6.60	0.89	14.20	2.39	2.60	0.55
Empty nest	4	84.25	9.88	5.50	1.00	46.25	2.50	−0.75	
First rejection	4	97.25	4.86	6.50	0.58	7.50	7.78	−3.00	0.00
The 'right' job	4	81.25	8.54	6.75	0.50	30.00	0.00	3.00	0.00
First contact	4	96.25	4.79	6.75	0.50	1.00	1.15	1.50	1.73
Baptism	4	77.50	9.57	4.75	1.50	0.00	0.00	1.50	1.29
Earn first money	4	95.00	4.08	5.75	0.96	16.25	4.79	0.75	0.50
Other	40	87.47	17.17	5.97	1.13	20.56	18.96	0.75	2.10

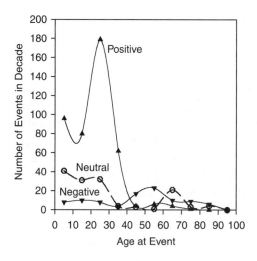

FIGURE 3.2. The distribution of age estimates for positive, negative and neutral life script events, reproduced from Berntsen and Rubin (2004, figure 2).

undergraduates to conduct the life script task as described earlier. In addition, they were asked the question that we presented at the beginning of this chapter. They were asked to come up with the seven most important events to be included if they were to tell their life story to a new friend. The life script findings largely replicated those of Berntsen and Rubin (2004). For the Danish sample, this replication was close to perfect, whereas some relatively minor differences were observed in relation to the life script generated by the American students, reflecting differences between the two cultures. For example, getting a driver's license was mentioned by a substantial number of Americans but not mentioned by the Danes. In both samples, the events generated for the life story showed a substantial overlap with events in the life script for each population.

Erdoğan, Baran, Avlar, Cağlar Taş, and Tekcan (2008) replicated Berntsen and Rubin's study (2004) in a Turkish sample of 220 university students. They found a substantial overlap between the Danish and the Turkish life script, as well as some cultural differences (i.e., "circumcision" in the Turkish life script vs. "confirmation" in the Danish life script).

Collins, Pillemer, Ivcevic, and Gooze (2007) asked 92 participants to describe two positive and two negative memories from when they were between 8 and 18 years old. They found that the negative memories were flatly distributed across the years, whereas the positive memories were clustered around life script events such as the highschool/college transition, with about half of all positive memories happening around age 17–18. They repeated this study for an age range without obvious cultural life script events (age 10–15) and found a flat distribution for both memories of negative and positive events.

In short, the studies reviewed so far have found evidence for the existence of a life script as a shared cognitive structure. When this structure is measured, it shows much overlap with the distribution of autobiographical memories. However, the fact that these two phenomena show highly similar characteristics regarding their distribution of events across the life span need not mean that one (the life script) is shaping the other (the life story). Alternatively, a common underlying factor could shape both. What would be a reasonable candidate for such an underlying factor? The only possible candidate we can think of would be the way life actually is for most people. According to this alternative account, because autobiographical memories deal with life and because life scripts give a realistic picture of the way life is, the distributions of autobiographical memories and life script events are highly similar.

However, this explanation is contradicted by several facts. First, many important and common events (e.g., accidents, menarche, menopause, assaults, losing a job) are not present in Table 3.1. Second, ratings of real-life prevalence were unrelated to how frequently an event was recorded in Berntsen and Rubin (2004, Study 2). Third, as mentioned earlier, the dominance of positive events in the bump period is not found when people are asked to retrieve memories in response to cue words (e.g., Rubin & Schulkind, 1997). Fourth, the dominance of positive events in the bump period and negative events expected to come later in life is also contrary to studies on the development of affect across the life span, which have shown that older adults experience less negative affect, both in terms of frequency and intensity (e.g., Charles, Reynolds, & Gatz, 2001; Mroczek, 2001, for reviews). Given that a reference to real life is unable to provide a satisfactory alternative explanation, it seems reasonable to conclude based on the review so far that shared cultural life scripts have a major influence on how adults remember and narrate their personal lives. In the next section, we examine to what extent the ability to construct a personal life story in childhood is related to the internalization of a culturally shared life script.

CULTURAL LIFE SCRIPTS AND THE DEVELOPMENT OF PERSONAL LIFE STORIES

Generally, there seems to be consent among researchers on autobiographical memory that the development of autobiographical memories happens through close encounters between the individual and the culture in which he or she grows up in (see Nelson & Fivush, 2004; Reese, 2002, for overviews). However, the ability to remember and recount autobiographical memories is not the same as being able to narrate one's life story coherently (Habermas & Bluck, 2000), and only few developmental memory researchers have considered the relationship between the surrounding culture and the development of the ability to tell one's life story.

Habermas and Bluck theorized that one of the prerequisites for telling a coherent life story is the internalization of a cultural concept of biography, which together with temporal coherence is "used to form a basic, skeletal life narrative consisting of an ordered sequence of culturally defined, major life events" (2000, p. 750). However, according to Habermas (2007), the cultural concept of biography includes more features than the cultural life script, as it also refers to knowledge about narrative conventions and goals pertaining to the telling of autobiographies. Similarly, Nelson describes the emergence of a "cultural self" as the prerequisite for the child's ability to construct an autobiography. This "cultural self" consists, on the one hand, of "the sociocultural temporal frame of one's life" (2003, p. 21) – namely, life script events such as "school, jobs, marriage" (p. 21) – but it also, on the other hand, consists of cultural myths and collective memories. Whereas Habermas and Bluck (2000) predict the emergence of a cultural concept of biography in late childhood or early adolescence, Nelson (2003) sets the emergence of the cultural self in the early school years (5–7 years). Even though these autobiographical memory researchers stress the importance of the development of a cultural framework for the child's ability to construct a life story, empirical studies have been scarce (Habermas, 2007). However, the introduction of the cultural life script by Berntsen and Rubin (2004) has made it easier to operationalize the idea of a cultural frame for the construction of life stories, thus making it much more feasable to test the relationship between the acquisition of a cultural life script and the ability to construct one's life story.

We (Bohn & Berntsen, 2008) studied the development of cultural life scripts and the relationship between this and the development of the ability to coherently tell one's life story in children and adolescents. Participants in our study were 140 Danish grade school and high school students. We collected data from 3rd graders (9–10 years old), a group of 5th and 6th graders (11–13 years old), and from 8th graders (14–15 years old).

In three sessions of 45 minutes each, we collected written reports of a recent autobiographical event, the childrens' life stories, and cultural life scripts. For the recent autobiographical event, we asked the children and adolescents to write about an event that had happened during their fall vacation. We chose this topic, because it ensured that we got stories about events that had happened at the same time, and these stories would encompass similar events for all children. This strategy proved to be successful, as most of the children wrote about family outings, vacation trips, or going shopping or to the movies with their families or friends. We used the vacation stories as a baseline measurement for the childrens' ability to tell about an autobiographical event. For the life story, the children received oral and written instructions to write their life story to a person who would like to know more about them and about the events that had happened to them since they were born. For the cultural life scripts, the children and adolescents were asked to imagine a newborn of their own sex and to write down the 10 most important events that they thought would happen in this newborn's life across the life span. They also were asked to give the approximate age of when the events would happen. The children were told that there were no right or wrong answers for this task but that we were interested in their opinion.

Measures

In order to measure the development of cultural life scripts, a norm was established by collecting cultural life scripts from an adult group. The adult group consisted of 111 Danish psychology majors who were, on average, 28.5 years old. We decided to collect new data to use as the adult norm instead of the cultural life script norms established by Berntsen and Rubin (2004) because the children had been asked to generate 10 events, whereas Berntsen and Rubin had asked their participants to provide only seven life events. Nevertheless, the adult group in our study generated life scripts highly similar to those found in the studies by Berntsen and Rubin (2004, see Table 3.1), and Rubin, Berntsen, and Hutson (2009). The fit of the childrens' life scripts to the adult life script norm was measured by the following two scores:

(1) a typicality score based on how often a life script event had been mentioned by the adult group. Thus, the higher a child scored on the typicality score, the closer his/her life script is to the adult norm.

(2) An idiosyncrasy score based on the assumption that a shared cognitive structure such as a life script should not vary too much across individuals. The individual variation of the life script was measured by the number of idiosyncratic events mentioned in the life script. Idiosyncratic events are all those events, which were mentioned by three or less adult participants in the study. Some examples of idiosyncratic life events mentioned by adults are "first promotion," "second marriage," and "being robbed." Children

mentioned idiosyncratic events such as "grow teeth," "begin to think," "stops using pacifier," "gets own cell phone," or "becomes famous."

The fall vacation stories were scored on general coherence, using a scale from 0 to 3 (adapted from Peterson & McCabe, 1983; see also Fivush et al., 2002). As life stories are more complex and involve more than one auto-biographical event memory, life story coherence was measured on various parameters such as beginning and ending of the stories, the number of life script events mentioned in the life story, as well as on general life story coherence.

Findings

The following is a brief summary of the main results of our study based on findings reported by Bohn and Berntsen (2008). We found that the typicality of cultural life scripts increased systematically across childhood and adolescence, and, at the same time, that the idiosyncrasy of the life scripts decreased. Third graders had on average almost twice as many idiosyncratic events included in their life scripts than the older children, and more than four times as many as the adult control group. The cultural life scripts of our participants became more and more adultlike with increasing age. However, even at age 14, not all participants had reached the adult norm for cultural life scripts.

We found large individual differences in the typicality of the cultural life scripts and in the coherence of life stories written by the children. Although there were significant correlations between the typicality of the cultural life script and life story coherence, no relationship was found between the coherence of fall vacation stories and the typicality of the life script. This pattern of relationship was present, even when the age of the participants and the length of their vacation and life stories were taken into account. Thus, it seems that children with less typical and more idiosyncratic cultural life scripts write less coherent life stories, whereas children with more typical life scripts are able to write more coherent life stories.

In the following paragraphs, we focus on the qualitative data to illustrate these points (for analyses of the numerical data, see Bohn and Berntsen, 2008). To illustrate the findings, we will present the life scripts and life stories of two nine-year-old boys named Jakob and Erik.

In accordance with earlier findings (for an overview, see Habermas & Bluck, 2000), both boys were able to write coherent stories about their fall vacations of about equal length. Jakob told about his vacation in Turkey, whereas Erik wrote about a day spent at a large tropical indoor swimming pool. Table 3.2 shows Jakob's and Erik's cultural life scripts. Jakob's life

TABLE 3.2. *An idiosyncratic and a normative life script*

Idiosyncratic life script ("Jakob")	Age at event
Is run over by a car	29
Becomes a professional soccer player	20
Birth	0
Plays for Brøndby Soccer club	24
Finishes school	16
Buys a new house	34
Member of the National Soccer Team	23
Team Captain Brøndby Soccer Club	26
He wins National Championship with Brøndby	27
He lifts the trophy	28

Normative life script ("Erik")	Age at event
Birth	0
Baptism	2
Learns to walk	3
Learns to talk	3
Begins daycare	3
Begins in school	6
Gets a job	19
Girlfriend	18
Marriage	29
Death	99

script is highly idiosyncratic and not ordered chronologically, whereas Erik's life script is in almost perfect chronological order and highly normative, that is, it includes events frequently mentioned by the adult group and does not contain any idiosyncratic events at all.

Even though both boys had reported autobiographical memories about their fall vacation of about equal length and coherence, their life stories are strikingly different:

- "Jakob" (boy with idiosyncratic life script): Down on Mallorca, I got lost from my mother and father on the beach. And they had to ask other people to help search for me. And then they finally found me down on the beach, and then we had to go home.

- "Erik" (boy with normative life script): I was born on October 25th, 1996. I love soccer and handball. I have two younger brothers. One is called Per, and the other is called Gustav. I have always liked to go to school. I was four when I learned how to ride a bike.

Jakob describes a single autobiographical memory, the almost classical or prototypical "nightmare event" for children (and parents) of getting lost: He gets lost and found on the beach. We get to know that this event took place on the Spanish island of Mallorca, but we do not learn how old Jakob was, when this event took place, or any other details from his life. Erik's life story is as short as Jakob's, but he is able to convey information about himself, his family, and even his personality. It seems that Erik's internalization of the cultural life script enables him to generate a more coherent and informative life story.

These examples illustrate the general pattern in our results of a relation between the ability to generate a normative life script and to tell a coherent life story (Bohn & Berntsen, 2008), suggesting that cultural life scripts are important for the development of the ability to tell a coherent life story. Although empirical studies with adults provide evidence for the use of cultural life scripts as "search machines" when providing one's life story (Collins et al., 2007; Rubin, Berntsen & Hutson, under review), our study suggests that the development of the shared cognitive structure of a cultural life script is an important prerequisite for establishing the story of one's life.

Even though the idiosyncratic events violated the shared life script norms, they were in many cases not entirely unique to the child but quite influenced by other cultural stereotypical ideas. Nelson (2003) includes in her model of the cultural self the absorbtion of cultural myths and representative stories as part of the developmental process. As an example for this, she refers to a study by Nicolopoulou and Weintraub (1998), who found that preschool boys tended to tell stories about superheroes, whereas preschool girls were more inclined to talk about home and family life or kings and queens. We found patterns akin to these in some of the life scripts. Some boys (such as Jakob, see Table 3.2) presented the life of a sports star (soccer, boxing) – arguably today's superheroes – in their cultural life scripts, whereas one girl actually presented the fairy tale life of a princess. Here are the sports star life scripts by another nine-year-old boy and the princess life script of a nine-year-old girl. (Note that AGF is a Danish soccer club; to understand the girl's life script, it is important to know that Denmark actually has a Crown Prince.)

Life Script Event (boy)	Age at Event
He starts playing soccer	4
He gets a playstation	6
He becomes professional soccer player	18
He plays for AGF	19
He gets into the national team	22
Wins Danish Soccer League Championship	25
Wins World Championship	28
Gets a child	30
He gets ill	75
He drops dead	95

Life Script Event (girl)	Age at Event
She travels to Croatia	3
She begins in school	6
She gets a boyfriend	10
She finishes school	15
She wants to be an actress	20
She plays in the Royal Theatre	30
The Crown Prince falls in love with her	32
He marries her	32
She becomes pregnant	36
She dies	59

Even though these two life scripts differ from the adult norm of a cultural life script because of their high degree of idiosyncrasy, they do follow the timeline of the normal life script, that is, they begin very early in life and progress chronologically until death. This chronological order can be found in the majority of the cultural life scripts at all age levels participating in this study, which is in agreement with findings from previous studies on the ablity to order events chronologically (for a review, see Habermas & Bluck, 2000). Generally, our study indicates that the major developmental differences in cultural life scripts are less to be found in the chronological order or in the perceived timing of the life script events but more in the type of events chosen for the life scripts.

As mentioned earlier, younger children were much more inclined to use idiosyncratic events in their life scripts. Many of these events can be accounted for by the "fairy tale" and "superhero" life myths. Another source of inspiration for idiosyncratic events seems to stem from the childrens' personal experiences or familiar topics, as many children use personally important or current events for their life scripts. For example, some children mentioned "First Christmas" or "First New Year's Eve" as a life script event. This choice was probably inspired by the fact that data collection took place in late November and early December. Events such as "going on vacation" or "moving" reflect personal events in the childrens' life that are important to them and that they have experienced themselves. To illustrate, consider the following series of events generated by a nine-year-old girl in response to a request for a life script for a girl within her culture: (1) "She gets two rabbits" (2) "The rabbits die" (3) "She gets two guinea pigs." Another nine-year-old girl, whose mother is a nurse in an intensive care unit, mentioned "needs oxygen from a bottle after birth" as a life script event. Here, stories she has heard her mother tell about her workplace might have led the girl to include this idiosyncratic event.

The tendency to choose life script events from a life fantasy or from currently important events and topics in one's personal life declines across middle childhood toward adolescence. At the same time, the idiosyncratic events are replaced by more normative cultural life events.

SUMMARY AND CONCLUDING COMMENTS

Even though we may be inclined to think about life stories as highly personal endeavors, life stories are greatly influenced by collectively shared norms within a given culture. Cultural life scripts are schemas for culturally expected transitional events and their timing in the average life course. In addition to influencing peoples' plans for their future, cultural life scripts structure recall from autobiographical memory and influence what we choose to include in our personal life stories. In this chapter, we have reviewed evidence showing great overlap between the distribution of autobiographical memories over the life span, on the one hand, when people are asked for memories of important or highly emotional events and, on the other hand, the distribution of normative life events when people are asked to produce life scripts. In both cases, an increase of reported events is found in young adulthood, and in both cases, this increase or bump is limited to events with a positive emotional content. Life scripts have to be learned in the same way as other forms of cultural knowledge are acquired. We have reviewed findings showing that knowledge of cultural life scripts develops throughout childhood and adolescence. Although school-aged children are able to remember and narrate about single events, they have great difficulty in telling their life story. It seems that an important prerequisite for life story abilities is the internalization of a cultural life script. Generally, the more typical life scripts children in our study produced, the more coherent life stories they constructed, whereas the ability to narrate about a single vacation event was unaffected by the degree of typicality of a life script. Children with less normative life scripts had interesting and unconventional suggestions for life script events, such as becoming a soccer star or queen of the country. Such idiosyncratic events could be seen as derived from cultural myths. Another source for idiosyncratic life events were unique experiences from the child's personal life that became projected into the normative life.

Future studies on this topic may examine cultural differences and generational differences in the contents of life scripts and how such differences may affect the content and structure of life stories in the same populations.

ACKNOWLEDGMENTS

We thank *Memory & Cognition* for the permission to reproduce Table 3.1 and Figure 3.2 from Berntsen and Rubin (2004), and Figure 3.1 from Rubin and Berntsen (2003). An extensive account of the life script notion is found in Berntsen and Rubin (2004), on which parts of this chapter is based. This work was supported by a grant from the Danish Research Council for the Humanities (273–05–0185).

REFERENCES

Abelson, R. P. (1981). Psychological status of the script concept. *American Psychologist, 36*, 715–729.

Berntsen, D., & Rubin, D. C. (2002). Emotionally charged autobiographical memories across the life span: The recall of happy, sad, traumatic, and involuntary memories. *Psychology and Aging, 17*, 636–652.

(2004). Cultural life scripts structure recall from autobiographical memory. *Memory & Cognition, 32*, 427–442.

Bluck, S., & Harbermas, T. (2000). The life story schema. *Motivation and Emotion, 24*, 121–145.

Bohn, A., & Berntsen, D. (under review).Culture and Coherence: Life story development and the acquisition of cultural life scripts in childhood and adolescence. *Developmental Psychology, 44*, 1135–1147

Charles, S. T., Reynolds, C. A., & Gatz, M. (2001). Age related differences and change in positive and negative affect over 23 years. *Journal of Personality and Social Psychology, 80*, 136–151.

Cohen, G., & Faulkner, D. (1988). Life span changes in autobiographical memory. In M. M. Gruenberg, P. E. Morris, & R. N. Sykes (Eds.), *Practical aspects of memory: Current research and issues: Vol. 1. Memory in everyday life* (pp. 277–282). New York: Wiley.

Collins, K. A., Pillemer. D. B., Ivcevic, Z., & Gooze, R. A. (2007). Cultural scripts guide recall of intensely positive life events. *Memory & Cognition, 35*(4), 651–659.

Conway, M. A., & Pleydell-Pearce, C. W. (2000). The construction of autobiographical memories in the self-memory system. *Psychological Review, 107*, 261–288.

Erdoğan, A., Baran, B., Avlar, B., Cağlar Taş, A., & Tekcan, A. I. (in press). On the persistence of positive events in life scripts. *Applied Cognitive Psychology, 22*(1), 95–112

Fitzgerald, J. M. (1992). Autobiographical memory and conceptualizations of the self. In M. A. Conway, D. C. Rubin, H. Spinnler, & W. Wagenaar (Eds.), *Theoretical perspectives on autobiographical memory* (pp. 99–114). Utrecht: Kluwer Academic Publishers.

Fivush, R., Hazzard, A., McDermott Sales, J., Sarfati, D., & Brown, T. (2003). Creating Coherence out of chaos? Children's narratives of emotionally positive and negative events. *Applied Cognitive Psychology, 17*, 1–19.

Giddens, A. (1991). *Modernity and self-identity. Self and society on the late modern age.* Cambridge: Polity Press.

Habermas, T. (2007). How to tell a life: The development of the cultural concept of biography. *Journal of Cognition and Development*, 1–31.

Habermas, T., & Bluck, S. (2000). Getting a life: The emergence of the life story in adolescence. *Psychological Bulletin, 126*, 748–769.

Luborsky, M. R. (1993). The romance with personal meaning in gerontology: Cultural aspects of life themes. *Gerontologist, 33* (4), 445–452.

Mroczek, D. K. (2001). Age and emotion in adulthood. *Current Directions in Psychological Science, 10*, 87–90.

Nelson, K. (2003). Narrative and self, myth and memory: Emergence of the cultural self. In: Fivush, R. & Haden, C. A. (Eds). *Autobiographical memory and the construction of a narrative self: Developmental and cultural perspectives* (pp. 3–28). Mahwah, NJ: Lawrence Erlbaum Associates Publisher.

Nelson, K., & Fivush, R. (2004). The emergence of autobiographical memory: A social cultural developmental theory. *Psychological Review, 111*(2), 486–511.

Neugarten, B. L., & Hagestad, G. O. (1976). Age and the life course. In R. Binstock & E. Shanas (Eds.), *Handbook of aging and social sciences* (pp. 35–55). New York: Van Nostrand Reinhold.

Neugarten, B. L., Moore, J. W., & Lowe, J. C. (1965). Age norms, age constraints, and adult socialization. *The American Journal of Sociology, 70*, 710–717.

Nicolopoulou, A., & Weintraub, J. (1998). Individual and collective representations in social context: A modest contribution to resuming the interrupted project of a sociocultural developmental psychology. *Human Development, 41*, 215–235.

Peterson, C., & McCabe, A. (1983). *Developmental psycholinguistics: Three ways of looking at a narrative.* New York: Plenum.

Reese, E. (2002). Social factors in the development of autobiographical memory: The state of the art. *Social Development, 11*(1), 124–142.

Robinson, J. A. (1992). First experiences: Contexts and functions in personal histories. In M. A. Conway, D. C. Rubin, H. Spinnler, & W. Wagenaar (Eds.), *Theoretical perspectives on autobiographical memory* (pp. 223–239). Utrecht: Kluwer Academic Publishers.

Robinson, J. A., & Taylor, L. R. (1998). Autobiographical memory and self-narratives: A tale of two stories. In C. P. Thompson, D. J. Herrmann, D. Bruce, J. D. Read, D. G. Payne, & M. P. Toglia (Eds.) *Autobiographical memory: Theoretical and applied perspectives* (pp. 125–143). Mahwah, NJ: Lawrence Erlbaum Associates.

Rubin, D. C. (2002). Autobiographical memory across the lifespan. In P. Graf & N. Ohta (Eds.), *Lifespan development of human memory* (pp. 159–184). Cambridge, MA: MIT Press.

Rubin, D. C., & Berntsen, D. (2003). Life scripts help to maintain autobiographical memories of highly positive, but not highly negative, events. *Memory & Cognition, 31,* 1–14.

Rubin, D. C., Berntsen, D., & Hutson, M. (2009 under review). The normative and the personal life: Individual differences in life scripts and life story events among USA and Danish undergraduates. *Memory, 17,* 54–68

Rubin, D. C., & Schulkind, M. D. (1997). Distribution of important and word-cued autobiographical memories in 20, 35, and 70 year-old adults. *Psychology and Aging, 12,* 524–535.

Rubin, D. C., Wetzler, S. E., & Nebes, R. D. (1986). Autobiographical memory across the adult lifespan. In D. C. Rubin (Ed.), *Autobiographical memory* (pp. 202–221). New York: Cambridge University Press.

Schank, R. C. (1982). *Dynamic memory.* New York: Cambridge University Press.

(1999). *Dynamic memory revisited.* New York: Cambridge University Press.

Schank, R. C., & Abelson, R. P. (1977). Scripts, plan, and knowledge. In P. N. Johnson-Laird & P. C. Wason (Eds.) *Thinking. Readings in cognitive science* (pp. 421–435). Cambridge: Cambridge University Press.

Ziehe, T., & Stubenrauch, H. (1982). *Plädoyer für ungewöhnliches Lernen. Ideen zur Jugendsituation.* [A pledge for unusual learning. Ideas for the situation of the young]. Reinbek: Rowohlt.

4

Specificity of Memory: Implications for Individual and Collective Remembering

DANIEL L. SCHACTER, ANGELA H. GUTCHESS, &
ELIZABETH A. KENSINGER

A great deal of research has attempted to clarify the nature and mechanisms underlying memory in individuals, and there is an increasing amount of work concerning collective remembering by societies and cultures. However, there have been few attempts to bridge the gap between these two levels of analysis, and the present volume represents a welcome step in that direction. There are, of course, many possible ways to try to bridge the divide between individual and collective memory. In the present chapter, we adopt an approach that reflects our backgrounds as researchers in the area of individual memory: we focus on a broad concept that has important implications for how we think about individual memory and that, we suggest, might also be relevant to the understanding of collective memory.

We refer to this concept as the *specificity of memory*: the extent to which, and sense in which, an individual's memory is based on retention of specific features of a past experience, or reflects the operation of specialized, highly specific memory processes. In some situations, memory is highly specific, and may include the precise details of a previous experience; in other situations, memory may be much more generic, including retention of only the general sense or gist of what happened. For example, when asked about last year's summer vacation, we may be able to recall in detail the exact meal we ate at a favorite restaurant, where we sat, who else was present, what the room looked like, and how we felt about the food we ate. But when asked about how we arrived at our vacation destination, we might remember only the general outlines of the airplane trip we took, recalling little more than a generic image of a large jet or an airport waiting area. Consider also another

We thank Alana Wong for help with preparation of the chapter. The chapter was supported by grants NIMH MH60941 and NIA AG08441 (to D.L.S.), NIA AG026920 (to A.H.G.) and MH070199 (to E.A.K.).

domain where specificity is important, albeit in a very different sense: skill learning. Sometimes practicing a skill produces a highly specific type of improvement, such as when practicing the piano results in an improved ability to play a specific piece, even though no general improvement transfers to other pieces. But some piano exercises will result in acquired skills that apply quite generally to many pieces. Just as recall can range from specific to general, so, too, can the benefits of practicing a skill.

In view of these considerations, it may not be surprising that questions concerning the specificity of memory loom large in a number of different areas of individual memory research (Schacter, Dobbins, & Schnyer, 2004; Schacter, Gallo, & Kensinger, in press). Although a comprehensive review of all aspects of memory specificity is beyond the scope of this chapter, we will attempt to convey a sense of some of the important findings and concepts that have arisen in regard to memory specificity in several domains of research. First, we will provide a brief overview of specificity issues in relation to one of the most intensively studied phenomena of human memory during the past two decades, known as *priming*: a facilitation or change in the ability of an individual to identify or produce a stimulus as a result of a recent exposure to that stimulus (Tulving & Schacter, 1990). Priming is an example of implicit memory, that is, a nonconscious form of memory that need not involve conscious or explicit recollection of a prior experience (Graf & Schacter, 1985; Schacter, 1987). We will focus on the specificity of priming – that is, when priming reflects retention of specific features of previously perceived items or specific responses made to those items (Schacter et al., 2004). Questions concerning the specificity of priming effects have been the focus of empirical and theoretical attention for nearly 30 years, and considering this research will allow us to refine exactly what we mean when we refer to the specificity of memory. We will then consider how some recent findings concerning the specificity of priming relate to specificity in the encoding of new memories, thereby illustrating how thinking about memory specificity can potentially provide links between different domains of memory research.

Continuing to focus on encoding processes, we will next consider a topic that is relevant to both individual and collective memory research: the role of the self in encoding of memories. Issues concerning the self are at the interface between individual and collective memories, so the topic is especially germane to the present volume. Memory researchers have focused in particular on the benefits of encoding new information with respect to the self, and have attempted to elucidate whether those benefits reflect processes specifically related to the self, or reflect more general benefits associated with any type of meaningful encoding activity.

Finally, we will turn to the effects of emotion on memory. We will review studies that address the question of whether emotion enhances the specificity (and accuracy) of memory, or whether it enhances the ability to remember general features of past experiences. We consider research that focuses on the role of emotion in modulating memory errors, and ask whether such modulations depend on emotion-specific processes rather than on more generalized memory mechanisms.

In each of the sections in this chapter, we will consider cognitive studies that delineate the psychological/behavioral properties of the various memory phenomena, and will also discuss recent neuroimaging studies, using techniques such as functional magnetic resonance imaging (fMRI), that provide insights into the neural correlates of memory and other cognitive processes. We believe that neuroimaging evidence can help to shape our theoretical understanding of memory specificity in various domains, and we will attempt to illustrate this point in each section.

PRIMING: LESSONS FROM SPECIFICITY EFFECTS

As noted earlier, priming refers to a change in the ability to identify, produce, or classify an item as a result of a prior encounter with that item or a related item. On priming tests, subjects are not asked to remember any particular prior experience. Instead, they may be asked to identify a briefly presented object, produce a word in response to a three-letter word stem, or classify a letter string on a lexical decision according to whether it is a word (e.g., table) or a nonword (e.g., bltae). Priming occurs when subjects perform the task more accurately or faster for previously studied items than for new, nonstudied items. Work on priming began in the 1970s, largely separate from mainstream memory research, when researchers interested in the nature of word and language processing reported priming effects on lexical decisions that were thought to provide insight into the nature and structure of word representations (e.g., Scarborough, Cortese, & Scarborough, 1977). Memory researchers became interested in priming partly as a result of studies of amnesic patients, who exhibit little or no ability to remember their recent experiences (usually as a result of damage to the hippocampus and related structures in the temporal lobe; e.g., Squire, Stark, & Clark, 2004). Surprisingly, despite patients' severe impairments of explicit memory, studies conducted during the 1970s and 1980s demonstrated that they often show normal priming effects when given a task that does not require conscious recollection, such as word stem completion, where subjects are instructed to complete three-letter word stems with the first word that pops to mind (e.g., Graf, Squire, & Mandler, 1984; Schacter, 1985; Warrington & Weiskrantz, 1974). At around the same time, research with healthy young adults revealed that a number of experimental manipulations, such as the length of the delay between study and test, or the type of encoding task performed, produced very different effects on priming tasks compared with explicit memory tasks such as recall or recognition (e.g., Jacoby & Dallas, 1981; Graf & Mandler, 1984; Tulving, Schacter, & Stark, 1982).

Almost from the beginning of research on priming, theoretical and experimental interest focused heavily on the specificity of the observed effects: the extent to which priming reflects retention of detailed information acquired during a specific prior episode, versus activation of a pre-existing abstract representation in long-term memory. Thus, for example, when subjects study a word (e.g., table) and later show priming by completing a stem (e.g., tab___) with a studied word rather than with an unstudied alternative (e.g., tablet), does such priming reflect memory for the specific features of the word presented on the list, or does it indicate that a more generic long-term representation of "table" was activated during the study task and affected later test performance? A number of important experimental papers revealed that priming effects show modality specificity on various tests (i.e., priming is reduced significantly by study-to-test changes in sensory modality), and also sometimes show specificity within a modality (e.g., changes in case or font of a word between study and test can reduce priming; see, for example, Roediger & Blaxton, 1987; Weldon & Roediger, 1987).

Since these early studies, numerous experiments have examined the nature and extent of specificity in priming (Bowers 2000). A number of different types of specificity effects have been distinguished. For example, Schacter et al. (2004) recently proposed a distinction among three types of specificity: stimulus, associative, and response. *Stimulus specificity* occurs when priming is reduced by changing physical properties of a stimulus between study and test, such as the typefont of a word or shape of an object; *associative specificity* occurs when priming is reduced because associations between target items are changed between study and test (e.g., subjects who form an association between a pair of words such as "*officer-garden*" or "*table-cloud*" show more priming when tested with "*officer-garden*" than "*officer-cloud*"); and *response specificity* occurs when priming is reduced because subjects make different responses to the same stimulus item at study and test. Stimulus and associative specificity effects have been thoroughly documented and explored in cognitive studies of priming, and more recently, by neuroimaging studies. Response specificity, by contrast, has only recently been the target of experimental investigation. We will first consider briefly neuroimaging evidence pertaining to response specificity, and then consider neuroimaging studies of stimulus specificity.

Response Specificity

Implications for Mechanisms of Priming
Recent studies of response specificity in priming have been conducted with a view toward testing ideas that have been advanced to explain priming-related changes in brain activity observed in neuroimaging studies. In such studies, participants are scanned while they carry out a task used to assess priming, such as completing three-letter word stems with the first word that comes to mind or making judgments about pictures of familiar objects. During primed scans, participants are given target items (e.g., word stems or objects) that appeared previously during the experiment; during unprimed scans, the target items did not appear previously. Virtually all studies using such materials and procedures report *decreased* activity in several cortical regions during primed scans compared to unprimed scans, most consistently in areas within the frontal lobes and the extrastriate visual cortex (for reviews, see Henson, 2003; Schacter & Buckner, 1998; Wiggs & Martin, 1998).

Wiggs and Martin (1998; see also Grill-Spector & Malach, 2001; Schacter & Buckner, 1998) contended that priming-related decreases in human neuroimaging that neural representations of objects, words, or other stimuli are sharpened or "tuned" with repetition (for more recent discussion, see Grill-Spector, Henson, & Martin, 2006). By this view, when an object is presented repeatedly, the neurons that code features that are not essential for recognizing the object show decreased responding; in so doing, they weaken their connections with other neurons involved in coding the object. Thus, the network of neurons that codes the object becomes more selective, and this neural "tuning" or sharpening is linked with faster and more efficient responding (Wiggs & Martin, 1998).

Although the neural tuning account emerges from studies concerned with perceptual priming of visual objects, it can be extended to other priming-like phenomena. For example, Raichle et al. (1994) reported that generating verbal associates to cue words yielded increased activation in several brain regions compared with simple reading of stimuli. Importantly, activation declined with repetition of the verb generation task, and this reduction correlated with reduced reaction times. Consistent with a neural tuning account, the activation reductions and associated reaction time decreases could indicate that semantic analysis of the materials is sharpened or streamlined with repetition. An alternative possibility, however, is that semantic analysis of the repeated stimuli is largely bypassed in favor of rapid retrieval of previous instances that directly indicate the appropriate response. More generally, it is possible that activation reductions in some previous priming studies could reflect such response-specific effects rather than neural tuning.

Dobbins, Schnyer, Verfaellie, and Schacter (2004) attempted to directly contrast tuning and response accounts with an object decision priming task that had been used in previous neuroimaging research, in which subjects indicated whether an object is "bigger than a shoebox"; this task had yielded evidence of reductions in priming-related activation in regions of prefrontal and fusiform cortex (e.g., Koutstaal et al., 2001). However, in previous studies subjects made the same response to repeated objects; Dobbins et al. modified the task so that sometimes subjects made the same response to repeated objects, and sometimes they made different responses to repeated objects. In the first scanning phase, pictures of common objects were either shown once or repeated three times, and subjects indicated whether each stimulus was bigger than a shoebox using a "yes" or "no" response. In the next phase, the cue was changed so that subjects were now required to indicate whether each item was "smaller than a shoebox"; they made this judgment about new items, and a subset of those that had been shown earlier. In the final scanning phase, the cue was restored to "bigger than a shoebox" and subjects were tested on new items and the remaining items from the initial phase.

If priming-related reductions in neural activity that are typically produced by this task represent facilitated size processing, attributable to "tuning" relevant aspects of neural representations, then changing the cue and associated response should have little effect on priming (although it could disrupt overall task performance by affecting both new and primed items). According to the neural tuning account, the same representations of object size should be accessed whether the question focuses on "bigger" or "smaller" than a shoebox. By contrast, if subjects come to rapidly recover prior responses, and this response learning mechanism bypasses the need to recover size representations, then the cue/response change should disrupt priming-related reductions. When the cue is changed, subjects would have to abandon learned responses and instead reengage the target objects in a controlled manner in order to recover size information.

Both fMRI and behavioral data supported the latter account. During the first scanning phase, standard priming-related activation reductions were observed in regions previously linked with priming, including left prefrontal and fusiform regions. When the cue was reversed, however, these reductions were eliminated in the left fusiform cortex and disrupted in prefrontal cortex; there was a parallel effect on behavioral response times. But when the cue was restored to the original format, priming-related reductions returned, and again there was a parallel effect on behavioral response times. These results suggest that the reductions depended on the ability of subjects to use prior responses during trials (note, however, that the effect was seen most clearly for items repeated three times before cue reversal; for further discussion of the important implications of this point, see more recent studies by Schnyer, Dobbins, Nicholls, Schacter, & Verfaellie, 2006; Schnyer et al., 2007).

This evidence for response specificity in neural priming, as indexed by fMRI signal changes, and in behavioral priming, as indexed by changes in response latencies, is perhaps surprising because previous priming research had neither documented such effects nor even considered their possible existence (for discussion of prior studies related to response specificity, see Dobbins et al., 2004; Schacter et al., 2004). Clearly, there must be limitations on response specificity: a number of well-established priming effects occur when participants make different responses during study and test. For instance, priming effects on the stem completion task, in which subjects respond with the first word that comes to mind in response to a three-letter word beginning, are typically observed after semantic or perceptual encoding tasks that require a different response. Nonetheless, the existence of response specificity poses a challenge for various theoretical accounts of priming-related decreases in fMRI signal as well as for theories aimed at purely behavioral data (for further discussion of this point, see Schacter et al., 2006).

Stimulus Specificity Links to Encoding Processes

Whereas neuroimaging evidence concerning response specificity was without much prior precedent in purely cognitive studies, neuroimaging evidence concerning stimulus specificity was preceded by a good deal of cognitive research. Much of this research involved studies in which words were used as target stimuli; the evidence showed that conditions exist in which there is an effect of changing sensory modality (auditory/visual) or within-modality perceptual features (case, typefont) on the magnitude of priming. Other studies used pictures of common objects as experimental stimuli, and showed that priming could be reduced by showing different exemplars of the same object at study and test (e.g., pictures of two different tables, dogs, cars, and so forth) or by changing specific features of the same object, such as its orientation (for review, see Schacter et al., 2004; Tenpenny, 1995).

Koutstaal et al. (2001) reported one of the first neuroimaging stud-ies to examine specificity of object priming. Previous studies had shown that repeated processing of visual objects yields activation reductions in a number of cortical regions, including fusiform and lateral occipital corti-ces as well as several regions within inferior prefrontal cortex (see Henson, 2003; Schacter & Buckner, 1998; Wiggs & Martin, 1998). Koutstaal et al. compared priming for identical objects and different exemplars with the same name, using a task in which objects were presented repeatedly, and on each presentation, subjects judged whether the object was larger than a 13" square box. Overall, subjects responded more quickly to repeated objects compared with initial presentation, indicating the presence of behavioral priming. Such priming was accompanied by reduced activity in a number of brain regions. Most important, speed of responding and correspond-ing activation reductions were greater when the same object was repeated than when a different exemplar of the object was repeated, documenting stimulus specificity. The neural specificity effect was observed in various regions involved in visual processing, including bilateral occipital and fusi-form cortices. Perhaps the most intriguing data came from a comparison of activation reductions in the right and left fusiform region for same and dif-ferent exemplars: visually specific activation reductions for object priming were greater in the right than the left fusiform cortex, suggesting that the right fusiform region is involved in processing of and memory for highly specific perceptual features of repeated objects. This pattern was of interest because earlier behavioral studies of word priming effects, in which stimuli were projected to either the left hemisphere or the right hemisphere, had indicated that stimulus specificity effects (e.g., effects of changing typefont between study and test) are greater in the right than the left hemisphere (e.g., Marsolek, Schacter, & Nicholas, 1996).

The pattern of results reported by Koutstaal et al. (2001) – greater activa-tion reduction for same than different object exemplars in the right than the left fusiform region – was replicated in a subsequent study by Simons et al. (2003), who also showed that activation reduction in the left fusiform region is sensitive to semantic (rather than perceptual) properties of studied objects. In a related study, Vuilleumier et al. (2002) used a behavioral task in which subjects decide whether pictorial images depict real or nonsense objects. Repeated stimuli were either identical, differed in size or viewpoint, or were different exemplars with the same name. Priming-related activation reductions in right fusiform cortex were sensitive to changes in both exemplars and viewpoint. Overall, then, the neuroimaging data indicate strong stimulus specificity effects of a visual nature in the right fusiform region.

Are these effects restricted to priming paradigms, or do they indicate a wider role for the right fusiform region related to memory for the specific visual features of object stimuli? Garoff, Slotnick, and Schacter (2005) examined this issue in a neuroimaging study that focused on the encoding and subsequent recognition of visual objects. They drew a distinction between specific recognition, in which one remembers the exact visual details of a previously presented object, and nonspecific recognition, in which one remembers general information about an object but not the specific visual details. For example, if an individual studies a picture of a tiger, she might later remember the visual details of the object, and thereby exhibit specific recognition of the exact tiger that had been studied. Alternatively, she might remember in general having seen a picture of a tiger, without remembering any specific visual details, thereby exhibiting nonspecific recognition. Garoff et al. reasoned that if the right fusiform cortex plays a role in encoding of specific object features, then it should be more active at the time of encoding when an individual subsequently shows specific recognition for the object compared with nonspecific recognition.

To examine the issue, Garoff et al. used what is known in neuroimaging research as a "subsequent memory" paradigm (e.g., Wagner et al., 1998). In a subsequent memory paradigm, subjects encode a list of items, and researchers measure brain activity associated with each of the individual items in the list; later, subjects are given a memory test for the previously studied items. These latter data are used to sort the items based on subjects' responses into bins comprised of remembered and forgotten items. Then, brain activity at the time of encoding is compared for the two types of items. If brain activity at the time of encoding in a particular region is greater for a subsequently remembered than for a forgotten item, then researchers infer that the region plays a role in the encoding process. In the Garoff et al. study, subjects encoded a series of pictures of common objects while in the fMRI scanner. The next day, they were given a test that included some of the same items seen the previous day, similar items that resembled the previously studied pictures (e.g., if the subject saw a picture of a tiger on the list, a different tiger would be presented on the test), and new pictures that were unrelated to any of the pictures subjects had seen previously on the study list. Subjects were instructed to respond "same" when they thought that a picture was identical to the one they had studied the previous day, "similar" when they thought that the picture was a different example with the same name as a previously studied picture (e.g., a different tiger than the one that had been seen on the list), and "new" when they thought that no picture with the same name had appeared previously on the study list. "Same" responses to same items indicate specific recognition, whereas "same" responses to similar items, and "similar" responses to same items both indicate some type of nonspecific recognition.

Garoff et al. reasoned that if the right fusiform region is involved in encoding of visual details of object, then it should be more active at the time of encoding for trials associated with subsequent specific recognition than with subsequent nonspecific recognition. This is precisely what was found: the right fusiform region was significantly more active at encoding for same pictures that receive a "same" response the next day, compared with same pictures that received a "similar" response or similar pictures that received a "same" response. Moreover, the right fusiform region was the only region in the entire brain to exhibit this pattern of greater activation at encoding for subsequent specific versus nonspecific recognition.

These results not only provide insight into the neural mechanism of encoding processes that support specific recognition, they also suggest a previously unsuspected link between the processes that subserve stimulus specificity in priming and encoding/recognition. This study thus provides one example of how thinking about specificity of memory may provide a conceptual bridge across areas that might be otherwise treated separately.

We next turn to a research domain in which neuroimaging has also played a useful role in allowing researchers to address a rather different type of issue concerning memory specificity: the specificity of encoding processes involved in making judgments that relate new information to the self.

SPECIFICITY, THE SELF, AND ENCODING PROCESSES

In the previous section, we considered neuroimaging evidence from subsequent memory paradigms concerning the encoding origins of specific and nonspecific recognition. Although this line of research has developed relatively recently, memory researchers have long been interested in how encoding processes influence memory. For example, the influential depth of processing framework (Craik & Lockhart, 1972) maintains that memories are closely linked to, and are the natural by-products of, encoding operations that are performed during the analysis of incoming information. According to this framework, deep or semantic encoding operations that elaborate the meaning of incoming information tend to produce higher levels of subsequent memory than do shallow encoding operations that focus on more superficial, nonsemantic information. However, soon after the appearance of the depth of processing framework, it was reported that encoding operations that relate information to the self support even higher levels of subsequent retention than do semantic encoding operation that do not involve reference to the self.

For example, in an early study (Rogers, Kuiper, & Kirker, 1977), participants answered orienting probes about a series of words. Some probes directed participants' attention to the words' reference to oneself (e.g., "does this word describe you?"), others directed participants to the word's semantic meaning ("is this word a synonym of 'happy'?"), and other probes focused participants on the structural features of the words ("is this word in uppercase font?"). Recall was highest in the condition that referenced the self compared to the remaining conditions. Whereas the depth of processing framework would lead to the prediction that any task that focuses on meaning should similarly enhance memory, the words that were self-referenced were recognized more frequently than those encoded through other meaning-based judgments, such as the synonym condition. Further studies established that the enhancement was specific to referencing the self, rather than any person or type of social information (e.g., Kuiper & Rogers, 1979).

Identification of the so-called self-reference effect, that is, enhanced memory for information encoded in relation to oneself, was interpreted to suggest that the self constitutes a unique and special structure in memory. The rich schema evoked by the self (Cantor & Mischel, 1977; Markus, 1977) was postulated to afford detailed cues and organizational structure to support memory, features that are unmatched by other types of semantic information (e.g., Rogers et al., 1977). This led to claims that the self was "special" and constituted a unique structure capable of enhancing memory.

Subsequent research, however, challenged the notion of self as special. The self-reference effect could be minimized, or even eliminated, when compared to tasks orienting to a personally known, intimate other (Bower & Gilligan, 1979; Ferguson, Rule, & Carlson, 1983) or social desirability (Ferguson et al., 1983). These results suggest that any rich, highly familiar cognitive structure could be used to enhance memory, although an advantage for self-referencing over these comparison conditions does emerge in within-subjects designs (McCaul & Maki, 1984) and was documented in a meta-analysis (Symons & Johnson, 1997). Evaluative dimensions, such as good/bad, could be the primary organizing principle to enhance memory, and underlie the self-reference effect because the concept of "self" spontaneously orients one to these evaluative aspects. Thus, the self-reference effect might simply represent another example of a depth of encoding manipulation (Craik & Lockhart, 1972; Craik & Tulving, 1975).

These considerations raised doubts about whether the self plays a specific role in enhancing memory; thinking about the self might instead engage processes that could enhance memory for any type of information. For example, in the adjective judgment task used by Rogers et al. (1977), self-referencing offers a relational organizational structure into the implicit categories of "me" and "not me" (Klein & Kihlstrom, 1986). In this case, recall of one self-relevant word can cue recall of another item based on their common organization around the concept of "self" (Einstein & Hunt, 1980). When the semantic conditions also share categorical relationships, recall and organization (defined as the order of output in recall) is similar for self-referenced and semantically related words. Klein and Loftus (1988) illustrated the effects of item-specific elaborative processes, extending Klein and Kihlstrom's work to suggest that organization is not the only way in which self-referencing benefits memory. Elaboration can drive the effects under some circumstances, a claim that was further supported by a meta-analysis (Symons & Johnson, 1997). These findings led Greenwald and Banaji (1989) to conclude that self-referencing relies on "ordinary" memory systems and to suggest that the self is analogous to other mnemonic structures in that arbitrary novel information can be meaningfully associated and easily accessed when rich cues are generated. In the case of self-referencing, the cues are memorable because they are self-generated, based on highly elaborated and organized existing knowledge.

The debate over self as a "special" structure in memory effectively reached a standstill when studies could not identify a unique process that caused the self to be memorable. With the advent of functional neuroimaging, which provided researchers with a new tool to examine possible dissociations between self-encoding and other forms of encoding, the debate was re-introduced. In a study using positron emission tomography (PET) to compare self and semantic encoding, participants were scanned as they judged whether adjectives described themselves, described Brain Mulroney (a former Canadian prime minister), described socially desirable traits, or counted the number of syllables in a nonsemantic control condition (Craik et al., 1999). The authors found a boost in memory for the self condition relative to the other conditions, but the neural activation pattern was quite similar for all three semantic conditions compared to the syllable judgments. Although a unique signature associated with the self did not emerge in the primary analyses, partial least squares analysis identified a predominantly right-hemisphere prefrontal activation associated with self judgments.

Because in the literature to date encoding processes had been observed primarily in the left hemisphere, the localization of self judgments to the right hemisphere was surprising because the hemisphere had been largely associated with retrieval processes (Tulving, Kapur, Craik, Moscovitch, & Houle, 1994). The authors interpreted the location of the self judgments to suggest that episodic retrieval draws heavily on self-referencing.

A later study extended these findings using a larger sample size and fMRI, which is not subject to some of the constraints on task design and spatial localization that are associated with PET. The authors identified neural regions that respond to self-judgments as distinct from neural regions that respond to judgments about semantics or another person (Kelley et al., 2002). In their study, participants viewed a series of adjectives, and alternated between judging whether the word described them (self-reference condition), described George Bush (other-reference condition), or was presented in upper- or lowercase font (case condition). Some regions (i.e., left inferior prefrontal cortex and anterior cingulate) tracked the meaningfulness of the judgments, with self and other judgments increasing activity relative to case judgments. Critically, there were also regions (i.e., medial prefrontal cortex and posterior cingulate) where self differed from the other and case conditions. If depth of encoding alone mediated the advantage for self-referencing, a single region, such as left inferior prefrontal cortex, would be expected to increase its activity across the different encoding manipulations, with maximal activation during the self judgments. Instead, Kelley et al.'s findings suggest that distinct neural regions are associated with self-referential encoding, compared to other social and nonsocial encoding manipulations, and these unique neural regions likely indicate a discrete set of cognitive operations engaged by the self.

Although this study suggests an intriguing distinction between processing of self and other, Kelley et al. (2002) did not directly link the medial prefrontal activity to memory performance; thus, the medial prefrontal activity could reflect a response to thinking about oneself but could be unrelated to successful memory encoding. In a follow-up study, Macrae and colleagues adopted a subsequent memory approach in order to investigate the role of medial prefrontal cortex in encoding processes (Macrae, Moran, Heatherton, Banfield, & Kelley, 2004). When words initially were judged for self-description, those items that were later remembered activated medial prefrontal cortex, as well as parahippocampal gyrus, more than those items later forgotten. These data suggest that the medial prefrontal regions associated with the self *do* play a functional and specific role in encoding processes. Macrae et al. posit that medial prefrontal cortex could represent a module analogous to the role of the amygdala in emotional memory, contributing as a "critical component of the human memory system" (p. 651). What is not known is whether it is most appropriate to consider medial prefrontal cortex a memory structure per se, recruited solely in the service of self-relevant information, or whether the region may prioritize self-relevant information as it interacts with the episodic memory system. Regardless of the precise mechanism, it seems clear that the contribution of medial prefrontal cortex is essential to self-referential memory, much as the research from our laboratory, reviewed in other sections of this chapter, suggests roles for the right fusiform in forming and retrieving precise perceptual memories, or the amygdala for emotional memories.

Many other studies show that the distinction between self and other is robust, and often reflected in the activity of medial prefrontal cortex. During recognition of previously studied positive and negative words, a region of medial prefrontal cortex was more active for self-referenced negative words compared to other-referenced negative words (Fossati et al., 2004). A second peak in medial prefrontal cortex responded to the valence of previously studied self-referenced words (positive > negative). Medial prefrontal cortex is activated during self-reference judgments of both positive and negative traits (Fossati et al., 2003), and activity in the region is heightened for self-descriptive traits (Moran, Macrae, Heatherton, Wyland, & Kelley, 2006), although further research is needed to test the contributions of valence and self-descriptiveness to encoding processes. Despite extensive cognitive changes, the self/other distinction holds with age, with younger and older adults similarly recruiting medial prefrontal regions and better recognizing self-referenced relative to other-referenced words (Gutchess, Kensinger, & Schacter, 2006).

Converging evidence from a number of other methods also supports the distinction between self and other recognition that has been established using neuroimaging. Many of these studies involve recognition of morphed faces, in which the faces of the subject and a familiar or famous other are blended into a single face. In these tasks, participants must recognize each morphed face as closer to their own face or the other person's face, across varying degrees of morphs (e.g., 80% self, 20% other). Wada testing, in which the left or right hemisphere is anesthetized in patients, reveals that the right hemisphere governs self-recognition (Keenan, Nelson, O'Connor, & Pascual-Leone, 2001), consistent with the initial PET study by Craik et al. (1999). Transcranial magnetic stimulation (a method that uses magnetic currents to interfere with neurotransmission in localized brain regions), also identifies a distinction across hemispheres, with temporary lesions of right inferior parietal regions disrupting self recognition (Uddin,

Molnar-Szakacs, Zaidel, & Iacoboni, 2006) and evidence for greater motor-evoked potentials in the right hemisphere associated with self recognition (Keenan et al., 2001). Evidence from split-brain patients, for whom the hemispheres have been separated by cutting the corpus callosum to restrict seizure activity, supports a self-other distinction. However, the studies are inconsistent regarding the role of the left and right hemispheres, with some supporting the idea of a right hemisphere advantage for self (Keenan, Wheeler, Platek, Lardi, & Lassonde, 2003) and others revealing a left hemisphere advantage for self recognition (Turk et al., 2002). The different findings across studies regarding the role of left and right hemispheres may reflect differences across tasks, or even individual differences across the split-brain patients. Critically, unique neural regions associated with the self emerge consistently across multiple methods.

Thus far, self has been primarily targeted as a structure with which to bolster memory performance at a general level. In contrast to the types of memory discussed in the other sections of this chapter, there has been little attention to the amount of detail associated with those memories, and whether that detail is a veridical representation of prior experience. If the benefit of self-referencing is derived primarily from the schematic nature of the self, then the retrieved information may rely on gist rather than detailed representations. Furthermore, reliance on the schematic self should also lead to systematic patterns of errors and distortions of memory. Some evidence for this comes from an investigation of the "false alarm effect," which refers to high levels of false alarms for novel information that is related to the prototype, in this case, of the self (Rogers, Rogers, & Kuiper, 1979). In this study, participants rated adjectives on a scale to denote whether the adjective was like them, or unlike them. Two and a half months later, the same participants incidentally studied a subset of these adjectives and received an old/new recognition test on the entire set of adjectives. Based on initial ratings of self-description, each participant's data were divided into quartiles, with sets ranging from the most self-descriptive to the least self-descriptive. Whereas hit rates were unaffected by the degree of self-reference, false alarms to new items were lowest for the items that were the least self-relevant, and tended to increase across quartiles as items became more self-relevant. This finding suggests that the self contributes to memory not only by enriching retrieval cues and organization but also can lead to memory errors, perhaps through a sense of familiarity as a result of chronic activation of self-relevant information.

The challenge still lies ahead for future work to clarify the impact of the self on memory through systematic consideration of the way in which it distorts memory. For example, does information closely related to the self concept lead to false alarms due to a feeling of familiarity (i.e., "'Friendliness' is a chronically activated trait for me because it is important to my self concept"), or does it actually convey recollective qualities based on one's autobiographical experience (i.e., "When I see the word 'friendly', I vividly recall many past episodes of my friendly behaviors")? It is also possible that the false alarms are more related to social desirability, rather than the self per se (Ferguson et al., 1983). The tendency to endorse positive items as self-relevant may lead to heightened levels of false alarms for positive traits, and suggests a close relationship between the memory systems associated with self and emotion (although distinct neural regions underlie these effects; Moran et al., 2006).

The studies discussed throughout this section demonstrate that the self engages specialized structures for the encoding and retrieval of self-relevant information. However, there is not consensus in the literature that self represents a "special" modality in memory (e.g., Gillihan & Farah, 2005). More work remains to be done in order to characterize the nature of the self representation and its relationship with other processes. The types of paradigms used in neuroimaging studies of self and memory are limited. It could be the case that the designs employed thus far inflate the appearance of the self as "special", much as was the case for the initial behavioral literature. For example, regions of medial prefrontal cortex have been shown to respond broadly to social information (e.g., Mitchell, Heatherton, & Macrae, 2002). In order to provide convincing evidence that the self is specifically associated with a distinct type of memory, broader exploration of these interrelated processes, as well as the specificity and qualities of self-referenced memories, is needed within the domain of memory. In addition, the roles of medial prefrontal cortex and other regions must be detailed during the formation and retrieval of self-relevant true memories, and false memories, under a variety of conditions.

SPECIFICITY AND ACCURACY OF EMOTIONAL MEMORIES

In *The Principles of Psychology*, William James stated, "It is a notorious fact that what interests us most vividly at the time is, other things equal, what we remember best. An impression may be so exciting emotionally as almost to leave a scar upon the cerebral tissues." Many people share James's intuition that when an event contains emotional importance, we remember that event in a highly specific manner, with extensive detail and clarity. The term "flashbulb memory," coined by Brown and Kulik (1977), captures the picturelike vividness that individuals often believe to accompany their memories of highly surprising and emotionally evocative events. For example, when individuals are asked what they remember about the personal circumstances in which they learned of an emotional event (e.g., the death of Princess Diana or the terrorist attacks of September 11, 2001), they often will claim to remember very specific details, such as where they were and what they were doing (e.g., Budson et al., 2004; Christianson, 1989; Kensinger, Krendl, & Corkin, 2006; Paradis et al., 2004). Studies of emotional remembering, then, raise important issues concerning memory specificity. We will address these issues by considering first research that has examined the accuracy of emotional memories and whether they are subject to distortion, and then turning to studies that have attempted to compare directly the specificity of emotional and non-emotional memories.

Numerous studies have demonstrated that these memories of emotional events are prone to significant distortions over time. Individuals often report details after a 6- or 12-month delay that conflict with those that they reported soon after the event. Moreover, although individuals can be highly confident about their memories, there often is little or no correlation between their confidence and the consistency of their memories (Neisser & Harsch, 1992; Schmidt, 2004; Schmolck et al., 2000; Talarico & Rubin, 2003). These data emphasize that emotional events do not leave indelible traces; rather, emotional memories, like nonemotional ones, are susceptible to distortion. However, studies of flashbulb memories have not allowed strong conclusions to be drawn regarding whether emotional memories are more accurate (and therefore specific) than nonemotional memories. It is nearly impossible to find nonemotional public events that are wholly comparable to the emotional ones (e.g., in media coverage, time spent discussing the event, etc.). It also is difficult (if not impossible) to assess the objective accuracy of participants' memories, requiring measures of consistency to be used as a proxy for memory accuracy.

In a recent study (Kensinger & Schacter, 2006e), we tried to circumvent the first difficulty by examining how participants' memories for an event were affected by the emotional importance of that event to them. In particular, we assessed participants' memories for the final game of the 2004 American League Championship Series between the Boston Red Sox and the New York Yankees. The Red Sox had come back from a 3–0 series deficit to overcome the New York Yankees, reversing decades of defeat by the Yankees. We asked young adults to tell us what they remembered about the game (e.g., important plays), and about the personal context in which they watched the game (e.g., who they were with, where they were), both within a few days of the event and after an approximately six-month delay. By examining the memories of participants who found the outcome of the game to be positive (i.e., Red Sox fans), negative (i.e., Yankees fans) or non-emotional (i.e., fans of neither team), we were able to examine the effect of emotion on memory consistency. The critical finding from this study was that participants who found the game to be negative were more consistent in their responses at the two time points than were other participants. The individuals who found the game to be positive, in contrast, showed more inconsistencies in their reports, and they also were overconfident in the accuracy of their responses (i.e., they demonstrated high confidence in their answers even when those responses were incorrect or inconsistent with their initial reports; see also Levine & Bluck, 2004 for a demonstration of overconfidence in individuals who were happy about the verdict in the O. J. Simpson trial). These data provide intriguing evidence that, although emotional events may not be immune to distortion, negative emotion may nevertheless provide some benefits in terms of memory accuracy.

Corroborating evidence for beneficial effects of negative emotion on memory accuracy has come from laboratory investigations. In one of the first studies to examine the effects of emotion on memory accuracy, participants were presented with lists of words that were orthographically associated to nonpresented lure words. Some of the lists were associated with emotional lures (e.g., cape, nape, tape all are associated with rape) whereas other lists were associated with neutral lures (e.g., book, look, cook all are associated with hook). After studying these lists of orthographic associates, participants were less likely to falsely recall or to falsely recognize the emotional lure words than the nonemotional ones (Kensinger & Corkin, 2004a; Pesta, Murphy, & Sanders, 2001).

These data provided suggestive evidence for an effect of emotion on memory accuracy. However, in the orthographic-list paradigm, the majority of the studied items always were neutral. Thus, the emotional lures may have been rejected due to their conceptual incongruence with the studied items rather than because of specific effects of emotion. In other words, participants may have been able to reject that rape had been on the study list because the word was not consistent with the types of (nonemotional) words that had been presented during the study phase. More direct evidence for effects of emotional salience on memory distortion has come from examinations of the effect of emotion on reality monitoring ability (the ability to distinguish what has been perceived from what has been imagined; Johnson & Raye, 1981).

Accurate assignment to an external or internal source typically can be made by remembering the types of information associated with an event: memories that originate from perception or experience usually are remembered with more perceptual detail (e.g., color, sound) and with more contextual information about the time and place of presentation. In contrast, memories originating from introspection or imagination include more detail about the cognitive operations that guided the generation of the information (Johnson, Hashtroudi, & Lindsay, 1993; Johnson & Raye, 1981). It has been proposed that participants rely on the types of information retrieved in order to decide whether an item has been perceived or imagined, and recent neuroimaging evidence has confirmed that individuals tend to believe that an item was perceived if its retrieval is associated with enhanced activation in sensory cortices, whereas they are likely to attribute an item to imagination if the item's retrieval is associated with enhanced activity in regions thought to support self-generated reflection and self-referential processing (Kensinger & Schacter, 2006b). Although remembering these characteristics typically allows accurate memory attributions, reality-monitoring errors sometimes can occur.

Kensinger and Schacter (2006d) investigated the effect of emotion on reality-monitoring performance, adapting a paradigm that had been shown to elicit high levels of reality-monitoring errors (see Gonsalves & Paller, 2000). We asked participants to view words, half of which were negative (e.g., snake, grenade) and half of which were neutral (e.g., barometer, blender). Participants formed a mental image of the named object. Half of the time, the name was followed by its photo, whereas the other half of the time it was followed only by a blank square. At retrieval, participants listened as words were pronounced over a headset, and they were instructed to indicate whether or not they had seen the corresponding photo. The critical finding from this study was that reality-monitoring errors occurred less frequently for negative arousing items compared to nonemotional ones. This enhanced discrimination for negative arousing items existed whether or not participants were informed about the memory task that would follow, and the effect was present for both verbal stimuli and single objects.

This finding is consistent with evidence indicating that emotional content enhances the linking or binding of many types of item and event details. For example, emotionally arousing items are more likely to be remembered with details such as the color of font in which a word was written or the location of a word on a screen (D'Argembeau & Van der Linden, 2004; Doerksen & Shimamura, 2001; Kensinger & Corkin, 2003; MacKay et al., 2004; MacKay & Ahmetzanov, 2005). Enhanced binding could combat reality-monitoring errors in a number of ways. It could increase the likelihood that participants remember the critical event details needed to distinguish presented from imagined events (e.g., sensory, perceptual, semantic details; Johnson et al., 1993). It also could prevent stimulus confusion. For example, after studying a picture of a tomato, a person may later falsely believe that they saw a picture of an apple if they remember only general information about that object (e.g., a red, round food). In contrast, this confusion may result less frequently for emotional items if they tend to be remembered with more detail, allowing them to be distinguished from other items.

To directly examine whether individuals are more likely to remember the specific visual details of a negative item's presentation, Kensinger, Garoff-Eaton, and Schacter (2006) presented participants with colored objects at study, some of which were negative and some of which were neutral. At retrieval, we used the previously described procedure from Garoff et al. (2005), and showed participants three different types of exemplars: "same" exemplars that were identical to the studied exemplars, "similar" exemplars that shared the same verbal labels as studied objects but that differed in any number of visual features (e.g., color, size, shape, or orientation), and "new" exemplars that were unrelated to studied objects. The data revealed that participants were better able to discriminate the "same" from "similar" exemplars when the objects were negative than when they were neutral.

These behavioral studies demonstrate that items with negative emotional content can be remembered with more detail than items lacking emotional meaning. But they leave open the question of whether this increased memory accuracy for the negative arousing information is specifically related to the processing of the emotional information, or whether it stems from engagement of the same processes that reduce memory distortion for neutral information. In other words, do the effects of emotion on memory accuracy result from increased engagement of domain-general processes that serve to boost memory accuracy for emotional and nonemotional information, or do they arise from engagement of emotion-specific processes?

This question is difficult to answer behaviorally, and so recent research has turned to neuroimaging to examine the neural processes that are engaged during the accurate encoding and retrieval of emotional and nonemotional information. Kensinger and Schacter (2005a, 2005b) asked participants to perform the reality-monitoring task, described earlier, while in the MRI scanner. As in the behavioral studies discussed above, reality-monitoring errors occurred less frequently for the negative items than for the neutral items. The critical question was whether distinct neural processes influenced the frequency of reality-monitoring errors for the two types of items.

The study revealed some overlap in the neural processes that were related to successful encoding and retrieval for the negative and neutral items. Most notably, activity in the left posterior hippocampus showed a relation to accurate encoding for both item types (i.e., greater activity during the encoding of items later correctly attributed to a presented or nonpresented source than during the encoding of items later misattributed; Kensinger & Schacter, 2005a), and activity in the anterior hippocampus showed a relation to accurate retrieval for both item types (Kensinger & Schacter, 2005b). These data suggest that there are some mnemonic processes that are broadly engaged during the successful encoding and retrieval of all items, regardless of their emotional content.

However, there also were distinctions in the neural processes that were related to accurate memory for the emotional and neutral items: enhanced activity in the amygdala and the orbitofrontal cortex corresponded with a reduction in the likelihood of memory misattributions specifically for the negative items. Activity in these regions showed a strong relation to memory accuracy for the negative items both during encoding (Kensinger & Schacter, 2005a) and during retrieval (Kensinger & Schacter, 2005b), but neither region showed a relation to memory accuracy for the neutral items. Both the amygdala and the orbitofrontal cortex are regions that frequently are engaged during the processing of emotional information (Bechara, Damasio, & Damasio, 2000; Kensinger & Schacter, 2006c; Phan et al., 2002; Zald, 2003). Thus, it appears that the way in which emotional information is processed can result in a memory accuracy advantage.

Part of the effect of these emotion-specific processes appeared to be exerted via their interactions with regions that promote accurate encoding of both emotional and nonemotional items. Activity in the amygdala was highly correlated with activity in the hippocampus during the encoding of emotional items later accurately attributed (Kensinger & Schacter, 2005a), consistent with a number of other studies that have found evidence for interactions between the amygdala and the hippocampus during the encoding on emotional information (Dolcos, LaBar, & Cabeza, 2004; Kensinger & Corkin, 2004b; Kilpatrick & Cahill, 2003; Richardson et al., 2004).

The results provide strong evidence that the enhancement in memory accuracy for emotional items does not stem solely from the additional engagement of domain-general processes that enhance accuracy for all items. Rather, domain-specific processes (in the amygdala and orbitofrontal cortex), engaged during encoding, serve to enhance memory accuracy for the emotional items. Nevertheless, the results also suggest that items with emotional content are not remembered because of engagement of processes that are entirely distinct from those that support memory for nonemotional information. Rather, there seems to be some overlap in the medial temporal-lobe mnemonic processes that support memory for information with and without emotional content (see also Kensinger & Schacter, 2006a).

Taken together, these studies demonstrate that information with negatively emotional content is more likely to be remembered accurately and specifically than is information lacking emotional salience. This boost in memory accuracy occurs across a range of behavioral paradigms and appears to result from the engagement of emotion-specific processes, particularly in the amygdala and the orbitofrontal cortex, during both encoding and retrieval.

CONCLUDING COMMENTS

In this chapter, we have reviewed evidence from several domains of individual memory in which issues regarding the specificity of memory have been salient. We discussed evidence showing the stimulus and response specificity of priming effects, and considered the relation of such specificity to memory encoding. We then discussed the role of the self in memory encoding, focusing on recent data from neuroimaging studies that suggest that self-reference encoding may constitute a specific, specialized type of memory process, rather than simply reflecting the operation of general processes that operate across a numbers of domains. Finally, we considered evidence highlighting the specificity of emotional memory.

Although we cannot say very much about how research concerning the specificity of individual memory is related to collective memory, it seems likely that specificity is a relevant dimension for collective memory research: whether a society remembers its past in a specific or general manner should have important consequences for how that society views itself. Societal differences in values and orientations to the world could dictate which dimensions are distinct and valued in memory. For example, cultures differ in the extent to which they consider the self to be an independent entity that is separate from the group, and this can also guide the expression and experience of emotion (Markus & Kitayama, 1991). It may be the case that cultures vary in the degree to which emotional and self-referential memory engage specific and special processes. Moreover, it seems to us that an important challenge would be to develop a means of assessing specificity in collective memory. Although individual memory researchers have developed a variety of techniques for assessing memory specificity in several domains, we are unaware of analogous research in the area of collective memory.

Although we have focused on specificity as an important dimension of how individuals remember their personal pasts, there is also evidence that specificity is relevant to how individuals envisage their personal futures. For example, Williams et al. (1996) gave word cues to depressed patients and healthy controls, and instructed them to recall an episode from the past or imagine a future episode. Depressed patients showed reduced specificity in their retrieval of both past and future autobiographical events – that is, they retrieved or imagined vaguer, more general events than did the controls. Furthermore, Williams and colleagues demonstrated that they could induce healthy individuals to retrieve more general events through task instructions that encouraged them to adopt a general retrieval style. Such instructions produced a comparable reduction in the specificity of subsequently generated future events. These findings, along with much other evidence from both behavioral and neuroimaging studies, suggest that remembering the past and imagining the future depend, to a large extent, on shared cognitive and neural processes (for recent review and discussion, see Atance & O'Neill, 2005; Buckner & Carroll, 2007; Schacter & Addis, 2007; Suddendorf & Busby, 2005).

It is intriguing to consider whether such a link in specificity of past and future events holds within the domain of collective memory. It seems only reasonable to assume that the specificity with which societies remember their pasts is related to how, and how specifically, they envisage their futures. Further examination of the specificity of remembering past events, and envisaging future events, would appear to be a promising possible link between research on individual and collective memories.

REFERENCES

Atance, C. M., & O'Neill, D. K. (2005). The emergence of episodic future thinking in humans. *Learning and Motivation, 36*, 126–144.

Bechara, A., Damasio, H., & Damasio, A. R. (2000). Emotion, decision making and the orbitofrontal cortex. *Cerebral Cortex, 10*, 295–307.

Bower, G. H., & Gilligan, S. G. (1979). Remembering information related to one's self. *Journal of Research in Personality, 13*, 420–432.

Bowers, J. S. (2000). In defense of abstractionist theories of repetition priming and word identification. *Psychonomic Bulletin and Review, 7*, 83–99.

Brown, R., & Kulik, J. (1977). Flashbulb memories. *Cognition, 5*, 73–99.

Buckner, R. L., & Carroll, D. C. (2007). Self-projection and the brain. *Trends in Cognitive Sciences, 11*, 49–57.

Budson, A. E., Simons, J. S., Sullivan, A. L., Beier, J. S., Solomon, P. R., Scinto, et al. (2004). Memory and emotions for the 9/11/01 terrorist attacks in patients with Alzheimer's disease, mild cognitive impairment, and healthy older adults. *Neuropsychology, 18,* 315–327.

Cantor, N., & Mischel, W. (1977). Traits as prototypes: Effects on recognition memory. *Journal of Personality and Social Psychology, 35,* 38–48.

Christianson, S.-A. (1989). Flashbulb memories: Special, but not so special. *Memory and Cognition, 17,* 435–443.

Craik, F. I. M., & Lockhart, R. S. (1972). Levels of processing: A framework for memory research. *Journal of Verbal Learning & Verbal Behavior, 11,* 671–684.

Craik, F. I. M., Moroz, T. M., Moscovitch, M., Stuss, D. T., Winocur, G., Tulving, E., et al. (1999). In search of the self: A positron emission tomography study. *Psychological Science, 10,* 26–34.

Craik, F. I. M., & Tulving, E. (1975). Depth of processing and the retention of words in episodic memory. *Journal of Experimental Psychology: General, 104,* 268–294.

D'Argembeau, A., & Van der Linden, M. (2004). Influence of affective meaning on memory for contextual information. *Emotion, 4,* 173–188.

Dobbins, I. G., Schnyer, D. M., Verfaellie, M, & Schacter, D. L. (2004). Cortical activity reductions during repetition priming can result from rapid response learning. *Nature, 428,* 316–319.

Doerksen, S., & Shimamura, A. (2001). Source memory enhancement for emotional words. *Emotion, 1,* 5–11.

Dolcos, F., LaBar, K. S, & Cabeza, R. (2004). Interaction between the amygdala and the medial temporal lobe memory system predicts better memory for emotional events. *Neuron, 5,* 855–63.

Einstein, G. O., & Hunt, R. R. (1980). Levels of processing and organization: Additive effects of individual-item and relational processing. *Journal of Experimental Psychology: Human Learning and Memory, 6,* 588–598.

Ferguson, T. J., Rule, B. G., & Carlson, D. (1983). Memory for personally relevant information. *Journal of Personality and Social Psychology, 44,* 251–261.

Fossati, P., Hevenor, S. J., Graham, S. J., Grady, C., Keightley, M L., Craik, F., et al. (2003). In search of the emotional self: An fMRI study using positive and negative emotional words. *American Journal of Psychiatry, 160,* 1938–1945.

Fossati, P., Hevenor, S. J., Lepage, M., Graham, S. J., Grady, C., Keightley, M. L., et al. (2004). Distributed self in episodic memory: Neural correlates of successful retrieval of self-encoded positive and negative personality traits. *NeuroImage, 22,* 1596–1604.

Garoff, R. J., Slotnick, S. D., & Schacter, D. L. (2005). The neural origins of specific and general memory: The role of fusiform cortex. *Neuropsychologia, 43,* 847–859.

Gillihan, S. J., & Farah, M. J. (2005). Is self special? A critical review of evidence from experimental psychology and cognitive neuroscience. *Psychological Bulletin, 131,* 76–97.

Gonsalves, B., & Paller, K. A. (2000). Neural events that underlie remembering something that never happened. *Nature Neuroscience, 3,* 1316–1321.

Graf, P., & Mandler, G. (1984). Activation makes words more accessible, but not necessarily more retrievable. *Journal of Verbal Learning and Verbal Behavior, 23,* 553–568.

Graf, P., & Schacter, D. L. (1985). Implicit and explicit memory for new associations in normal and amnesic subjects. *Journal of Experimental Psychology: Learning, Memory, and Cognition, 11*, 501–518.

Graf, P., Squire, L. R., & Mandler, G. (1984). The information that amnesic patients do not forget. *Journal of Experimental Psychology: Learning, Memory, and Cognition, 10*, 164–178.

Greenwald, A. G., & Banaji, M. R. (1989). The self as a memory system: Powerful, but Ordinary. *Journal of Personality and Social Psychology, 57*, 41–54.

Grill-Spector, K., Henson, R., & Martin, A. (2006). Repetition and the brain: Neural models of stimulus-specific effects. *Trends in Cognitive Sciences, 10*, 14–23.

Grill-Spector, K., & Malach, R. (2001). Fmr-adaptation: A tool for studying the functional properties of neurons. *Acta Psychologica, 107*, 293–321.

Gutchess, A. H., Kensinger, E. A., & Schacter, D. L. (2006). Aging and memory for self and social contexts. Presentation at the 4th International Conference on Memory, Sydney, Australia.

Henson, R. N. (2003). Neuroimaging studies of priming. *Progress in Neurobiology, 70*, 53–81.

Jacoby, L. L., & Dallas, M. (1981). On the relationship between autobiographical memory and perceptual learning. *Journal of Experimental Psychology: General, 110*, 306–340.

Johnson, M. K., Hashtroudi, S., & Lindsay, D. S. (1993). Source monitoring. *Psychological Bulletin, 114*, 3–28.

Johnson, M. K., & Raye, C. L. (1981). Reality monitoring. *Psychological Review, 88*, 67–85.

Keenan, J. P., Nelson, A., O'Connor, M., & Pascual-Leone, A. (2001). Self-recognition and the right hemisphere. *Nature, 409*, 305.

Keenan, J. P., Wheeler, M., Platek, S. M., Lardi, G., & Lassonde, M. (2003). Self-face processing in a callosotomy patient. *European Journal of Neuroscience, 18*, 2391–2395.

Kelley, W. M., Macrae, C. N., Wyland, C. L., Caglar, S., Inati, S., & Heatherton, T. F. (2002). Finding the self? An event-related fMRI study. *Journal of Cognitive Neuroscience, 14*, 785–794.

Kensinger, E. A., & Corkin, S. (2004a). The effects of emotional content and aging on false memories. *Cognitive, Affective, and Behavioral Neuroscience, 4*, 1–9.

(2004b). Two routes to emotional memory: Distinct neural processes for valence and arousal. *Proceedings of the National Academy of Sciences, USA, 101*, 3310–3315.

(2003). Memory enhancement for emotional words: Are emotional words more vividly remembered than neutral words? *Memory and Cognition, 31*, 1169–1180.

Kensinger, E. A., Garoff-Eaton, R. J., & Schacter, D. L. (2006). Memory for specific visual details can be enhanced by negative arousing content. *Journal of Memory and Language, 54*, 99–112.

Kensinger, E. A., Krendl, A. C., & Corkin, S. (2006). Memories of an emotional and a nonemotional event: Effects of aging and delay interval. *Experimental Aging Research, 32*, 23–45.

Kensinger, E. A., & Schacter, D. L. (2005a). Emotional content and reality-monitoring ability: FMRI evidence for the influence of encoding processes. *Neuropsychologia, 43*, 1429–1443.

(2005b). Retrieving accurate and distorted memories: Neuroimaging evidence for effects of emotion. *NeuroImage, 27,* 167–177.

(2006a). Amygdala activity is associated with the successful encoding of item, but not source, information for positive and negative stimuli. *Journal of Neuroscience, 26,* 2564–70.

(2006b). Neural processes underlying memory attribution on a reality-monitoring task. *Cerebral Cortex, 16,* 1126–1133.

(2006c). Processing emotional pictures and words: Effects of valence and arousal. *Cognitive, Affective, and Behavioral Neuroscience, 6,* 110–127.

(2006d). Reality monitoring and memory distortion: Effects of negative, arousing content. *Memory and Cognition, 34,* 251–260.

(2006e). When the Red Sox shocked the Yankees: Comparing negative and positive memories. *Psychonomic Bulletin and Review, 13,* 757–763.

Kilpatrick, L., & Cahill, L. (2003). Amygdala modulation of parahippocampal and frontal regions during emotionally influenced memory storage. *NeuroImage, 20,* 2091–2099.

Klein, S. B., & Kihlstrom, J. F. (1986). Elaboration, organization, and the self-reference effect in memory. *Journal of Experimental Psychology: General, 115,* 26–38.

Klein, S. B., & Loftus, J. (1988). The nature of self-referent encoding: The contribution of elaborative and organizational processes. *Journal of Personality and Social Psychology, 55,* 5–11.

Koutstaal, W., Wagner, A. D., Rotte, M., Maril, A., Buckner, R. L., & Schacter, D. L. (2001). Perceptual specificity in visual object priming: fMRI evidence for a laterality difference in fusiform cortex. *Neuropsychologia, 39,*184–199.

Kuiper, N. A., & Rogers, T. B. (1979). Encoding of personal information: Self-other differences. *Journal of Personality and Social Psychology, 37,* 499–514.

Levine, L. J., & Bluck, S. (2004). Painting with broad strokes: Happiness and the malleability of event memory. *Cognition and Emotion, 18,* 559–574.

MacKay, D. G., & Ahmetzanov (2005). Emotion, memory and attention in the taboo Stroop paradigm: An experimental analogue of flashbulb memories. *Psychological Science, 16,* 25–32.

MacKay, D. G., Shafto, M., Taylor, J. K., Marian, D. E., Abrams, L., & Dyer, J. R. (2004). Relations between emotion, memory, and attention: Evidence from taboo stroop, lexical decision, and immediate memory tasks. *Memory and Cognition, 32,* 474–488.

Macrae, C. N., Moran, J. M., Heatherton, T. F., Banfield, J. F., & Kelley, W. M. (2004). Medial prefrontal activity predicts memory for self. *Cerebral Cortex, 14,* 647–654.

Markus, H. (1977). Self-schemata and processing information about the self. *Journal of Personality and Social Psychology, 35,* 63–78.

Markus, H. R., & Kitayama, S. (1991). Culture and the self: Implications for cognition, emotion, and motivation. *Psychological Review, 98,* 224–253.

Marsolek, C. J, Schacter, D. L., & Nicholas, C. (1996). Form-specific visual priming for new associations in the right cerebral hemisphere. *Memory and Cognition, 24,* 539–556.

McCaul, K. D., & Maki, R. H. (1984). Self-reference versus desirability ratings and memory for traits. *Journal of Personality and Social Psychology, 47,* 953–955.

Mitchell, J. P., Heatherton, T. F., & Macrae, C. N. (2002). Distinct neural systems subserve person and object knowledge. *Proceedings of the National Academy of Sciences USA, 99*, 15238–15243.

Moran, J. M., Macrae, C. N., Heatherton, T. F., Wyland, C. L., & Kelley, W. M. (2006). Neuroanatomical evidence for distinct cognitive and affective components of self. *Journal of Cognitive Neuroscience, 18*, 1586–1594.

Neisser, U., & Harsch, N. (1992). Phantom flashbulbs: False recollections of hearing the news about Challenger. In E. Winograd & U. Neisser (Eds.), *Affect and accuracy in recall: Studies of "flashbulb" memories*. New York: Cambridge University Press.

Paradis, C. M., Solomon, L. Z., Florer, F., & Thompson, T. (2004). Flashbulb memories of personal events of 9/11 and the day after for a sample of New York City residents. *Psychological Reports, 95*, 304–310.

Pesta, B. J., Murphy, M. D., & Sanders, R. E. (2001). Are emotionally charged lures immune to false memory? *Journal of Experimental Psychology: Learning, Memory, and Cognition, 27*, 328–338.

Phan, K. L., Wager, T., Taylor, S. F., & Liberzon, I. (2002). Functional neuroanatomy of emotion: A meta-analysis of emotion activation studies in PET and fMRI. *Neuroimage, 16*, 331–348.

Raichle, M. E., Fiez, J. A., Videen, T. O., Macleod, A. M., Pardo, J. V., Fox, P. T., et al. (1994). Practice-related changes in human brain functional anatomy during nonmotor learning. *Cerebral Cortex, 4*, 8–26.

Richardson, M. P., Strange, B. A., & Dolan, R. J. (2004). Encoding of emotional memories depends on amygdala and hippocampus and their interactions. *Nature Neuroscience, 7*, 278–285.

Roediger, H. L. III, & Blaxton, T. A. (1987). Effects of varying modality, surface features, and retention interval on priming in word fragment completion. *Memory & Cognition, 15*, 379–388.

Rogers, T. B., Kuiper, N. A., & Kirker, W. S. (1977). Self-reference and the encoding of personal information. *Journal of Personality and Social Psychology, 35*, 677–688.

Rogers, T. B., Rogers, P. J., & Kuiper, N. A. (1979). Evidence for the self as a cognitive prototype: The "false alarms effect". *Personality and Social Psychology Bulletin, 5*, 53–56.

Scarborough, D., Cortese, C., & Scarborough, H. (1977). Frequency and repetition effects in lexical memory. *Journal of Experimental Psychology: Human Perception and Performance, 3*, 1–17.

Schacter, D. L. (1985). Priming of old and new knowledge in amnesic patients and normal subjects. *Annals of the New York Academy of Sciences, 444*, 44–53.

    (1987). Implicit memory: History and current status. *Journal of Experimental Psychology: Learning, Memory, and Cognition, 13*, 501–518.

Schacter, D. L., & Addis, D. R. (2007). The cognitive neuroscience of constructive memory: Remembering the past and imagining the future. Philosophical Transactions of the Royal Scoeity (B), 362, 773–86.

Schacter, D. L., & Buckner, R. L. (1998). Priming and the brain. *Neuron, 20*, 185–195.

Schacter, D. L., Dobbins, I. G., & Schnyer, D. M. (2004). Specificity of priming: A cognitive neuroscience perspective. *Nature Reviews Neuroscience, 5*, 853–862.

Schacter, D. L., Gallo, D. A., & Kensinger, E. A. (2006). The cognitive neuroscience of implicit and false memories: Perspectives on processing specificity. In J. S. Naime (Ed.), *The foundations of remembering: Essays honoring Henry L. Roediger III* (pp. 353–377). New York: Psychology Press.

Schmidt, S. R. (2004). Autobiographical memories for the September 11th attacks: Reconstructive errors and emotional impairment of memory. *Memory and Cognition, 32*, 443–454.

Schmolck, H., Buffalo, E. A., & Squire, L. R. (2000). Memory distortions develop over time: Recollections of the O. J. Simpson trial verdict after 15 and 32 months. *Psychological Science, 11*, 39–45.

Schnyer, D. M., Dobbins, I. G., Nicholls. L., Davis, S., Verfaellie, M., & Schacter, D. L. (2007). Item to decision mapping in rapid response learning. *Memory and Cognition, 35*, 1472–1482.

Schnyer, D. M., Dobbins, I. G., Nicholls, L., Schacter, D. L., & Verfaellie, M. (2006). Rapid response learning in amnesia: Delineating associative learning components in repetition priming. *Neuropsychologia, 44*, 140–149.

Simons, J. S., Koutstaal, W., Prince, S., Wagner, A. D., & Schacter, D. L. (2003). Neural mechanisms of visual object priming: Evidence for perceptual and semantic distinctions in fusiform cortex. *NeuroImage, 19*, 613–626.

Suddendorf, T., & Busby, J. (2005). Making decisions with the future in mind: Developmental and comparative identification of mental time travel. *Learning and Motivation, 36*, 110–125.

Squire, L. R., Stark, C. E. L., & Clark, R. E. (2004). The medial temporal lobe. *Annual Review of Neuroscience, 27*, 279–306.

Symons, C. S., & Johnson, B. T. (1997). The self-reference effect in memory: A meta-analysis. *Psychological Bulletin, 121*, 371–394.

Talarico, J. M., LaBar, K. S., & Rubin, D. C. (2004). Emotional intensity predicts autobiographical memory experience. *Memory and Cognition, 32*, 1118–1132.

Tenpenny, P. L. (1995). Abstractionist versus episodic theories of repetition priming and word identification. *Psychonomic Bulletin & Review, 2*, 339–363.

Tulving, E., Kapur, S., Craik, F. I. M., Moscovitch, M., & Houle, S. (1994). Hemispheric encoding retrieval asymmetry in episodic memory: Positron emission tomography findings. *Proceedings of the National Academy of Sciences, USA, 91*, 2016–2020.

Tulving, E., & Schacter, D. L. (1990). Priming and human memory systems. *Science, 247*, 301–306.

Tulving, E., Schacter, D. L., & Stark, H. (1982). Priming effects in word-fragment completion are independent of recognition memory. *Journal of Experimental Psychology: Learning, Memory, and Cognition, 8*, 336–342.

Turk, D. J., Heatherton, T. F., Kelley, W. M., Funnell, M. G., Gazzaniga, M. S., & Macrae, C. N. (2002). Mike or me? Self-recognition in a split-brain patient. *Nature Neuroscience, 5*, 841–842.

Uddin, L. Q., Molnar-Szakacs, I., Zaidel, E., & Iacoboni, M. (2006). rTMS to the right inferior parietal lobule disrupts self-other discrimination. *Social Cognitive and Affective Neuroscience, 1*, 65–71.

Vuilleumier, P., Henson, R. N., Driver, J., & Dolan, R. J. (2002). Multiple levels of visual object constancy revealed by event-related fMRI of repetition priming. *Nature Neuroscience, 5*, 491–499.

Wagner, A. D., Schacter, D. L., Rotte, M., Koutstaal, W., Maril, A., Dale, A. M., et al. (1998). Building memories: Remembering and forgetting of verbal experiences as predicted by brain activity. *Science, 281*, 1188–1190.

Warrington, E. K., & Weiskrantz, L. (1974). The effect of prior learning on subsequent retention in amnesic patients. *Neuropsychologia, 12*, 419–428.

Weldon, M. S., & Roediger, H. L. (1987). Altering retrieval demands reverses the picture superiority effect. *Memory & Cognition, 15*, 269–280.

Wiggs, C. L., & Martin, A. (1998). Properties and mechanisms of perceptual priming. *Current Opinion in Neurobiology, 8*, 227–33.

Williams, J. M., Ellis, N. C., Tyers, C., Healy, H., Rose, G., & MacLeod, A. K. (1996). The specificity of autobiographical memory and imageability of the future. *Memory & Cognition, 24*, 116–125.

Zald, D. H. (2003). The human amygdala and the emotional evaluation of sensory stimuli. *Brain Research: Brain Research Review, 41*, 88–123.

PART III

HOW DO WE BUILD SHARED
COLLECTIVE MEMORIES?

We all know that in many human groups people have created a particular version of their own collective past, represented by most members in
roughly similar ways, and passed on from generation to generation. So far
so good. But how does that occur?

Vague notions, especially when they seem profound and richly evocative,
often stand in the way of precise empirical investigation. That is a common
occurrence in the social and behavioral sciences, and nowhere is a warning
against such seductive concepts more apposite than in the study of shared
memories and the collective past. It is not clear in precisely what manner
the notion of "collective memory" helps us make sense of how people create
distinctive versions of their collective past and come to share these versions.
The metaphor is not just unclear but also misleading, as James Wertsch
points out (this volume). First, talking about memory rather than remembering obscures the fact that there are agents here, people who actively listen, select, modify, or rigidify particular versions of their past. Second, it
also blurs the functions of such memories, which are not about the past but
emphatically about present interests and conflicts. This marks the simplest
contrast between scholarly history and collective remembering – the latter has an agenda rather than a method, particular goals but no explicit
standards (Wertsch, 2002). The process of construction, as in the case of
individual memories, is largely implicit. Apart from the limiting-case of
deliberate propaganda, people are not usually aware of the many ways in
which psychological processes shape their traditions. For instance, particular scripts or idealized scenarios make specific versions of national histories
particularly compelling, as Werstch demonstrates on the Russian case.

This is only one example of the many ways in which the memory processes usually studied by psychologists directly shape the contents and
transmission of cultural knowledge of the past. As Roddy Roediger and

colleagues demonstrate (this volume), many standard manipulations of experimental psychology have their counterpart in the domain of representations of the collective past. Experimental protocols show the effects of retrieval on recall – information that is accessed, and is accessed often, is more likely to be retained in a roughly faithful manner – this is why we should expect recurrent memorial occasions to support strong identification with a common past. Also, laboratory studies show the effects of feedback on memory – and lead us to expect social feedback, for example, through the teaching of national histories in schools, to have particular effects on representations of the past. Finally, particular emotions and the parameters of the emotional scenes or information predict particular recall patterns – an effect demonstrated by the famous "flashbulb memories," usually so vividly recalled (e.g., "Where were you when you heard of the 9/11 attacks?") and with such confidence (Neisser & Harsch, 1993).

This kind of systematic description of individual processes and their effects on shared representations shows us how far we can go, beyond the vagueness of collective memory, towards an empirical explanation of recurrent properties of people's notions of their past. Another indispensable study is the actual observation of historical memories in the making, that is, tracking the individual processes triggered by the event and gradually leading to a collectively accepted version. Very few psychologists or social scientists have undertaken such field studies, with the notable exception of Jamie Pennebaker (Pennebaker, Páez, & Rimé, 1997, and this volume). His naturalistic studies of such historical disasters as the 9/11 attacks or presidential assassinations, as well as many other traumatic events, illustrate the important role of implicit processes, and consequently of implicit methods, in this domain. The gradual construction of a shared history goes through particular phases and processes that are far from obvious to the actors themselves – see, for instance, how people's use of the personal pronouns "I" and "we" changes quickly after such a dramatic event (Pennebaker & Gonzales, this volume), or how their narratives of the event change over time.

Such implicit processes are not usually considered in the social science and history of shared representations, focused as these disciplines often are on what actors actually say about historical processes and their consequences. In the political field, too, experimental studies illuminate some of the implicit processes at work, as demonstrated by Alan Lambert and colleagues. Dramatic historical events often usher in equally dramatic political changes – but traditional political science has little to say about the microprocesses underpinning such changes. Rational choice models of actors with complete information and clearly expressed preferences only account for part of the variance in political attitudes, which motivated the recent development of an empirical, indeed experimental political psychology (Lane, 2003). Lambert and colleagues demonstrated how a familiar political phenomenon – "rallying the flag" in situations of perceived national danger – is the outcome of complex cognitive processes, to do with the particular identification of perceived threat, the identification of which particular coalition is threatened, and strong intuitions about the logic of threat and counterthreat (Navarrete, Kurzban, Fessler, & Kirkpatrick, 2004).

REFERENCES

Lang, R. E. (2003). Rescueing Political Science from Itself. In D. O. Sears, L. Huddy & R. Jervis (Eds.), *Oxford Handbook of Political Psychology* (pp. 755–794). Oxford: University Press.

Navarrete, C. D., Kurzban, R., Fessler, D. M. T., & Kirkpatrick, L. A. (2004). Anxiety and Intergroup Bias: Terror Management or Coalitional Psychology? *Group Processes & Intergroup Relations*, 7(4), 370–397.

Neisser, U., & Harsch, N. (1993). Phantom flashbulbs: False recollections of hearing the news about Challenger. In E. Winograd & U. Neisser (Eds.), *Affect and accuracy in recall: Studies of "flashbulb" memories* (pp. 9–31). New York, NY: Cambridge University Press.

Pennebaker, J. W., Páez, D., & Rimé, B. (1997). *Collective memory of political events: Social psychological perspectives.* Mahwah, NJ: Lawrence Erlbaum Associates.

Wertsch, J. V. (2002). *Voices of collective remembering.* New York: Cambridge University Press.

5

Collective Memory

JAMES V. WERTSCH

"Collective memory" is a term that appears frequently in the media and everyday conversation. We use it when talking about the causes of ethnic violence and geopolitical miscalculation, political leaders invoke it in times of crisis, and it is behind massive expenditures on museums and holidays. In general, it is hard to go more than a few days without encountering the notion somewhere, but when we try to say just what collective memory is, we realize how little we understand about its workings.

Despite – or perhaps because of – this conceptual muddle, a renewed "memory industry" (Klein, 2000) has sprung up over the past two decades. The open-ended nature of this enterprise is reflected in the plethora of terms that can be found in writings on the topic, terms such as "public memory" (Bodnar, 1992), "social memory" (Burke, 1989; Connerton, 1989), "cultural memory" (Berliner, 2005), "bodily memory" (Young, 1996), "historical consciousness" (Seixas, 2004), and "mnemonic battles" (Zerubavel, 2003).

Part of the difficulty in bringing together all these strands of inquiry stems from the number of disciplines involves. The list includes anthropology (Berliner, 2005; Cole, 2001), history (Novick, 1999), psychology (Pennebaker, Paez, & Rimé, 1997), and sociology (e.g., Schuman, Schwartz, & D'Arcy, 2005). Further complications arise from the fact that collective memory can be at the center of debates – often quite heated – in the public arena and popular media where little attention is given to clear definitions. Consider, for example, the dispute between Estonia and Russia over how the 1939 Molotov-Ribbentrop Pact should be remembered, the mnemonic standoff between Turks and Armenians over what happened to Ottoman Armenians in 1915, or unresolved differences in the United States over slavery.

In short, collective memory is a notion that is widely invoked and discussed, yet it is little understood. Instead of having a commonly accepted definition, there may be as many definitions as there are parties discussing it, and these definitions may overlap, conflict, or simply be unrelated. It would be a tall order – if not simply misguided – to try to fit these competing notions into a tightly structured conceptual framework, and I shall not attempt to do so here. Instead, I shall present some basic oppositions intended to outline the conceptual field on which the debate over collective memory is carried out. These oppositions are best viewed as continua, as tensions and overlap – rather than ironclad distinctions – are often involved. The hope is to create a conceptual field that allows productive engagement in memory studies.

The oppositions outlined in the sections that follow are strong versus distributed accounts of collective memory, collective versus individual memory, history versus memory, and specific memory versus deep memory.

STRONG VERSUS DISTRIBUTED ACCOUNTS OF COLLECTIVE MEMORY

When discussing collective memory, it is all too tempting to approach it in terms of loose analogies with individual memory. Discussions of America's memory about Vietnam, for example, often seem to presuppose that America is some sort of large being that has intentions, desires, memories, and beliefs just as individuals do. Such presuppositions lie behind statements such as "America's memory of Vietnam makes it sensitive to charges that Iraq may be a quagmire."

Assumptions of this sort have often been the object of legitimate critiques. Frederic Bartlett, the father of modern memory studies in psychology, was critical of the "more or less absolute likeness [that] has been drawn between social groups and the human individual" (1995, p. 293), and he warned that collectives, in and of themselves, do not have some sort of memory. Bartlett's critique was aimed at the French sociologist Maurice Halbwachs, who is usually credited with founding the modern study of collective memory. As Mary Douglas (1980) has noted, Bartlett's "travestied account" (p. 16) of Halbwachs may have misinterpreted him, but the general observation behind Bartlett's comments is on the mark and worth understanding.

Indeed, Bartlett himself was quite concerned with the social dimension of memory. Much of his argument was about how the memory of individuals is fundamentally influenced by the social context in which they function. One of his central claims in this regard was that "social organisation gives a persistent framework into which all detailed recall must fit, and it very powerfully influences both the manner and the matter of recall" (1995, p. 296).

What he espoused in the end is a position that recognizes "memory *in* the group, [but] not memory *of* the group" (p. 294) and in reality does not fundamentally contradict Halbwachs (Wertsch, 2002). Misguided assumptions about memory "*of* the group" continue to surface, however, and they constitute what can be termed a "strong version" of collective memory (Wertsch, 2002). When made explicit, these claims are often rejected, but implicit analogies between individual and collective processes continue to emerge in many discussions.

An alternative that recognizes memory in the group without slipping into questionable assumptions about memory of the group is a "distributed version" of collective memory. From this perspective, memory is viewed as being distributed: (a) socially in small group interaction, as well as (b) "instrumentally" in the sense that it involves both active agents and instruments that mediate remembering (Wertsch, 2002). In the case of social distribution, for example, Mary Sue Weldon (2001) has examined the "collaborative remembering" that occurs when groups of individuals work together to recall information or events from the past.

Instrumental distribution, which is the primary focus of what follows, involves active agents, on the one hand, and cultural tools such as calendars, written records, computers, and narratives, on the other. It is a notion that derives from the ideas of Lev Semënovich Vygotsky about the "instrumental method" in psychology (Vygotsky, 1981). By introducing the notion of mediation, Vygotsky sought to move beyond the "methodological individualism" (Lukes, 1977) that characterized the psychology of his day and continues to be part of the discipline. His basic point was that human action, including mental processes, can be understood only by appreciating its reliance on tools and signs. This attempt to avoid individualistic reductionism should not be taken to amount to a kind of "instrumental reductionism" in which active agents are sidelined to the point of being mere pawns of the tools they employ. Instead, the point is to approach human action, including thinking, remembering, and other mental processes, from the perspective of how it involves an irreducible tension between active agent and cultural tool (Wertsch, 1998).

The emphasis on mediated *action* entailed in this view means that it would be preferable to speak of collective *remembering* rather than collective memory, and in this connection it is noteworthy that Bartlett's classic work has "remembering" rather than "memory" in the title. With this in mind, the term "remembering" will often be used in what follows, but the widespread practice of using "memory" and "collective memory" means that it is nearly impossible to avoid these terms altogether.

Given this focus on mediated action and instrumentally distributed collective remembering, a crucial consideration is the type of instruments, or "cultural tools" (Wertsch, 1998) used to remember the past. Several different instruments, each suggesting a particular form of remembering, have been put forth as being important. Although making no attempt to provide a complete inventory of these cultural tools, it is worth noting a basic divide between two forms of mediation that have emerged in this discussion. This is the divide between explicit linguistic forms, especially narratives, that represent the past, on the one hand, and forms of mediation that rely less on explicit linguistic representation and more on embodied practices, on the other.

In many accounts of collective remembering it is assumed that narrative or other linguistic forms are the basic tools involved, and indeed language will be the focus of what follows. However, it is worth noting the critique of this assumption that has been leveled by analysts such as Paul Connerton. In *How Societies Remember* (1989), he noted the strong bias toward assuming recollection is "something that is inscribed." He viewed this as a limitation that derives from a linguistic bias in hermeneutic scholarship, arguing that "although bodily practices are in principle included as possible objects of hermeneutic inquiry, in practice hermeneutics has taken inscription as its privileged object" (p. 4).

This critique provided the foundation for Connerton's notion of "habit memory." In his view "If there is such a thing as social memory … , we are likely to find it in commemorative ceremonies; but commemorative ceremonies prove to be commemorative only in so far as they are performative; performativity cannot be thought of without a concept of habit; and habit cannot be thought without a notion of bodily automatisms" (pp. 4–5). Like Halbwachs, Connerton derives crucial aspects of his account of memory from the social theory of Emile Durkheim, something that led to a focus on ritual and ritualistic practice.

Notions of habits and patterns of action clearly deserve a place in the study of collective remembering, and as I shall argue in the analysis of specific versus deep memory, they actually play a role in linguistic mediation. I begin, however, by focusing on linguistic mediation, especially in the form of narrative. Jerome Bruner (1990) has noted that narratives occupy a particularly important place in the "toolkit" of human cognition in general, and they can also be expected to be a crucial cultural tool for representing the past, both in history and in memory. From this perspective, what makes collective memory collective is the fact that members of a group share the same narrative resources. By harnessing and discussing these narrative resources, the group is shaped into what Brian Stock (1990) has called a "textual community."

The centrality of narratives and other forms of linguistic mediation in a distributed version of collective remembering has several implications. To say that narratives and other forms of linguistic mediation do some of the remembering for us would suggest the sort of instrumental reductionism rejected earlier, but such a formulation does provide a reminder of how central cultural tools are in the process.

COLLECTIVE VERSUS INDIVIDUAL REMEMBERING

The study of collective and individual remembering differs greatly in terms of the disciplines involved and the methods employed. Individual memory has been a central topic in psychology for over a century, and the result is that relatively well established and accepted terms and methods have emerged. To be sure, many disagreements remain, but psychologists begin their discussion with the working assumption that terms like "short-term memory," "long-term memory," "semantic memory," and "episodic memory" can be used with some shared understanding.

There are two additional defining features of the psychological study of memory worth noting when contrasting it with the study of collective memory. The first is the assumption that memory can be studied in isolation from other aspects of mental life, and the second is that a basic metric for assessment is accuracy. Assuming that memory can be studied in isolation is consistent with views of it as a faculty or specialized skill, sometimes coupled with claims about specific regions of the brain or neural networks. But even more important than such conceptual commitments are the methods employed in psychology to study memory. As in the study of cognition, attention, and other aspects of mental functioning, the disciplinary norm for examining memory is to employ experimental settings where variables can be controlled and hypotheses tested.

This control of variables approach imposes major limitations on what can be studied, but it clearly has yielded conceptual and empirical breakthroughs. As an example of this, consider the phenomenon of "memory distortion" outlined by Henry Roediger and Kathleen McDermott (1995). Without the experimental methods they employed, it is doubtful that this phenomenon could have been uncovered. Using carefully controlled lists of words and experimental conditions, these researchers demonstrated that subjects are likely to systematically, but falsely recognize certain words in recall and recognition experiments. For instance, when presented with a list such as *door, glass, pane, ledge, sill, house, open, curtain, frame, view, breeze, sash, screen,* and *shutter,* subjects are likely to "remember" that *window* was in the list – even when they are explicitly warned that they would be tempted to include incorrect items.

As is the case for much of the psychological research on memory, the methodological standards employed in this case are linked to the assumption that memory is a distinct phenomenon that can be studied in relative isolation from other mental functions. From this perspective, it is entirely legitimate – indeed, preferable – to study memory in and of itself, and it is also assumed that there are settings in which individuals can engage in remembering strictly for the sake of remembering.

This approach contrasts with that often employed in most discussions of collective memory. Instead of assuming that one can study remembering in and of itself, the guiding assumption is that it is invariably bound up with something else. Partly for this reason, collective remembering seldom lends itself to being studied with a methodology grounded in the control of variables. Instead, it is viewed as existing in a complex setting and in the service of providing a "usable past" (a notion that derives from Nietzsche, 1874). A usable past is almost invariably part of some identity project such as mobilizing a nation to resist an enemy. As such, collective remembering is taken to be part of some broader agenda, and any attempt to consider it in isolation or view it as amenable to an experimental paradigm would be viewed as destroying the very phenomenon to be studied.

These observations are related to an additional point that distinguishes the study of individual and collective memory – what will be termed here the "accuracy criterion." The very notion of memory presupposes some representation (in the broadest sense) of the past, and it is usually assumed that this representation makes some claim to being accurate. As already noted in the case of collective remembering, however, other competing functions and hence other criteria for assessing the appropriateness and power of memory may be involved. The issue, then, is the degree to which accuracy is a criterion by which to assess a memory performance.

In the psychological study of individual memory, the accuracy criterion takes a front seat. This is not to claim that psychologists believe individual memory to be particularly accurate. If anything, decades of research have shown myriad ways that memory can be *in*accurate. But the point remains that the basic metric by which many memory studies in psychology is assessed is accuracy. One cannot talk about memory "distortion" (Roediger & McDermott, 1995), "false" memory (Schacter, 1996, chapter 9), or many other major topics in the field without presupposing accurate representation of past events as a comparison point.

Things stand somewhat differently when it comes to the study of collective remembering. As already noted, most research traditions concerned with this topic have assumed that collective remembering can only be understood as part of a larger picture. For example, in studies that focus on socially distributed (as opposed to instrumentally distributed) memory, David Middleton and his colleagues (Middleton & Edwards, 1990) have argued that remembering often occurs in the context of the discursive negotiation of social differences and identity. And in another line of research concerning "public memory," John Bodnar (1992) views remembering as part of a never-ending struggle between "official culture" and "vernacular culture" in a society.

The larger picture of which collective memory is a part is usually formulated in terms of conflict and negotiation rather than approximation to accurate representation. Such conflict and negotiation occur in the social and political sphere (Bodnar, 1992; Wertsch, 2002) of "memory politics" (Hacking, 1996) and are carried out in the service of providing a usable past that serves some identity project. This is not to say that accuracy is not important or is not assumed by those doing the remembering, but it does mean that accuracy is of secondary importance and may be sacrificed to the extent required to serve other functions.

A psychologist whose research of individual memory provides a sort of bridge to this discussion in collective memory studies is Martin Conway (e.g., Conway & Playdell-Pearce, 2000; Williams & Conway, this volume). In contrast to many analyses in psychology that assume memory can be studied in isolation from other aspects of mental life, Conway and Playdell-Pearce argued for the need to examine autobiographical memory as part of a larger system of self and life goals. Another researcher who has developed a related line of research is Michael Ross (1989), who has argued that the "implicit theories" we have about ourselves shape our autobiographical memory. Like many psychologists, Ross assumes that remembering is often not very accurate, at least with regard to details, but he goes beyond many others in viewing the recall of personal histories as being systematically shaped by powerful biasing factors, including implicit theories.

In sum, the study of collective memory stands in contrast to research on individual memory in several ways, many of which have to do with disciplines and the methods associated with them. Psychological research on individual memory has tended to rely on laboratory methods that allow for controlled experimentation, and this has encouraged it to focus on memory as an isolated mental process. Furthermore, it has encouraged the privileging of the criterion of accuracy when formulating research questions. In contrast, studies of collective remembering have tended to focus on how memory is part of complex processes such as the negotiation of group identity, and this has led to a view of remembering as contestation and negotiation in social and political spheres. This focus, in turn, has placed issues of accuracy in a secondary position.

The different methods employed in the study individual and collective remembering have given rise to different notions of what remembering is, but several scholars have provided analyses that seem to serve both orientations. Perhaps the most prescient of these – once again – was Frederic Bartlett, the father of the modern memory studies in psychology. He emphasized that the active processes of remembering involves an "effort after meaning" (1995, p. 20), a formulation that applies to the kind of laboratory experiments by Roediger and McDermott as well as the account of public memory outlined by Bodnar.

HISTORY VERSUS MEMORY

The understanding of history and memory has itself undergone transformation over the past several centuries. In particular, the rise of mass literacy and the mental habits associated with it have had a profound impact on human memory. Literacy makes possible what cognitive scientists call the "off-loading" of information (Bechtel & Abrahamsen, 1991) into written texts, and the history of this process has been explored by analysts such as Merlin Donald (1991). The crucial point in what follows, however, is that the emergence of literacy – especially its widespread dissemination during the Enlightenment – has been associated with privileging new forms of critical thought and discourse. This, in turn, has been associated with a new way of representing the past.

This way of representing the past is usually termed "history" and stands in opposition to memory. In the 1920s, Halbwachs formulated a version of this in his comments about how "formal history" differs from collective memory (1950, p. 78), and in one form or another, the opposition continues to be a part of the discussion today. In many such discussions, however, the notion of collective memory remains underexplored, if not nebulous. In the words of the historian Kerwin Lee Klein, "Much current historiography pits memory against history even though few authors openly claim to be engaged in building a world in which memory can serve as an alternative to history" (2000, p. 128).

As a starting point for discussing this distinction, consider the following comments by Peter Novick (1999), a historian who has built on the ideas of Halbwachs in arguing:

To understand something historically is to be aware of its complexity, to have sufficient detachment to see it from multiple perspectives, to accept the ambiguities, including moral ambiguities, of protagonists' motives and behavior. Collective memory simplifies; sees events from a single, committed perspective; is impatient with ambiguities of any kind; reduces events to mythic archetypes. (pp. 3–4)

Contemporary discussions of how formal or analytic history differs from memory have been at the heart of recent debates carried on by Pierre Nora (1989), who has argued that "real memory" has been largely pushed aside, if not eradicated by the practices of creating analytic historical accounts of the past. The result is that "we speak so much of memory because there is so little of it left" (p. 7), and we have a felt need to create *lieux de mémoire* (sites of memory) "because there are no longer *milieux de mémoire*, real environments of memory" (p. 7).

In Nora's view, memory and history are not just different; they stand in fundamental, even implacable opposition. For him, memory "remains in permanent evolution" and is "unconscious of its successive deformations, vulnerable to manipulation" (p. 8). In contrast, "history, because it is an intellectual and secular production, calls for analysis and criticism... At the heart of history is a critical discourse that is antithetical to spontaneous memory" (pp. 8–9). The nature of this opposition is such that "history is perpetually suspicious of memory, and its true mission is to suppress and destroy it" (p. 9). Nora's line of reasoning does not entail that analytic history simply supplants memory. Instead, the implicit contrast with history resulted in an ongoing differentiation and redefinition of what memory is, and the struggle over this issue continues in the renewed debates that have emerged over the past few decades.

The upshot of this ongoing differentiation of history from memory is that it is often difficult to categorize accounts unequivocally as either one or other. Instead, they typically need to be positioned on a continuum, thereby recognizing that they are typically a mixture of both ways of relating to the past. For example, official histories produced by modern states clearly include elements of collective remembering as well as history. Indeed, scholars such as Louis Mink (1978) and Hayden White (1987) have raised questions about whether *any* representation of the past – including those generated by those most concerned with objectivity in analytic history – can be genuinely distanced and objective and hence whether this distinction can be maintained.

But even those who are most critical of the distinction between history and memory accept that it must be accepted in some form. For example,

Novick (1988), a figure who has produced a major critique of the "noble dream" of objectivity in history, contrasts history's willingness to deal with complexity and multiple perspectives with the tendency of collective memory to simplify, to see events from a "single committed perspective," and to be "impatient with ambiguities of any kind" (1999, pp. 3–4).

In developing his version of the distinction between history and collective memory, Novick goes so far as to assert that the latter "is in crucial senses ahistorical, even anti-historical" (p. 3). This is so because

> Historical consciousness, by its nature, focuses on the *historicity* of events – that they took place then and not now, that they grew out of circumstances different from those that now obtain. Memory, by contrast, has no sense of the passage of time; it denies the "pastness" of its objects and insists on their continuing presence. Typically a collective memory … is understood to express some eternal or essential truth about the group – usually tragic. A memory, once established, comes to define that eternal truth, and, along with it, an eternal identity, for the members of the group. (p. 4)

Recent studies of commemoration, a practice closely tied to collective remembering, have made similar points about the tendency to eschew ambiguity and to present the past from a single committed perspective. In his discussion of the distinction between the commemorative voice and the historical voice in history museum exhibits, for example, Edward Linenthal (1996) touched on this point in analyzing the dispute over the Enola Gay exhibit in the National Air and Space Museum in 1995, a case that escalated into a "history war" (Linenthal & Engelhardt, 1996). Linenthal concluded that accepting a single committed perspective results in viewing the museum as a "temple" (p. 23), whereas encouraging the exploration of ambiguity presupposes that the museum is a "forum." In the museum as a forum there is a tendency to take into consideration the "complicated motives of actions and consequences often hardly considered at the moment of the event itself" (pp. 9–10). Instead of being a "reverently held story," it should involve "later reappraisal" (p. 10) of these complicated motives, actions, and consequences.

In another analysis of the forces that gave rise to the history wars around the Enola Gay exhibit, the historian John Dower (1996) provided additional insight into how history differs from commemoration and memory more generally. Specifically, he discussed "two notions that most historians take for granted that controversy is inherent in any ongoing process of historical interpretation, and that policymaking is driven by multiple considerations and imperatives" (p. 80). In formulating ways in which commemoration and collective remembering stand in opposition to history Dower outlined a notion of heroic narrative as being inherently hostile to the assumptions guiding the historian.

Heroic narratives demand a simple, unilinear story line. In popular retellings, that simple line often takes the form of an intimate human-interest story.... In the case of the atomic bombs, the American narrative almost invariably gravitates to Colonel Paul W. Tibbets Jr., who piloted the famous plane, and his crew – brave and loyal men, as they surely were. And the pilot and his crew tell us, truthfully, what we know they will: that they carried out their mission without a second thought in order to save their comrades and help end the war. Such accounts ... tell us little if anything about how top-level decisions were made – about who moved these men, who gave them their orders, and why. To seriously ask these questions is to enter the realm of multiple imperatives (pp. 80–81).

By way of summarizing these points, consider a set of oppositions that can be used to distinguish collective memory from analytic history. At the risk of reinforcing the mistaken impression that the two can be easily and neatly separated, these are listed below. It is essential to keep in mind that the oppositions outlined here are *tendencies* and *aspirations* of collective memory and history rather than ironclad attributes and that the opposing tendencies often operate in tension with one another.

Collective Memory	History
"Subjective"	"Objective"
Single committed perspective	Distanced from any particular perspective
Reflects a particular group's framework	Reflects no particular social framework
Unself-conscious	Critical, reflective stance
Impatient with ambiguities about motives and the interpretation of events	Recognizes ambiguity
Denies "pastness" of events	Focus on historicity
Links the past with the present	Differentiates the past from the present
Ahistorical, antihistorical	Views past events as "then and not now"
Commemorative voice	Historical voice
Museum as a temple	Museum as a forum
Unquestionable heroic narratives	Disagreement, change, and controversy as part of ongoing historical interpretation

SPECIFIC MEMORY VERSUS DEEP MEMORY

Schacter, Gutchess, and Kensinger (this volume) outline an account of "specificity" in individual memory, and they suggest that a parallel effort would be of interest for collective remembering. They define specificity in terms of "the extent to which, and sense in which, an individual's memory is based on retention of specific features of a past experience, or reflects the operation of specialized, highly specific memory processes." And they go on to note: "In some situations, memory is highly specific, and may include the precise details of a previous experience; in other situations, memory may be much more generic, including retention of only the general sense or gist of what happened."

In keeping with earlier comments about the hazards of reducing collective to individual remembering, the point in what follows is not to argue that specificity on the individual plane can be expected to have exact parallels on the collective plane. There are important differences, especially when it comes to collective memory for events that occurred beyond the living memory of the members of a group. As Winter (this volume) notes, for example, events from the past and the sites of memory associated with them vary greatly, depending on where they are positioned vis-à-vis a generation's life experience. Nonetheless, Schacter et al.'s suggestion that "it seems likely that specificity is a relevant dimension for collective memory research" is suggestive and deserves attention.

In accordance with the notion of instrumental distribution, an account of specificity in collective remembering needs to take into account the cultural tools involved, especially narratives. And in this regard it is useful to make a distinction between "specific narratives" and "schematic narrative templates" (Wertsch, 2002). Under the heading of the former I have in mind items in what the moral philosopher Alisdair MacIntyre (1984) called the "stock of stories" that shape a society. These stories may be nonfictional accounts of the past, or they may be parables or fiction such as those in the Western tradition "about wicked stepmothers, lost children, good but misguided kings, wolves that suckle twin boys, youngest sons who receive no inheritance but must make their own way in the world and eldest sons who waste their inheritance on riotous living and go into exile to live with the swine" (p. 216). Regardless of their claims to truth, the point is that such stories refer to specific settings, characters, and events.

Specific narratives contrast with more generalized, abstract versions, or what can be termed "schematic narrative templates" (Wertsch, 2002). The notion of a schematic narrative template finds its conceptual roots in several theoretical traditions and figures, the most important perhaps being the Russian folklorist Vladimir Propp (1928). In developing his account of Russian folktales, Propp argued for the need to focus on generalized "functions" that characterize an entire set of narratives, as opposed to the particular events and actors that occur in specific narratives. These "recurrent constants ... of dramatis personae are basic components of the tale" (p. 21). This focus on generalized functions means that several different specific events and actors may fulfill a more abstract role in a narrative: "*Functions of characters serve as stable, constant elements of a tale, independent of how and by whom they are fulfilled*" (p. 21, italics in the original).

Propp identified an extensive network of generalized functions, including items such as "The Villian Receives Information about His Victim" (p. 28) and "The Villian Is Defeated" (p. 53) and used them to create a typology of Russian folktales. When exploring the implications of his ideas for collective remembering, what is crucial is his general line of reasoning rather than his detailed claims about particular functions or how they apply to folktales.

Switching from folklore to psychology, a related line of reasoning may be found in the writings of Bartlett (1995). Although there is no reason to assume that he was familiar with Propp's writings, Bartlett did develop some strikingly similar claims. In his view remembering is usually more of a "constructive" process (p. 312) than a product of stimuli, and this led him to examine the generalized patterns or "schemata" brought to this process by the agent doing the constructing.

The writings of Propp and Bartlett contribute different points to an understanding of schematic narrative templates. The common points that can be extracted from their ideas are (a) narrative templates are schematic in the sense that they concern abstract, generalized functions of the sort that Propp discussed in his structural analysis of folk tales or that Bartlett discussed under the heading of schemalike knowledge structures; (b) the organizing form is narrative, a point that is explicit in Propp's writings and consistent with what Bartlett proposed; and (c) the notion of template is involved because these abstract structures can underlie an entire set of specific narratives, each of which has a particular setting, cast of characters, dates, and so forth.

The writings of Propp and Bartlett suggest a couple of additional properties worth keeping in mind when dealing with narrative templates. First, they are not taken to be some sort of universal archetypes. Instead, they are specific to particular narrative traditions that can be expected to differ from one sociocultural setting to another. Indeed, they are key to understanding Halbwachs's basic maxim that there are as many collective memories as collectives. And, second, narrative templates are not readily accessible to the conscious reflection of those using them. As Bartlett noted, they are used in an "unreflective, unanalytical and unwitting manner" (1985, p. 45).

The unreflective nature of narrative templates stems in part from the "transparency" of narrative tools more generally (Wertsch, 2002); it is as if those using them look right through them without recognizing their power to shape how we represent the past. In Bruner's formulation, it is easy to assume "that the story form is a transparent window on reality, not a cookie cutter imposing a shape on it" (2002, pp. 6–7). Along with the fact that these narrative tools are typically interwoven with identity commitments, this means that schematic narrative templates act as unnoticed, yet very powerful "coauthors" when we attempt to recount what "really happened" in the past (Wertsch, 2002, chapter 1).

Schematic narrative templates function to exert a conservative, yet often unrecognized force on collective memory, making it quite resistant to change (Wertsch, 2008a). This reflects the fact that they are deeply embedded, both in the sense of being transparent and nonconscious and in the sense of being part of deeply held identity commitments. Taken together these characteristics suggest that narrative templates operate at a level that can be called "deep collective memory."

Hence the opposition Schacter and his colleagues (Schacter, 1996; Schacter et al. this volume) outline between specificity and "the general sense or gist of what happened" has a counterpart in collective remembering. The parallel is not exact, however, because instead of focusing on *the* gist of what happened, the focus is on how different collectives may have *different* gists. Collectives may differ – often quite substantially – in the general sense they make of one and the same past event, and it is in this connection that schematic narrative templates for one society can give rise to deep memories that are quite different from those of others.

Consider a schematic narrative template that has been outlined by Wertsch (2002). It is one that occupies a place of particular importance in Russian understanding of crucial historical episodes, and as such it imposes a basic plot structure on a range of specific characters, events, and circumstances. This can be called the "expulsion of foreign enemies" schematic narrative template and includes the following elements:

1. An "initial situation" (Propp, 1968, p. 26) in which Russia is peaceful and not interfering with others
2. The initiation of trouble in which a foreign enemy viciously and wantonly attacks Russia without provocation

3. Russia almost loses everything in total defeat as it suffers from the enemy's attempts to destroy it as a civilization
4. Through heroism and exceptionalism, and against all odds, Russia, acting alone, triumphs and succeeds in expelling the foreign enemy

At first glance, it may appear that there is nothing peculiarly Russian about this narrative template. For example, by replacing "Russia" with "America," it would seem to provide a foundation for American collective memory of the Japanese attack on Pearl Harbor in 1941. This points to the fact that the claim is not that this narrative template is available only to members of the Russian narrative tradition or that it is the only one available to this group. However, there are several indications that it plays a particularly important role in the Russian narrative tradition and collective remembering.

The first of these concerns its ubiquity. Whereas the United States and many other societies have accounts of past events that are compatible with some points of this narrative template, it seems to be employed more widely in the Russian tradition than elsewhere. In this connection consider the comments of Musatova (2002) about Russia's past. In remarking on the fate of having to learn "the lessons of conquests and enslavement by foreigners" (p. 139), she lists several groups who are viewed as having perpetrated similar events in Russia's history "Tartars, Germans, Swedes, Poles, Turks, Germans again" (p. 139). She reeled this list off in a way suggesting that whereas the particular actors, dates, and setting may change, the same basic plot applies to all these episodes. They have all been stamped out of the same basic template, suggesting a "generalized gist" that plays an especially important role for Russia.

Some observers would go so far as to say that the expulsion of foreign enemies narrative template is *the* underlying story of Russian collective remembering, and this provides a basic point of contrast with other groups. For example, it is strikingly different from American items such as the "mystique of Manifest Destiny" (Lowenthal, 1994, p. 53), the "reluctant hegemon" story (Kagan, 2006), or a "quest for freedom" narrative (Wertsch and O'Connor, 1994). The expulsion-of-foreign-enemies template clearly plays a central role in Russian collective memory, even in instances where it would not seem relevant, at least to those who are not "native speakers" (Lotman & Uspenskii, 1985) of this tradition.

This schematic narrative template has had a powerful impact on the state-sponsored official history in Soviet and post-Soviet Russia (Wertsch, 2002), yielding a striking continuity in this official account (which, like all state-sponsored official histories, functions as part of an identity project and hence incorporates ingredients of memory as well as history). For example, it provides a foundation for interpreting episodes such as the Molotov-Ribbentrop Pact that have remained largely intact despite the disclosure of archival materials that clearly contradict the specific narrative that had been promulgated for decades (Wertsch, 2008a). And the tenacity of this schematic narrative template was so great that Stalin dusted it off and employed it to mobilize the Soviet population during World War II, even though he had just spent decades downplaying, indeed repressing it (Wertsch, 2008b).

The conservative nature of deep memory and claims about the schematic narrative templates that underlie it suggest that it may represent a distinct way of representing the past in comparison with specific memory. Something like habit memory, as outlined by Connerton, may play a more important role in deep memory than specific memory. Claims of distinct forms of memory can be traced back to the work of Henri Bergson (1911), another figure who, along with Durkheim, had a powerful influence on Maurice Halbwachs, and hence on collective memory studies. Bergson wrote of "habits" and "motor mechanisms," on the one hand, and "personal memory-images," on the other (p. 96), thereby laying out an issue that continues to be quite open today.

THE SOCIAL ORGANIZATION OF COLLECTIVE REMEMBERING

By definition, collective remembering involves a collective of some sort, and hence is inherently social. But the organization of the social processes involved is envisioned quite differently by different scholars. The distributed version of collective remembering outlined above begins with the assumption that a memory community is built around a shared set of textual means, especially narratives. This does not mean, however, that everyone in the community has a single system of uniform knowledge and belief. Instead, as outlined by Brian Stock (1990), "textual communities" are shaped as much by internal differentiation and institutionalization as by the texts around which they are formed. In this process a variety of social and political dynamics typically give rise to a complex, differentiated collective.

In some cases, scholars highlight these dynamics to such a degree that collective remembering is viewed largely as a forum for political negotiation and contestation rather than a body of knowledge. For example, in his account of "public memory" Bodnar (1992) views remembering primarily in terms of the struggle between "official culture" and "vernacular culture," one result being that the accuracy criterion that guides such a central role in psychological studies plays a distinctly secondary role.

Considerations of social structure have long been part of the sociological study of collective remembering. For example, in his classic article "The Problem of Generations," first published in 1928, Karl Mannheim (1952) argued that each generation develops a distinctive picture of political and social reality depending on the experiences it has during the formative years of young adulthood. Included in this line of reasoning was the claim that a generation is a social rather than a biological construct, one upshot being that distinctive generations may be less distinct in traditional societies where novel events may be rare and change slow.

Howard Schuman and Jacqueline Scott (1989) used Mannheim's notions to formulate hypotheses about different generations recall events like World War II, the Vietnam War, and the Civil Rights era. They found that American subjects recalled as especially important events that occurred in their teens or early 20s, hence supporting the generational hypothesis that memories of important political events and social changes are structured by age.

Complementing such studies in sociology is research in psychology on reminiscence. Studies by David Rubin and his colleagues (Rubin, Wetzler, & Nebes, 1986; Berntsen & Rubin, 2002) and others including Joseph Fitzgerald (1988, 1995) have given rise to the notion of a "reminiscence bump" that challenges usual assumptions about how memories decay over the life span. Instead of a steady decline in memories for more distant events, this research has consistently shown that older adults' memories for events that occurred during their young adult years are more detailed than are memories for events that happened before or after this formative age. The cause of the reminiscence bump is still being debated, but analyses have focused on issues of self and identity development (Conway & Playdell-Pearce, 2000; Williams & Conway, this volume) and crucial stages in the formation of a living narrative (Fitzgerald, 1988). Regardless of the final outcome of this debate in life-span psychology, this is one topic on which this discipline has the potential of coming into productive collaboration with sociological analyses of collective remembering.

More recently, Howard Schuman, Barry Schwartz, and Nancy D'Arcy (2005) have outlined other dimensions of social structure that influence collective remembering. Analyzing responses from a national sample of Americans, they identified varying ideas about Columbus and his place in American history based on race, religion, and a critical stance toward the United States. For example, they concluded that "among white respondents, the characterization of Columbus as villainous draws on a larger receptivity to non-normative beliefs generally, presumably in a liberal or radical direction" (p. 16).

What is perhaps most interesting about the study by Schuman et al., however, is how little change there has been more generally in Americans' ideas about Columbus over the past few decades, even in the face of radically new, critical portrayals of him in connection with the 500th anniversary of his arrival in the Americas. They report that "most Americans continue to admire Columbus because, as tradition puts it, 'he discovered America', although only a small number of mainly older respondents speak of him in the heroic terms common in earlier years" (p. 2).

This "inertia of memory" noted by Schuman et al. echoes the resistance to change characteristic of deep memory. This perhaps should come as no surprise, given the extent to which collective remembering is typically tied to identity and the threat that changes in accounts of the past could pose to the group. In contrast to analytic history, in which enough countervailing evidence at least occasionally gives rise to a new narrative, collective memory seems to be nearly impervious to such transformation. This appears to be the case even in the face of major revisions of official history, revisions such as those that occurred in how Columbus is presented in U.S. education (Schuman et al., 2005) and those that occurred in the radical rewriting of Russian history after the Soviet period.

CONCLUSION

In comparison with individual memory, collective remembering has been little conceptualized, and hence a major goal of this chapter has been to lay out a framework for pursuing theoretical and empirical inquiry. Rather than trying to provide a definition of collective remembering – which would inevitably be overly simple, if not downright misguided at this point – the goal has been to lay out a few basic oppositions and issues that shape the current debate. These are the conceptual oppositions strong versus distributed versions of collective memory, individual versus collective remembering, history versus memory, and specific versus deep collective memory.

At several points, parallels between individual and collective memory have been identified, but this always involves a note of caution, given the need to avoid reducing collective to individual processes. There are obvious points of contact between the study of individual and collective remembering, and these need to be the focus of future efforts to flesh out a general approach to memory studies. For example, the sociological analysis of generations can be profitably related tied to findings in psychology on the reminiscence bump, and the contrast between specific and deep forms of memory calls for further collaboration between those focusing on individual remembering and those concerned with collective phenomena. At a more general level, this chapter suggests that a distributed approach to collective remembering requires broader collaboration as we seek to formulate the broadly conceived field of memory studies.

REFERENCES

Bartlett, F. C. (1995). *Remembering: A study in experimental and social psychology.* Cambridge: Cambridge University Press. (first published in 1932).

Bechtel, W., & Abrahamsen, A. (1991). *Connectionism and the mind: An introduction to parallel processing in networks.* Oxford: Blackwell.

Bergson, H. (1911). *Matter and memory.* London: George Allen and Unwin. (Trans. by Nancy Margaret Paul and W. Scott Palmer).

Berntsen, D., & Rubin, D. C. (2002). Emotionally charged autobiographical memories across the life span: The recall of happy, sad, traumatic, and involuntary memories. *Psychology and Aging, 17,* 636–652.

Bodnar, J. (1992). *Remaking America: Public memory, commemoration, and patriotism in the twentieth century.* Princeton: Princeton University Press.

Burke, P. (1989). History as social memory. In T. Butler (Ed.), *Memory: History, culture and the mind* (pp. 97–113). Oxford: Basil Blackwell.

Bruner, J. (1990). *Acts of meaning.* Cambridge, MA: Harvard University Press.

Cole, J. (2001). *Forget colonialism? Sacrifice and the art of memory in Madagascar.* Berkeley: University of California Press.

Connerton, P. (1989). *How societies remember.* Cambridge: Cambridge University Press.

Conway, M. A. (1997). The inventory of experience: Memory and identity. In J. W. Pennebaker, D. Paez, & B. Rimé (Eds.), *Collective memory of political events: Social psychological perspectives* (pp. 21–45). Mahwah, NJ: Lawrence Erlbaum Associates.

Conway, M. A., & Playdell-Pearce, C. W. (2000). The construction of autobiographical memories in the self-memory system. *Psychological Review, 107*(2), 261–288.

Donald, M. (1991). *Origins of the modern mind.* Cambridge, MA: Harvard University Press.

Douglas, M. (1980). Introduction: Maurice Halbwachs (1877–1945). In Halbwachs, M. (Eds.), *The collective memory.* New York: Harper & Row. (Trans by Francis J. Didder, Jr. & Vida Yazdi Ditter).

Dower, J. W. (1996). Three narratives of our humanity. In Linenthal, E. T. & Engelhardt, T. (Eds.), *History wars: The Enola Gay and other battles for America's past* (pp. 63–96). New York: Metropolitan Books.

Fitzgerald, J. M. (1988). Vivid memories and the reminiscence phenomenon: The role of a self narrative. *Human Development, 31,* 261–273.

(1995). Intersecting meanings of reminiscence in adult development and aging. In D. C. Rubin (Ed.), *Remembering our past: Studies in autobiographical memory* (pp. 360–383). Cambridge: Cambridge University Press.

Hacking, I. (1996). Memory sciences, memory politics. In P. Antze & M. Lambek (Eds.), *Tense past: Cultural essays in trauma and memory* (pp. 67–87). New York: Routledge.

Halbwachs, M. (1980). *The collective memory*. New York: Harper & Row. (Trans. by Francis J. Didder, Jr. & Vida Yazdi Ditter).

(1992). *On collective memory*. Chicago: University of Chicago Press. (Ed. and Trans. by Lewis A. Coser).

Klein, K. L. (2000). On the emergence of memory in historical discourse. *Representations, 69,* 127–150.

Leont'ev, A. N. (1981). The problem of activity in psychology. In J. V. Wertsch (Ed.), *The concept of activity in Soviet psychology* (pp. 37–71). Armonk, NY: M.E. Sharpe.

Linenthal, E. T. (1996). Anatomy of a controversy. In Linenthal, E. T. & Engelhardt, T. (Eds.), *History wars: The Enola Gay and other battles for America's past* (pp. 9–62). New York: Metropolitan Books.

Linenthal, E. T., & Engelhardt, T. (Eds.) (1996). *History wars: The Enola Gay and other battles for America's past*. New York: Metropolitan Books.

Lotman, Yu. M., & Uspenskii, B. A. (1985). Binary models in the dynamics of Russian culture (to the end of the eighteenth century). In A. D. Nakhimovsky & A. S. Nakhimovsky (Eds.), *The semiotics of Russian cultural history. Essays by Iurii M. Lotman, Lidiia Ia. Ginsburg, Boris A. Uspenskii* (pp. 30–66). Ithaca: Cornell University Press.

Lowenthal, D. (1994). Identity, heritage, and history. In J. R. Gillis (Ed.), *Commemorations: The politics of national identity* (pp. 41–57). Princeton: Princeton University Press.

Lukes, S. (1977). Methodological individualism reconsidered. In S. Lukes (Ed.), *Essays in social theory* (pp. 177–186). New York: Columbia University Press.

MacIntyre, A. (1984). *After virtue: A study in moral theory*. Notre Dame, Indiana: University of Notre Dame Press.

Mannheim, K. (1952). *The problem of generations. Chapter VII in: K. Mannheim. Essays on the sociology of knowledge* (pp. 276–320). London: Routledge & Kegan Paul Ltd. (Ed. by Paul Kecskemeti).

Middleton, D., & Edwards, D. (1990). Conversational remembering: A social psychological approach. In D. Middleton & D. Edwards (Eds.), *Collective remembering* (pp. 23–45). London: Sage Publications.

Mink, L. O. (1978). Narrative form as a cognitive instrument. In R. H. Canary & H. Kozicki (Eds.), *The writing of history: Literary form and historical understanding* (pp. 129–149). Madison: University of Wisconsin Press.

Nora, P. (1989). Between memory and history: *Les lieux de mémoire. Representations,* 26, 7–25.

Novick, P. (1999). *The Holocaust in American life*. Boston: Houghton Mifflin Company.

Pennebaker, J. W., Paez, D., & Rimé, B. (Eds.). (1997). *Collective memory of political events: Social psychological perspectives*. Mahwah, NJ: Lawrence Erlbaum Associates Publishers.

Propp, V. (1968). *Morphology of the folktale*. Austin, TX: University of Texas Press. (Trans. by Laurence Scott).

Roediger, H. L., & K. B. McDermott (1995). Creating false memories: Remembering words not presented in lists. *Journal of Experimental Psychology: Learning, Memory, and Cognition, 21*, 803–814.

Ross, M. (1989). Relation of implicit theories to the construction of personal histories. *Psychological Review, 96*(2) 341–357.

Rubin, D. C., Wetzler, S. E., & Nebes, R. D. (1986). Autobiographical memory across the adult lifespan. In D. C. Rubin (Ed.), *Autobiographical memory* (pp. 202–221). New York: Cambridge University Press.

Schacter, D. L. (1996). *Searching for memory: The brain, the mind, and the past.* New York: Basic Books.

Schuman, H., B. Schwartz, & H. D'Arcy. (2005). Elite revisionists and popular beliefs: Christopher Columbus, hero or villain? *Public Opinion Quarterly, 69*(1), 2–29.

Schuman, H., & J. Scott. (1989). Generations and collective memories. *American Sociological Review, 4* (54), 359–381.

Seixas, P. (Ed.). (2004). *Theorizing historical consciousness.* Toronto: University of Toronto Press.

Stock, B. (1990). *Listening for the text: On the uses of the past.* Philadelphia: University of Pennsylvania Press.

Vygotsky, L. S. (1981). The instrumental method in psychology. In J. V. Wertsch (Ed.), *The concept of activity in Soviet psychology* (pp. 134–143). Armonk, NY: M.E. Sharpe.

Weldon, M. S. (2001). Remembering as a social process. In D. L. Medin (Ed.), *The psychology of learning and motivation* (pp. 67–120). San Diego: Academic Press.

Wertsch, J. V., & O'Connor, K. (1994). Multivoicedness in historical representation: American college students' accounts of the origins of the U.S. *Journal of Narrative and Life History, 4*(4), 295–310.

Wertsch, J. V. (1998). *Mind as action.* New York: Oxford University Press.

(2002). *Voices of collective remembering.* New York: Cambridge University Press.

(2008a). Blank spots in collective memory: A case study of Russia. *The Annals of the American Academy of Political and Social Science, 617* (May), 58–71.

(2008b). *A clash of deep memories. Profession 2008.* New York: Modern Language Association, 2008, pp. 46–53.

White, H. (1987). *The content of the form: Narrative discourse and historical representation.* Baltimore: The Johns Hopkins University Press.

Young, A. (1996). Bodily memory and traumatic memory. In P. Antze & M. Lambek (Eds.), *Tense past: Cultural essays in trauma and memory* (pp. 89–102). New York: Routledge.

6

The Role of Repeated Retrieval in Shaping Collective Memory

HENRY L. ROEDIGER III, FRANKLIN M. ZAROMB, &
ANDREW C. BUTLER

This book is about culture and memory, about how the society and culture in which people grow up helps to determine their individual memories, collective memories, and identity. We will emphasize how the process of repeated retrieval helps to shape our memories. Before we get to our main story, we need to provide some background.

Many different cultures exist within the community of scholars who study memory, from humanistic approaches to a whole variety of scientific approaches to the field (see Roediger, Dudai & Fitzpatrick, 2007). In our chapter, we attempt to blend some insights from several approaches to studying memory. In particular, we apply the principles that have emerged from research in experimental cognitive psychology to issues in collective memory in hopes that combining insights from various disciplines may point the way to progress in understanding larger issues in the study of memory.

Our chapter has six parts. First, we discuss issues in collective memory – how we conceive the topic – by considering three conceptual oppositions (following Wertsch & Roediger, 2008). We then discuss how these issues might play out in learning about history from textbooks. Next, we describe three main mechanisms that we believe play a critical role in shaping collective memory: the act of retrieving information from memory; repeated retrieval of information over long periods of time; and finally the role of feedback in modifying memories. The third, fourth, and fifth sections of the chapter spell out these mechanisms and how they might contribute to the creation of collective memories. The sixth section explores the issue of accuracy in collective memory, and how it is affected by the mechanisms of retrieval and feedback. Finally, we end with some conclusions.

WHAT IS COLLECTIVE MEMORY?

Collective memory is not a term with a precise definition. Since Maurice Halbwachs introduced the term in the 1920s, it has been used in many different ways. Historians, sociologists, anthropologists, psychologists, and literary analysts all have slightly different definitions of what constitutes a collective memory. The general feature that unites all uses of the term is that collective memory is a form of memory that transcends individuals and is shared by the group. In our treatment in this section, we rely heavily on observations of Dudai (2002) and Wertsch and Roediger (2008).

In *Memory from A to Z,* Yadin Dudai (2002) noted that "The term 'collective memory' actually refers to three entities: a body of knowledge, an attribute, and a process" (p. 51). The body of knowledge refers to the common knowledge of a society or culture (a European) that can be divided further into subgroups (Italians, Florentines, Florentine women over 60). Of course, one can go further to the level of families, friends, and even pairs of people, where the collective memories are even more specialized. Regardless of the size of the group, each individual in the group will share various memories with other members of that group. Importantly, the collective memory is present in each individual; that is, each member of the group would produce roughly the same information if asked about the memory individually. In this sense, it is different from the concept of transactive memory, in which people serve as external memory aids to one another (Wegner, 1986). The attribute to which Dudai refers is "the distinctive holistic image of the past in the group" (such as World War II veterans in the United States, to whom some refer as the "greatest generation" of Americans; Brokaw, 2001). Finally, the process is the continual evolution in understanding between the individual and the group. That is, individuals may influence and change the collective memory of the group, and the group can change the individual's understanding of being a member of the group and of the group's past.

These three features – body of knowledge, attribute, and process – are critical to understanding collective memory. To flesh out the concept more fully, we follow Wertsch and Roediger (2008) in briefly considering a set of three oppositions that highlight different uses of the term.

Collective Memory versus Collective Remembering

The term collective memory is sometimes used to refer to a relatively static set of knowledge, as in Dudai's (2002) "body of knowledge" feature or Tulving's (1972) semantic memory. This might refer to what people in England know about what happened in 1066, or what most Americans know about their Revolutionary War or about the events of 9/11, and so on. By contrast, collective remembering refers to a dynamic process, how different perspectives and reconstructions over the years can provide a contentious process of representing the past. Examples in U.S. history include how the view of Native Americans ("Indians") and African Americans has changed over the years, often with the "new" view espoused by each group opposing that of the dominant culture. Such disputes over how some central event is to be remembered erupt during construction of museums and monuments, the writing of textbooks, and creation of national holidays. These disputes over how the past is to be remembered that are fought among groups with different interests have been termed "the politics of memory" (Kramer, 1996).

History versus Collective Remembering

Halbwachs (1980, 1992) raised the issue of how collective memory – a representation of the past – might be different from history. In contemporary thinking, history and collective memory are often considered to be conflicting. The reason is that the two modes of knowing have different aspirations of representing the past. History aspires to provide an accurate account of the past, even when that record may reflect poorly on the people being represented. In contrast, in collective remembering, the past is often tied to the present, so that a person's self identity and group identity are buoyed by the glorious past history of the people. In collective memory, negative aspects of the past may be omitted or suppressed in the service of representing what kind of people we are. Americans today grapple with how to reconcile "America the good" with atrocities committed in the past against Native Americans and African slaves, as well as to many immigrant groups soon after they arrived (not to mention scandals more recently involving abuse of prisoners). As noted by the historian Peter Novick (1999):

> To understand something historically is to be aware of its complexity, to have sufficient detachment to see it from multiple perspectives, to accept the ambiguities, including moral ambiguities, of protagonists' motives and behavior. Collective memory simplifies; sees events from a single, committed perspective; is impatient with ambiguities of any kind; reduces events to mythic archetypes. (pp. 3–4)

Individual versus Collective Remembering

Remembering is often conceived as occurring within an individual: some cue reminds one of events or facts of the past. Bartlett (1932) even raised the issue of whether collective remembering can exist, at least in the strong sense that a group (as a group) "can be usefully characterized as having some sort of memory in its own right" (Wertsch, 2002, p. 22). After all, memories must be carried in individual nervous systems. In contrast to this position, Schudson (1992) has questioned whether memory can be anything but collective in that "memory is social … it is located in institutions rather than in individual human minds in the form of rules, laws, standardized procedures and records, a whole set of cultural practices through which people recognize a debt to the past" (p. 347). These views are quite different, but the point of contact may be "agreement on the point that socially situated individuals are the agents of remembering" (Wertsch & Roediger, 2008).

As Wertsch (2002) has pointed out, individuals use a set of cultural tools to aid in representing the past – written symbols in books, paintings and icons, museums and monuments, and today the huge amount of information distributed on the internet. Most readers doubtless have used Google or Wikipedia to help remember some event or fact. Furthermore, our memories are socially constructed in that we rely on others to provide information to update our memories of events, which can both improve our recollections and can insert errors, depending on the information provided (Roediger, Bergman & Meade, 2001). In short, individuals remember, but with much help from social and cultural aids including reports of memories from other people. Collective memories may ultimately reside in individual nervous systems, but complex social processes provide the basis for our memories and their nature.

The foregoing provides our reflections on the nature of collective memory (see Wertsch [2002; 2008] for admirable overviews of the field). We turn now to specific processes by which we believe collective memories (indeed, all memories) are created and maintained over long periods of time. We refer first to retrieval of memories. Much evidence points to the critical role of retrieval in future remembering (e.g., Roediger & Karpicke, 2006a). Although we do not have evidence to completely back up this point, we strongly suspect that the only events occurring today that can be retrieved far into the future are ones that will have been retrieved previously. That is, it is probably impossible if you are over 20 to ever accurately retrieve an event from when you were 10 unless you have retrieved it during the interim. We next turn to repeated retrieval and spaced retrieval as keys in maintaining memories over long periods of time, with the theme being a "use it or lose it" point of view. Furthermore, the process of retrieval is itself shaped by feedback given, either from other people or from sources such as history books, novels, television, and the like. We consider these issues in turn before continuing on to the issue of truth and myth (accuracies and inaccuracies) in collective memory.

HISTORY TEXTBOOKS: A POTENTIAL SOURCE OF COLLECTIVE MEMORIES

The classroom is a setting in which many collective memories are likely to be created, because people learn much of their historical knowledge through formal schooling. Although students are sometimes taught to consider multiple perspectives on historical events, the historical information presented to students is often closer to the aims of collective remembering than to those of history (as discussed earlier). That is, historical information is often portrayed in ways that conform to present cultural values or political objectives, rather than providing an objective account of the past. Indeed, when it comes to teaching history in educational settings, students primarily learn accounts of the past that reflect the current biases, goals, and beliefs of a particular social group or nation-state (Loewen, 1995; see Blatz & Ross, this volume). This contrast can also be observed in a variety of other contexts in which history is taught, commemorated, or symbolically represented, such as museums and national holidays (see Blatz & Ross, this volume; Blight, this volume; Pennebaker & Gonzales, this volume; Winter, this volume).

In the classroom, the textbook used by the teacher usually dictates the account of history that is taught and, as a result, textbooks are likely to be a primary source of information for collective memories. Although one might assume that the information about and perspective taken on historical events has remained largely consistent over time, there is actually a high degree of variability. In a recent survey of U.S. history textbooks from 1794 to 1999, Ward (2006) analyzed how textbooks have portrayed seminal events in United States and modern world history over time. History textbooks are especially useful for studying collective memory, because, as Ward argues, they typically reflect the most widely read historical accounts in any country at a given time and are studied during a student's formative adolescent years.

This point is confirmed by a study conducted in our lab in which we asked American college students to recall the 10 most important events that occurred during the U.S. Civil War (1861–1865), World War II (1939–1945), and the current Iraq War (2003–present). Afterward, students answered a series of questions about their knowledge and attitudes concerning the specific events they recalled. When asked about the particular source from which they first learned about each of the recalled events, students recollected having first learned 85 percent of the events listed for the U.S. Civil War from either textbooks (55%) or teachers (30%). Similarly, 77 percent of the events listed for World War II were first learned from textbooks (48%) or teachers (29%). Of course, given that the Iraq War is too recent to have been taught in the classroom, students instead recollected having first learned of the majority of listed Iraq War events from media sources (87%) such as television (62%), print media (19%), and the Internet (6%).

Ward (2006) further argues about the importance of textbooks in shaping our collective knowledge and conceptions of history:

> Unlike independently authored historical accounts, textbooks are a quasi-official story, a sort of state-sanctioned version of history. In nearly all countries the government takes some role in setting the standards for an acceptable cultural, political, and social history – i.e., what the authorities want the next generation to learn about its own national heritage – enfolding them, as it were, into a collective national identity. The fundamental contribution of any textbook is, of course, the story, an account that reveals much about a nation's priorities and values. Because history textbooks contain national narratives written by national authors for a national audience, they model the national identity in a very profound and unique way. (pp. xviii–xix)

Consider the events surrounding the dropping of the atomic bomb on Hiroshima and Nagasaki in 1945. Although there is no doubt as to when and where this occurred and the identity of the principal actors, over the past 60 years, U.S. history textbooks have described the rationale and significance of these events in ways that appear to reflect prevailing attitudes in American society at different times toward nuclear weapons and the consequences of their use. In 1947, U.S. history textbooks emphasized the role that the atomic bombs played in hastening Japanese surrender, but by 1954, near the height of the Cold War nuclear arms race, textbooks emphasized the development of the bombs themselves, skipping the subject of their strategic role in ending the war (Ward, 2006, pp. 289–292). In the wake of the 1961 Cuban Missile Crisis in which the United States and the Soviet Union reached the brink of a nuclear war, one textbook from 1966 informed students in its discussion of the 1945 atomic bombings that "a nuclear holocaust might be the end result, if a 'lasting peace' was not found" (pp. 291). It was not until the 1990s, in the aftermath of the Cold War and the breakup of the Soviet Union that U.S. textbooks began to provide students with several interpretations as to why the atomic bomb was used at the end of World War II.

Even more striking are the differences in historical accounts revealed by comparing textbooks used around the world. Contemporary Japanese textbooks question the U.S. motives for dropping the atomic bombs and emphasize the devastating impact of the bombs and the cost in human lives. Canadian textbooks highlight the role that Canadians played in mining and enriching the uranium for the atomic bomb. Likewise, British textbooks remind students of the contributions of British and other European scientists to developing the atomic bomb. By contrast, Italian textbooks focus on U.S. motivations by explicitly stating that there was no military justification for using nuclear weapons, and that President Truman was primarily concerned with ensuring a dominant role for the United States in postwar international affairs, especially with respect to the Soviet Union (Lindaman & Ward, 2004, pp. 238–244).

Judging by the information that is both emphasized and omitted in history textbooks, it comes as no surprise that students' knowledge and understanding of history can dramatically vary from generation to generation or from country to country (e.g., Liu et al., 2005; Wertsch, 2002). For example, Wertsch (2002) reported cases that pitted the recollections of World War II of Russian and American students that revealed striking differences in the specific events the two groups recalled as well as the basic structure used to recount the war's narrative.

Wertsch (2002; see also Wertsch, 2008) described one exercise that required participants to list the most important events of World War II. Among American students, the most frequently listed events were: (a) the attack on Pearl Harbor (December 7, 1941); (b) the Battle of Midway (June, 1942); (c) D-Day (June 6, 1944); (d) the Battle of the Bulge (Winter 1944–1945); (e) the Holocaust (throughout the war); and (f) the atomic bombing of Hiroshima and Nagasaki (August 1945). Data collected in our lab from American college students generally replicated these findings, with the following events listed most frequently (a) the atomic bombing of Hiroshima and Nagasaki; (b) the attack on Pearl Harbor; (c) D-Day; (d) the Holocaust; (e) the German invasion of Poland (September, 1939); and (f) the United States entering World War II. In contrast, Russian students surveyed during the 1990s generated a completely different list of events, which included: (a) the German attack on the U.S.S.R. (June 22, 1941); (b) the Battle of

Moscow (Winter 1941–1942); (c) the Battle of Stalingrad (Winter 1942–1943); (d) the Battle of Kursk Salient (Summer 1943); (e) the Siege of Leningrad (1942–1944); and (e) the Final Battle for Berlin (1945).

What is most striking about these lists of events is the fact that there is no overlap. Wertsch (2008) explains that the lack of overlap does not imply that participants in either of the two groups have no knowledge of the others' listed items. Rather, the events listed for one group are considered much less important than those listed by the other group. For example, what is listed as "D-Day" by American students is known to Russians as the "opening of the second front" in June of 1944. The first and primary front in their eyes was the Eastern front.

Although group-related differences in historical memory may be explained in terms of what students learn in the classrooms of different countries, it is of equal if not greater importance to consider how students learn history. That is, what educational practices enhance learning of materials taught in the classroom? We now turn to exploring how the mechanisms of retrieval, repeated retrieval (or spacing), and feedback can help to create, maintain, and shape collective memories, respectively. For each of these mechanisms, we will first review some of the research from the laboratory and then discuss how the principles that emerge can be applied to collective memory.

RETRIEVAL: A MECHANISM FOR CREATING COLLECTIVE MEMORIES

One way in which people learn information is through the process of retrieving that information from memory. We now review findings from the laboratory that demonstrate the powerful effect of retrieval on long-term retention. Of course, the mnemonic benefits of retrieval are not confined to the laboratory. For example, retrieval practice is regularly incorporated in the classroom in the form of tests. Accordingly, we also explore how the mechanism of retrieval may play a role in the creation of collective memories.

Laboratory Research on the Testing Effect

A robust finding in the cognitive and educational psychology literature is that testing subjects on their ability to remember previously learned material improves long-term retention relative to restudying it for an equivalent amount of time (e.g., Carrier & Pashler, 1992; for review, see Roediger &

Karpicke, 2006a). This finding, known as the testing effect, occurs even when neither feedback nor further study opportunities are provided (Gates, 1917; Glover, 1989; Roediger & Karpicke, 2006b; Spitzer, 1939). Interestingly, the benefits of testing have also been shown to promote retention of related, but untested information (Chan, McDermott, & Roediger, 2006). More important, the benefits of testing have been shown to be quite powerful, both in the laboratory and the classroom (for a meta-analysis, see Bangert-Drowns, Kulik, & Kulik, 1991). For example, Jones (1923–1924) reported that when students were tested after a classroom lecture, they scored twice as high as untested students on a retention test given eight weeks later.

In a recent review of the steadily growing body of research on the testing effect, Roediger and Karpicke (2006a) argued that testing has a direct, positive effect on learning, as well as many indirect benefits. The direct effect of testing derives from the use of retrieval as a mechanism to enhance the long-term retention of information. Retrieving information from memory is not a neutral event; rather, it leads to a modification of the memory trace (Bjork, 1975). As a result, the act of retrieving information from memory produces a memory trace that is more resistant to forgetting. The indirect benefits of testing might include helping students to direct the focus of their subsequent studying strategies (i.e., "learning to learn"), encouraging students to study more frequently, and reducing students' anxiety about taking tests because their grade is not completely dependent on a small number of tests (e.g., a midterm and final) and they are familiar with the types of questions that might appear on the test.

Although most of the testing effect studies reported in the research literature have been obtained in laboratory settings using discrete verbal study materials (e.g., lists of words), several classic studies conducted with relatively large populations of grade-school students have also shown strong, positive effects of testing (Gates, 1917; Jones, 1923–1924; Spitzer, 1939). Recent years have also seen a flurry of studies that have investigated the testing effect using more educationally relevant materials, such as prose passages and textbooks (e.g., Foos & Fisher, 1988; Kang, McDermott, & Roediger, 2007; McDaniel, Roediger & McDermott, 2007; Roediger & Karpicke, 2006b).

Of relevance to history education, Butler and Roediger (2007) examined the benefits of testing on long-term retention of history lectures in a simulated classroom setting. Subjects viewed a series of lectures on consecutive days and, following each lecture, engaged in one of three types of activities (a) studying a lecture summary, (b) taking a multiple-choice test, or (c) taking a short answer test. One month later, students completed a final short answer test. Not surprisingly, studying the lecture summaries or taking a multiple-choice test led to better performance on the final recall test than a no activity control condition. More importantly, taking an initial short-answer test significantly improved final recall relative to studying the lecture summary or taking an initial multiple-choice test. The superiority of the short answer testing condition compared to the study and no activity conditions indicates a direct long-term benefit of testing. However, the advantage of short answer testing over multiple-choice testing suggests that test format, and more specifically, the cognitive demands of particular tests on retrieval processes are critical in determining testing effects (Kang et al., 2007). Whereas students may rely on the familiarity of responses to answer multiple-choice test questions, they must engage in effortful retrieval in order to complete short-answer recall tests.

Retrieval Creates Collective Memories

Although it has not been empirically investigated, one might reasonably argue that tests play an additional role of designating the historical information and perspectives that are important to know (as well as the information that is of secondary or little importance). This is especially true of standardized or AP exams that are administered at the state or national level. For instance, American students are much more likely to be tested on their knowledge of the Japanese attack on Pearl Harbor than the German siege on Leningrad, even though both events were significant in their own right in determining the course of World War II. In other words, tests may determine the importance of particular historical events and concepts in the minds of students.

Returning to the comparison of American and Russian students' recollections of World War II, Wertsch (2002) noticed distinct patterns in the basic narrative structure of their recall testimonies. He argued that these patterns reflect the use of what he terms a "schematic narrative template" to recount historical episodes. Similar to Bartlett's (1932) conception of schema, schematic narrative templates are abstract knowledge representations that are readily accessible to the narrator and guide the reconstructive process of remembering. As an example, Wertsch (2002) proposed a schematic narrative template for Russians entitled the "Triumph over Alien Forces" narrative. It may be distilled from accounts of events that occurred throughout Russian history such as Napolean's invasion of Russia in the early 1800s and the German invasion of World War II. The basic elements of the schematic narrative template are (a) Russia is peaceful and not interfering with others, (b) Russia is viciously and wantonly attacked without provocation,

(c) Russia almost loses everything in total defeat, and (d) through heroism and exceptional bravery, and against all odds, Russia triumphs.

To the extent that tests either reflect or emphasize the importance of particular historical facts, they force students to actively retrieve historical knowledge and attempt to relate that information to the larger scope of national or world history as well as to the present. As such, tests might even serve a function that is not unlike commemorative holidays such as President's Day, the Fourth of July, Veteran's Day, or Martin Luther King Jr.'s Birthday in the U.S., because, in essence, national holidays stress the role of particular historical events and figures in shaping national history. As days of remembrance, national holidays are designed to encourage citizens to recollect, discuss, and ponder the significance of past wars, leaders, national tragedies, or the birth of political institutions. Together, the testing of history in the classroom and the yearly remembrance of key historical events and figures can serve as important tools for promoting the long-term retention of historical knowledge and the shaping of a collective memory.

REPEATED RETRIEVAL AND STRENGTHENING OF COLLECTIVE MEMORIES

If retrieval is a mechanism that creates collective memories, repeated retrieval is the process through which these collective memories are strengthened and maintained over long periods of time. The repeated retrieval of information from memory has been shown to produce better long-term retention than a single retrieval attempt (e.g., Wheeler & Roediger, 1992). In addition, when the repeated retrieval attempts are spaced over a period of time, much greater retention is produced than when the attempts are massed together. This finding, which occurs when items are presented for study as well as when they are retrieved, is commonly referred as the spacing effect and is one of the oldest in the literature, dating back to the first empirical studies of memory (Ebbinghaus 1885/1967; see Roediger, 1985). We now review some of the findings from the laboratory on repeated retrieval and spacing, and then attempt to apply the idea to the long-term maintenance of collective memories.

Laboratory Research on Repeated Retrieval and Spacing

Cognitive psychologists have investigated how the timing and spacing of repeated retrieval influences long-term retention using the experimental paradigm of paired-associated learning. Specifically, if subjects learn a pair of associates (A–B), where A might be "horse" and B its Spanish equivalent "caballo," is it best to practice retrieving the A–B pair in massed fashion with retrieval attempts occurring in immediate succession, or is it better to space the retrieval attempts over intervals of time? At first blush, massed retrieval practice is appealing, because it occurs shortly after initial learning when little forgetting has occurred, and as a result, retrieval may be errorless. On the other hand, spaced retrieval may be superior, just as repeated study benefits long-term retention when the presentation of the to-be-learned items is repeated in spaced as opposed to massed fashion (Glenberg, 1976; Melton, 1970; for a review, see Cepeda, Pashler, Vul, Wixted, & Rohrer, 2006; Dempster, 1989). Moreover, if spaced retrieval is beneficial, what schedule of spacing should be used? Should individuals practice retrieving information using equal spacing intervals or, rather, should the interval vary, such as in an expanding schedule with longer times before successive retrievals?

Landauer and Bjork (1978) conducted two experiments that compared these schedules of repeated retrieval. In their experiments, subjects studied pairs of items (e.g., names paired with surnames or names paired with faces) and then took a series of cued recall tests (without feedback) for each of the study pairs distributed according to massed or spaced (equal and expanding interval) schedules in a continuous paired-associates learning task. Subjects then completed a final recall test 30 minutes after the learning phase. They found that the equal-interval retrieval schedule produced better final recall test performance than did massed retrieval. A number of subsequent studies have replicated this long-term memorial advantage of spaced versus massed retrieval practice (e.g., Cull, 2000; Cull, Shaughnessy, & Zechmeister, 1996). In addition, the expanding-interval schedule produced better final recall test performance than the equal-interval schedule. However, many subsequent studies have failed to demonstrate an advantage of one type of spacing schedule over the other (see Balota, Duchek, & Logan, 2007).

Recent work has sought to break the impasse by redirecting the focus of attention to the timing of the initial test, or retrieval attempt (e.g., Karpicke & Roediger, 2007a; Logan & Balota, 2007). These studies have shown that the timing of the initial recall test in a spaced, repeated retrieval schedule may enhance or detract from the success of the schedule. If the first test occurs immediately after learning, as is usually the case in expanding retrieval schedules, then the memorial benefit of such a test is minimal, because little retrieval effort is required to successfully recall the just-presented information. However, if the initial test occurs after a delay (provided that it is not too long) as is customary with equal-interval schedules, then the first test will require some retrieval effort, thereby promoting long-term retention.

Repeated Retrieval Maintains Collective Memories

To the extent that repeated retrieval does play an important role in the formation and shaping of collective memory, laboratory studies of repeated retrieval and spacing have important implications for remembering historical events. First, the spacing effect literature underscores the importance of considering the different times in which historical knowledge is learned and remembered in society. For instance, many historical facts taught in schools at the primary and secondary level are learned and tested in massed fashion and may not be encountered again for many years. By contrast, holidays such as the Fourth of July encourage individuals to recollect the events surrounding the signing of the Declaration of Independence at equally spaced yearly intervals. Other remembrance occasions such as school reunions may first take place shortly after schooling (e.g., 5 years), then continue to be held at expanding intervals (e.g., 10 years, 25 years, 50 years). Given the variety of schedules, it is worth asking how the timing with which individuals repeatedly think about or discuss their recollections of a particular historical event in relation to when it was first learned or experienced influence their memory for the event. To address this question, we will discuss several studies of the "flashbulb memory" phenomenon, because they provide some evidence for the influence of repeated retrieval, as well as the frequency and timing of retrieval, on the formation and long-term maintenance of collective memories.

Although the educational practices and collective rituals of social groups play a significant role in the development and shaping of collective memory, they do not have absolute control over the process. This is because many events that have greatly affected the course of history have occurred unexpectedly. Such events might include the stock market crash of 1929, the assassination of John F. Kennedy in the United States or Yitzhak Rabin in Israel, or the terrorist attacks of 9/11. As revealed by studies of the "flashbulb memory" phenomenon, the psychological impact of shocking public historical events can have long-term memorial consequences, not only for individuals but for larger social groups as well.

Flashbulb memories are memories for specific events that are so vivid and personal that an individual seems to remember exact details of the context in which he or she first learned or experienced the event for a long period of time (Brown & Kulik, 1977). As Brown and Kulik (1977) reported in their pioneering study, individuals can develop flashbulb memories in response to any event that is very surprising or shocking and of personal significance, such as learning about the death of the close relative. However, in many cases, flashbulb memories develop in a large number of individuals in response to shocking public events, such as the assassination or attempted assassination of a political leader. For young adult participants in the Brown and Kulik study in the late 1970s, the assassination of President John F. Kennedy in 1963 was such an event and to this day serves as the best known example of the flashbulb memory phenomenon. Over the past 30 years, researchers have debated the existence, accuracy, and methods for assessing flashbulb memories (e.g., Conway, 1995; Neisser & Harsch, 1992; Rubin & Kozin, 1984). Nevertheless, for our purposes, it is worth highlighting findings that elucidate the role that retrieval processes may play in the formation and shaping of memories for historical events such as 9/11 among social groups.

Less well known is the fact that Brown and Kulik (1977) examined whether flashbulb memories tend to arise differently in distinct groups of people. The authors administered questionnaires to white and African American participants that asked whether they remembered events associated with various contemporary political leaders. Whereas some leaders were political officials in government, others were leaders in the Civil Rights movement, and although most of the listed events were assassinations or assassination attempts, one event involved an accidental drowning (Mary Jo Kopeckne, riding in Ted Kennedy's car) and another was a death as a result of natural causes (General Francisco Franco of Spain). Participants were also asked to remember a personal, unexpected shock, such as the death of a friend or relative, serious accident, and so on. If they remembered a particular event, they composed a detailed narrative describing the circumstances in which they learned of it. Last, they were asked to rate the importance or consequentiality of the event and the number of times they repeated telling others about it.

Brown and Kulik (1977) found that events that were quite surprising and highly consequential tended to elicit flashbulb memories. Such events were also more likely to be retold numerous times to others. More importantly, there was a greater tendency for African American participants to report flashbulb memories for the assassinations of Medger Evers, Malcolm X, Martin Luther King Jr., and George Wallace than white participants.

Following this initial study, a number of recent studies have also reported similar types of group differences in memory for historical events. For instance, Berntsen and Thomsen (2005) examined Danes' memories for the German invasion of Denmark in 1940 and its liberation in 1945. The study investigated differences between the memory of individuals who had ties to the resistance movement and those who did not. Berntsen and

Thomsen (2005) found that participants who reported ties to the Danish resistance movement had more vivid and accurate memories than the other participants. Danes with ties to the resistance movement also reported ruminating on and discussing these events with other people more than Danes not involved in the resistance movement. Repeated retrieval probably helped consolidate the vivid memories.

Curci and Luminet (2006) examined influence of national identity on the accuracy, durability, and subjective experiences associated with memories for the terrorist attacks of 9/11 (see also Luminet et al., 2004). Participants in six countries (France, Italy, the Netherlands, Romania, Japan, and the United States) were asked to complete questionnaires that assessed their memories for the 9/11 attacks. They answered questions about the context in which they first learned of the attacks and their knowledge of the event itself. In addition, they rated the novelty, surprise, importance, or consequentiality of the attacks, as well their emotional reactions and background knowledge. In order to examine the consistency and retention of subjects' flashbulb memories, questionnaires were administered a few weeks after the attacks and again about a year later.

As expected, Americans' recollections of the 9/11 attacks were more accurate and displayed more of the specific attributes associated with flashbulb memories than people of other nationalities. In addition, Americans reported stronger emotional responses to the event, more background knowledge, and an increased tendency to ruminate (with the exception of Dutch participants) than other nationalities. Interestingly, the pattern of results for Americans was similar to those for the Italian and Dutch participants, who displayed high specificity and consistency in their flashbulb memories and whose event recollections were generally accurate. All three groups reported strong emotional reactions on learning of the attacks and frequently rehearsing news about the event by sharing it with others, ruminating, and following relevant media coverage. By contrast, the remaining participants from Belgium, Romania, and Japan, while still having reported highly specific and consistent flashbulb memories of the 9/11 attacks, were much less accurate in their recollections of the events themselves.

These results highlight three group-related differences in historical memory. First, although previous studies of flashbulb memories for earthquakes have shown that physical proximity to the event influenced participants' recollections (Er, 2003; Neisser et al., 1996), the findings of Curci and Luminet (2006) were only partially consistent with this finding. Although Americans reported the most specific, consistent, and accurate memories, flashbulb memories were frequent and consistent across all national groups. Second, some of the idiosyncratic results are difficult to interpret without considering culturally-specific explanations. For example, Japanese participants reported having the weakest emotional response to the 9/11 attacks. Romanian participants were least likely to share news of the attacks with others and to follow media coverage of the event, perhaps reflecting the enduring cultural legacy of past dictatorships. Third, there were significant national differences in event recall accuracy.

It should be noted that at the outset Brown and Kulik (1977) offered little justification for comparing the recollections of whites and African Americans except for making the assumption that differences might be observed between individuals in any two social, professional or racial groups; their intuitions led them to predict that some of the recent assassinations of political leaders involved in the Civil Rights Movement would resonate more among African Americans than among whites (see Brown and Kulik 1977). Brown and Kulik offered no further explanation as to what specific aspects of group identification were associated with group differences in historical memory. However, they did argue that a surprising or highly consequential event is of biological significance and, therefore, may activate neural mechanisms that enhance the encoding of contextual information related to the circumstances in which the event was originally experienced. To the extent that individuals in groups differ in their interests, different events will seem more surprising or consequential depending on group membership. Furthermore, the psychological impact of such events may lead individuals to rehearse their memories for those experiences in both covert (i.e., rumination) and overt manners (i.e., by writing or verbally discussing recollections with others), which in turn, may directly influence how elaborate a person's recollections are of the original event.

Although one might argue along the lines of Brown and Kulik (1977) that the observed group differences in historical memory were primarily determined by the memorial encoding conditions – that is, the initial impact of the event and the influence of group identification on that experience. Alternatively, we argue that of equal if not greater importance may be the role that retrieval plays in the formation and retention of memories across groups over time. For instance, in the studies mentioned earlier, memory for historical events was enhanced for groups that tended to retrieve covertly (to ruminate over) and to recollect those events in social contexts (overt retrieval). Probably the repeated retrieval of events is critical to their long-term retention, as has been shown in laboratory studies by Karpicke and Roediger (2007b).

THE TIMING AND EFFECTS OF SPACED RETRIEVAL

Shapiro (2006) has offered some further insight into the effects of retrieval by examining college students' recollections of the terrorist attacks on September 11, 2001, over a two-year period of time. Specifically, she asked whether flashbulb memory (memory for reception context) and event recall were differentially affected by retention interval. In addition, she investigated whether the frequency and temporal spacing of repeated recollections moderated the effects of retention interval on recall. In one experiment, three groups were tested either one or three times for their recollections of 9/11. Three recall tests were completed by the first two groups at either expanding or equally spaced intervals. In the expanding interval group, subjects were tested 1–2 days, 2 weeks, and 11 weeks after the attacks of 9/11. The equal spacing group was tested 1–2 days, 6 weeks, and 11 weeks following 9/11. The third group served as a control and was tested only one time, 11 weeks after 9/11.

The memory tests were designed to determine whether subjects developed flashbulb memories for the events surrounding 9/11, as well as assess their knowledge of the events themselves. Based on the original criteria proposed by Brown and Kulik (1977), flashbulb memory reports were based on subjects' ability to report their location when they first learned of the 9/11 attacks; what activity they were doing at the time, the source of the information from which they first learned about the attacks, and any personal relevance. For the first two groups, the same queries were made during the follow-up assessments in order to evaluate the consistency of their recollections over time. To assess knowledge of the events themselves, subjects were instructed to write down everything they knew about the 9/11 attacks.

Shapiro (2006) found that the length of the retention interval did not affect recall elaboration or consistency for details of the reception context of 9/11. By contrast, recall for various aspects of the events pertaining to 9/11 was detrimentally affected by a long retention interval. Long-term retention of the events of 9/11 was enhanced by covert retrieval, or rehearsal, as indicated by elevated recall performance and degree of elaboration in the groups assessed three times. However, somewhat surprisingly, the spacing of the assessments did not significantly affect event recall, which suggests that it was the frequency, and not the temporal spacing, of the retrieval attempts that mattered.

In a follow-up experiment, Shapiro (2006) examined the effects of using longer retention intervals of 23 weeks, 1 year, and 2 years on memory for the reception context and events of 9/11. Similar to the results of her first experiment, neither retention interval nor the number of retrieval attempts affected the amount and consistency of reception context information recalled. By contrast, event recall performance, but not consistency, was detrimentally affected by the longer retention intervals. However, even following the longer retention intervals, event recall showed improvement with subsequent retrieval attempts. Using additional questionnaires to probe the subjective experiences associated with subjects' recollections, Shapiro observed that recall was enhanced for subjects that reported their memories as vivid, frozen, or encompassing a longer period of time. Furthermore, recall performance was positively correlated with measures of confidence in accuracy and reported frequency of rehearsal through discussion. The latter provides further support for the idea that repeated overt retrieval aids maintenance of flashbulb memories.

Taken together, these findings are consistent with the notion that the processes underlying the formation of flashbulb memories are different from those involved in the learning and retention of historical event information. Whereas variations in retention interval and retrieval schedules had little impact on flashbulb memories, these variables significantly influenced recollections of what events had actually occurred on 9/11. These findings lend indirect support to Brown and Kulik's (1977) original theory of flashbulb memories, in which encoding mechanisms play a determining role in the formation of memories, but then repeated retrieval helps to maintain memories for the event itself, but not for the surrounding context. If, as Shapiro (2006) observed, repeated retrieval has little influence on one's memory for reception context, then the primary determinants of flashbulb memories must interact at the encoding stage.

By contrasting the durability of flashbulb memories with the fragility of historical event memory, one can appreciate the paradox that societies face when coming to terms with national tragedies such as 9/11. On the one hand, certain subjective features of the event are seemingly unforgettable, whereas, on the other hand, core information is readily forgotten, unless it is rehearsed on a frequent basis. Of course, only the single study by Shapiro (2006) has yet tackled these issues, so further evidence on these points would be welcome.

FEEDBACK: A MECHANISM FOR SHAPING COLLECTIVE MEMORIES

Feedback consists of information provided or generated after recollection of an event (or the performance of a behavior) that allows the learner to improve future recollection or performance. Feedback can be provided by either an external or internal source. With such a broad definition, the term feedback applies to many different phenomena: from signals generated by the somatosensory system after fine motor movements to comments made by audience members after hearing a presentation. For the purpose of the present chapter, we focus on feedback that is given in the context of acquiring and using declarative knowledge. More specifically, feedback is conceptualized as information about the accuracy of a person's performance on a task that requires retrieval from memory (e.g., recalling the name of the 16th President of the United States on a test, remembering one's 18th birthday, etc.). We first review research from the laboratory on the effect of post-test feedback on learning and retention. Then, we describe how the same feedback mechanisms that influence learning in the laboratory may also shape collective memories outside the laboratory.

Laboratory Research on Feedback

Laboratory studies have investigated a multitude of different factors that influence the effectiveness of feedback after a test (for reviews see Bangert-Drowns, Kulik, Kulik, & Morgan, 1991; Butler & Winne, 1995; Hattie & Timperley, 2007; Kulhavy & Stock, 1989), including the timing of feedback, the type of to-be-learned material, the format of the test, the retention interval, and the amount of prior learning (to name but a few). Of these many factors, the most important is the nature of the information provided. In its most basic form, the feedback message must provide learners with information about the veracity of the response (i.e., whether it is correct or incorrect). When additional content is included, the basic feedback message can be expanded along three dimensions: type, form, and load (Kulhavy & Stock, 1989). The different types of feedback are generally classified as a function of the type of information included. When information from the test is used in the feedback message, such as re-presenting the question along with the correct response, it is generally referred to as task-specific feedback. The feedback message can also include a re-presentation of the original study materials, such as a text read before the test, in which case feedback is called instruction-based. Finally, additional information that was not presented during the initial learning or the subsequent test can be included in the feedback message, such as relating the to-be-learned material to a familiar concept from another knowledge domain. This type of feedback is called extra-instructional. The form of feedback refers to the degree of similarity (both structural and superficial) between the original test question and the feedback message. For example, if a multiple-choice item is followed by feedback that consisted of a re-presentation of that item (including all of the potential alternatives) with the correct answer highlighted, the form of the feedback message would be essentially unchanged. However, if the order of the alternatives were rearranged, it would constitute an elaboration of feedback form. Finally, the term feedback load is used to describe the amount of information contained in the feedback message. A simple indication of right or wrong would constitute a small load, whereas a re-presentation of the original study materials would be a large load.

Perhaps the single most important piece of information that can be included in the feedback message is the correct response. When an incorrect response is made on a test, providing the learner with the correct response allows that error to be corrected. For this reason, correct answer feedback (the re-presentation of the question stem along with the correct response) almost always results in superior learning relative to simple right/wrong feedback. For example, Pashler et al. (2005) had subjects study a list of 20 Luganda–English word pairs (e.g., leero – today) and then tested them twice on each pair (leero – ?) during an initial learning session. After each response on the initial learning tests, subjects received either no feedback, right/wrong feedback, or correct answer feedback. When subjects were tested again a week later, they produced a significantly higher proportion of correct responses in the correct answer condition relative to the right/wrong and no feedback conditions (which did not differ statistically). The advantage of correct answer feedback over right/wrong feedback replicates many other studies in the feedback literature (e.g., Gilman, 1969; Roper, 1977). In addition, the lack of a benefit of providing right/wrong feedback relative to no feedback is also a common finding (for a meta-analysis see Bangert-Drowns, Kulik, Kulik, & Morgan, 2001). Presumably, this outcome occurs because knowledge that a particular response is incorrect does not help the learner correct the error, unless there is the opportunity to re-study the material or some other way of determining the correct answer. Thus, one clear implication of the feedback literature is that the feedback message must at least include the correct response in order to promote successful learning.

Although there is consensus with regard to the importance of including the correct response, the effectiveness of further expanding the feedback message along the dimensions of type, form, and load varies considerably. Some ways of expanding upon the basic feedback message appear to have a positive effect on learning, whereas others have no effect or, occasionally, a negative effect. We provide a few examples of expansions that have yielded positive effects. Along the type of feedback dimension, some studies have found that a self-grading feedback procedure in which students are re-presented with the original materials or required to correct their own test is superior to simply providing the correct answer (e.g., Fazio, Huelser, Johnson & Marsh, under review; Andre & Thieman, 1988). Presumably, this effect results from the active processing of the material engendered in the self-grading task, which may boost the retention of information relative to the passive processing involved in receiving correct answer feedback. In terms of the form, feedback messages that require the subject to generate the correct answer by rearranging letters have been found to be more effective than re-presenting the question and correct answer in the original form (Lhyle & Kulhavy, 1987). For the feedback load dimension, the best example may be the benefit of correct answer feedback relative to right/wrong feedback described earlier. Expansion of the feedback message beyond the inclusion of the correct response has yielded mixed results. Some studies have found that including an elaborative explanation of why a particular response is wrong improves learning (Peeck, 1979; Phye, 1979), but others have found no effect of elaboration (e.g., McDaniel & Fisher, 1991; Kulhavy et al., 1985). It may be that the benefits of increasing the feedback message load depend on the nature of the to-be-learned material. Correct answer feedback may be all that is needed for relatively discrete, factual material (e.g., names, dates, foreign language vocabulary, etc.), whereas learning more complex materials (e.g., concepts, applications, etc.) may necessitate an elaborate explanation of the correct answer.

The primary function of feedback is to correct memory errors (Bangert-Drowns, Kulik, Kulik, & Morgan, 2001; Kulhavy & Stock, 1989). When people retrieve information from memory, they can make two kinds of errors: (1) errors of commission and (2) errors of omission. Errors of commission occur when incorrect information is retrieved and volunteered under the assumption that it is correct (or as a guess). Errors of omission occur when information that should be reported is either retrieved but not volunteered because it is presumed to be incorrect (or irrelevant) or not retrieved at all because it is inaccessible in memory. Feedback plays a critical role in correcting both these types of errors. After an error of commission, feedback allows the learner to replace the incorrect response with the correct response. When an error of omission is made, feedback informs the learner of the information that should have been reported and allows that information to be encoded if it was not previously known.

With the ability to correct both these types of errors, feedback is a powerful tool in promoting the retention of information after tests. For example, Butler and Roediger (2008) had subjects study prose passages on a variety of topics and then take a multiple-choice test on information from the passages. Correct answer feedback was provided immediately after some questions, while no feedback was given for other questions. One week later, subjects took a final short answer test that included questions previously tested on the initial multiple-choice test as well as new questions about information from the passages that were not tested earlier to serve as a control condition. The results showed that taking the initial multiple-choice test without feedback led to a higher proportion of correct responses on the final test relative to the no test condition, another example of the testing effect. However, taking an initial test without feedback also led to a higher proportion of intrusions (incorrect responses that were used as lures on the initial multiple-choice test) on the final test than in the no test condition. Nevertheless, the test with feedback condition led to best performance, both increasing the proportion of correct response and decreasing the proportion of intrusions on the final test.

Another function of feedback is to correct metacognitive errors. Metacognition refers to what people know about their own cognitive processes. When people retrieve information from memory, they assess the correctness of that information, a process referred to as metacognitive monitoring (Barnes, Nelson, Dunlosky, Mazzoni, & Narens, 1999; Koriat & Goldsmith, 1996; Nelson & Narens, 1990). The level of confidence placed in a response is a major determinent of how subsequent feedback will be utilized. For example, when feedback study time is self-paced, subjects spend more time studying high confidence incorrect responses than low confidence incorrect responses (see Kulhavy, 1977; Kulhavy & Stock, 1989), probably because they are surprised that something they were sure is right turned out to be wrong. In general, when people are asked to assess their confidence in the correctness of a response, they are generally quite accurate. This is especially true when people have the option to volunteer or withhold responses (i.e., free report) because they tend to volunteer high confidence responses and withhold low confidence responses (see Barnes et al., 1999; Kelley & Sahakyan, 2003; Koriat & Goldsmith, 1996). However, sometimes there is a large discrepancy between actual and perceived correctness of a response, such as when an incorrect response is given in high confidence or a correct response is given in low confidence. Feedback can help to correct such metacognitive errors by reducing the discrepancy between actual and perceived correctness in a response. Research has shown that high confidence incorrect responses are particularly likely to be corrected with feedback, a finding called the hypercorrection effect (Butterfield & Metcalfe, 2001; 2006). Presumably, the surprise associated with finding out a high confidence response is incorrect increases processing of the feedback and makes the correct response more memorable. Along the same lines, feedback seems to be critical in correcting the metacognitive error inherent in low confidence correct responses (Butler, Karpicke, & Roediger, 2008).

In summary, laboratory research clearly shows that feedback enhances the benefits of testing. Throughout the feedback literature, the effect of providing feedback is overwhelmingly positive. The few studies that show a negative effect have generally provided feedback in a manner that undermines learning. For example, many early programmed instruction experiments, operating on the principle that learning should be errorless, provided both the question and feedback simultaneously (i.e., instead of waiting until after the question had been answered to provide feedback). As a result, subjects could answer the question by looking at the correct answer at the bottom of the screen rather than trying to retrieve it from memory (see Bangert-Drowns, Kulik, Kulik, & Morgan, 2001; Kulhavy, 1977). By helping to correct errors, both in memory and metacognitive monitoring, feedback enables learners to progress toward the desired state of knowledge. We now turn to describing how feedback might shape collective memories outside the laboratory.

Feedback Shapes Collective Memories

Much as the mechanisms of retrieval and spacing are critical to the creation and maintenance of collective memories, feedback may serve as a mechanism to shape collective memories into stable, schematized narratives. When individuals in a group retrieve memories for a shared event, feedback is generated by both external (e.g., other members of the group) and internal sources (i.e., each individual listening to others and checking his or her own recollections). The feedback consists of information about both the accuracy of the retrieved memories as well as important aspects of the event (details, subevents, etc.) that may not be recalled (errors of commission and omission, respectively). Through the process of repeatedly retrieving memories and receiving feedback from the group, the critical aspects of the event are selected by the group and eventually coalesce into a collective memory.

To illustrate this process, imagine a married couple reminiscing about their wedding. On the way to the honeymoon, they begin to share their memories of the wedding day. The husband remembers how his wife looked as she walked down the aisle, the toast his father gave during the reception, and saying thank you to all the guests at the end of the night. In turn, the wife remembers their first kiss after the ceremony, the taste of the wedding cake, and dancing with her friends to a favorite song. As they go back and forth sharing memories, each one corrects any inaccuracies in the other's recall of the events (errors of commission). For example, the husband may have attributed a funny one-liner from a toast to his father, but the wife reminds him that it was his uncle that made everyone laugh with the joke. They also remind each other of certain details and subevents that they might not have otherwise recalled (errors of omission). For example, the wife recalled walking down the aisle, but the husband reminds her that she stumbled briefly because of her long wedding dress. Over the course of their marriage this process is repeated countless times: retelling the story of their wedding to a new friend, looking through their photo album, reminiscing during an anniversary dinner, etc. As a result, the particular details and subevents that are remembered become more consistent and uniform over time until a collective memory for the event that is shared by the husband and wife exists.

Of course, this example of feedback shaping a collective memory in a dyad represents the simplest group possible. The idea could be expanded to larger groups, such as members of a championship football team reminiscing about the big game, war veterans from the same platoon sharing memories from their military service, and residents of a town recalling a horrible snowstorm. The critical point is that during the process of repeated retrieval of an event by members of a group, individuals receive feedback about the accuracy of their memories and any important aspects of the event that they failed to recall. Presumably, much of this feedback is given directly by other members of the group during collaborative remembering, as in the earlier example. However, feedback can certainly be given indirectly as well. Art, books, films, television, and other manifestations of popular culture are all prime examples of such indirect feedback. For instance, most (if not all) Americans have a collective memory for the series of events surrounding the terrorist attacks in New York City and Washington, DC on September 11, 2001. In this context, reading the 9/11 Commission Report or watching the controversial film *Fahrenheit 9/11* might be an indirect way for some members of the group to influence the way in which other members of the group remember the events of 9/11. As in laboratory research, the feedback that helps to shape collective memories can take on many forms and be delivered by numerous different methods, but its function is still to correct both errors of commission and omission.

To date, no research has investigated the influence of feedback on collective memories outside the laboratory. Hence, our extensions of research to this arena as in the previous paragraphs are speculative. However, some research exists on remembering in groups (usually two or three people) that suggests that collaborative remembering facilitates subsequent individual remembering (e.g., Basden, Basden, & Henry, 2000; Weldon & Bellinger, 1997). For example, Rajaram and Pereira-Pasarin (2007) had subjects study pictures and words, and then gave them a recognition test in one of two conditions. In the collaborative condition, the group of three subjects would first discuss each item (i.e., indicating to each other whether or not they had studied it previously), then made an individual decision (yes/ no) about the word. In the noncollaborative condition, subjects just made a decision about the item without any discussion. The results indicated that when subjects had the opportunity to discuss the items in a group before making their decision, they performed better on the recognition test than when tested individually. Presumably, subjects in the collaborative group benefited from the feedback that was generated during the discussion of each item by allowing them to correct errors of commission and omission.

ACCURACY AND INACCURACY IN COLLECTIVE MEMORIES

The accuracy of collective memories is a major issue for historians, anthropologists, psychologists, and the many other groups of researchers who work on this topic – not to mention the groups of people who share these memories. At best, agreement about the accuracy of a collective memory can unite a group, such as the yearly commemoration of the Declaration of Independence by Americans on July 4. At worst, disputes about the accuracy of a collective memory between groups can have dire consequences. For example, a centuries-old disagreement between the Sunni and Shiite Muslims about the legitimate successors of the Prophet Mohammed continues to spark violence. Whereas Shiite Muslims maintain that the Prophet Mohammed explicitly designated his son-in-law Ali as successor, the Sunnis claim that Mohammed wished that his successor be appointed by the Muslim community. Regardless of whether there is consensus or disagreement about the accuracy of a collective memory, it is quite difficult (if not impossible) to determine the truth in any objective sense. In addition, even if consensus exists, the agreed upon version of events can change over time, like in the example of history textbooks given earlier. Thus, we will put aside the question of whether collective memories are generally accurate or inaccurate, and instead briefly discuss how the mechanisms of retrieval, spacing, and feedback described in this chapter might influence the accuracy collective memories.

Retrieval of information from memory helps people to better remember that information over long periods of time. However, taken alone, this mechanism for promoting long-term retention is completely indifferent to the accuracy of information. If incorrect information is retrieved, then memory for that incorrect information is strengthened. For example, Roediger, Jacoby, and McDermott (1996) had subjects view slides depicting a crime and then read a narrative from another witness that contained misinformation. Immediately after the narrative, they were given a forced recall test and told to recall information either only from the slides or from both the slides and the narrative. Subjects who were asked to recall information from either source produced more misinformation than those in the slides-only condition on this immediate test. A final recall test was given 2 days later with instructions to recall information from the slides only. Across both conditions, misinformation from the narrative that was (falsely) recalled on the initial test was more likely to be recalled on final test. That is, the act of producing information on the forced recall test seemed to strengthen the memories (the testing effect) and led subjects to be more likely to erroneously recall the information later even when they were told to be sure only to recall information from the slides (see too McDermott, 2006).

Another example comes from the literature on multiple-choice testing: when subjects (incorrectly) select a lure item, they often will produce that lure again on a subsequent test (e.g., Butler, Marsh, Goode, & Roediger, 2006; Roediger & Marsh, 2005) unless feedback is given (Butler & Roediger, 2008). Critically, this effect is not a result of simple ignorance: the lure is more likely to be retained and reproduced later if it is selected through faulty reasoning than as a random guess (Huelser & Marsh, 2006). Overall, these findings clearly show that retrieving incorrect information on a test can lead to the learning and retention of that incorrect information. Thus, it is the accuracy of the to-be-retrieved information that determines the accuracy of the collective memories that are created.

Just as the mechanism of retrieval is blind to accuracy of information, repeated retrieval (especially when spaced) serves to increase retention of information, regardless of its accuracy. If incorrect information is repeatedly retrieved over time, it will lead to an even stronger memory for that incorrect information. Although no study has specifically investigated the effects of repeated retrieval of incorrect information, many studies have looked at how repeated exposure to misinformation influences subsequent memory. For instance, using a paradigm similar to Roediger et al. (1996), Zaragoza and Mitchell (1996) varied the number of exposures to misinformation after viewing slides of a crime. Subjects were presented with the

misinformation either once or three times. A greater number of presenta-
tions of the misinformation led to the production of more misinformation
on a final recall test. In fact, the effect of repeated exposure to misinformation is so strong that subjects often retain the misinformation even if
it is subsequently corrected (Lewandowsky, Stritzke, Oberauer, & Morales,
2005) or explicitly labeled at the time of exposure (Skurnik, Yoon, Park, &
Schwartz, 2005). One explanation for this effect is that repeated exposure
to misinformation increases the fluency with which that misinformation
can be retrieved from memory. After a long delay, people forget that the
information has been labeled incorrect, but the fluency remains and people
attribute this fluency to the correctness of the information. These findings
suggest that the repeated retrieval involved in creating collective memories
will increase the retention of incorrect information in the exact same way as
correct information. Again, the accuracy of the repeatedly retrieved information is the critical component, not the mechanism of spacing.

In contrast to retrieval and spacing, feedback can be a mechanism for
reducing inaccuracy. As described earlier, feedback enables people to correct memory errors as they engage in repeated retrieval and form collective
memories. However, feedback will only help to correct errors if the feedback
succeeds in labeling the errors as incorrect. Moreover, if the information
from the source of the feedback is incorrect, feedback can actually cause
people to acquire incorrect information. Roediger, Meade, and Bergman
(2001) conducted a study that illustrates this point. Using a relatively new
paradigm for studying false memories, they had pairs of people study six
common household scenes (e.g., a kitchen). One person was a naive subject
and the other was a confederate of the experimenter with instructions on
how to respond. After studying a scene, each person took turns recalling
items from the scenes. During this collaborative recall phase, the confederate reported either true items only or both some true items and some
erroneous items, ones that did not appear any of the scenes. Later, when
subjects were again asked to recall items from the scenes, they reported
more erroneous items if the confederate had suggested erroneous items
during the collaborative recall phase, an effect they termed the "social contagion of memory." Subjects in this study treated recall by the confederate
as feedback about items that they had not recalled. Unaware that some of
the items recalled were erroneous, they used this feedback to correct what
they perceived to be errors of omission. Accordingly, feedback can promote
accuracy in collective memories, but only when information can be identified as incorrect. If incorrect information is deemed to be correct by other
members of the group, feedback will help to promote the retention of that

incorrect information and, as a result, inaccuracy in collective memories. Some collective memories may have errors introduced in this way, when one vocal member of the group remembers an event and gets some details or facts wrong.

In conclusion, the mechanisms described earlier each serve to promote the creation, retention, and composition of collective memories, irrespective of their accuracy. As previously discussed, one source of information that contributes to the creation of collective memories is history textbooks used in schools. If these textbooks contain inaccuracies, either intentionally or unintentionally, then students who must learn the information in those textbooks will repeatedly retrieve incorrect information and receive feedback from teachers (among other sources) that suggest that the information is correct. The result will be an inaccurate collective memory, because the mechanisms of retrieval, spacing, and feedback are largely blind to the accuracy of the information placed into the system. Although many of the inaccuracies included in history textbooks are minor or simply a matter of opinion, some inaccuracies are so blatant that they might constitute misinformation. For instance, the Kremlin has recently begun to promote a textbook entitled *A Modern History of Russia: 1945–2006: A Manual for History Teachers* that presents a new view of recent Russian history, which, among other revisions, justifies Stalin's dictatorship as a "necessary evil." Another example is the genocide of Native Americans by European settlers, which was omitted largely from (or else finessed) in American history textbooks until recent years. Thus, the accuracy of the information that is repeatedly retrieved and confirmed by feedback is the prime determinant of the accuracy of the subsequent collective memory.

CONCLUSION

In some ways, the study of collective memory is still in its beginning phases. Much has been written about the topic, but systematic exploration of the issues and the relation of issues in collective memory to the empirical study of memory by psychologists are just starting. Our aim in this chapter has been to show how lessons learned from laboratory experiments may be extended to help our framing of issues in the field of collective memory. We have discussed how repeated retrieval and feedback, in particular, are critical topics in both laboratory and real-world settings. Repeated retrieval and the feedback one receives from others in discussing some event are critical in developing what Wertsch (2002) calls schematic narrative templates that people use to organize and retrieve their collective memories.

REFERENCES

Andre, T., & Thieman, A. (1988). Level of adjunct question, type of feedback, and learning concepts by reading. *Contemporary Educational Psychology, 13,* 296–307.

Balota, D. A., Duchek, J. M., & Logan, J. M. (2007). Is expanded retrieval practice a superior form of spaced retrieval? A critical review of the extant literature. In J. S. Nairne (Ed.), *The foundations of remembering: Essays in honor of Henry L. Roediger, III* (pp. 83–105). New York: Psychology Press.

Bangert-Drowns, R. L., Kulik, J. A., & Kulik, C. C. (1991). Effects of frequent classroom testing. *Journal of Educational Research, 85,* 89–99.

Bangert-Drowns, R. L., Kulik, C. C., Kulik, J. A., & Morgan, M. (1991). The instructional effect of feedback in test-like events. *Review of Educational Research, 61,* 213–238.

Barnes, A. E., Nelson, T. O., Dunlosky, J., Mazzoni, G., & Narens, L. (1999). An integrative system of metamemory components involved in retrieval. In D. Gopher & A. Koriat (Eds.), *Attention and Performance XVII – Cognitive regulation of performance: Interaction of theory and application* (pp. 287–313). Cambridge, MA: MIT Press.

Bartlett, F. C. (1932). *Remembering: A study in experimental and social psychology.* Cambridge, UK: Cambridge University Press.

Basden, B. H., Basden, D. R., & Henry, S. (2000). Costs and benefits of collaborative remembering. *Applied Cognitive Psychology, 14,* 497–507.

Berntsen, D., & Thomsen, D. K. (2005). Personal memories for remote historical events: Accuracy and clarity of flashbulb memories related to World War II. *Journal of Experimental Psychology: General, 134,* 242–257.

Bjork, R. A. (1975). Retrieval as a memory modifier: An interpretation of negative recency and related phenomena. In R. L. Solso (Ed.), *Information processing and cognition* (pp. 123–144). New York: Wiley.

Brokaw, T. (2001). *The greatest generation.* New York: Random House.

Brown, R., & Kulik, J. (1977). Flashbulb memories. *Cognition, 5,* 73–99.

Butler, A. C., Karpicke, J. D., & Roediger, H. L., III (2008). Correcting a meta-cognitive error: Feedback enhances retention of low confidence correct responses. *Journal of Experimental Psychology: Learning, Memory and Cognition, 34,* 918–928.

Butler, A. C., Marsh, E. J., Goode, M. K., & Roediger, H. L., III (2006). When additional multiple-choice lures aid versus hinder later memory. *Applied Cognitive Psychology, 20,* 941–956.

Butler, A. C., & Roediger, H. L., III (2007). Testing improves long-term retention in a simulated classroom setting. *European Journal of Cognitive Psychology, 19,* 514–527.

  (2008). Feedback enhances the positive effects and reduces the negative effects of multiple-choice testing. *Memory & Cognition, 36,* 604–616,

Butler, D. L., & Winne, P. H. (2005). Feedback and self-regulated learning: A theoretical synthesis. *Review of Educational Research, 65,* 245–281.

Butterfield, B., & Metcalfe, J. (2001). Errors committed with high confidence are hypercorrected. *Journal of Experimental Psychology: Learning, Memory, and Cognition, 27,* 1491–1494.

(2006). The correction of errors committed with high confidence. *Metacognition & Learning, 1,* 69–84.

Carrier, M., & Pashler, H. (1992). The influence of retrieval on retention. *Memory & Cognition, 20,* 633–642.

Cepeda, N. J., Pashler, H., Vul, E., Wixted, J. T., & Rohrer, D. (2006). Distributed practice in verbal recall tasks: A review and quantitative synthesis. *Psychological Bulletin, 132,* 354–380.

Chan, C. K., McDermott, K. B., & Roediger, H. L., III (2006). Retrieval induced facilitation: Initially nontested material can benefit from prior testing. *Journal of Experimental Psychology: General, 135,* 533–571.

Conway, M. A. (1995). *Flashbulb memories.* Hillsdale, NJ: Lawrence Erlbaum Associates, Inc.

Cull, W. L. (2000). Untangling the benefits of multiple study opportunities and repeated testing for cued recall. *Applied Cognitive Psychology, 14,* 215–235.

Cull, W. L., Shaughnessy, J. J., & Zechmeister, E. B. (1996). Expanding understanding of the expanding-pattern-of-retrieval mnemonic: Toward confidence in applicability. *Journal of Experimental Psychology: Applied, 2,* 365–378.

Curci, A., & Luminet, O. (2006). Follow-up of a cross-national comparison on flashbulb and event memory for the September 11th attacks. *Memory, 14,* 329–344.

Dempster, F. N. (1989). Spacing effects and their implications for theory and practice. *Educational Psychology Review, 1,* 309–330.

Dudai, Y. (2002). *Memory from A to Z: Keywords, concepts and beyond.* Oxford, UK: Oxford University Press.

Ebbinghaus, H. (1967). *Memory: A contribution to experimental psychology* (H. A. Ruger & C. E. Bussenius, Trans.). New York: Dover. (Original work published 1885).

Er, N. (2003). A new flashbulb memory model applied to the Marmara earthquake. *Applied Cognitive Psychology, 17,* 503–517.

Fazio, L. K., Huelser, B. J., Johnson, A. & Marsh, E. J. (under review). Receiving partial feedback: Consequences for learning.

Foos, P. W., & Fisher, R. P. (1988). Using tests as learning opportunities. *Journal of Educational Psychology, 80,* 179–183.

Gates, A. I. (1917). Recitation as a factor in memorizing. *Archives of Psychology, 6*(40), 1–104.

Gilman, D. A. (1969). Comparison of several feedback methods for correcting errors by computer-assisted instruction *Journal of Educational Psychology, 60,* 503–508.

Glenberg, A. M. (1976). Monotonic and nonmonotonic lag effects in paired-associate and recognition memory paradigms. *Journal of Verbal Learning and Verbal Behavior, 15,* 1–16.

Glover, J. A. (1989). The "testing" phenomenon: Not gone but nearly forgotten. *Journal of Educational Psychology, 81,* 392–399.

Halbwachs, M. (1980). *The collective memory.* New York: Harper & Row. (Trans. by Francis J. Didder, Jr. and Vida Yazdi Ditter).

(1992). *On collective memory.* Chicago: University of Chicago Press. (Ed. and Trans. by Lewis A. Coser).

Hattie, J., & Timperley, H. (2007). The power of feedback. *Review of Educational Research, 77*, 81–112.

Huelser, B. J., & Marsh, E. J. (2006, November). Does guessing on a multiple-choice test affect later cued recall? Poster presented at the Annual Meeting of the Psychonomic Society, Houston, TX.

Jones, H. E. (1923–1924). The effects of examination n the performance of learning. *Archives of Psychology, 10*, 1–70.

Kang, S. H. K., McDermott, K. B., & Roediger, H. L., III (2007). Test format and corrective feedback modulate the effect of testing on memory retention. *The European Journal of Cognitive Psychology, 19*, 528–558.

Karpicke, J. D., & Roediger, H. L., III (2007a). Expanding retrieval practice promotes short-term retention, but equally spaced retrieval enhances long-term retention. *Journal of Experimental Psychology: Learning, Memory and Cognition, 33*, 704–719.

(2007b). Repeated retrieval during learning is the key to long-term retention. *Journal of Memory and Language, 57*, 151–162.

Kelley, C. M., & Sahakyan, L. (2003). Memory, monitoring and control in the attainment of memory accuracy. *Journal of Memory and Language, 48*, 704–721.

Koriat, A., & Goldsmith, M. (1996). Monitoring and control processes in strategic regulation of memory accuracy. *Psychological Review, 103*, 490–517.

Kramer, J. (1996). *The politics of memory: Looking for Germany in the New Germany.* New York: Random House.

Kulhavy, R. W. (1977). Feedback in written instruction. *Review of Educational Research, 47*, 211–232.

Kulhavy, R. W., & Stock, W. A. (1989). Feedback in written instruction: The place of response certitude. *Educational Psychology Review, 1*, 279–308.

Kulhavy, R. W., White, M. T., Topp, B. W., Chan, A. L., & Adams, J. (1985). Feedback complexity and corrective efficiency. *Contemporary Educational Pscyhology, 10*, 285–291.

Landauer, T. K., & Bjork, R. A. (1978). Optimum rehearsal patterns and name learning. In M. M. Gruneberg, P. E. Morris, & R. N. Sykes (Eds.), *Practical aspects of memory* (pp. 625–632). London: Academic Press.

Lewandowsky, S., Stritzke, W., Oberauer, K., & Morales, M. (2005). Memory for fact, fiction, and misinformation: The Iraq War 2003. *Psychological Science, 16*, 190–195.

Lhyle, K. G., & Kulhavy, R. W. (1987). Feedback processing and error correction. *Journal of Educational Psychology, 79*, 320–322.

Lindaman, D., & Ward, K. (2004). *History lessons: How textbooks from around the world portray U.S. history.* New York: The New Press.

Liu, J. H., Goldstein-Hawes, R., Hilton, D., Huang, L-L., Gastardo-Conaco, C., Dresler-Hawke, E., et al. (2005). Social representations of events and people in world history across 12 cultures. *Journal of Cross-Cultural Psychology, 36*, 1–21.

Logan, J. M., & Balota, D. A. (2008). Expanded versus. equal interval spaced retrieval practice: Exploring different schedules of spacing and retention interval in younger and older adults. *Aging, Neuropsychology, and Cognition, 15*, 257–280.

Loewen, J. (1995). *Lies my teacher told me: Everything your American history textbook got wrong.* New York: W.W. Norton and Company.

Luminet, O., Curci, A., Marsh, E. J., Wessel, I., Constantin, T., Gencoz, F., & Yogo, M. (2004). The cognitive, emotional, and social impacts of the September 11 attacks: Group difference in memory for the reception context and the determinants of flashbulb memory. *The Journal of General Psychology, 131,* 197–224.

McDaniel, M. A., Anderson, J. L., Derbish, M. H., & Morrisette, N. (2007). Testing the testing effect in the classroom. *European Journal of Cognitive Psychology. 19,* 494–513.

McDaniel, M. A., & Fisher, R. P. (1991). Tests and test feedback as learning sources. *Contemporary Educational Psychology, 16,* 192–201.

McDaniel, M. A., Roediger, H. L., III, & McDermott, K. B. (2007). Generalizing test-enhanced learning from the laboratory to the classroom. *Psychonomic Bulletin & Review, 14,* 200–206.

McDermott, K. B. (2006). Paradoxical effects of testing: Repeated retrieval attempts enhance the likelihood of later accurate and false recall. *Memory & Cognition, 34,* 261–267.

Melton, A. W. (1970). The situation with respect to the spacing of repetitions and memory. *Journal of Verbal Learning and Verbal Behavior, 9,* 596–606.

Neisser, U., & Harsch, N. (1992). Phantom flashbulbs: False recollections of hearing the news about *Challenger.* In E. Winograd & U. Neisser (Eds.), *Affect and accuracy in recall: Studies of flashbulb memories* (pp. 9–31). New York: Cambridge University Press.

Neisser, U., Winograd, E., Bergman, E. T., Schreiber, C. A., Palmer, S. E., & Weldon, M. S. (1996). Remembering the earthquake: Direct experience vs. hearing the news. *Memory, 4,* 337–357.

Nelson, T. O., & Narens, L. (1990). Metamemory: A theoretical framework and new findings. In G. H. Bower (Ed.), *The psychology of learning and motivation* (Vol. 26, pp. 125–141). New York: Academic Press.

Novick, P. (1999). *The Holocaust in American life.* Boston: Houghton Mifflin Company.

Pashler, H., Cepeda, N. J., Wixted, J. T., & Rohrer, D. (2005). When does feedback facilitate learning of words? *Journal of Experimental Psychology: Learning, Memory, and Cognition, 31,* 3–8.

Peeck, J. (1979). Effects of differential feedback on the answering of two types of questions by fifth- and sixth-graders. *British Journal of Educational Psychology, 49,* 87–92.

Phye, G. D. (1979). The processing of informative feedback about multiple-choice test performance. *Contemporary Educational Psychology, 4,* 381–394.

Rajaram, S., & Pereira-Pasarin, L. (2007). Collaboration can improve individual recognition memory: Evidence from immediate and delayed tests. *Psychonomic Bulletin & Review, 14,* 95–100.

Roediger, H. L., III (1985). Remembering Ebbinghaus. *Contemporary Psychology, 30,* 519–523.

Roediger, H. L., III, Bergman, E. T., & Meade, M. L. (2000). Repeated reproduction from memory. In A. Saito (Ed.), *Bartlett, culture, and cognition.* Cambridge, UK: Psychology Press.

Roediger, H. L., III, Dudai, Y., & Fitzpatrick, S. M. (Eds.). (2007). *Science of memory: Concepts.* Oxford, UK: Oxford University Press.

Roediger, H. L., III, Jacoby, D., & McDermott, K. B. (1996). Misinformation effects in recall: Creating false memories through repeated retrieval. *Journal of Memory and Language, 35,* 300–318.

Roediger, H. L., III, & Karpicke, J. D. (2006a). The power of testing memory: Basic research and implications for educational practice. *Perspectives on Psychological Science, 1,* 181–210.

(2006b). Test-enhanced learning: Taking memory tests improves long-term retention. *Psychological Science, 17,* 249–255.

Roediger, H. L., III, & Marsh, E. J. (2005). The positive and negative consequences of multiple-choice testing. *Journal of Experimental Psychology: Learning, Memory, & Cognition, 31,* 1155–1159.

Roediger, H. L., III, Meade, M. L., & Bergman, E. T. (2001). Social contagion of memory. *Psychonomic Bulletin & Review, 8,* 365–371.

Roper, W. J. (1977). Feedback in computer assisted instruction. *Programmed Learning and Educational Technology, 14,* 43–79.

Rubin, D. C., & Kozin, M. (1984). Vivid memories. *Cognition, 16,* 81–95.

Schudson, M. (1992). *Watergate in American memory: How we remember, forget, and reconstruct the past.* New York: Basic Books.

Shapiro (2006). Remembering September 11th: The role of retention interval and rehearsal on flashbulb and event memory. *Memory, 14,* 129–147.

Skurnik, I., Yoon, C., Park, D. C., & Schwarz, N. (2005). How warnings about false claims become recommendations. *Journal of Consumer Research, 31,* 713–724.

Spitzer, H. F. (1939). Studies in retention. *Journal of Educational Psychology, 30,* 641–656.

Tulving, E. (1972). Episodic and semantic memory. In E. Tulving & W. Donaldson (Eds.), *Organization and memory* (pp. 381–403). New York: Academic Press.

Ward, K. (2006). *History in the making: An absorbing look at how American history has changed in the telling over the last 200 years.* New York: The New Press.

Wegner, D. M. (1986). Transactive memory: A contemporary analysis of the group mind. In B. Mullen & G. R. Goethals (Eds.), *Theories of Group Behavior* (pp. 185–205). New York: Springer-Verlag.

Weldon, M. S., & Bellinger, K. D. (1997). Collective memory: Collaborative and individual processes in remembering. *Journal of Experimental Psychology: Learning, Memory, and Cognition, 23,* 1160–1175.

Wertsch, J. W. (2002). *Voices of collective remembering.* Cambridge, UK: Cambridge University Press.

(2008). Collective memory. In J. H. Byrne (Ed.), *Learning and Memory: A Comprehensive Reference.* (pp. 927–939). Oxford, UK: Elsevier Ltd.

Wertsch, J. V., & Roediger, H. L., III (2008). Collective memory: Conceptual foundations and theoretical approaches. *Memory, 16,* 318–326.

Wheeler, M. A., & Roediger, H. L., III. (1992). Disparate effects of repeated testing: Reconciling Ballard's (1913) and Bartlett's (1932) results. *Psychological Science, 3,* 240–245.

Zaragoza, M. S., & Mitchell, K. J. (1996). Repeated exposure to suggestion and the creation of false memories. *Psychological Science, 7,* 294–300.

7

Making History: Social and Psychological Processes Underlying Collective Memory

JAMES W. PENNEBAKER & AMY L. GONZALES

The field of history is premised on the idea that knowledge of our past can inform our behaviors in the future. Indeed, this idea is central to many assumptions within personality, developmental, and clinical psychology. Implicit in this thinking is that history is somehow made up of immutable facts that are set in stone in society's memory. Who, after all, could doubt the accuracy of America's role in World War II, the facts surrounding the discovery of the New World by Columbus in 1492, the bravery and upstanding characters of the men who defended the Alamo in 1845, or the profound effect of the Magna Carta in 1215? These events, of course, are not as straightforward as we were taught in grade school. Events such as these undergo rethinking, reinterpreting, and even forgetting to become part of the permanent fabric of collective memory. But the transition from cultural upheaval to history does not happen all at once. The macrocosm of how a collective memory is built over centuries takes place on a much smaller scale beginning in the days, weeks, and months following an event.

The purpose of this chapter is to suggest that our current psychological state shapes our thinking about historical events in the same way that historical events shape our current thinking. Just as the key to the future may be the past, the key to the past may be the present. What about an event that makes it memorable? How does memory of an event change over time? What are the psychological effects that accompany the integration of events in memory? Whereas most memory research focuses on the processes of individual memory, history is constructed through the shared memories of multiple people.

HOW ARE HISTORICAL MEMORIES FORMED?

To answer this question, we must first ask how individual memories are created and retained. As described in much greater detail by others in this volume, we tend to remember events that are vivid, novel, personal, emotional, affect multiple sensory systems, have behavioral relevance, and are rehearsed. If we are presented with a serial word list, we are more likely to remember words like *sex, kill,* and *fudge* than words such as *cup, type,* and *process.* We should also be more likely to remember unexpected events associated with vivid images and emotional upheaval, than more predictable pallid ones. Ten years later, most of us would be more likely to remember an event like September 11, 2001, than the deaths of thousands of people who died that same year from an influenza outbreak.

Historical memory requires long-term change. Another factor associated with historical memory is that we are more likely to remember events that change our lives. American wars such as World War II and Vietnam tended to change the course of U.S. history far more than the Korean War or the 1991 Persian Gulf War. Indeed, if a large event has only minimal long-term impact, it is easily forgotten. A rich example of this is the 1991 Persian Gulf War. When it occurred, much of the United States came to a halt. During the first week of the war, American streets were empty each night because people were glued to their television sets. Just before, during, and following the six-week war, our research team tracked the responses of several hundred people in Dallas, Texas (Pennebaker & Harber, 1993). In random digit dialing (RDD) telephone surveys with hundreds of people, as well as repeated questionnaires with over two hundred college students, the average person reported talking about the Persian Gulf War 7.1 times per day, and thinking about it 11.2 times per day. The vast majority agreed that the war was historically significant because for the first time a united post-Soviet world had come together to fight for justice, freedom, and democracy.

But one year later, all the troops had gone home, the same regime was in power in Iraq, and no long-term consensus in the world was apparent. Two years after the war, we contacted 76 students who had completed multiple questionnaires about the war when it was underway. In our telephone follow-up survey, we asked people a series of questions about the war – who the U.S.-led coalition was fighting (Iraq), how long the invasion of Iraq lasted (six weeks), how many Americans were killed in combat (approximately 150), and so on. Even though two years earlier our students talked about the war several times per day, heard about it in most of their classes, and filled out multiple questionnaires concerning it, their memories for the war had evaporated. For example, only 81 percent could identify Iraq as the country we were fighting, 28 percent accurately estimated the American deaths (within ± 150 people), and only 6 percent were correct in guessing how long the war lasted (within a ± three-week margin). In mid-1993 when asked when the invasion of Iraq started (January 17, 1991), only 57 percent accurately identified the month, and 68 percent the year. Interestingly, several students, after not being able to answer the first questions about the war, hung up on us to avoid any more embarrassment (Crow & Pennebaker, 2000).

Although we didn't know it at the time, the Persian Gulf War didn't significantly change the students' worlds. Because of this, it quickly diminished in their (and most of our) memories. The formation, maintenance, and reinterpretation of both memories and history change over time depending on new information. In the years to come, the 1991 Persian Gulf War may indeed be newly remembered depending on the ultimate outcome of the subsequent Iraq invasion in 2003.

Historical Events Must Touch the Right Cohort: Ages 13–25

Ask most anyone over the age of 40 what are the three most important songs ever written and they will likely list songs that were popular when they were between the ages of 13 and 25. Conway (1990) describes a series of studies on autobiographical memory wherein elderly people were asked to list their most significant personal memories. Overwhelmingly, these events occurred during their teenage years. Sociologists have independently reported that events that occur during the age window between 13 and 25 are most likely to be commemorated in the future (e.g., Schuman, Belli, & Bischoping, 1997). This is consistent with findings by Rubin and colleagues (Rubin, Wetzler, & Nebes, 1986) who found that random word cues produce memories from events that occurred between the ages of 11 and 20. The second most likely age from which memories stem are from events that occurred between the ages of 21 and 30. In general, memories that are formed between the ages of 13 and 25 are the most striking events in our personal histories. It is not surprising, then, that historical memories are largely retained and passed on by people within this cohort.

The tendency toward recall of events that occur during adolescence and early adulthood has been explored by various authors. According to Erik Erikson (1950), experiences between 12 and 19 are important because they contribute to development of an integrated, single identity. After one's mid-20s, in Erikson's view (see also Levinson, Darrow, Klein, Levinson, & McKee, 1978), most life transitions are less critical to the developing identity. Moreover, memories may be strongest for events from one's late teens and early 20s because they are more disruptive, often being the first of many major life events. In Mannheim's (1952) words, these events constitute a "fresh" experience.

Historical Memories Must Be Shared

Talking forms the core of historical memories by generating the content, but it also serves to reinforce memory. On an individual level, objects or events are most likely to be consolidated in memory if they are verbally rehearsed. Furthermore, verbally rehearsing the details of an event influences how it is organized in memory and, perhaps, recalled in the future. This same process takes place at a social level as well. In fact, Shils (1981) claims that for a society to exist over time, its communications must be said, said again, and reenacted repeatedly.

Part of the reason major events are socially rehearsed is because events that are significant enough to change our lives typically involve a certain level of stress. Writing or talking about upsetting experiences is a common response that can help people to understand, organize, or resolve their effects (Pennebaker & Chung, 2007). In other cases, talking has been associated with a prolongation of the emotional distress (Rimé, 1995), as has rumination about the event (Nolen-Hoeksema, Morrow, & Fredrickson, 1993). In either case, increased communication seems to be a natural reaction to social stress. In two related studies, on the Loma Prieta earthquake that occurred in the San Francisco Bay Area in 1989, and the Persian Gulf War in 1991, the degree of self-reported talking and thinking was exceptionally high during the first two weeks following each event (Pennebaker & Harber, 1993). Similar findings emerged in natural recorded conversations among students in the aftermath of the 9/11 attacks. As these and other studies indicate, significant emotional events are discussed with others and, through these discussions, are interpreted and shaped in order to better understand their occurrence. This rehashing process, then, serves as the groundwork for future memories of the event.

Historical Events Must Reflect Well on the Culture

At some points in time, historical events are celebrated and, at others, the same events are forgotten – or at least not acknowledged. Events that are embarrassing, shameful, or in some way reflect negatively on people are more likely to be forgotten than more self-affirming events. The massacre of American Indians, slavery, and lynchings within the United States are generally given short shrift in most history textbooks. As described later in this chapter, more subtle are events that occur in a community or culture that may not be any residents' fault but reflect negatively on the community. The assassinations of John F. Kennedy in Dallas in 1963 and Martin Luther

King Jr. in Memphis in 1968 are good examples. In both cases, the cities initially responded by minimizing the effects of the murders (Pennebaker, 1997). Similar phenomena have been reported among Chileans in the aftermath of the Pinochet regime (Lira, 1997).

THE SOCIAL DYNAMICS OF TRAUMATIC EVENTS

Most historical events grow out of traumatic upheavals. Wars and revolutions entail death, loss, and adapting to a new order. Creating new ways to think of things by definition shakes up those who cling to the old ways of thinking. Given the close links between memory of emotional experiences and history, the study of people's responses to traumatic events is a productive way to examine the processes of creating historical memories.

Traumatic events are ultimately social events. Personal upheavals such as death of a loved one, a sexual trauma, or the diagnosis of a major illness have the ability to influence every part of a person's life. Over the last two decades, we have asked thousands of students and nonstudents to write about the most traumatic experiences of their lives. Even the most private traumas affect others. When keeping an important and potentially explosive secret from close friends, the secret can create a subtle rift in those relationships. The person often feels guarded and not free to discuss a personal topic that normally would be shared (cf., Bok, 1983). This is not to say that sharing secret traumas is always a good idea. Often when embarrassing or shameful experiences are shared, the person's social network is permanently disrupted. More public traumas also have social consequences as well. The death of a family member, for example, typically results in friends talking with, cooking for, and watching out for the bereaved for days or weeks. In certain circumstances, such as the death of a child, the event may sufficiently upset close friends as to cause them to avoid the family that is bereaved (Pennebaker, 1997).

Socially shared traumas such as natural or man-made disasters provide some of the cleanest evidence for appreciating the social dynamics of upheavals. Over the last several years, our research team has attempted to track the social changes that occur as a public trauma unfolds. The projects with the most fine-grained analyses include September 11, the Texas A&M Bonfire disaster, the death of Princess Diana, the Loma Prieta earthquake, and the U.S. response to the Persian Gulf War. Broader, and less fine-grained, analyses have been conducted on responses to the assassinations of John F. Kennedy in Dallas and Martin Luther King Jr. in Memphis. Our goal in these studies has been to track people's lives as closely and as accurately as possible while major events are unfolding.

As outlined later in this chapter, culturally shared traumas can have very different social footprints depending on the perceived cause and implications of the event. Of particular importance is the awareness of the time frame of a trauma. The social processes of traumas are quite dynamic with constant shifts in the ways people relate to one another, and to the trauma, in the days, weeks, months, years, and even generations after a significant experience has occurred.

Based on previous research with the Loma Prieta earthquake in the San Francisco Bay area in 1989, and U.S. citizens' responses to the Persian Gulf War in 1991, we posited that three distinct social stages to traumatic experience occur (Pennebaker & Harber, 1993). Unlike psychological stage models such as those proposed by Piaget for cognitive development, or Kübler-Ross for dealing with news about one's own death, a social stage model assumes that one's social environment changes over time when collectively confronting emotional upheavals.

The *emergency stage* typically occurs during the first two to three weeks after an event. For both the earthquake and Persian Gulf War projects, we found that people reported talking and thinking about the event at very high rates during this initial stage. Indeed, this was a time of social bonding, where many people reported talking with neighbors or strangers in ways they never had done before. A heightened rate of talking with others after an upheaval is common across multiple events. An elevated desire to share one's perspective is evidenced among cancer patients (Mitchell & Glickman, 1977), or for those who have recently experienced the death of a loved one (Schoenberg, Carr, Peretz, Kutscher, & Cherico, 1975). Increased levels of socialization during times of distress are consistent with theories of social coping (Cohen & Willis, 1985; Psyzczynski, Solomon, & Greenberg, 2002; Schachter, 1959), and are expressed by people across different cultures (Rimé, Philippot, Boca, & Mesquita, 1998).

The *inhibition stage* lasts from two to three to two or more months after an event occurs. In this phase individuals gradually reduced their talking about the event although they continued to think about it. Our sense was that people still wanted to tell their stories but were tired of hearing other people's stories. A compelling example was that a month after the Loma Prieta earthquake, t-shirts began appearing in San Francisco saying "Thank you for not sharing your earthquake experience." Most interesting has been that the inhibition phase was associated with increased rates of dreams about the event, higher illness rates, and more reports of assaults as well as fights with friends and coworkers. In the two to six weeks after the earthquake, aggravated assault rates increased 10 percent over the previous year in San Francisco (Pennebaker, 1992). A comparable jump in assaults was apparent in Dallas two to six weeks after the war started.

More startling is what happened approximately two weeks after the war ended. Recall that the Persian Gulf War was declared to be a striking victory six weeks after it started. However, within a week of its conclusion, it became quite apparent to most Americans that the Iraq government was essentially unchanged and that the brutal treatment of Kurdish residents was, if anything, intensified. Our surveys indicated that people simply no longer wanted to hear or think about the war. It was at this time that aggravated assaults jumped 70 percent above the previous year (Pennebaker & Harber, 1993).

The *adaptation stage* was an admittedly vague postinhibition label that signaled that people were getting on with life. In retrospect, this was not a particularly important theoretical advance. Since our original formulation, we now appreciate that there are a number of additional processes that unfold in the months and years after an event.

As more studies have been conducted, it is clear that the social stages model is a preliminary model at best. The project was based on studies where a powerful event disrupted a group of people for a relatively brief time with little disruption to the infrastructure. Anyone familiar with the long-term effects of an extended war, the 2004 Tsunami, or Hurricane Katrina appreciates how a truly massive upheaval rips the social fabric at every level for years rather than weeks or months.

A related consideration is that cultural upheavals are rarely single events occurring at one point in time. The 9/11 attacks were soon followed by other events that were tied to them such as the anthrax-tainted letters to public officials and the U.S. invasions of Afghanistan and Iraq. When Mt. St. Helens volcano erupted in 1981, it was followed by another series of eruptions over the next few months, arousing fears for those living closest to the mountain (Pennebaker & Newtson, 1983). In his naturalist tests of cognitive dissonance theory, Leon Festinger (1964) was intrigued by how major disruptive events typically spark rumors of even more disruptive events in the future. Historical events are generally historical because one large upheaval unleashes a series of subsequent events that change large groups of people for generations.

Although no two events are the same, it is important to begin to track how cultural upheavals unfold over time. In the remainder of the chapter, we examine a series of culturally significant events with different temporal lenses, with the understanding that traumatic experiences, like all historical events, are ultimately social. The first series of studies explore what happens in the first days and weeks after an upheaval. The second section tracks changes over the first years after its occurrence. The final section glimpses at how generations of people think about events as they decide what is historically significant.

HISTORY IN THE MAKING: THE FIRST DAYS, WEEKS, AND MONTHS

How do people's social worlds change once they learn of massive upheavals? Note that our focus is on the "audience" of disasters and upheavals – not those directly affected by them. Over the last few years, we have employed two overlapping methodologies to track people's thoughts and behaviors as they learn about and react to the news of an upheaval. The first involved a serendipitous digital recording project surrounding the 9/11 attacks. The second tracked the ways people talked about upheavals on the Internet. Both methodologies point to consistent social shifts whereby people's interactions change over time.

Social Behaviors in the Hours Surrounding the 9/11 Attacks

The September 11, 2001, attacks on New York City and Washington, DC, stunned people across the United States. Through a series of coincidences, our lab in Austin, Texas had just started a two-day project on September 10 using ambulatory blood pressure machines and a device called the Electronically Activated Recorder (EAR). The EAR is an unobtrusive recording device that is programmed to record all ambient sound for 30 seconds at 12.5 minute intervals (Mehl, Pennebaker, Crow, Dabbs & Price, 2001). In addition to transcribing what people are saying, judges listening to the recordings are able to accurately assess where participants are, what they are doing, and who they are with. Six participants had started wearing the EAR and blood pressure machine on the morning of September 10 and another five had worn the EAR in the prior weeks and were able to join our study within hours of the attacks. Although the study only consisted of a small sample of 11 college students, we were able to track their lives at a culturally pivotal point.

Results from the study revealed that group interactions with at least two other people were quite high immediately after learning of the attacks. However, this group behavior decreased in a linear fashion in the days after the attack, whereas dyadic interactions increased (Mehl & Pennebaker, 2003). That is, in the days after the attacks, people spent an increasing amount of time at home with one other person rather than congregating in large or moderate-sized groups. Moreover, self-report measures taken at the end of the study revealed that dyadic interactions were associated with less avoidance and psychological intrusion from the attacks, while continued group interactions were related to the persistence of post-traumatic stress. In other words, the desire to talk about the events of September 11 did not help people cope unless time was spent one-on-one with other people. This suggests that the socialization inherent in the building of a historical memory happens first on a very small scale. People must develop their stories with trusted others, and through this they can gradually integrate their own stories into the historical memory.

Recall that for six of the participants, we were also able to capture ambulatory blood pressure and heart rate, language use, and television/radio exposure at the same time that the 9/11 saga was unfolding (Liehr, Mehl, Summers, & Pennebaker, 2004). This full data set was only available for September 10, as well as the morning (when the attacks occurred) and the afternoon of September 11. Although the sample size was quite small, there was a significant elevation in people's heart rate from 79 beats per minute (bpm) on the 10th to 84 bpm on the morning of the 11th and 87 bpm in the afternoon. A similar trend held for systolic blood pressure. The percentage of EAR recording periods where radio or television was detected jumped from 14 percent of the time on the 10th to 42percent and 51 percent, respectively, for the morning and afternoon of the 11th. Linguistically, the only significant change was for the use of first person plural pronouns – we, us, and our. People's use of "we" words increased from 0.62 percent of all words used on the 10th to 0.96 percent in the morning and 1.90 percent in the afternoon of the 11th.

Language Use in the Weeks Surrounding an Upheaval

The ways people use language in their writing and speaking reflects their social and psychological states. Recent work suggests that an important distinction can be made between content and function words (Miller, 1995). Content words, which include nouns and regular verbs, reflect what people are talking about. Function words, which include pronouns, prepositions, articles, and auxiliary verbs, convey how people are talking. Particularly striking is that function words subtly reflect people's mood states, hormone levels, social relationships with others, and a variety of other psychological processes (Chung & Pennebaker, 2007; Pennebaker, Mehl, & Niederhoffer, 2003).

The converging technologies of the Internet and computer-based text analysis programs have opened new ways to study the social and cultural impact of large-scale traumatic experiences. On the Internet, several interactive systems have evolved that have attracted millions of people of all ages. One of the most common is the use of Web logs, or blogs. Generally, people essentially create an online diary where they are apt to post their thoughts about the world, their favorite recipes, what happened on last night's date, their plans for the day, and so on. Another more immediate forum is the chat room where groups of people get together at the same time and send one to two line messages to everyone in the "room." Chat rooms function much like cocktail parties with multiple overlapping conversations occurring at once. As described later in this chapter, we used several thousand blogs to track responses to 9/11 (Cohn, Mehl, & Pennebaker, 2004) and thousands of chat room entries to study the death of Princess Diana in 1998 (Stone & Pennebaker, 2002).

In 2001, one of the largest blog sites was LiveJournal.com, which boasted several million active members with at least tens of thousands of posts each hour. Working with the LiveJournal developers, we were able to download approximately 75,000 blog posts from over 1,000 frequent users from between July 11, through November 10, 2001. All posts were analyzed using the computer text analysis program Linguistic Inquiry and Word Count, or LIWC (Pennebaker, Francis, & Booth, 2001) to determine the degree people used various function and emotion words. Most relevant for this chapter were the results of first person singular and plural pronouns (Figures 7.1 and 7.2).

People's use of I-words and we-words shifted dramatically once they learned about the 9/11 attacks. Specifically, use of I-related words dropped by over 15 percent after the attacks, gradually returning to about 5 percent below baseline over the next two months. It should be noted that use of first person singular is linked to self-focus, depression, and low self-esteem (see Chung & Pennebaker, 2007, for review of literature). It is of interest that people reported feeling sad, afraid, angry, and a host of other negative emotions in the days after 9/11 but their use of I-words dropped rather than increased. A virtual identical pattern emerged for chat rooms on America Online (AOL) in the hours and days after people learned of Princess Diana's death (Stone & Pennebaker, 2002). One argument is that when dealing with an overwhelming negative experience, a good short-term coping strategy is to direct attention away from the self (Carver, 2007).

Consistent with the EAR study described earlier, people increased in their use of we-words by over 75 percent. Interestingly, the "we" increases were not attributable to greater nationalism but, rather, to greater attention to family and close friends. That is, in the days and weeks after 9/11, people were much more likely to talk about "my boyfriend and me" or "our neighbors" than they previously had been. Again, a similar – although less dramatic – pattern emerged for the Princess Diana chatroom data.

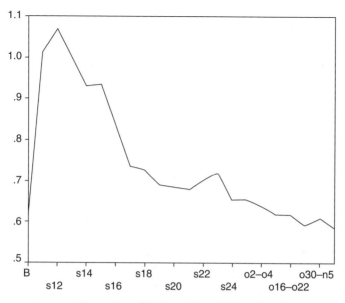

FIGURE 7.1. Percentage of total word use dedicated to first person singular pronouns in blogs from July 11, 2001, to November 11, 2001. [B=aggregated baseline of all blogs prior to September, 11, 2001]

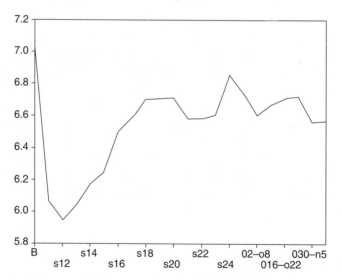

FIGURE 7.2. Percentage of total word use dedicated to first person plural pronouns in blogs from July 11, 2001, to November 11, 2001. [B=aggregated baseline of all blogs prior to September, 11, 2001]

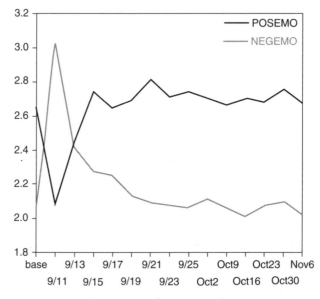

FIGURE 7.3.   Percentage of positive and negative emotion
words in blogs from July 11, 2001, to November 11, 2001.

One other 9/11 finding deserves mention – use of positive and negative
emotion words. Positive emotion words include any words that have a positive
connotation (e.g., happy, good, tasty, friend) just as negative emotion words
have negative connotations (e.g., sad, kill, ugly). As seen in Figure 7.3, negative
emotion words greatly increased as of September 11 and returned to baseline
within two weeks. More interesting is the pattern for positive emotion words.
Although there was an immediate drop in positive emotion words, it only lasted
for 4 days. By the fifth day, positive emotion words were slightly above baseline
and remain at that level for the duration of the study – two months later.

Taken together, the language analyses paint a somewhat different picture
of 9/11 than has traditionally been painted in research (e.g., Silver et al.,
2003). Rather than a monolithic negative experience, September 11 aroused
a sense of community and positive feelings.

Social and Health Processes in the First Year of an Event
Whereas the first few days after a major upheaval are devoted to learning
about and making sense of it, the subsequent months have a different focus.
The rates at which people talked about 9/11 after several months dropped
significantly. Indeed, virtually all events have a natural half-life of only a few
weeks. We must admit that we do not have a clear picture of what generally

happens during the first year after an event has occurred. Some data suggest that the natural order falls apart, resulting in conflict and strife – as occurred in Chicago after the Great Chicago Fire of 1871 (Sawislak, 1995). Other data, although not showing strife per se, suggest a great deal of internal tension among the residents. For example, in the year following the assassination of John F. Kennedy in Dallas, the death rates caused by heart disease increased 4 percent (compared to a drop of 2 percent nationwide and in other Texas cities). Murder and suicide rates increased significantly in Dallas in the two years following the assassination compared to control cities as well (Pennebaker & Banasik, 1997).

At least one other example suggests an opposite pattern. In the fall of 1999, Texas A&M students had almost finished their month-long project to build a giant bonfire that they were to set afire before their annual football game against their arch-rivals, the University of Texas at Austin. Around 3:00 in the morning, some cables snapped causing the entire wooden structure to collapse resulting in the deaths of 12 students. Language analyses of the school newspaper showed the same I and we changes as reported with 9/11 and the Princess Diana project.

More intriguing were the findings on the students' use of campus health centers (Gortner & Pennebaker, 2003). Students' use of campus health center visits for illness was tracked during the 8 months following the bonfire at both Texas A&M and its neighbor, the University of Texas at Austin. For the University of Texas, health center visits remained stable in comparison to illness rates the year before. At A&M, by contrast, there was a brief one-month increase in illness visits by about 15 percent compared to a year earlier. However, in the following four months, illness visits dropped by 40 percent. Ultimately, the bonfire disaster was associated with improvements in the student body's physical health.

Explanations from this unexpected reversal of health may be the high levels of social support found in the A&M community. Indeed, social networks have been found to help reduce poor health following other types of disasters (Cohen & McKay, 1984). Turnarounds in physical health following a disaster suggests that whereas in some cases social strife degrades the quality of life in a community, a strongly unified response not only acts as a buffer, but may actually increase health from levels before the event occurred.

HISTORY MADE: DECADES AND CENTURIES

As time passes, some events remain at the forefront of the culture's memory and others mysteriously fade. What determines when, and how, an event becomes important for a community? What fuels the process of creating a lasting memory? Over the last few years, we have begun addressing this question by looking at various indicators of popular culture within the United States. Much of this work was the outgrowth of the Kennedy assassination project. In the years following the assassination, there was very little open acknowledgment that Kennedy's death took place within Dallas itself. Virtually no landmarks were erected. Unlike most other cities in the United States, no schools, streets, or buildings were named after Kennedy. Oddly, a similar phenomenon occurred in Memphis, Tennessee – the city where Martin Luther King Jr. was assassinated in 1968. In Memphis, unlike the rest of the country, no schools, buildings, or streets were named after King. (Dallas named several buildings or streets after King soon after his death; Memphis named schools, streets, and buildings soon after Kennedy's assassination.)

Approximately 25 years after the Kennedy assassination, Dallas opened an impressive museum/exhibit acknowledging Kennedy's murder in the downtown area where the shooting took place. Earlier attempts to open similar exhibits in the city had been met with opposition. Approximately 25 years after the assassination of King, Memphis opened a large exhibit commemorating the death of the famous civil rights leader. Similarly, the Vietnam Memorial Wall commemorating people who fought in Vietnam was opened in 1982, almost 25 years after the first Americans died in the war.

Is this 25-year lapse between a traumatic experience and the building of a monument real or coincidental? To test this idea, we sought to find monuments that had been erected within the previous 100 years in the United States that commemorated a single discreet event (e.g., disaster, battle, or similar event – either positive or negative). We then computed the time between the event and the erection of the monument. The data showed that monuments tend to be erected either immediately after an event or in 20–30 year cycles thereafter. Interestingly, whether the event commemorated was positive or negative does not make a tremendous difference in whether or not the 20–30 years was required to pass before acting (Pennebaker & Banasik, 1997).

Although monument building is one form of tracking the emergence of history, other cultural data exist as well. Indeed, movies and books often reflect cultural interest in occurrences from the past. Vietnam War movies in the United States provide a good example. Arguably, the upswell of debate and coverage of the Vietnam War peaked in 1968. Yet, no commercially viable movies existed about Vietnam until *Platoon* was released in 1986. Within the next two to three years, there were approximately 12 other motion pictures about the Vietnam War (Adams, 1989). Our own lab embarked on a larger more systematic study linking the time period that movies depicted. In the study, a random sample of 1,400 popular movies from a pool of over 20,000 made between 1920 and 1990 were coded for date of release and the era which the movie depicted. Not surprisingly, the majority of movies depict the present (i.e., the time period when the movie was released). However, movies not depicting the present tend to take place about 20–25 years earlier. This pattern is actually stronger for top grossing movies (in terms of ticket sales) than movies in general. United States film watchers, and probably those elsewhere around the world, seek to remember what was happening 22 years earlier.

Why does it take 20–30 years to construct a monument or make a movie surrounding an important event? On a certain level, the erection of monuments or the making of expensive movies are complex coordinated social activities. For example, there usually must be some consensus and very little overt opposition among residents to build a monument and a large potential audience for a movie. Typically, numerous committees must be coordinated to acquire funding for the project. Whether the building of a monument is a sign of enthusiasm, or a lack of opposition is unknown. There is also the thorny problem of deciding how to interpret an event. As has been apparent over the last several years in New York City since the 1991 attacks, different constituencies are demanding different interpretations. Should the monument be dedicated to the people working there, the rescue workers who died, the country/city that will not be intimidated, a rebuke of the terrorists themselves? Different groups of people have alternative visions that can only be reconciled with time.

Groups of individuals and entire societies collectively look back at specific times. During these times of looking back, people openly talk about and acknowledge the relevance of these events to their own personal development. What accounts for the emergence of the 20–30 year cycle in looking back? To answer that, we must revisit our original question about how memories are formed. As mentioned earlier, four components of memory must be considered: having a significant change on long-term history, influencing people of a critical age, having an active dialogue about the event, and assuming that the event reflects well on a culture. Yet, as we have seen with the Persian Gulf War study, sometimes talking is actually conducive to forgetting, rather than remembering.

What, then, must occur for an event to re-enter social awareness? Two explanations are relevant – the cohort effect and psychological distancing.

The cohort effect suggests that those most affected (people between ages 13 and 25) do not have the resources to memorialize the event for another few decades. Once they reach the ages of 38–50, they have the financial and political clout to build monuments and influence popular culture.

The psychological distancing effect is based on the clinical observation that people tend to distance themselves from traumatic experiences. Reminders of the trauma can arouse anxiety and distress (e.g., Horowitz, 1976). Healthy coping typically involves people engaging with their worlds and, within weeks or months, moving beyond the event. There is a wide range of ways individuals deal with a loss, however, and the issue becomes more complex when looking at groups of people dealing with the same loss. In Dallas after the assassination of Kennedy, for example, some individuals sought to openly discuss the event. Others increased their donations to worthy causes (perhaps a form of sublimation). Yet others murdered, committed suicide, or died quietly from heart disease. Statistically, then, a community or culture can show a number of seemingly inconsistent patterns in the months, and even years following an unwanted tragedy.

Based on the Dallas example, a sizable minority will support the building of a monument, whereas a separate group will oppose it. One group seeks to remember, the other to forget. Interestingly, the impact of these two forces changes over time in different ways. The desire to look back slowly increases as people begin to acknowledge the event's effects on their own lives and on that of their society. The members of society who initially oppose the building of a monument do so because the event arouses too much anxiety and distress. These negative emotions, however, tend to dissipate over time. The driving emotional force of the opposition to any monument, then, quietly diminishes. The net effect is that society builds a consensus for the erection of a monument and an acknowledgment of the importance of the given collective memory. Over time, as events assume a more realistic perspective and as the factual memory becomes more blurred, it may be easier to reach a consensus on how the event should be remembered.

History: The Long View

Being distanced from an event can do more than allow wounds to heal. With enough time, historical memories are reinterpreted and changed to match the needs of the culture. With time, the memories can often evolve into something mythlike, with positive outcomes emphasized and the costs forgotten. Interestingly, this phenomenon occurs across time and cultures.

As the year 2000 approached, an international group of researchers decided to ask over 1,300 college students from seven different countries what were the three most important events that had occurred in the last 100 and 1,000 years (Pennebaker, Páez, & Deschamps, 2006). Results show that historical memories are influenced by recency and self-relevance. With one exception, the most important historical events of the last 1,000 years occurred in the second half of the millennium; with one exception, the most important historical events of the last century occurred beginning after about 1935. The bias toward recall of more recent events may be perpetuated by generational recall in the form of communicative memories (Laszlo, 2003). Unlike semantic and cultural memory, communicative memories are those memories that are being actively transmitted between three living generations. No events in the top 10 of either list occurred in the Southern Hemisphere. Indeed, most of the historical events happened to have occurred in the very countries where our participants lived. Imagine that. It appears that humans reflect a common tendency to temporally and physically link personal experience to past historical events.

Averaged across all countries, the most important event of the last 1,000 years was the French Revolution. Interestingly, of over 1,000 American students' entries about important events, only seven listed the French Revolution. Why was the French Revolution of interest to everyone else in the world, whereas the American Revolution was uniquely important for people in the United States? Given that all of the participants from other countries were living in countries ruled by monarchs during the French Revolution, one can immediately surmise why the overthrow of the ruling king had far more resonance than the overthrow of an occupying force (Table 7.1).

Historical memories are shaped by the interests and subjective experiences unique to each culture and era. Other analyses asked participants to rate the degree to which different events were considered positive or negative. For example, World War II was rated very negatively for Poles but neutral, and even positively, for some Russians. It is interesting to ponder Table 7.2 to appreciate the degree to which the majority of events that are viewed in a positive light are done so by the participating country.

As the tables suggest, history is indeed fickle. What people viewed as historically significant at the end of the twentieth century will undoubtedly change over the next generation. The dynamic nature of historical events is wonderfully illustrated by tracking the cyclical popularity of Christopher Columbus. In a compelling analysis, Wilford (1991) chronicles how the legacy of Columbus has risen and fallen century after century. For example, on his return to Spain

TABLE 7.1. *Top 10 Rated Historical Events across Six Countries.*
For the last 1000 and 100 years.
Note: *Rankings are based on student samples from England, Germany, Italy, Japan,*
Spain, and the United States. USSR collapse refers to both the break-up of the USSR
as well as the reunification of Germany.

Rank	1,000 Years	100 Years
1	New world discovery	WW2
2	French revolution	WW1
3	Industrial revolution	Space exploration
4	WW2	USSR collapse
5	WW1	Wars in general
6	Religion, reformation	Cold war
7	Wars in general	Vietnam
8	US revolution	Spanish Civil war
9	Science theory	Great depression
10	Space exploration	Computers

in the late 1400s, Columbus was praised as a hero. By the early 1500s, his conquest was dismissed or ignored by other explorers, such as Cortez, who returned with gold and fantastical stories of the New World. By the mid-1500s, Columbus's star was again rising and he was viewed as a man of vision. Within the United States, Columbus emerged as a national hero around the time of the American Revolution. By the late 1800s, the Americans had reengineered his image as a rags-to-riches story exemplifying the American dream. In France at about the same time, he was viewed as a religious icon who had exported Christianity to the New World. At this time, the French were active in promoting Columbus for sainthood. But, by the mid-1900s, Columbus's star was falling. He was considered a symbol of globalization, imperialism, and genocide. The 500th anniversary of his "discovery" of America was virtually ignored by countries on both sides of the Atlantic.

CONCLUSIONS

We have broadly traced how individuals and groups think and talk about emotional upheavals. Our purpose has been to capture the unfolding of historical events to better understand how we collectively construct important events. By understanding the basic processes of individual memory, we can begin to see what boundary conditions are necessary for any event to be remembered over time.

TABLE 7.2 *Top 10 Rated Historical Events for the Last 100 Years (top panel) and 1,000 years (bottom panel) by country.*

Note: *Questionnaires were completed in October, 1998, and are based on student samples only. Most religion entries refer to the reformation or changes in the Roman Catholic Church. Misc Germany, Misc Italy, and Misc Spain refer to specific political controversies in that particular country.*

Rank	England (N = 86)	Germany (N = 248)	Italy (N = 91)	Japan (N = 167)	Switzerland (N = 80)	Spain (N = 129)	United States (N = 351)
1	New World	New World	French rev.	WW2	New World	New World	New World
2	Industrial rev.	French rev.	New World	French rev.	French rev.	Industrial rev.	US rev.
3	WW2	Industrial rev.	WW2	Industrial rev.	Printing invention	French rev.	WW2
4	WW1	WW2	Misc Italy	New World	Wars in general	Wars in general	Industrial rev.
5	Battle of Hastings	Religion	Industrial rev.	US rev.	WW2	WW1	US Civil war
6	Racial conflict	Communication	Religion	WW1	WW1	WW2	Renaissance
7	Electricity	30 years war	WW1	Atomic bomb	Russian rev	Medical advances	Colonization
8	French rev.	Wars in general	Wars in general	Religion	Colonization	Space	Space
9	Science theory	Science theory	Science theory	Renaissance	Space	Communication	WW1
10	Religion	Crusades, rel. wars	Arts & Literature	Racial conflict	Protestant reform	Crusades, re. wars	Wars in general

Rank	England	Germany	Italy	Japan	Switzerland	Spain	United States
1	WW2	WW2	WW2	WW2	WW2	Spanish Civil war	WW2
2	WW1	WW1	WW1	WW1	WW1	WW2	WW1

(continued)

TABLE 7.2 (continued)

Rank	England (N = 86)	Germany (N = 248)	Italy (N = 91)	Japan (N = 167)	Switzerland (N = 80)	Spain (N = 129)	United States (N = 351)
3	Space exploration	Wars in general	USSR Collapse	USSR Collapse	May 68	WW1	Space
4	Cold war	Space	Wars in general	Space	Wars	Wars in general	Vietnam
5	Wars in general	Cold war	Space technology	Great Depress	Vietnam War	Space	Great Depress
6	Women's movement	USSR Collapse	Misc Italy	Gulf War	USSR collapse	USSR Collapse	Computers
7	Computers	Industrial rev.	Fascism	Vietnam	AIDS	democracy	Racial conflict
8	Man-made disasters	Transportation	Gulf War	Atomic bomb	Technology	communication	Wars in general
9	Technology, misc	Atomic bomb	Religion	JFK death	Women's movement	AIDS	JFK death
10	Racial conflict	Medical advances	Vietnam	Korean war	Space	Women's movement	Holocaust

190

In addition to traditional memory processes, however, the role of basic social dynamics cannot be underestimated. Cultural upheavals are ultimately emotional and result in people talking about them in a variety of ways. Frequent discussions of events help to shape and reinforce how they are interpreted. In the weeks and months after the upheavals, the groundwork for future collective memories is laid through further cultural shifts resulting from the initial upheaval. The more that people use a specific cultural event as a memory-based bookmark, the more likely it will take on long-term historical significance. By a memory-based bookmark, we mean a common cultural reference point: "ever since 9/11" or "since Vietnam."

Columbus, the French Revolution for people living in monarchies, the American Revolution for people in the United States, and World War II are all bookmarks that undoubtedly shared many of the same short-term social dynamics that we have seen with our analyses of 9/11, the Loma Prieta Earthquake, and the Persian Gulf War. Only a small number of today's upheavals will ultimately be more than footnotes in history texts in a hundred years. For something like 9/11 to be historically significant, there must be long-term cultural changes linked to it. In addition, those between 13 and 25 years old in 2001 must be active in writing books, movie scripts, and building monuments. Their children and grandchildren, too, must be motivated to learn more about and promote that fateful day.

Ultimately, collective memories reflect the self-serving biases of human nature. With the passage of time, painful events become more tolerable and are reconceptualized to reflect the desired identity of a culture. Painful or shameful events are either forgotten or are morphed into experiences that reflect well on the society. Just as historians, sociologists, and psychologists have inferred how Americans have felt about themselves over the past centuries by examining how the country remembered Christopher Columbus, the future interpretations of events such as 9/11 will serve as windows into the souls of future generations.

REFERENCES

Adams, W. (1989). War stories: Movies, memory, and the Vietnam War. *Comparative Social Research, 11*, 165–189.

Bok, S. (1983). *Secrets: On the ethics of concealment and revelation*. New York: Pantheon.

Carver, C. S. (2007). Stress, coping, and health. In H. Friedman and R. Silver (Eds.), *Foundations of health psychology* (pp 117–144). New York: Oxford University Press.

Chung, C. K., & Pennebaker, J. W. (2007). The psychological function of function words. In K. Fiedler (Ed.), *Social communication: Frontiers of social psychology* (pp 343–359). New York: Psychology Press.

Cohen, S., & McKay, G. (1984). Social support, stress, and the buffering hypothesis: A theoretical analysis. In A.Baum, S. E. Taylor, & J. E. Singer (Eds.), *Handbook of psychology and health, Volume IV: Social psychological aspects of health* (pp. 253–268). Hillsdale, NJ: Lawrence Erlbaum Associates.

Cohen, S., & Wills, T. A. (1985). Stress, social support, and the buffering hypothesis. *Psychological Bulletin, 98*, 310–357.

Cohn, M. A., Mehl, M. R., & Pennebaker, J. W. (2004). Linguistic markers of psychological change surrounding September 11, 2001. *Psychological Science, 15*, 687–693.

Conway, M. A. (1990). *Autobiographical memory: An introduction.* Philadelphia: Open University Press.

Crow, D. M., & Pennebaker, J. W. (1998). *Talking about, remembering, and forgetting the Persian Gulf War.* Department of Psychology, University of Texas at Austin: Unpublished technical report.

Erikson, E. (1950). *Childhood and society.* New York: Norton.

Festinger, L. (1964). *When prophecy fails: A social and psychological study.* New York: Harper-Collins.

Gortner, E., & Pennebaker, J. W. (2003). The archival anatomy of a disaster: Media coverage and community-wide health effects of the Texas A&M bonfire tragedy. *Journal of Social and Clinical Psychology, 22*, 580–603.

Horowitz, M. (1976). *Stress response syndromes.* New York: Jacob Aronson.

Laszlo, J. (2003). History, identity, and narratives. In J. Laszlo-W. Wagner (Eds.), *Theories and controversies in societal psychology.* Budapest: New Mandate Publishers, 180–192.

Levinson, D. J., Darrow, C. M., Klein, E. B., Levinson, M. H., & McKee, B. (1978). *The seasons of a man's life.* New York: Knopf.

Liehr, P., Mehl, M. R., Summers, L. C., & Pennebaker, J. W. (2004). Connecting with others in the midst of a stressful upheaval on September 11, 2001. *Applied Nursing Research, 17*, 2–9.

Lira, E. (1997). Remembering: Passing back through the heart. In: Pennebaker, J., Paez, D., & Rimé, B. (Eds.), *Collective memory of political events: Social psychological perspectives* (pp. 223–235). Hillsdale, NJ, England: Lawrence Erlbaum Associates, Inc.

Mannheim, K. (1968). *Essays on the sociology of knowledge.* London, England: Routledge & Kegan Paul Ltd. (originally published 1952).

Mehl, M. R. (2004). *The sounds of social life: Exploring students' daily social environments and natural conversations.* Unpublished Doctoral Dissertation.

Mehl, M., Pennebaker, J. W., Crow, D. M., Dabbs, J., & Price, J. (2001). The Electronically Activated Recorder (EAR): A device for sampling naturalistic daily activities and conversations. *Behavior Research Methods, Instruments, & Computers, 33*, 517–523.

Miller, G. A. (1995). *The science of words.* New York: Scientific American Library.

Mitchell, G. W., & Glickman, A. S. (1977). Cancer patients: Knowledge and Attitude. *Cancer, 40*, 61–66.

Nolen-Hoeksema, S., Morrow, J., & Fredrickson, B., (1993). Response styles and the duration of episodes of depressed mood. *Journal of Abnormal Psychology, 102,* 20–28.

Pennebaker, J. W., Francis, M. E., & Booth, R. J. (2001). *Linguistic inquiry and word count (LIWC): LIWC2001 (this includes the manual only).* Mahwah, NJ: Erlbaum Publishers.

Pennebaker, J. W., & Harber, K. (1993). A social stage model of collective coping: The Persian Gulf and other natural disasters. *Journal of Social Issues, 49,* 125–145.

Pennebaker, J. W., Mehl, M. R., & Niederhoffer, K. (2003). Psychological aspects of natural language use: Our words, our selves. *Annual Review of Psychology, 54,* 547–577.

Pennebaker, J. W., Páez, D., & Deschamps, J. C. (2006). The social psychology of history. *Psicologia Política, 32,* 15–32.

Pyszczynski, T. A., Solomon, S., & Greenberg, J. (2002). *In the wake of 9/11: The psychology of terror.* Washington, DC: American Psychological Association.

Rimé, B. (1995). Mental rumination, social sharing, and the recovery from emotional exposure. In J. W. Pennebaker (Ed.), *Emotion, disclosure, and health* (pp 271–292). Washington, DC: American Psychological Association.

Rimé, B., Philippot, P., & Boca, S. (1991). Beyond the emotional event: Six studies on social sharing of emotion. *Cognition and Emotion, 5,* 435–465.

Rubin, D. C., Wetzler, S. E., & Nebes, R. D. (1986). Autobiographical memory across the life span. In D. C. Rubin (Ed.), *Autobiographical memory* (pp 202–221). Cambridge, England: Cambridge University Press.

Sawislak, K. (1995). *Smoldering City: Chicagoans and the Great Fire, 1871–1874.* Chicago: University of Chicago Press.

Schachter, S. (1959). *The psychology of affiliation.* Stanford, CA: Stanford University Press.

Schoenberg, B. B., Carr, A. C., Peretz, D., Kutscher, A. H., & Cherico, D. J. (1975). Advice of the bereaved for the bereaved. In B. Schoenberg, I. Gerbner, A. Wiener, A. Kutscher, D. Peretz, & A. Carr (Eds.), *Bereavement: Its psychological aspects* (pp 362–367). New York: Columbia University Press.

Schuman, H., Belli, & Bischoping (1997). The generational basis of historical knowledge. In J. W. Pennebaker, D. Paez, & B. Rimé, (Eds.), *Collective memory of political events: Social psychological perspectives* (pp 47–77). Mahwah, NJ: Lawrence Erlbaum, Assoc.

Shils, E. A. (1981). *Tradition.* Chicago: University of Chicago Press.

Silver, R. C., Holman, E. A., McIntosh, D. N., Poulin, M., & Gil-Rivas, V. (2002). Nationwide longitudinal study of psychological responses to September 11. *JAMA: The Journal of the American Medical Association, 288,* 1235–1244.

Stone, L. D., & Pennebaker, J. W. (2002). Trauma in real time: Talking and avoiding online conversations about the death of Princess Diana. *Basic and Applied Social Psychology, 24,* 172–182.

Wilford, J. N. (1991). *The mysterious history of Columbus: An exploration of the man, the myth, the legacy.* New York: Knopf.

8

How Does Collective Memory Create a Sense
of the Collective?

ALAN J. LAMBERT, LAURA NESSE SCHERER, CHAD
ROGERS, & LARRY JACOBY

Where were you when you first heard about the 9/11 attacks? Do you remember what you were doing at the time? How did you feel when you first heard the news, and how does thinking about this event make you feel now? As of this writing, many Americans over the age of 15 most likely find these questions remarkably easy to answer. The fact that a singular event in history could be remembered so well, and by so many people, is relevant to at least two lines of research in the memory literature.

First, the very fact that people can answer such questions so easily is relevant to research and theory on "flashbulb memories" (Brown & Kulik, 1977; Kvavilashvili, Mirani, Schlagman, & Kornbrot, 2004; Sharot, Martorella, Delgado, & Phelps, 2006). As originally conceptualized, flashbulb memories were regarded as extraordinarily detailed, long-lasting, and unusually accurate "snapshots" of the specific context in which an unexpected, emotion-laden event occurred (Brown & Kulik, 1977). Over the years, research has qualified some of the early claims regarding such memories. For example, even though people often perceive that such memories are accurate, such recollections can contain the same sorts of distortions one finds with other types of memories (Neisser & Harsch, 1992). Nevertheless, more recent work has found that flashbulb memories can sometimes be extraordinarily accurate and detailed, provided that the event has direct, personal relevance to the perceiver (Bernsten & Thomsen, 2005). As we discuss in more detail later in this chapter, the vividness of these memories is important because it suggests that such recollections may be especially likely to trigger strong emotions.

Second, the fact that such vivid memories are distributed across literally millions of people has implications for research and theory on collective memory (Halbwachs, 1992). Although there is no single agreed-on definition of such memories (cf. Wertsch & Roediger, 2008), one of the important functions of such memories is that they have a remarkable capacity to create a sense of unity or "oneness" among people who would not otherwise see a meaningful sense of kinship. This certainly seems to be true of the 9/11 attacks in the sense that this event, as with other calamitous threats to a nation or its people, creates a "remembering collective that recollects and recounts itself through the unifying memory of catastrophes and suffering ... binding its members together by instilling in them a sense of common mission and destiny" (Zertal, 2005, p. 2) In other words, although memories of the 9/11 attacks are certainly important for many people, such memories are particularly important for Americans because they have become an important element of how they define themselves. To paraphrase an analogous point made by Balkin (1999), such memories bind Americans together because these memories are linked to a story that is their story.

COLLECTIVE MEMORY AND EMOTION

In our view, catastrophic events such as the 9/11 attacks are particularly valuable because they highlight the important relation of emotion to understanding collective memory. Although collective memory researchers have hardly ignored emotion (Cohn, Mehl, & Pennebaker, 2004), less is known about this factor than one might think. This is especially true in terms of the different types of consequences that emotion can have in shaping and guiding social attitudes and values.

We discuss these findings in more detail later in this chapter, but our interest in these matters was stimulated by a recent line of research in our laboratory that, over the past few years, has yielded some provocative and highly counterintuitive results (Lambert et al., 2008; Olson, 2003). In this paradigm, participants are randomly assigned to condition in which they either were, or were not, reminded of the 9/11 attacks. Perhaps not surprisingly, these reminders triggered a significant increase in negative emotion, including heightened levels of unhappiness, anger, and anxiety. Of greater interest, these emotional experiences led to systematic "shifts" in participants' support for key sociopolitical issues. For example, the anger elicited by memories of the 9/11 attacks led, in turn, to a general tendency to support "pro-military" positions, which included greater support for Bush's decision to invade Iraq as well as the president's "war on terror." Moreover, the direction and magnitude of this effect were completely unaffected by participants' own political ideology (measured earlier in the experiment). This meant that, even among the most "superliberal" Bush-hating participants in our sample, reminders of the 9/11 attacks led to increased support for the president's policies, as mediated through anger. For us, these and other aspects of our findings to be discussed later serve as a provocative illustration of the power of collective memories, and the important role that emotion might play in this regard.

The rest of this chapter is organized in the following way. We begin with a brief consideration of some basic theoretical issues regarding collective memory. This is not meant to be an exhaustive review of the literature but is meant to clarify a few key issues that are germane to some key points. We next discuss two different "senses" of emotion as it relates to collective memory, namely, memories of emotion as opposed to the effects of memory on emotion. Following this, we consider some interesting but understudied implications of emotion as it might apply to the passage of time, and how such passage could ultimately yield striking incongruities between the ways that people felt about an event in the past, as opposed to how they might feel later. In the final section of the chapter, we discuss in more detail the recent findings we have obtained in our own laboratory that, as suggested earlier, provide specific documentation of the interactive roles of collective memory and emotion in shaping important sociopolitical attitudes.

Theoretical Background

Collective memories are often relevant to the citizens of a particular nation, but such memories can also be critical to other types of collectives, such as religious groups (e.g., Jewish memories of the Holocaust; cf. Novick, 1999). As for the sense of "togetherness" that collective memories might foster, such effects could operate at different levels. For example, such unity could refer to a global sense of identity (e.g., nationalism, patriotism) among members of a group. However, these effects might be more specific, anchored with respect to a specific attitude or decision, such as a decision to go to war. The process by which collections of individuals might vary increase in their "groupiness" is related to Campbell's (1958) concept of entitativity, which refers to the degree to which a collection of persons are bonded together in a coherent unit (Lickel et al., 2000). For example, groups high in entitativity tend to maintain greater cohesiveness and "feel" more like a collective compared to groups low in entitativity (McConnell, Sherman, & Hamilton, 1997). Entitativity is somewhat related to the concept of group homogeneity (Lambert & Wyer, 1990; Lambert, Barton, Lickel, & Wells, 1998; Tajfel, 1981; Park & Hastie, 1987), although the two concepts are not identical (Yzerbyt, Judd, & Corneille, 2003).

One of the long-running debates in the collective memory literature is whether studying the mechanisms underlying individually held memories – the kinds of memories most often studied by experimental psychologists – can lead to a greater understanding of collective memories, and vice versa (Velleman, 1997; Wilson, 2005). Although we do not subscribe to a strong "reductionistic" view (i.e., that collective memory can simply be reduced to individual memory processes), we believe that many of the findings obtained in the experimental psychological literature on "individual" memories are relevant to collective memories as well. In other words, a focus on the collective does not automatically preclude a focus on the individual, and vice versa.

In writing this chapter, we were particularly interested in those aspects of collective memory that are relevant to emotion. However, this does not imply that that all examples of collective memory must necessarily involve strong affective experience. For example, Americans memories of the Declaration of Independence or British memories of the Battle of Hastings both seem to qualify as excellent examples of collective memory. However, neither of these memories is likely to be associated with particularly strong emotions. Hence, emotion may be only one of several different sorts of factors that have the capacity to bind people together. In the two examples cited earlier, for instance, it is the symbolic meaning of these events that probably give the memories significance to their respective target populations. The factors that determine the presence/intensity of emotion in collective memory strikes us as an important issue in its own right. As far as we know, little formal work has been done on this topic. It may be useful in future work to delineate factors on the basis of whether they have to do with the nature of the event itself (e.g., how long ago it occurred, its vividness) or the properties of the person remembering it.

Finally, it is important to recognize that collective memories are, by their very nature, embedded in a singular historical/social context. For this reason, it is possible that some of the dynamics surrounding a given collective memory may be specific to that particular memory, and may not generalize to other memories that are relevant to events that occurred in a different context. Although we focus on a number of different collective memories in this chapter, our main attention is on the 9/11 attacks, as a "running theme" to illustrate some of the main points we wish to make here. Nevertheless, we believe that emotion is likely to play an important role in collective memory much of the time, and one of the overarching goals of this chapter is delineate the various ways that this might occur for various types of collective memory, including but not limited to those associated with the 9/11 attacks.

Emotions as Memorial Representations: On the Storage and Retrieval of Affective States

In the collective memory literature, emotion is often framed as something that is remembered. For example, the question we posed at the beginning of our chapter – How did you feel when you first heard the news about the 9/11 attacks? – represents a query about a past internal state. This sense of emotion can be understood as a type a memory within the declarative memory system, which "provides a basis for conscious recollection of facts and events" (Squire, 1994, p. 203). Hence, questions about one's past emotional state are, in principle, not appreciably different from asking people to remember other facts about that day (e.g., do you recall calling your parents?). Recalling information about a past emotional state may, or may not, correspond to how you currently feel. For example, a person may remember being extremely confused and upset when they first heard the news about the 9/11 attacks. However, this does not necessarily imply that they are feeling that way at the time they are answering the question.

In short, we speak here of memories about our emotions. Setting aside the issues surrounding collective memories for the moment, such memories are important for several reasons. For one thing, we have a huge number of them. If you took the time to write about all of the things that have happened to you over the last week, many of these events are likely to be associated with at least some kind emotional reaction (e.g., boredom, surprise, pleasure, irritation, happiness, sadness, impatience, etc.). There may be some truly mundane events that do not trigger any emotion at all, such as picking up a cup of coffee (unless it happens to be unexpectedly hot). For the most part, however, events of any consequence usually are associated with some emotion, even if such emotions are quite fleeting (cf. Zajonc, 1980). Moreover, memories of our own emotions almost certainly play a role in formation and construction of personal identity. In particular, the sense of who we are as a person, and our ability to predict our own future behavior, are likely to be based in part on our memories of our own affective responses to previous events (Stryker, 2004).

Implications for Collective Memory

How might these considerations be relevant to collective memories in particular? In the discussion to follow we first consider two distinct ways that memories for emotion could foster the "sense of the collective" that is often mentioned by researchers in this area. As we shall show, this sense of collectiveness does not necessarily have to be based on objective reality, insofar as people could potentially overestimate or exaggerate the extent to which others share one's own memories of affective experience. We continue this theme in the next section, exploring the various memory biases that might play a role here and the consequences that such biases might have.

Creation of the Collective through Interaction and Social Inference

Memories are obviously something that people share with one another during one-on-one interactions (Boyer, 1992) and such sharing can often include sharing of memories about emotional experiences (Harber & Cohen, 2005; Laurenceau, Barrett, and Pietromonaco, 1998; Rime, 2007). Such shared memories could focus on events that are specific to the people involved (e.g., "Remember that time when we took that road trip to Boston?") or could extend to a much more widely experienced event (e.g., "I can't believe it's been 40 years since we sat in front of the television and watched the funeral of President Kennedy"). In the latter case, sharing of memories about a widely experienced event could lead huge groups of people to feel a greater sense of kinship than they otherwise would. Again, we speak here of the sharing of memories about emotions, not the affective experience itself; we consider the latter in more detail presently. However, it would be a mistake to dismiss such memories as trivial or inconsequential. On the contrary, sharing how one "felt at the time" can be psychologically important and useful in its own right, even in the absence of actual emotions during the retelling.

A sense of the collective does not, however, necessarily have to be based on objective reality. In other words, a perception that other share one's recollections may be more important than whether that overlap is actually present. For example, many Americans are likely to feel that they have a psychological bond with at least some other Americans in terms of their emotional experiences surrounding several disparate historical events. Depending on their age and other demographic factors, this could include memories of the attack on Pearl Harbor (1941), launching of Sputnik (1957), the assassination of JFK (1963), the resignation of Richard Nixon (1974), the explosion of the *Challenger* shuttle (1986), or the start of the Persian Gulf War (1990).

In theory, there could be very high overlap across people in the vividness of people's memory of these and other events, along with the emotions associated with them. In practice, however, people may often perceive more consensus than is really the case. Research in the social psychological literature has shown that people tend to assume that others share their own attitudes and experiences, especially when we are not privy to any specific information about others (Ross, Greene, & House, 1977). In other words, in the absence of any information to the contrary, people often "default" to their own experiences when forming inferences about others. Hence, for example, a 50-something ex-hippy might tend to overestimate the extent to which people of his generation remembered and experienced Woodstock in the same way he did. Importantly, this could be true even if his experiences are, in fact, fairly idiosyncratic and are not shared by many people at all. In this sense, one could argue that one's subjective perception of the overlap of one's memories/emotions with others can, in certain cases, be most critical, independent of whether those perceptions are actually correct.

On the Role of Selective/Reconstructive Memory

The considerations listed here raise a related issue, namely, the extent to which memories for emotions are guided by selective or reconstructive biases. Although memories of events such as the 9/11 attacks might generally be accurate, this does not mean that such biases never exist in this domain. Such biases could certainly include memory for one's own previous emotions. In other words, as with other sorts of memories, recollection of one's own internal state could be systematically be distorted by considerations that are present at the time of retrieval.

As for where such biases might come from, it is heuristically useful to consider two general families of causation. On the one hand, such biases could be driven by "internal" factors specific to the person engaging in the recollection. Certainly, there is much evidence in the experimental psychological literature showing that memories for one's own previous emotions can be systematically biased by one's own personality traits (e.g., level of neuroticism) as well as chronically experienced or acute emotional experiences, such as feelings of anxiety (Feldman-Barrett, 1997; Safer, Levine, & Lench, 2006). Such considerations certainly could lead to collective memories. For example, if you happened to be anxious at the time you thought about the 9/11 attacks and your original reaction to them, this might lead you to selectively focus on, or perhaps even falsely "remember," previous experiences that were associated with anxious feelings as opposed to experiences associated with other emotions, such as anger (Levine, Whalen, Jamner & Henker, 2005).

On the other hand, emory for one's previous emotions could also be affected by considerations that are more "external" to the person doing the remembering. Of particular relevance to collective memory is the attempts of politicians to deliberately influence our memories through the use of propaganda, speeches, or other types of "political spin" (Ewen, 1996). It has long been recognized that politicians often have much to gain through manipulating the emotions of the people they seek to govern, and this could certainly include subtle or not-so-subtle attempts to distort memories for what people felt at any particular time. For example, political observers often observed that Hillary Clinton's campaign during the 2008 presidential election cycle relied, in part, on augmenting Americans' nostalgia for Bill Clinton's presidency during the 1990s. To the extent that such efforts were even partially successful, such effects could have been, in part, related to some distortion or exaggeration of people's memories for their positive emotions (e.g., economic well-being) during that period. Of course, politicians often have much to gain by deliberately manipulating and drawing people's current emotions, an issue that we consider in more detail later in this chapter.

The upshot of these considerations is that memories of emotions, like other types of memories, can often be constructed. To reiterate, this does not necessarily contradict the notion that vivid events can be remembered quite accurately. Some aspects of people's memories may, in fact, be remarkably accurate, especially when they pertain to overt "external" events, such as having a mental snapshot of the flow of events on a particular day. When it comes to our own internal experiences, however, memory biases may be more likely, although the extent to which this is true is likely to depend on the nature of the emotional experience and the extent to which the emotion was behaviorally expressed at the time.

On the Role of Memory in Triggering the Active Experience of Emotion

The previous discussion of the emotion-memory relationship focused on memory for past emotions. However, this is just one aspect of the interrelation between memory and emotion. In particular, remembering our past can also give rise to current emotional experience. Episodic memory is particularly likely to be involved in these considerations, for reasons that are captured well by Endel Tulving's (2002) famous essay in which he noted the "time capsule" essence of episodic memory:

With one singular exception, time's arrow is straight. Unidirectionality of time is one of nature's most fundamental laws. It has relentlessly governed all happenings in the universe – cosmic, geological, physical, biological, psychological – as long as the universe has existed. Galaxies and stars are born and they die, living creatures are young before they grow old, causes always precede effects, there is no return to yesterday, and so on and on. Time's flow is irreversible. The singular exception is provided by the human ability to remember past happenings. When one thinks today about what one did yesterday, time's arrow is bent into a loop. The rememberer has mentally traveled back into her past and thus violated the law of the irreversibility of the flow of time. She has not accomplished the feat in physical reality, of course, but rather in the reality of the mind, which, as everyone knows, is at least as important for human beings as is the physical reality. (Tulving, 2002, p. x)

Tulving does not specifically consider emotion in his analysis, but this view clearly suggests that episodic memory can play an important role not only in remembering, but also in reexperiencing, the emotional content of the initial event. For example, memories of the 9/11 attacks may not simply involve remembering being upset, it may subsequently lead one to actually be upset.

Readers familiar with the process-oriented literature on memory may have already noted that the sense of emotion emphasized here might bear some relevance to nondeclarative systems of memory (e.g., automatized, proceduralized processes such as classical conditioning; cf. Squire & Kandel, 1999). However, the problem in this analysis is that there is considerable debate in the literature as to what is the best way to frame the nature of these dual memory systems (e.g., explicit vs. implicit, as opposed to declarative vs. nondeclarative). As a related point, nondeclarative processes are sometimes assumed to be nonconscious but this assumption may not be applicable when speaking of the active experience of emotion (cf. Clore, 1994). For present purposes, the distinction that is most important is between memories of emotion (covered in an earlier section of this chapter) as opposed to the effects of memories on emotion, which is the focus of the current discussion.

Communication of Emotion, Redux

As with other internal nondeclarative states, human beings possess the ability to transform emotional experiences into verbal reports. However, some transformations can be more difficult than others. Researchers and poets alike have long known that the process of "putting emotions into words" can be inherently difficult and there can be a large gap between the words that we are using to describe an emotional state and the features of the emotional state itself. Nonetheless, human beings do seem to have a drive to express their current feelings and this fact has some important implications for many aspects of social behavior, including issues relevant to collective memory.

Earlier in this chapter, we had suggested that people might be inclined to share memories about their past emotional experiences, even when the retrieval process does not actually trigger any emotion per se. Such sharing may be even more likely when recollections of past events spontaneously activate strong emotions (Rime & Christophe, 1997). Classic work in the social psychological literature has shown that people often have a drive to affiliate with others when they are experiencing strong emotions (especially, negative emotions arising out of stress) as part of a larger effort to understand their own internal feelings (Schachter, 1959). In addition, the "urge to share" may be also driven by the psychological benefits of expressing one's emotional experiences to others (Harber & Pennebaker, 1992). The process of sharing/communicating such emotions seems likely to represent a specific social psychological mechanism, which could contribute to the "sense of the collective" that has been of such strong interest among researchers in the collective memory literature.

What Kinds of Memories are Likely to Trigger Emotions?

Before turning to the next section, it is useful to consider an interesting but understudied issue, namely, what kinds of collective memories are likely to involve emotion in either of the senses we have discussed thus far (i.e., emotion as a stored representation, or as an actively experienced affective state). Thus far, we have focused mostly on episodic memory, which includes "memory for specific events that were personally experienced and remembered" (Balota & Coane, in press). As noted earlier, such memories do not necessarily have to involve the direct experience of emotion. However, when memories do involve emotion, it seems intuitively likely that the memory in question is, in fact, an episodic memory. Certainly, our most powerful emotional reactions (e.g., feelings of grief, euphoria, depression, anger, happiness) seem to usually revolve around an event or series of events, that we more or less personally experienced.

The issue of what it means to "personally experience" an event is more complex than it might seem. To illustrate, consider three different settings that a person might acquire knowledge about the 9/11 attacks: (a) on the morning of September 11, 2001, a resident of New York City looks up and watches the second plane crash into the South Tower, (b) 1 hour later, a woman who lives in Seattle watches a rebroadcast of that event, (c) 10 years later, a child first learns about the 9/11 attacks by watching the same video rebroadcast in class. Most people would agree that the person in Seattle has an episodic memory of the attacks, even though she was not personally there and learned about it in after-the-fact fashion. If this is so, however, there seems no reason in principle why the child in the third scenario could not also be said to have an episodic memory of the event itself. These considerations arguably begin to blur the distinction between semantic and episodic memory. However, this complication is not of central concern for present purposes since, as we note later in this chapter, the distinction between these two types of memory may not necessarily be critical in the context of theory and research on collective memory.

By way of contrast, semantic memory pertains to an even broader base of memory, which could loosely be regarded as people's "general world knowledge," which would include, among other things, your understanding of concepts and words (e.g., the meaning of the concept of mammal), beliefs about objects in our environment (e.g., knowledge that tomatoes are red, edible, and are smaller than watermelons), as well as knowledge of facts about people and events, including those involving the self. For example, the knowledge that your mother gave birth to you is part of semantic, but not episodic, memory, as humans typically lack reliable episodic memory of events from the first year or so of life (cf. Newcombe, Lloyd, & Ratliff, 2007).

To what extent do emotions play a role in semantic memories? Certainly, we can have positive or negative appraisals of events and objects we have not had any personal experience at all. For example, semantic memory can include knowledge about all sorts of people and historical events (e.g., Adolf Hitler, Mahatma Gandhi, the crash of the *Hindenburg*, the coronation of King Louis VIII) about which we may have positive or negative feelings, even in the absence of any personal experience. Moreover, depending on the event in question and the type of knowledge that one has acquired about it, the intensity of such emotions can sometimes rival those associated with episodic memories. For example, few people alive at the current time personally experienced the Holocaust. However, knowledge of the event itself, and the vivid photographs that document its existence, can trigger exceptionally strong reactions in people, even if they were born long after the event took place.

Past–Present Emotional Discordance

The way that people felt about an event may not necessarily match their current feelings. For example, events that once elicited joy may now make us rather gloomy. Conversely, events that formerly elicited a sense of doom now may be more likely to make us rather cheery. In such cases, remembering the initial event could elicit a sense of conflict (e.g., "torn feelings"), such as a mixed sense of wistfulness, happiness, and anger that someone might feel in the context of bitter divorce, when reminiscing about a joyful marriage ceremony with one's former spouse. In such cases, the conflict may involve a sharp discrepancy between the emotions stored along with the original episodic trace (e.g., "I remember dancing all night with you in the garden") versus current emotions that are based on more recent events. Such discrepancies could include at least two "types," namely, circumstances in which (a) the original memory is associated with positive emotions but we feel more negative now, or (b) the original memory is associated with negative emotions but we feel more positively now. For example, the former might involve hating something we once loved, whereas the latter might involve loving something we once hated.

Setting aside the exact nature of the discordance, research has demonstrated that people have a remarkable tendency to engage in personal "revisionism" in their own personal histories in the service of alleviating or even eliminating such conflict. For example, work by Michael Ross and his colleagues (Ross & Wilson, 2003; Wilson & Ross, 2001) have shown that people often distort memories of their own past. This revisionism often occurs in the service of rendering a more evaluatively consistent balance between how we feel now and how we remember feeling then. This sort of process may generally be consistent with principles of cognitive dissonance (Festinger, 1957), which suggests that people find evaluative discord unpleasant and will be motivated to resolve the consistency by changing one or more of the elements that are contributing to it. In the case of conflict between present and (memories of) past emotions, one could resolve this dissonance either through modifying one's current feelings (e.g., "Perhaps I really still do love her, after all") or by revising one's sense of what one's original feelings were like (e.g., "Deep down, I guess I did have some serious doubts about the marriage").

Implications for Collective Memory

These considerations have some theoretically and practically important ramifications for collective memory. Take, for example, the fall of the Berlin Wall in 1989. As widely reported by the media, reunification of West and East Germany appeared to result in a general state of euphoria. However, Germans' current feelings tell a rather different story. Recent polls from various polling organizations indicate some sharply divided and remarkably disparate feelings among Germans, with a surprisingly high percentage of Germans (approximately 25 percent, as of 2004) expressing the opinion that Germany was better off with the wall intact. This is just one example, but we suspect that the experience is not uncommon. A large group of people might experience (more or less) the same emotional reaction to an event when it initially occurs. However, this in no way implies that the group will always have this kind of emotional consensus. Over time, groups are likely to become more heterogeneous in their emotions depending on the idiosyncratic trajectory of people's own personal lives. For example, Germans whose economic fortunes substantially improved with the fall of the Berlin Wall should, for obvious reasons, be more likely to retain their positive feelings regarding reunification compared to those who fared less well after that event.

This issue is important because it means that after-the-fact recollections of a key historical event may, or may not, increase the psychological sense of togetherness among a group of people, even if huge groups of people all felt more or less the same emotion at the time. Time has a tendency to change our views, but the exact track of revisionism may take different paths for different people over time. Memories that create a sense of collectiveness at one point in time may not necessarily have that property indefinitely.

The Power of Collective Betrayal

As noted earlier, emotional discord in individuals can produce strong emotions in its own right, such as feelings of disappointment or even betrayal. However, the existence of such bitterness in one person is one thing; the presence of such emotions among large groups of people, all at the same time, is quite another. The phenomenon of large groups of people all feeling strong emotions at the same time is relevant to several classic lines of research in the social science. This includes LeBon's (1895) classic work on "mob behavior" as well as numerous other theoretical models concerned with the psychology of crowds (e.g., Reicher, 2004). To be sure, groups do not always act in a coordinated manner, even when their members are feeling much the same emotion. However, there are important cases in which the collective experience of emotion can lead to dramatic and sudden changes. Indeed, history is filled with examples of nations whose citizens have experienced collective euphoria over a change in leadership or political structure, only to feel quite differently a relatively short time later, when optimism about the "new guard" quickly fades into a sense of disappointment, sometimes even betrayal. Again, it seems likely that the strength of these emotions is derived from a sharp discord between past and present, between what people felt at a particular time and how they feel now.

One very recent example of this emerged very recently in the former Soviet Republic of Georgia. In 2003, Mikheil Saakashvili received nearly unanimous support among Georgians as part of the nonviolent "Rose Revolution" in which Eduard Shevardnadze – a politician strongly associated with the corrupt practices of the Communist Party – was swept from office. Only 4 years later, however, Georgians engaged in massive and widescale protests demanding Saakashvilli's immediate resignation, fostered (ironically) by the widespread perception that he had engaged in many of the same sorts of corrupt actions that led to his predecessor being removed from office. We are not aware of any data that specifically speaks to this point, but it seems likely that the collective memory of the Rose Revolution – and in particular, the positive feelings and optimism surrounding that event – may, ironically, be one of the important reasons for the widespread existence of anger. Rapid changes in society often involve intense emotions. It seems likely that collective memories may often play a key role in eliciting the widespread activation and expression of these affective states.

IMPLICATIONS: THE "RALLY EFFECTS"

Just a few days after the 9/11 attacks, President George W. Bush saw his job approval ratings soar 39 points to 90 percent. This represents the highest approval rating ever recorded for an American president, besting the previous record of 89 percent, held by Bush's father, just after the commencement of the Gulf War in 1991. These events are familiar to American political theorists, who often use the term "rally effects" (short for "rally 'round the flag effect") to describe these dramatic boosts in approval ratings in response to a singular historical event (Mueller, 1970). We believe that there is a strong connection between rally effects and collective memories, for at least two reasons. First, although political scientists rarely mention memory processes in their discussion of rally effects, such effects are, by definition, shifts in political preferences that occur in "after-the-fact" fashion to historical events and these preference shifts can last for months or even years (Brody & Shapiro, 1989). Hence, rally effects are strongly rooted in collective memory of an historical event. Second – and even more important, to our mind – the consequences of rally effects are directly relevant to the "sense of the collective" that is so central to the idea of collective memory in the first place. For example, it is difficult to imagine that George W. Bush could have galvanized support for the subsequent war in Iraq without broad support for his presidency, and the 9/11 attacks certainly provided that support in the form of recordbreaking levels of presidential approval.

Political criticisms of Bush aside (e.g., whether he "misused" the 9/11 attacks for his own agenda in Iraq) the fact remains: rally effects provide presidents with a base of support that can be used to launch enormously important policies and executive decisions which can, in turn, have dramatic implications not only for Americans but for other people around the world as well. We cannot imagine any better illustration of the importance of collective memory and why social scientists should study it. In the remainder of this chapter, we consider in greater detail some relevant data that speak to these issues.

Brief Overview of Theory and Research on Rally Effects

Early models of such effects (Mueller, 1970) suggested that any sudden international crisis could trigger sustained boosts in presidential popularity. However, Baker and O'Neal (2001) have cast some doubt on this assumption, suggesting that rally effects are much rarer than was thought at first. For example, even the most severe financial crises do not reliably lead to significant changes in support for the president. On the basis of their review, Baker and O'Neal (2001) suggest that an emerging military crisis – especially if it is sudden, dramatic, and international in scope – is one of the few factors known to be sufficient, in and of itself, to trigger sustained increases in support for the president. In line with this view, there are only a small handful of well-documented rally effects aside from those following the attacks of 9/11, and all of these fit the criteria laid out by Baker and O'Neal, namely, (a) the attack on Pearl Harbor (1941); (b) the Bay of Pigs crisis (1962); (c) the earlier-mentioned entry of the United States into the Gulf War (1991); and (d) the invasion of Iraq (2003).

Although rally effects have been well documented empirically, the psychological dynamics underlying rally effects are poorly understood. This is, in part, because rally effects have been studied almost exclusively through analyses of presidential surveys (often through telephone polls). Such polls undoubtedly possess many strengths, such as the ability to generate huge, nationally representative samples overnight. However, pollsters have only a limited window of opportunity – often, less than a minute – to pose questions to the respondent. This obviously limits the scope of questions to be posed and, of those that are included, these can sometimes yield ambiguous results. For example, the ubiquitous "job approval ratings" that form the basis for many presidential approval polls are often interpreted as revealing general support for the president, but it also might indicate much more narrow approval of the president's specific role as military commander-in-chief.

Throughout this chapter, we have emphasized why and how emotion might be relevant to collective memory. Here, too, we see emotions playing a large role as well, insofar as emotions have the capacity to exert a strong impact on social attitudes and values. However, the precise nature of this impact should depend on the precise type of emotion that is activated. We probe this issue in more detail later in this chapter.

The "Functional Approach" to Emotions and Social Judgment

Once a particular emotion is activated, such emotions can powerfully shape our understanding of our environment (Forgas, 2002). This can lead to context-based shifts in our attitudes and values, that is, how we appraise the "goodness" and "badness" of our environment. In other words, social psychological preferences are not fixed; rather, they are often dependent on situational context. This is not a novel idea (Mischel, 1968; Wicker, 1969) in and of itself. However, recent research has only begun to uncover the specific way that emotion plays a role in this regard.

As it turns out, emotions can affect judgment and behavior in several, and not just one, way. For example, emotions can play a role at a relatively "early" stage of processing, such as influencing the kinds of stimuli which we notice, and influencing how ambiguous stimuli are interpreted. Of particular interest for our concerns, there is a rapidly growing line of research on the functional approach to emotion, which assumes that affective experience is often connected to one or more psychological goals or motives (Frijda & Mesquita, 1994; Harmon-Jones, 2004; Keltner & Gross, 1999; Schwarz, 1990). One question to arise from this functional approach is whether the activation of motives precedes the experience of emotions, or whether emotions precede the activation of motives. For example, does the motive of retaliation trigger anger, or does anger activate motives for retaliation? This issue has long been debated among theorists in this area and, hence, for present purposes, it is heuristically useful to regard motives and emotions as psychological clusters or "bundles" in which the activation of goals often leads to activation of emotions, and vice versa.

The functional approach to emotions becomes particularly important and interesting in those cases where a singular event can trigger two or more distinct motive/emotion clusters, each of which could exert very different effects on judgment and behavior. Consider the example of threat. On the one hand, many – although perhaps not all – threatening contexts are likely to be associated with motives of retaliation and retribution, which are likely to be associated with anger. On the other hand, threatening contexts may also be associated with motives for protection and security, which are likely to involve anxiety and fear. Hence, although anger and anxiety may often be correlated as a result of their shared negative valence (Lerner & Keltner, 2001), they nevertheless have the capacity to affect behaviors and judgments in rather different ways.

An Experimental Study of the Consequences of Collective Memory

Experimental methodologies are not often used in the collective memory literature. However, there is no reason why such an approach could not be used fruitfully to study such memories, particularly with respect to assessing their consequences. This perspective rests on the assumption that the salience of collective memories, like other sorts of memories, can vary in terms of their salience (i.e., their cognitive accessibility). As a number of scholars have noted, anniversaries represent a "natural manipulation" of the salience of collective memories (Pennebaker & Banasik, 1997; Schwalbe, 2006). However, laboratory-based priming procedures afford the opportunity to study the consequences of such differences in salience under more controlled conditions. In particular, one can randomly assign participants to conditions in which their memories of a particular event either are or are not made more salient. Although rather straightforward, this approach can be extremely valuable insofar as it provides causal evidence regarding the effects of any given memory on judgment and behavior.

This is, in fact, the approach we have used over the last few years in our laboratory, in an attempt to better understand the consequences of people's memories of the 9/11 attacks (Lambert et al., 2008; Olson, 2003). Across several studies conducted between 2002 and 2007, we employed two different kinds of memory manipulations designed to affect the salience of participants' memories of this event. In some experiments, participants were assigned either to watch an eight-minute clip of the 9/11 attacks (excerpted from a CNN-produced video entitled *America Remembers*) or to solve a series of anagrams. In other studies, participants were asked to write an autobiographical account either of the 9/11 attacks or of the mundane events that occurred during a typical day. Importantly, both types of memory manipulations produced similar effects, showing that our results were not due to the idiosyncratic way that memories were activated.

Immediately after being reminded of the 9/11 attacks, we assessed participants' current emotional experience on the basis of a battery of self-report items adapted from the PANAS (Watson & Tellegen, 1985), perhaps the most widely used self-report instrument designed to assess emotional experience. Among the large number of studies using the PANAS (or modifications of it), the usual approach is to form two very general indices of affect and, in particular, positive versus negative affect. Although such broadband indices can be useful in some contexts, we were interested in the possibility that memories for traumatic events could elicit different types of negative emotion which could exert different types of effects on judgments and attitudes. To this end, we constructed two multi-item indices, including (a) an anger index (based on an average of angry, mad, and irate) and (b) an anxiety index (based on an average of anxious, jittery, nervous, worried, relaxed, comfort, and calm, after reverse scoring where necessary). These two indices tended to correlate moderately with another, ranging between .30 and .50, depending on the experiment. Perhaps not surprisingly, participants reported significantly higher levels of anger and anxiety if they had been induced to think about the 9/11 attacks than if they had not. Nevertheless, despite this overlap in emotion, the now-activated emotions of anger and anxiety led to different sorts of "shifts" with respect to sociopolitical attitudes, as we note later in this chapter.

Following assessment of emotion, we typically had our participants complete a large, randomized battery of questions which tapped a number of different sociopolitical attitudes. This battery included attitude queries about the president and his policies (including but not limited to those pertaining to the Iraq War) as well as more general items relevant to liberalism and conservatism. We then conducted tests of mediation, which allowed us to examine any effects of the experimental manipulation on attitudes and whether such effects were mediated by emotion. By and large, most of our effects were in fact mediated by emotion. That is, the memory manipulation produced strong differences in emotion across condition, and these differences in emotion then produced systematic changes in attitudes and values. Once changes in emotion were statistically controlled for, the effects of the memory manipulation usually but not always disappeared; see Lambert et al., 2008 for further details).

One of the more interesting aspects of our research is that we found evidence of double dissociation in terms of the effects of anger versus anxiety on attitudes. That is, anger affected attitudes that were unaffected by anxiety, whereas anxiety affected attitudes that were unaffected by anger. As for anger, increased levels of this emotion were associated with a general rise in support for the president (reminiscent of the classic rally effects as conceptualized by political scientists) but this effect occurred in the larger context of a general rise in "militant aggressiveness," including enhanced support for the war in Iraq along with more favorable attitudes toward people, groups and institutions associated with a pro-military position, as well as a general surge in punitiveness, even in domains completely unrelated to the ongoing war in Iraq. Again, all of these effects were mediated by anger. In contrast, anxiety led to more favorable attitudes toward culturally defined "traditional" institutions and attitude objects associated with security, order, and stability, including more positive attitudes toward powerful government and traditional religious values. (For a more thorough discussion of these results and their relation to other models of social attitudes, see Lambert et al., 2008.)

Another interesting aspect of these results is that the effects of making these collective memories salient were essentially identical, and did not depend on individual differences in either (a) political ideology, that is, where participants fell along the liberal-conservative dimension or (b) political expertise, conceptualized here as general knowledge about the identity of political figures within and outside the United States. This was true in two important areas of the data. First, the extremity of anger and anxiety as triggered by the memory manipulations was the same regardless of these individual differences (for example, liberals were just as angered by these memories as conservatives, and vice versa). Second, the consequences of the memory on sociopolitical attitudes, mediated by emotion, were the same regardless of a priori ideology and political expertise. The upshot of these considerations is that increasing the salience of memories of the 9/11 attacks, even years after the fact, had remarkably similar effects, regardless of the kinds of personal attitudes and opinions that participants had when they first walked into our laboratory.

To reiterate a theme running throughout this chapter, these findings are especially important because they shed light on the specific mechanisms by which collective memories about the past can have implications for how people respond to currently unfolding events in their lives. In short, these findings suggest the implications of collective memories for the "collective present," the latter of which refers to unusual consensus among otherwise disparate individuals in terms of their attitudes and opinions about people and events.

BROADER IMPLICATIONS OF OUR RESEARCH

We began our discussion by specifically focusing on the 9/11 attacks, but we believe that our findings speak more broadly to some larger issues that may transcend that event in particular. It is extremely unusual to see large numbers (i.e., millions) of people all feeling essentially the same emotion at the same time, but memories for historical events can lead to just this sort of scenario.

As we have noted, memories for certain types of historical events can trigger strong emotions, regardless of whether the event occurred in the recent or distant past, and regardless of whether the person personally experienced the event or not. Once activated, such emotion can have enormously important implications for social policy that can, in turn, affect large portions of the population.

Quite apart from the circumstances surrounding the 9/11 attacks, a rather different illustration of the interconnected roles of collective memory, emotion, and public policy is afforded by the recently released tapes of conversations between President Lyndon Johnson and Martin Luther King Jr., just four days after John Kennedy had been assassinated (Beschloss, 1997). One key element of this conversation is Johnson and King's awareness that Americans were essentially in a state of collective mourning. For his part, Johnson clearly believed that this provided a golden opportunity to work for swift passage of civil rights legislation (which Kennedy had obviously played a large part in developing) and history shows that he was essentially correct. Thus, here again we see that collective memory of a singular, powerful event led to important consequences and that these consequences were almost certainly, in large part, a result of emotional experience.

In summary, we believe that these considerations nicely highlight the reasons why studying emotion may engender a greater understanding of collective memory, especially in terms of the powerful effects that such memories can have on many elements of behavior and judgment. By the same token, however, studying emotion in the context of collective memory is likely to afford a greater understanding of emotion, which is often studied in relatively controlled, arguably sterile laboratories. There is a long history of research on the connection between emotion and memory, but many of the nuances and complexities of this relationship have yet to be fully understood, especially in the collective memory literature. It is our hope that the present chapter highlights the need to further explore this relationship along with the theoretical and practical implications that are relevant to it.

ACKNOWLEDGMENT

We would like to acknowledge the insightful comments of Franklin Zaromb on an earlier draft of this chapter.

REFERENCES

Baker, W. D., & O'Neal, J. R. (2001). Patriotism or opinion leadership?: The nature and origins of the "Rally 'Round the Flag' Effect. *Journal of Conflict Resolution*," 45, 661–687.

Balkin, J. M. (1999). *The Declaration and the promise of a democratic culture. Unpublished manuscript.* Yale University: New Haven, CT.

Bernsten, D., & Thomsen, D. (2005). Personal memories for remote historical events: Accuracy and clarity of flashbulb memories related to World War II. *Journal of Experimental Psychology: General. 134*, 242–257.

Beschloss, M. R. (1997). *Taking charge: The Johnson white house tapes, 1963–1964.* New York: Simon & Schuster.

Boyer, P. (1992). *Tradition as truth and communication.* Cambridge: Cambridge University Press.

Brody, R., & Shapiro (1989). Policy failure and public support: The Iran-ContraPolicy Failure and Public Support: The Iran-Contra affair and assessments of President Reagan. *Political Behavior, 11*, 353–370.

Brown, R., & Kulik, J. (1977). Flashbulb memories. *Cognition, 5*, 73–99.

Cohn, M. A., Mehl, M. R., & Pennebaker, J. W. (2004). Linguistic markers of psychological change surrounding September 11, 2001. *Psychological Science, 15*(10), 687–693.

Clore, G. L. (1994). Why emotions are never unconscious. In P. Ekman & R. J. Davidson (Eds.), *The nature of emotion: Fundamental questions* (pp. 285–290). New York: Oxford University Press.

Ewen, S. (1996). *A social history of spin.* New York: Basic Books.

Festinger, L. (1957). *A theory of cognitive dissonance.* New York: Oxford University Press.

Foote, K. (1990). To remember and forget: Archives, memory, and culture. *American Archivist, 53*, 378–392.

Forgas, J. P. (2002). Feeling and thinking: The influence of affect on social cognition and behavior. In L. Bäckman, E. Lars, & C. von Hofsten (Eds.), *Psychology at the turn of the millennium, Vol. 1: Cognitive, biological, and health perspectives* (pp. 455–480). Hove, England: Psychology Press.

Frijda, N. H., & Mesquita, B. (1994). The social roles and functions of emotions. In S. Kitayama & H. Markus (Eds.), *Emotion and culture: Empirical studies of mutual influence* (pp. 51–87). Washington, DC: American Psychological Association.

Halbwachs, M. (1992). *On collective memory.* Chicago: University of Chicago Press.

Harber K., & Pennebaker, J. (1992) Overcoming traumatic memories. In S. Christianson (Ed.), *The handbook of emotion and memory: Research and theory* (pp. 359–387). Hillsdale, NJ: Erlbaum.

Harber, K. D., & Cohen, D. J. (2005). The emotional broadcaster theory of social sharing. *Journal of Language and Social Psychology, 24*, 382–400.

Harmon-Jones, E. (2004). From cognitive dissonance to the motivational functions of emotions. In R. A. Wright, J. Greenberg, & S. S. Brehm (Eds.), *Motivation and emotion in social contexts: Jack Brehm's influence on contemporary psychological thought* (pp. 39–55). Mahwah, New Jersey: Lawrence Erlbaum Associates.

Keltner, D., & Gross, J. J. (1999). Functional accounts of emotions. *Cognition and Emotion*, 13, 467–480.

Kvavilashvili, L., Mirani, J., Schlagman, S., & Kornbrot, D. (2004). Comparing flashbulb memories of September 11 and the death of Princess Diana: Effects of time delays and nationality. *Applied Cognitive Psychology*, 17, 1017–1031.

Kunst-Wilson, W. R., & Zajonc, R. B. (1980). Affective discrimination of stimuli that cannot be recognized. *Science*, 207, 557–558.

Lambert, A. J., & Wyer, R. S. (1990). Stereotypes and social judgment: The effects of typicality and group heterogeneity. *Journal of Personality and Social Psychology*, 59, 676–691.

Lambert, A. J., Nesse, L., Olson, K., Andrews, R., Zisser, A., & Schott, J. P. (2008). A dual-emotion framework of threat and social attitudes. Manuscript under review.

Lambert, A. J., Barton, L., Lickel, B. A., & Wells, J. (1998). The influence of group variability and processing goals on the ease of making decisions about social categories. *Personality and Social Psychology Bulletin*, 24, 807–820.

Lerner, J. S., & Keltner, D. (2001). Fear, anger and risk. *Journal of Personality and Social Psychology*, 81, 146–159.

Le Bon, G. (1895) *The crowd: A study of the popular mind*. Mineola, NY: Dover Publications. (Originally published as *La psychologie des foule*.

Levine, L. J., Whalen, C. K., Jamner, L. D., & Henker, B. (2005). Looking back on September 11, 2001: Appraised impact on memory for emotions in adolescents and adults. *Journal of Adolescent Research*, 20, 497–523.

Levine, L. J., Safer, M. A., & Lench, H. C. (2006). Remembering and misremembering emotions. In L. J. Sanna & E. C. Chang (Eds.), *Judgments over time: The interplay of thoughts, feelings, and behaviors* (pp. 271–290). New York: Oxford University Press.

Lickel, B., Hamilton, D., Wieczorkowska, G., Lewis, A., Sherman, S., & Uhles, A. (2000). Varieties of groups and the perception of group entitativity. *Journal of Personality and Social Psychology*, 78, 223–246.

McConnell, A. R., Sherman, S. J., & Hamilton, D. L. (1997). Target entitativity: Implications for information processing about individual and group targets. *Journal of Personality and Social Psychology.* 72(4), 750–762.

Mischel, W. (1968). *Personality and assessment*. New Jersey: John Wiley & Sons Inc.

Mueller, J. E. (1970). Presidential popularity from Truman to Johnson. *The American Political Science Review*, 64, 18–34.

Neisser, U., & Harsch, N. (1992). Phantom flashbulbs: False recollections of hearing the news about Challenger. In E. Winograd & U. Neisser (Eds.), *Affect and accuracy in recall: Studies of "flashbulb" memories* (Vol. 4, pp. 9–31). New York: Cambridge University Press.

Newcombe, N. S., Lloyd, M. E., & Ratliff, K. R. (2007). Development of episodic and autobiographical memory: A cognitive neuroscience perspective. In

R. V. Kail (Ed.), *Advances in child development and behavior* (Vol. 35, pp. 37–85). San Diego, CA: Elsevier.

Novick, P. (1999). *The Holocaust in American life.* New York: Houghton Mifflin Co.

Olson, K., (2003). *Effects of priming 9–11 memories on social attitudes and values.* Undergraduate honors thesis, Washington University.

Pennebaker, J. W., & Banasik, B. (1997). On the creation and maintenance of collective memories: History as social psychology. In J. W. Pennebaker, D. Paez, & B. Rimé (Eds.), *Collective memory of political events: Social psychological perspectives* (pp. 3–20). Mahwah, NJ: Lawrence Erlbaum.

Reicher, S. (2004). The psychology of crowd dynamics. In M. B. Brewer & M. Hewstone (Eds.), *Self and social identity* (pp. 232–258). Malden, MA: Blackwell Publishing.

Rime, B., & Christophe, V. (1997). How individual emotional episodes feed collective memory. In J. W. Pennebaker, D. Paez, & B. Rim´e (Eds.), *Collective memory of political events: Social and psychological perspectives* (pp. 131–146). Hillsdale, NJ: Erlbaum.

Ross, M., & Wilson, A. E. (2003). Autobiographical memory and conceptions of self: Getting better all the time. *Current Directions in Psychological Science,* 12, 66–69.

Ross, L., Greene, D., & House, P. (1977). The false consensus effect: An egocentric bias in social perception and attribution processes. *Journal of Experimental Social Psychology,* 13, 279–301

Safer, M. A., Levine, L. J., & Drapalski, A. (2002). Distortion in memory for emotions: The contributions of personality and post-event knowledge. *Personality and Social Psychology Bulletin,* 28, 1495–1507.

Schachter, S. (1959). *The psychology of affiliation.* Stanford: Stanford University Press.

Schwalbe, C. B. (2006). Remembering our shared past: Visually framing the Iraq war on U.S. news websites. *Journal of Computer-Mediated Communication* 12(1), article 14.

Schwarz, N. (1990). Feelings as information: Informational and motivational functions of affective states. In E. T. Higgins & R. M. Sorrentino (Eds.), *Handbook of motivation and cognition: Foundations of social behavior* (Vol. 2, pp. 527–561). New York, NY: Guilford Press.

Sharot, T., Martorella, E. A., Delgado, M. R., & Phelps, E. A. (2006). How personal experience modulates the neural circuitry of memories of September 11. *Proceedings of the National Academy of Sciences,* 104, 389–394.

Squire, L. R., (1994). Declarative and nondeclarative memory: Multiple brain systems supporting learning and memory. In D. L. Schacter & E. Tulving (Eds.), *Memory systems 1994* (pp. 203–231). Cambridge, MA: The MIT Press.

Squire, L. R. & Kandel, E. R. (1999). *Memory: From mind to molecules.* New York: W. H. Freeman.

Stryker, S. (2004). Integrating emotion into identity theory. In J. Turner (Ed.), *Advances in group processes, Vol 21: Theory and research on human emotions* (pp. 1–23). US: Elsevier Science/JAI Press.

Tajfel, H. (1981). *Human groups and social categories.* Cambridge: Cambridge University Press.

Tulving, E. (1991). Concepts of human memory. In L. Squire, G. Lynch, N. M. Weinberger, & J. L. McGaugh (Eds.), *Memory: Organization and locus of change* (pp. 3–32). New York: Oxford University Press.

Velleman, D. (1997). How to share an intention. *Philosophy and Phenomenological Research* 57, 29–50.

Watson, D., & Tellegen, A. (1985). Toward a consensual structure of mood. *Psychological Bulletin*, 98, 219–235.

Wertsch, J. V., & Roediger, H. L. (2008). Collective memory: Conceptual foundations and theoretical approaches. *Memory*, 16, 318–326.

Wicker, A. W. (1969). Attitudes versus actions: The relationship of verbal and overt behavioral responses to attitude objects. *Journal of Social Issues*, 25, 41–78.

Wilson, R. A. (2005). Collective memory, group minds, and the extended mind thesis. *Cognitive Processing*, 6, 227–236.

Wilson, A. E., & Ross, M. (2001). From chump to champ: People's appraisals of their earlier and current selves. *Journal of Personality and Social Psychology*, 80, 572–584.

Yzerbyt, C., Judd, C., & Corneille, O. (2003). *The psychology of group perception: Contributions to the study of homogeneity, entitativity and essentialism.* Philadelphia, PA: Psychology Press.

Zajonc, R. B. (1980). Feeling and thinking. Preferences need no inferences. *American Psychologist*, 35, 151–175.

Zertal, I. (2005). *Israel's holocaust and the politics of nationhood.* Cambridge: Cambridge University Press.

PART IV

HOW DOES MEMORY SHAPE HISTORY?

According to the "Whig" narrative, world history is a series of long struggles and many detours that fortunately led to that apotheosis of mankind's political achievements, the British Empire of circa 1900 – as excellently demonstrated by (among many others) George Macaulay Trevelyan (see, for instance, Trevelyan, 1904). That is also the version of history gently satirized in the famous *1066 and All That*, which, as the authors added in their subtitle, provided the reader with *A Memorable History of England, comprising all the parts you can remember, including 103 Good Things, 5 Bad Kings and 2 Genuine Dates* (Sellar & Yeatman, 1930). The connection between memory and whiggish history is no coincidence. "Presentism," that bogeyman of historiographers, is an unfortunate and ever-present temptation to see past events in the light of current norms and conditions. But it also manifests itself in the idea that the present is necessary – that history had to happen the way it did (Hawthorne, 1991; Tetlock, Lebow, & Parker, 2006). And if the past proves to be rather embarrassing, it should be transmogrified or omitted altogether, lest it ruins the flattering self-image on which rests a sound polity.

All this may seem familiar, but the studies surveyed by Craig Blatz and Michael Ross show how deep-seated the biases are, and how they operate even in the most "historically aware" of places. In the early days of memory research, Frederic Bartlett had used a version of the "telephone" or "Chinese whispers" game, to show how a complex story is gradually simplified, but also made more culturally acceptable, as it passes along from one person to another along a long chain of transmission (Bartlett, 1932; Bergman & Roediger, 1999). Ross and his colleagues used a similar technique to show how historical narratives gradually acquire more flattering passages and distort or omit the embarrassing ones. As they point out, this is paradoxical in an age of "repentance," when governments and international institutions (but rarely the people) seem to compete in their apologies for past deeds.

What was a matter of satire to the Victorians acquired a much more sinister edge in the last century, by virtue of the sheer scale of atrocities and massacres. This, as David Blight points out, is one of the main reasons why we have witnessed such a "memory boom" in public discourse. Scholarly history was not the prime mover here. The spectacular development of memory studies in history is a consequence of a larger social phenomenon, an ever-increasing awareness that shared historical memories are generally contentious and contested. An early source for this awareness is, of course, the intractable problem of Holocaust memory. Modern Germany may provide the only example in history of a society that has faced collective responsibility in the most explicit manner, in contrast to other participants in World War II atrocities (Buruma, 1994). To this day, the issue of what to make of the past and of the entanglements of personal and collective responsibility, is a major theme of public debate in countries as diverse as South Africa, Spain, Argentina, and postcommunist European democracies.

These debates, as Blight points out, often reveal the inescapable tensions between collective remembering of the kind described in previous chapters of this volume, and the exigencies of scholarly history – especially around the dimension of trust. After all, historians pride themselves in having a *metier*, a series of procedures rather than a set of goals. This focus on methods, on how to do scholarly work rather than on what to demonstrate, is very similar to the shift in religious exegesis, from theological demonstration of dogma (we know that the text is true, and we can use any available methods to demonstrate it) to historical philology (we must use specific methods to analyze texts, whatever conclusions that leads us to) (Todorov, 1982). This should remind us that it takes particular historical conditions, to create and foster such an unnatural form of remembering – unnatural in that it goes against the grain of our cognitive tendencies. What those conditions are is still somewhat mysterious; it is at least clear that an emphasis on factual chronology, explicitly distinguished from myth and epic, is not an exclusively Western achievement (Brown, 1988; Goody, 2006).

The development of a politics of memory has led historians to treat collective remembering as an object of study, rather than an annoyingly ill-mannered competitor. Jay Winter is among those historians whose focus has shifted from historiography to a history of memory (Winter, 1995). In particular, Winter describes the socialization, or the appropriation, of a collective past through the consecration of particular places – those statues, museums, and memorials that are supposed to provide us with a material representation of shared history (see also Nora, 1984, 1986). These places serve specific social functions, ritual ones in particular, but they also express more than we realize of shared ways of construing the past. Consider, for instance, the striking difference between most World War II memorials – heroic and hieratic statues, explicit warlike imagery, emphasis on effort and victory – and the Washington, DC, Vietnam memorial – a simple list of names, with not a single comment or illustration. The shift in public representations, from war as collective triumph to war as individual catastrophe, is a psychological one – in the connections people establish between their own past and history.

REFERENCES

Bartlett, F. C. (1932). *Remembering. A study in experimental and social psychology*. Cambridge: Cambridge University Press.

Bergman, E. T., & Roediger, H. L. I. (1999). Can Bartlett's repeated reproduction experiments be replicated? *Memory and Cognition, 27*, 937–947.

Brown, D. E. (1988). *Hierarchy, history, and human nature: The social origins of historical consciousness*. Tucson: University of Arizona Press.

Buruma, I. (1994). *The wages of guilt: Memories of war in Germany and Japan* (1st ed.). New York: Farrar, Straus, Giroux.

Goody, J. (2006). *Theft of history*. Cambridge: Cambridge University Press.

Hawthorne, G. (1991). *Plausible worlds: Possibility and understanding in history and the social sciences*. Cambridge: Cambridge University Press.

Nora, P. (1984). *Les Lieux de mémoire. I, La République*. Paris: Gallimard.

Nora, P. (1986). *Les Lieux de mémoire. II, La Nation*. Paris: Gallimard.

Sellar, W. C., & Yeatman, R. J. (1930). *1066 and all that: A memorable history of England, comprising all the parts you can remember, including 103 good things, 5 bad Kings and 2 genuine dates*. London: Methuen London.

Tetlock, P., Lebow, R. N., & Parker, G. (2006). *Unmaking the West: "what-if" scenarios that rewrite world history*. Ann Arbor: University of Michigan Press.

Todorov, T. (1982). *Symbolism and interpretation*. Ithaca, NY: Cornell University Press.

Trevelyan, G. M. (1904). *England under the Stuarts*. London: Methuen & Co.

Vidal-Naquet, P. (1992). *Assassins of memory: Essays on the denial of the Holocaust*. New York: Columbia University Press.

Winter, J. M. (1995). *Sites of memory, sites of mourning: The Great War in European cultural history*. Cambridge; New York: Cambridge University Press.

9

Historical Memories

CRAIG W. BLATZ & MICHAEL ROSS

After the attacks on the World Trade Center and Pentagon on September 11, 2001, the Princeton historian Bernard Lewis explained the thinking and behavior of Muslims to the American public in a *New Yorker* article (Lewis, 2001). Lewis wrote that, unlike Americans, Muslims know and care about history:

> In current American usage, the phrase "that's history" is commonly used to dismiss something as unimportant, of no relevance to current concerns. ... Middle Easterner's perception of history is nourished from the pulpit, by the schools, and by the media, and although it may be – indeed, often is – slanted and inaccurate, it is nevertheless vivid and powerfully resonant. (p. 51)

Lewis implies that Americans' (and presumably most Westerners') historical memories are not "nourished from the pulpit, by the schools, and by the media." He further implies that Americans' historical memories are accurate, even if they do not care much about history.

In this chapter, we dispute each of these claims. Muslims are not unique in their use or abuse of history. People's memories of the histories of the national, ethnic, or religious groups to which they belong (ingroups) are often tilted in favor of their ingroups and against other groups. We present evidence that historical memories are skewed, in part, because children and adults are presented with selective and biased depictions of the past. Educators, religious leaders, politicians, and media all play an important role by influencing the knowledge available. We also show that people's response to the information available further affects their historical memories. People's memories are influenced by how they attend to, process, and retrieve the information that they receive. Individuals create historical memories that depict their valued ingroups favorably, even after reading unfavorable information. We reason that favorable memories of ingroups satisfy important group and individual needs. We conclude by discussing a recent surge in government apologies for past injustices. Government redress is important because it can possibly satisfy group and individual concerns, and contribute to more balanced historical memories.

LEARNING HISTORY

The histories taught in schools and presented in the media are not impartial renderings of past events; rather, these histories reflect a bias to report the past in a way that confirms current preferences, goals, and beliefs (Loewen, 1995). Conceptions of the past are flexible and succeeding generations rewrite history to reflect their own beliefs and achieve their current goals (Barkan, 2000; Mead, 1929/1964). Historians use the term "presentism" to describe these biased portrayals of the past (Butterfield, 1959). As a consequence of presentism, young people everywhere commonly learn versions of history that justify and glorify the actions of their own national, ethnic, and religious groups. Episodes that highlight the superiority of the present group are emphasized; whereas episodes potentially damaging to the group's image are deemphasized or omitted (Frijda, 1997; Loewen, 1995; Paris, 2000).

There are many examples of the selective presentation of history in school texts and the media. Recently, Japanese government officials announced their intention to revise textbooks to delete descriptions of how the Japanese army ordered civilians to commit mass suicide in the Battle of Okinawa during World War II (Onishi, 2007). Fitzgerald (1979) analyzed school history texts used in the United States during different decades. Until the Civil Rights era in the 1960s, slaves were depicted as appearing "magically" at some unspecified time and disappearing after the Civil War (p. 83). History texts failed to mention that slaves were forcibly abducted and removed from their families and homes. Furthermore, slave owners were commonly portrayed as generous and the Ku Klux Klan as having "a worse reputation than it deserved" (p. 86). Fitzgerald also described how Native Americans were represented favorably in texts in the 1830s and 1840s, more negatively after the Civil War ("savages," "half-civilized"), and then omitted entirely from textbooks between the 1930s and 1960s.

Similar editing of history occurs in our home country, Canada. Backhouse, a Canadian legal scholar, recently observed that Canadians have a "stupefying innocence" (Backhouse, 1999, p. 278) about the extensive record of racism in their country, partly because such information is often omitted from history texts. Also, Canadian history textbooks tend to glorify the Canadian army's contributions in World War I and World War II. For example, many texts describe a four-day battle in which Canadian soldiers led the Allied conquest of the highly fortified Vimy Ridge during World War I. This military success is often portrayed as a founding moment in Canadian history. One historical Web site emphasizes Canadian heroism by presenting the reactions of a French soldier when he learned that the heavily fortified Vimy Ridge had been captured by the Allies. Supposedly, the soldier first exclaimed, "C'est impossible!" Then, on learning it was the Canadians who had won battle, he continued "Ah! Les Canadiens. C'est possible!" (*Return to Vimy Ridge*, 2007). These accounts of the conquest of Vimy Ridge typically omit details that reflect less favorably on the contributions of Canadian troops. Canadian forces won the conflict at Vimy in large part because of months of intense planning and artillery support by French and British troops. Furthermore, the capture of Vimy Ridge was a limited victory in the Battle of Arras, which the Allies eventually lost (Valpy, 2007).

Additional examples of the the cleansing and glorification of military history are easy to find. Japanese government officials recently announced that they were no longer going to discuss the Japanese army's complicity in creating the "comfort women" system (Onishi, 2007). The U.S. military concocted a story concerning the death of Corporal Pat Tillman in Afganistan. An ex-NFL football player, Tillman was accidentally killed by a fellow American soldier. In the accounts that first emerged after his death, however, the military portrayed Tillman as dying bravely under enemy fire (Herbert, 2007). An official inquiry found some high-ranking military officials responsible for the false story, including a three-star general ("Demotion Expected," 2007).

Finally, like Muslim clerics, leaders of other religions offer accounts of the past that can influence the views and actions of their adherants. For centuries, Christian religious leaders tended to portray the death of Jesus as a Jewish crime, a rendering of history that caused Jews great harm. In 1987, Pope John Paul II acknowledged the destructive effects of church teachings about Jews and created a new Church doctrine that transformed Catholic-Jewish relations. Based on the new doctrine, the Catholic United States Bishops' Committee for Ecumenical and Interreligious Affairs declared in 1988 that passion plays must avoid unfavorable caricatures of Jews (Accattoli, 1998; Foxman, 2003). As these examples show, religious leaders regularly present and interpret stories of the past. They can create pasts that further negative or positive relations between religious groups.

The content and implications of public portrayals of history are readily documented, but the motivations behind efforts to control the past are more complex. Political elites use history to promote the viability, dynamism, and superiority of their group. Stories of the past help define and justify group values and goals, and guide group members' behaviors. In his novel *1984*, George Orwell wrote: "He who controls the present controls the past" (1949, p. 32). The reverse also holds: those who control the past control the present.

Although it is possible to understand the historical memories of individuals partly in terms of the information offered to them by various political elites, people's own psychological motivations are also important. People prefer not to hear and remember injustices committed by members of their ingroup. In the next section, we examine the psychological bases and implications of this preference.

INDIVIDUAL HISTORICAL MEMORIES

Memory is often described as a form of mental time travel (Kandel, 2006). According to this metaphor, people can travel back in time and recapture their original experiences. This metaphor is appealing, but misleading. People are often unable to recapture their original experiences because they cannot remember details. People sometimes recall only a few aspects of an episode; they may then use their current knowledge and preferences to fill in gaps and resolve ambiguities in their memories (Bartlett, 1932; Neisser, 1967; Ross, 1989). Memory is also selective. For example, in recalling the history of their country, people typically do not try to recover everything they might have learned. Like politicians and religious leaders, ordinary people tend to recall past events that offer support for their present knowledge, preferences and motivations (Blatz & Ross, 2009).

Lost in Transmission

People learn about most historical events from others rather than experience the episodes directly. We have already discussed the selective presentation of history in textbooks. But transmission of historical memories also occurs at a more personal level as recollections are transmitted from individual to individual and from parent to child. There is reason to suppose that biases can arise during the simple transmission of historical information from person to person. Psychologists have examined the transmission of memories using the method of serial reproduction (Allport & Postman, 1947; Bartlett, 1932; Lyons & Kashima, 2003). This approach is similar to a children's game called "Telephone" or "Chinese Whispers." Typically, the first person in a chain reads a text and, after a brief delay, recalls this text for a second participant. The second participant then listens to the first person's account and, after a brief delay, recalls it for a third individual. This process is repeated until the chain has three or more participants. Most studies examine the transmission of fictional stories rather than historical information, but the findings have implications for historical memories. Accounts become shorter as they move down the chain; peripheral details are lost, whereas central details remain; and elements that are unusual or that contradict stereotypical beliefs are lost or altered.

In a recent study, we examined how information about a historical injustice is transmitted from individual to individual in a three-person chain (Blatz & Ross, 2006). Participants learned about an episode that allegedly occurred either in the participants' home country (Canada) or in a distant land (Australia). The passage presented a series of events in which representatives of the government behaved in a prejudiced and cruel manner toward aboriginal children. The first participant in each chain listened to an audio recording that described how the Canadian or Australian government forcibly removed aboriginal children from their homes and communities and placed them in residential schools. The goal of the schools was to "civilize" the aboriginal children, who were strictly disciplined for speaking their native language and robbed of their cultural identity. Many children were physically, psychologically, or sexually abused. The passage was based on episodes that actually happened in Canada (Krotz, 2007), although similar events also occurred in Australia (Manne, 2006). The first person transmitted the passage from memory to a second individual, who then passed the information on to a third person. All participants were asked to repeat the information as accurately as possible.

As in past research, we expected the story of the event to become shorter as the description was passed along the chain. These changes should occur regardless of whether the events occurred in Canada or Australia. When the events happened in Canada, however, we expected the alterations of the passage to be systematic: the final version of the story should be more flattering to government officials and less damaging to the aboriginal children than the original passage. These changes would occur because of a feature of memory: people more readily remember information that is consistent with their beliefs and supports their preferences (e.g., Ross, 1989). If they have a positive attitude toward Canada, they should better remember aspects of the passage that are less damaging to Canada. Also, if they forget aspects of the passage, they may use their positive beliefs about Canada to reconstruct the missing information. For example, suppose participants forget exactly how many aboriginal children "attended" residential schools. Their favorable views of Canada might lead them to reconstruct a number that is lower, rather than higher than the actual number. When the events transpired in Australia, we expected alterations but not changes that would promote a more favorable evaluation of the episode. Presumably, Canadian students have not been exposed to as much positive propaganda about Australia as about Canada. Also, they should be more psychologically motivated to regard their own system of government as fair (Jost & Banaji, 1994; Tajfel & Turner, 1986).

We tested our ideas by coding the recollections of the passage for memory errors that reduced the degree of harm and distanced the episode from present-day Canadians or Australians. For example, some participants underestimated how many children were placed in residential schools or recalled that the events happened longer ago than the original passage described. If the events occurred long ago, people alive today are not directly implicated in the wrongdoing. When the story was located in Canada, such errors were rare for the first person (who heard the original passage), but errors became increasingly common as the memory proceeded down the chain. Each person remembered the passage as slightly less damning to the Canada of today than the preceding person did. No similar changes occurred when the events were located in Australia. This study indicates that ordinary people, and not just political elites, alter historical memories to serve their current motivations.

Social Identity and Historical Memory

Some people are more motivated than others to think favorably of their ingroup. One important influence is the degree to which individuals identify with their group. High identifiers feel strongly connected to their group. They are especially likely to value their group and feel psychologically threatened by their group's harmful actions (Ellemers, Spears, & Doosje, 2002; Hinkle & Brown, 1990). High identifiers may feel guilty about their group's misconduct, even if they, themselves, are innocent of wrongdoing and the incident happened decades earlier (Branscombe & Doosje, 2004; Doosje, Branscombe, Spears, & Manstead, 2006). Consequently, high identifiers should be particularly likely to exhibit positively biased historical memories.

Sahdra and Ross (2007) studied the historical memories of Sikhs and Hindus, two groups with a history of retaliatory, extremely violent acts against each other in India and elsewhere. Sikh and Hindu participants attempted to recall events in which Hindus committed acts of violence against Sikhs and Sikhs committed similar actions against Hindus. Sahdra and Ross also assessed the extent to which participants identified with their religious group. As expected, Sikhs and Hindus who identified highly with their religious group recalled fewer incidents of violence and hatred perpetrated by ingroup members than did low identifiers. Low identifiers showed no bias in historical memory; they were as likely to recall violence perpetrated by the ingroup against the outgroup as they were violence perpetrated by the outgroup against the ingroup.

High identifiers might report biased memories because they were exposed to biased historical information prior to the study. Alternatively, the bias could occur because of psychological processes occurring at the level of the individual. For example, high identifiers may be more motivated than low identifiers to recall events favorable to their group. To demonstrate the contribution of individual motivation, Sahdra and Ross (2007) experimentally varied Canadian participants' identification with Canada. Some participants were randomly assigned to read information that strengthened their identification with Canada. Others were randomly assigned to read information that lowered their identification with Canada. Participants in both groups were then asked to recall acts of violence and hatred committed by Canadians against members of other groups. As expected, participants who were experimentally induced to identify highly with Canada recalled fewer incidents of violence and hatred than did participants in the low identity condition. The historical bias revealed in this study seems to reflect high identifiers' motivation to view Canada favorably.

The results of these studies suggest that biases in historical memories can result from apparently unintentional, psychologically motivated alterations to memory. Yes, educators, governmental officials and other political elites often provide versions of history that flatter their ingroups. But everyday memory and communication processes also contribute to distortions in historical memory. Furthermore, biased historical memory is not limited to particular religious or ethnic groups, as suggested by the quote presented at the beginning of this chapter.

CONFRONTING HISTORICAL INJUSTICES

Remembering Ingroup Tragedies

Most religious, ethnic, and national groups stage annual festivals to recreate and celebrate past glories, such as independence days and military successes. These celebrations reflect the motivation to emphasize the favorable aspects of ingroup history. However, ethnic groups and nations also memorialize tragedies that occurred decades or even centuries ago. Jews commemorate the Holocaust, Armenians remember the Armenian genocide, Acadians memorialize their expulsion from Eastern Canada in 1755, and Palestinians memorialize the Great Catastrophe (land and lives lost during Israel's war of independence), and so forth.

Why do groups preserve memories of tragedies? One answer is that, like memories of former glories, recollections of ingroup suffering and associated rituals enhance ingroup solidarity (Devine-Wright, 2003; Irwin-Zarecka, 1994; Novick, 1999; Roe, 2003). The tragic history unites members of the ingroup and also sets them apart from other groups (Novick, 1999). The sometimes bizarre competition among groups to claim that their own tragedy is greater than others of its kind (Novick, 1999) perhaps reflects the motive to distinguish one's own group from the rest of the pack. Just as groups frequently represent their strengths and past glories as unique, they also emphasize the distinctiveness of their tragedies.

The downside of memorializing historical injustices committed against one's group is that such recollections can fuel bad feelings and intergroup hostility. Groups may fail to settle present conflicts because earlier grievances remain unresolved. The conflicting sides cannot put the past behind them as they attempt to deal with the present and future. For example, the second author of this chapter has engaged in causal discussions with ordinary Israelis and Palestinians about prospects for peace in the Middle East. The focus of the conversation often turns to discussion about events that happened decades and even centuries earlier. As conflict theorists commonly observe, if there is any hope for resolution, opponents need to switch from debating past wrongs to developing future plans for reconciliation (e.g., Ross, Ross, Stein, & Trabasso, 2006).

Governmental Apologies

Sometimes, leaders of previously victimized groups attempt to settle past grievances by demanding apologies and compensation for historical injustices. For example, members of the African American community have asked federal and state governments to apologize and atone for slavery for over a century (Brooks, 1999). Although the tendency to ask for redress is not a recent phenomenon, governments and some religious leaders are now showing an increased willingness to accede to such demands (Accattoli, 1998; Brooks, 1999). In 1988, Canada and the United States apologized and provided financial compensation to Japanese Canadians and Americans who were interned during World War II (Brooks, 1999), in 1993, the United States apologized to native Hawaiians for seizing their land one hundred years earlier ("Apology Passed," 1993), and in the last few years, the governments of Canada and New Zealand apologized and provided financial compensation for discriminatory taxes that their countries imposed on Chinese immigrants in the late nineteenth and early twentieth centuries ("Compensation Offered," 2006; "Government Offers Token Regret," 2004; "Government Sorry," 2002). As we write this chapter in 2007, a growing number of state legislatures in the United States are for the first time officially aknowledging and expressing regret for their role in perpetuating slavery (e.g., "Virginia Expresses 'Profound Regret'," 2007).

Efforts to acknowledge and apologize for distant injustices often ignite controversy. Proponents of redress argue that governmental apologies help heal the wounds of past injustices. In proposing that the Virginia House of delegates provide an apology for African slavery, one of the sponsors of the bill, Donald McEachin noted: "It is meant to be a resolution that is part of a healing process, a process that still needs to take place even today in 2007" (Gibson, 2007). Opponents argue, as they did with respect to the proposed Virginia apology, that the wounds should have healed long ago and the victim group should just "get over it" (this argument overlooks the fact that the victim group might have been seeking redress for many years). Opponents also argue against redress on the grounds that the people who should offer or receive an apology are dead (Thompson, 2002).

Governments may also hesitate to provide an apology for historical injustices against a minority because the majority opposes such offers. In a poll conducted in 2002, a majority of white Americans rejected a proposal that the government offer redress for slavery (Viles, 2002). Despite this opposition, governments today seem more inclined than their predecessors to apologize. The reasons for this willingness to apologize probably include the recognition that demands for redress will persist and that other governments have apologized for similar incidents without ill effects (Ross & Schumann, 2007). Also, members of the previously victimized minority often achieve greater political clout. In Virginia, the apology for slavery was sponsored by African American Virginia Delegates, at least two of whom were descended from slaves (Gibson, 2007). Following the Virginia expression of regret, the legislatures in Maryland, North Carolina, Alabama, and New York quickly issued their own apologies, and more are in the offing. Virginia broke the solid opposition to governmental apologies that had existed for more than a century.[1]

This increasing governmental willingness to apologize coincides with an emerging consensus among social scientists that redress is beneficial (Barkan, 2000; Blatz, Schumann, & Ross, 2007; Brooks, 1999; Dyzenhaus & Moran, 2006; Minow, 1998, 2002). By acknowledging an earlier injustice, governments affirm the historical memories of the victimized minority. The apology indicates that the government and majority are to blame for wrongs that caused great suffering among minority members. In its expression of regret, the State of Virginia explained that slavery was "sanctioned and perpetuated through the laws of Virginia and the United States." There was no mention of generous owners and happy slaves in this statement by the legislature, as there had been in some American history textbooks (Fitzgerald, 1979). Instead, the statement notes that slaves were "brutalized, humiliated, dehumanized" and that slavery "ranks as the most horrendous of all depredations of human rights and violations of our founding ideals in our nation's history."[2]

Such acknowledgments of the devastating effects of slavery might seem too obvious to warrant mentioning, but they can be psychologically important. In addition to confirming the memories of the minority, these acknowledgments may help to short-circuit any psychological tendency to justify government wrongs (Blatz et al., 2007). According to social psychologists, people are motivated to believe that they live in a just country, where people get what they deserve and deserve what they get (Jost, Banaji, & Nosek, 2004; Lerner, 1980). In the face of injustice, members of the nonvictimized majority sometimes maintain a belief in the fairness of their country and government by minimizing the degree of wrong or blaming the victims for their suffering (Lerner, 1980). As we have already observed, members of the majority may also bury historical facts to maintain their belief that they live in a just and fair country. Like members of the majority, members of the victimized minority also need to believe that they live in a fair and just country. To foster a sense of justice, they may hold their own group at least partly responsible for its problems. It is therefore important that governmental apologies explicitly verify the degree of harm, the innocence of the minority, and the fairness of the current system. The apology dissociates the current majority group and system from the earlier injustice; the apology

---

[1] Some writers argue that President Lincoln apologized for slavery in his second inaugural address (e.g., Lazare, 2004). Lincoln eloquently described the evils of slavery, but we do not see evidence of an explicit apology on behalf of the government.

[2] The Virginia statement also expressed regret for the State's treatment of Native Americans.

demonstrates the government's commitment to addressing even the injustices of previous generations (Blatz et al., 2007).

Government apologies sometimes also include praise for both the victim and majority groups (Blatz et al., 2007). For example, the Virginia statement emphasized "the faith, perseverance, hope, and endless triumphs of ... African Americans" and that "their significant contributions to this Commonwealth and the nation should be embraced, celebrated, and retold for generations to come." Virginians more broadly are praised for exemplifying "the founding ideals of liberty and equality ... by providing some of the nation's foremost trailblazers for civil rights and electing a grandson of slaves to the Commonwealth's highest elective office." Such praise may enhance the majority and minority's views of each other and of the fairness of their system of government, as well as increase their enthusiasm for the apology.

We have claimed a lot of potential benefits for governmental apologies. Is there any evidence that they actually deliver these benefits? There is little empirical research on this question. Some scholars have assessed the effectiveness of redress by contrasting how various countries respond to different historical injustices (e.g., Brooks, 1999). For example, they often compare how Japan's unwillingness to apologize for wartime atrocities has hindered reconciliation with its neighbors to how Germany's offers of apology and reparations fostered positive relations with its neighbors (Barkan, 2000). Although such research is instructive, the evidence is inconclusive because countries and past injustices diverge on many dimensions.

We conducted a more controlled study to evaluate the effects of redress. We surveyed Canadians of Chinese and non-Chinese descent to assess their reactions to the Chinese Head Tax (a discriminatory tax imposed on Chinese immigrants more than 80 years ago) one month before and one month after the Canadian government officially apologized and offered financial compensation for the Head Tax (Blatz, Ross, Day, & Schryer, 2007). Both Chinese and non-Chinese Canadians reported that the Head Tax reflected less poorly on the Canadian system of government and evaluated Canadians of European heritage more favorably after redress was offered than before. The apology had no effect on either group's evaluations of Chinese Canadians. When asked to evaluate the actual redress offer, both groups responded favorably, but non-Chinese participants were particularly enthusiastic.

The findings from this study confirm that redress is beneficial – but especially, in this case at least – for the nonvictimized majority. Clearly, one study is not definitive, but our results indicate that, once offered, reparations for historical injustices are supported by the majority. The minority also seems to benefit, though ironically to a lesser extent. Perhaps the advantages for the minority are more long term, however, as it and the majority forge a more respectful and harmonious relationship.

What is the impact of redress on historical memories, which are the focus of this paper? Do governmental offers of redress lead to a rewriting of history texts? Are shameful historical injustices discussed more openly following redress? Are the government's and majority's roles in the injustices examined? Is the impact of the injustices on the victims detailed? Anecdotally, we see some evidence that a governmental apology might increase awareness of a historical injustice even a long time after the apology is offered. As an annual class exercise, one of us (MR) asks his Canadian university students to indicate the degree to which they are aware of various historical injustices, and especially acts of racism and discrimination committed by the Canadian government. The students are generally ignorant of most of the events in the list. They are almost all familiar, however, with the government's internment of Japanese Canadians during World War II and its subsequent apology. Students seem to be most familiar with the one injustice in the list that received an official government apology and offer of reparations. Apologies may have the power to alter historical memories.

SUMMARY

Groups glorify their histories because recollections of the past serve important political and psychological purposes. Political elites intentionally misrepresent history and ordinary people unintentionally alter it. In recent years, governments have increasingly apologized and atoned for historical injustices. Although there is little research on the topic, it appears that the political and psychological motives that are met by manipulating history can be satisfied by apologizing and atoning for a group's past misdeeds. Redress for historical injustice could be an important step in producing more balanced historical memories as well as fostering harmony among groups.

ACKNOWLEDGMENTS

Preparation of this article was facilitated by a Natural Science and Engineering Research Council doctoral fellowship to Craig Blatz. Address correspondence to Craig Blatz, Department of Psychology, University of Waterloo, 200 University Avenue West, Waterloo, Ontario, Canada, N2L 3G1; e-mail: cwblatz@uwaterloo.ca.

REFERENCES

Accattoli, L. (1998). *When a pope asks forgiveness: The mea culpas of Pope John Paul II* (J. Auman Trans.). Boston: St. Paul Books & Media.

Allport, G. W., & Postman, L. (1947). *The psychology of rumor.* New York: Holt, Rinehart & Winston.

Apology for 1893 rebellion (1993, November 17). *The New York Times Online.* Retrieved April 18, 2007 from http://query.nytimes.com/gst/fullpage.html? res=9F0CE7D8153BF934A25752C1A965958260.

Backhouse, C. (1999). *Color coded: A legal history of racism in Canada.* Toronto, Ontario, Canada: University of Toronto Press.

Barkan, E. (2000). *The guilt of nations: Restitution and negotiating historical injustices.* New York: Norton.

Bartlett, F. C. (1932). *Remembering: A study in experimental and social psychology.* Cambridge: Cambridge University Press.

Blatz, C. W., & Ross, M. (2006). *Transmitting collective memories of historical events.* Unpublished data: University of Waterloo.

Blatz, C. W., Ross, M., Day, M., & Schryer, E. (2007). *Reactions to a real apology for a historical injustice.* Unpublished data: University of Waterloo.

Blatz, C. W., Schumann, K., & Ross, M. (2007). *Government apologies for historical injustices.* Manuscript submitted for publication.

Blatz, C. W., & Ross, M. (2009). Principled ideology or racism: Why do modern racists oppose race-based social justice programs? *Journal of Experimental Social Psychology, 45*(1), 258–261.

Branscombe, N. R., & Doosje, B. (2004). *Collective guilt: International perspectives.* New York: Cambridge University Press.

Brooks, R. L. (Ed.). (1999). *When sorry isn't enough: The controversy over apologies and reparations for human injustice.* New York: New York University Press.

Butterfield, H. (1959). *The Whig interpretation of history.* London: Bell.

"Compensation Offered". (2006, June 22). PM unveils redress for Head Tax on Chinese. *CBC news online.* Retrieved March 22, 2007 from: http://www.cbc. ca/canada/story/2006/06/22/chinese-apology.html.

"Demotion Expected". (2007, July 27). Demotion expected for role in Tillman case. *The New York Times Online.* Retrieved July 30, 2007 from http://www.nytimes. com/2007/07/27/us/27tillman.html?_r=1&oref=slogin.

Devine-Wright, P. (2003). A theoretical overview of memory and conflict. In E. Carins, & M. D. Roe (Eds.), *The role of memory in ethnic conflict* (pp. 9–33). New York: Palgrave Macmillan.

Doosje, B. E. J., Branscombe, N. R., Spears, R., & Manstead, A. S. R. (2006). Antecedents and consequences of group-based guilt: The effects of ingroup identification. *Group Processes & Intergroup Relations, 9*, 325–338.

Dyzenhaus, D., & Moran, M. (2006). *Calling power to account: Law, reparations and the Chinese Head Tax.* Toronto, Ontario, Canada: University of Toronto Press.

Ellemers, N., Spears, R., & Doosje, B. (2002). Self and social identity. *Annual Review of Psychology, 53*, 161–186.

Fitzgerald, F. (1979). *America revised: History schoolbooks in the twentieth century.* New York: Little, Brown, and Company.

Foxman, A. H. (2003). *Never again? The threat of the new anti-semitism*. New York: Harper.

Frijda, N. H. (1997). Commemorating. In J. W. Pennebaker, D. Paez, & B. Rime (Eds.), *Collective memory of political events: Social psychological perspectives* (pp. 103–127). Hillsdale, NJ, England: Lawrence Erblaum Associates.

Gibson, B. (2007, January 16). Slavery apology ignites legislative debate. *The Daily Progress*. Retrieved July 26, 2007 from http://www.dailyprogress.com/servlet/ Satellite? pagename=CDP/MGArticle/CDP_BasicArticle&c=MGArticle&cid= 1149192673260.

"Government Offers Token Regret." (2004, February 12). Government offers token of regret to Chinese. *The New Zealand Herald*. Retrieved July 26, 2007 from http://www.nzherald.co.nz/section/1/story.cfm?c_id=1&objectid=3548790.

"Government Sorry" (2002, February 12). Government to sorry for tax on Chinese. *The New Zealand Herald*. Retrieved July 26, 2007 from http://www.nzherald. co.nz/section/1/story.cfm?c_id=1&objectid=889867.

Herbert, B. (2007, April 30). Working the truth beat (Op-ed). *The New York Times,* p. A21.

Hinkle, S., & Brown, R. J. (1990). Intergroup comparisons and social identity: Some links and lacunae. In D. Abrams & M. A. Hogg (Eds.), *Social identity theory: Constructive and critical advances* (pp. 48–70). New York: Harvester Weatsheaf.

Irwin-Zarecka, I. (1994). *Frames of remembrance: The dynamics of collective memory*. New Brunswick, NJ: Transaction Publishers.

Jost, J. T., & Banaji, M. R. (1994). The role of stereotyping in system-justification and the production of false consciousness. *British Journal of Social Psychology, 33*, 1–27.

Jost, J. T., Banaji, M. R., & Nosek, B. A. (2004). A decade of system justification theory: Accumulated evidence of conscious and unconscious bolstering of the status quo. *Political Psychology, 25*, 881–920.

Kandel, E. R. (2006). *In search of memory*. New York: Norton.

Krotz, L. (2007, February). Separate and unequal: Money for crimes committed at residential schools may be forthcoming, but problems with the reserve system remain. *The Walrus*. Retrieved July 25, 2007 from http://www.walrusmagazine. com/articles/2007.02-national-affairs-separate-and-unequal/.

Lazare, A. (2004). *On apology*. New York: Oxford University Press.

Lerner, M. J. (1980). *The belief in a just world: A fundamental delusion*. New York: Plenum Press.

Lewis, B. (2001). The revolt of Islam. *The New Yorker, November 19*, 50–63.

Loewen, J. (1995). *Lies my teacher told me: Everything your American history textbook got wrong*. New York: W. W. Norton and Company.

Lyons, A., & Kashima, Y. (2003). How are stereotypes maintained through communication? The influence of stereotype sharedness. *Journal of Personality and Social Psychology, 85*, 989–1005.

Manne, R. (2006, September 9). The cruelty of denial. *The Age*. Retrieved July 26, 2007 from http://www.theage.com.au/news/robert-manne/the-cruelty-of-denial/2006/09/08/1157222325367.html.

Mead, G. H. (1929/1964). The nature of the past. Reprinted in Selected Writings: G. H. Mead. Andrew Reck (Ed.). Indianapolis: Bobbs-Merrill.

Minow, M. (1998). *Between vengeance and forgiveness: Facing history after genocide and mass violence.* Boston: Beacon Press.

(2002). *Breaking the cycles of hatred.* Princeton, NJ: Princeton University Press.

Neisser, U. (1967). *Cognitive psychology.* New York: Appleton-Century-Crofts.

Novick, P. (1999). *The holocaust in American life.* New York: Houghton Mifflin.

Onishi, N. (2007, April 1). Japan's textbooks reflect revised history. *The New York Times Online.* Retrieved July 25, 2007 from http://www.nytimes.com/2007/04/01/world/asia/01japan.html?ex=1333080000&en=5fa52832e2bd5db5&ei=5124&partner=digg&exprod=dig.

Orwell, G. (1949). *Nineteen eighty-four. A novel.* New York: Harcourt, Brace & Co.

Paris, E. (2000). *Long shadows: Truth, lies, and history.* London: Bloomsbury Publishing PLC.

"Return to Vimy Ridge" (2007). About Vimy Ridge (n.d.) Retrieved July 26, 2007 from: http://www.returntovimyridge.ca/aboutvimy.htm.

Roe, M. D. (2003). Cowlitz Indian ethnic identity, social memories and 150 years of conflict with the United States government. In E. Carins & M. D. Roe (Eds.), *The role of memory in ethnic conflict* (pp. 55–74). New York: Palgrave Macmillan.

Ross, H., Ross, M., Stein, N., & Trabasso, T. (2006). How siblings resolve their conflicts: The importance of first offers, planning, and limited opposition. *Child Development, 77,* 1730–1745.

Ross, M. (1989). The relation of implicit theories to the construction of personal histories. *Psychological Review, 96,* 341–357.

Ross, M., & Schumann (2007). How and why governments apologize. Talk presented at the *11th Ontario Symposium: The psychology of justice and legitimacy,* University of Waterloo, Waterloo, Ontario, Canada.

Sahdra, B., & Ross, M. (2007). Group identification and historical memory. *Personality and Social Psychology Bulletin, 33,* 384–395.

Tajfel, H., & Turner, J. C. (1986). The social identity theory of inter-group behavior. In S. Worchel and L. W. Austin (Eds.), *Psychology of intergroup relations* (pp. 2–24). Chicago: Nelson-Hall.

Thompson, J. (2002). *Taking responsibility for the past: Reparation and historical justice.* Cambridge, UK: Polity Press.

Valpy, M. (2007, April 7). Vimy Ridge: The making of a myth. *The Globe and Mail.* Retrieved July 30, 2007 from: http://www.theglobeandmail.com/servlet/story/RTGAM.20070406.cover07/BNStory/VimyRidge/home.

Viles, P. (2002, March 27). Suit seeks billions in reparations. *Cable News Network (CNN).* Retrieved August 24, 2006 from http://archives.cnn.com/2002/LAW/03/26/ slavery.reparations.

"Virginia Expresses 'Profound Regret'" (2007, February 24). Virginia expresses 'profound regret' for role in slave-trade. *CBC news online.* Retrieved April 14, 2007 from http://www.cbc.ca/world/story/2007/02/24/virginia-slavery.html.

10

The Memory Boom: Why and Why Now?

DAVID W. BLIGHT

> Memory is as the affection: we remember the things
> which we love and the things which we hate.
> Ralph Waldo Emerson

Almost nothing renders us human as much as our unique capacity for memory. Other animals surely have memory in biological and even social forms. They can do amazing things in flocks and herds. But no other creatures can use memory to create, to record experience, to forge self-conscious associations, to form and practice language, to know, collect, narrate, and write their pasts. We not only can know at least some of our past; we know that we can know it. Sometimes it seems that memory really is the root, the fountain of human intelligence. It is this deeply human power of memory that makes it so ubiquitous, so essential to human life, but also such a problem and such a subject of inquiry. As the Israeli philosopher Avishai Margalit has written: "Memory is knowledge from the past. It is not necessarily knowledge about the past" (Margalit, 2004). In everyday life, and in the world of scholarship (whether cognitive psychology, neuroscience, anthropology, literature, or history), all considerations of memory seem perpetually to ride on the teeter-totter of trust and distrust, up and down, with distrust carrying the most weight, and trust struggling to keep the teeter-totter moving at all. Can we believe what memory provides us? Can we afford not to? Is it part of human nature to perpetually struggle to live without memory only to be forever trapped in its tentacles or lost in its mists?

But memory's power is everywhere and the testimonies ancient. In *The Confessions,* St. Augustine refers to memory as the "vast court," the "treasury" in the mind. He stands in awe of its force – a great "chamber," he calls it, and no one had "sounded the bottom thereof." "Great is the power of memory," Augustine wrote, "a fearful thing. O my God, a deep and

boundless manifoldness; and this thing is the mind, and this am I myself."
Augustine seems convinced that we are our memories: they dictate to us,
we respond to them, and we endlessly revise them. Memory can control
us, overwhelm us, even poison us. Or it can save us from confusion and
despair. As individuals we cannot live effectively without it; but it is also
part of the agony of the human condition to live with it as well. Is all of this
equally true when memory takes on the collective, social, group form? How
do we know a collective memory when we meet one? Do whole societies
take their very sustenance from memory in similar ways as individuals?
Svetlana Boym, a scholar of nostalgia, aptly called collective memory "a
messy, unsystematic concept." We do indeed need to be careful with terms
such as popular and collective memory. We need to tie them to historical particulars and to specific contexts. But the idea of collective memory
is indispensable to understanding how people comprehend themselves in
time. Collective memories, writes Boym, provide the "common landmarks
of everyday life." Instinctively, and I think empirically, we know that memory has this powerful social dimension. We should worry about memory
collectively as Augustine worried personally. Contending social memories
explode in our faces every day in the world. Historians ignore the social
power of memory at their peril. Pierre Nora defined collective memory as
"what remains of the past in the lived reality of groups, or what these groups
make of the past" (Augustine, [398]1996; Boym 2001; Nora, 1989). This process of making collective memories goes on every day in all societies. It is
that making of collective memory, through all its many mediums, that is
our subject – why and how it happens, and who controls it?

Historians especially do not ordinarily trust memory, but we have been
captured by its charms, its significance, its role in helping us explain how
history is used and understood, how versions of the past endlessly contend
with one another for control over the sovereign present, and how the study
of memory is also the study of forgetting – willful, organized, or unconscious. In *The Hamlet*, William Faulkner reminds us of our human weakness when it comes to embarrassing or traumatic memory. "Only thank
God men have done learned how to forget quick," says one of his characters,
"what they ain't brave enough to try to cure." What a nice, succinct characterization of Civil War memory in the United States. And then there is
Mark Twain, warning us simply not to depend on memory at all as a human
faculty. "When I was a young man," said Twain, "I remembered everything
whether it happened or not. But now that I am an old man, I remember only
the things that never happened" (Faulkner, 1931; Rasmussen, 1995; http://
www.twainquotes.com). But even though we know the world is riven with

too much memory, too much war, nationalism, and exploitation enacted in the name of some kind of memory, in the balance sheet of remembrance versus forgetting, it is far more dangerous to forget.

When a tourist arrives at the Bahnhof in Weimar, in eastern Germany, he or she is confronted with a very rare orientation. A large sign reads: "Yes, this is the city where so much great art was created. It is also the city next to Buchenwald. Weimar is both, and we want you to be aware of this awful contradiction while you are here." (How adept are Americans at confronting their own deepest contradictions?) Heinrich Himmler had the famous Goethe oak tree cut down up in the gorgeous forested hills above Weimar to build the death camp of Buchenwald. The Nazis were perverted priests of contradiction. As James Young has written, Himmler and other Nazis were so adept at neutralizing and stealing Goethe's "cultural authority" (and German romanticism generally) and turning it into barbed wire and mass murder ("Weimar Claims," 2007; Young, 1993). So often, it seems, it is in the starkest or most brutal of historical contradictions that we find our deepest understanding of the obligation to remember.

Those without a sense of irony or tragedy will probably never understand the compelling power of historical memory. In metaphors of beauty and horror, we also know why we have art, and there may be no art without memory. Frederick Douglass's metaphors of freedom in his *Narrative* provide unforgettable reminders. He remembers standing as a lost and desperate teenage slave on a ridge overlooking Chesapeake Bay, viewing a multitude of sailing ships. "Those beautiful vessels, robed in purest white," he writes, were "so many shrouded ghosts, to terrify and torment me with thoughts of my wretched condition." As he pours out his "soul's complaint" in autobiographical remembrance, Douglass puts his own voice in quotation marks and speaks to the ships: "You are loosed from your moorings, and are free; I am fast in my chains and am a slave! You move merrily before the gale, and I sadly before the bloody whip! You are freedom's swift-winged angels that fly around the world; I am confined in bands of iron! O that I were free! O that I were on one of your gallant decks!" (Douglass, [1845]2003). In the depth of such remembered contradictions, and in the spirit to overcome them, we find our most compelling reasons why we remember in spite of ourselves. As readers of Douglass, or for that matter of Goethe, we can sit with the poets, in the dark nights of our own souls, along our own Chesapeake Bay or our own Ettersberg mountain above the valley of Weimar, and contemplate the deepest yearnings of our own tortured and distracted times.

For the past (nearly) two decades a "memory boom," or "memory industry" has swept over both scholarship and civic life. Among historians, the problem of what Patrick Hutton has called the "history/memory puzzle" seems to have first crept into our discourse in the 1960s and 1970s with the study of collective "mentalities" in European history (Hutton, 1993, 2005; Klein, 2000). The broad revolution in social history no doubt led us with time to social memory, although preoccupations with race, gender, and class have made many hard-boiled social historians suspicious of this turn toward something often too loosely and vaguely termed cultural memory. Before 1980, it was rare to see any citations with the word "memory" in the title; today, it appears everywhere and has caused somewhat of a backlash and accusations of trendiness. The linguistic turn in intellectual and cultural history in the 1970s and 1980s also no doubt ushered some historians down the memory road, as did a widespread debate over the nature and validity of the constructedness of narrative and knowledge itself. If hardly anyone believed anymore in the "noble dream" of neutral narratives, then the subject might as well be competing narratives – memories and counter-memories – and how they emerge in relation to social and political power.

Moreover, the bloody history of the twentieth century made us more concerned with how nations organize their pasts, how they forge creation stories, invent traditions, and how and why great violence can be committed in the name of memory. As national identity became a prime subject in many disciplines in the second half of the twentieth century, following on the disintegration of empires which themselves now had to explain their pasts to increasingly pluralistic and skeptical populations, how could "memory studies" be far behind? And years behind anthropologists, historians discovered the work of Maurice Halbwachs, whose insights into how we remember collectively in groups, associations, communities, frameworks, and ever-changing contexts served those historians who now wanted to discern how historical consciousness is formed in any given culture. In many ways, what historians used to suspiciously or derisively refer to as "myth" transformed in the 1980s and 1990s into the study of memory. We came to realize – again, or more than ever – that myths are the deeply encoded stories from history that acquire with time a symbolic power in any culture. We came to understand, with Roland Barthes, that myths are ideas, values, or stories that have lost "the memory that they were ever made" up. A myth, wrote Barthes, "organizes a world that is without contradictions ... a world ... wallowing in the evident ... a blissful clarity: things appear to mean something by themselves" (Barthes, 1957; Halbwachs, 1950). The role of the historian has always been to correct this "blissful clarity" in public knowledge – to push our noses into the contradictions – but we have to first know why and how such myths take hold and endure beyond our capacity to write and teach them away.

What historians studying memory have come to understand, simply put, is that the process by which societies or nations remember collectively itself has a history; and we have been writing, for better or worse, histories of memory. Some historians, notably my colleague at Yale, Jay Winter, have argued that we have just gotten too vague and loose with the ubiquitous use of the idea of memory. Winter suggests we replace the term "memory" with "acts of remembrance" in order to distinguish particular ways, sites, or practices in which memory is displayed. Because memory is so "unstable, plastic, synthetic, and reshaped," writes Winter, we need a better terminology and more attention to the historical detail, through good research, by which memory struggles unfold (Winter, 2006). I could not agree more that the study of memory needs careful research, in old fashioned and imaginative ways. Sometimes the study of memory can seem like just one damned commemoration or ritual after another with no framework, as though history is really nothing more than competing parades and monuments. But I see no good reason yet to abandon the term *memory*, and we cannot avoid contrasting it with the scholarly craft of history.

"Memory is today our inspiration," writes Paul Hutton, and "history as an art of memory will be remembered as the historiographical signature of our times." And Winter has called it the historians' "generational signature." That may be true, but history and memory have distinct boundaries, and we should maintain them as best we can. History and memory are two attitudes toward the past, two streams of historical consciousness that must at some point flow into one another. Historians are custodians of the past; we are the preservers and discoverers of the facts and stories out of which people imagine their civic lives. But we need a sense of both humility and engagement in the face of public-popular memory. "The remembered past," warned John Lukacs, "is a much larger category than the recorded past" (Hutton, 2005; Lukacs, 1968). We might wish the public would demonstrate a more critical sense of history, that they would listen to their professors and teachers and read good history; but shutting off antiquarianism is like stopping Niagara. And often a grandparent simply carries far more authority than we do, and a feel-good story can trump our tragedies and contradictions any day of the week on the History Channel.

History is what trained historians do, a reasoned reconstruction of the past rooted in research; it tends to be skeptical of human motive and action, and therefore more secular than what we commonly call memory. History can belong to or be read by everyone; it is more relative, and contingent on time, place, and scale. But if history is shared and secular, memory is often treated as a sacred set of absolute meanings and stories, possessed as the heritage or identity of a community. Memory is often owned, history interpreted. Memory is passed down through generations; history is revised generation after generation. Memory often coalesces in objects, sites, monuments; history seeks to understand contexts in all their complexity. History asserts the authority of academic training and rules of evidence; memory carries the more immediate authority of community membership or family experience. In an essay on the slave trade and memory, Bernard Bailyn aptly stated memory's appeal: "Its relation to the past is an embrace ... ultimately emotional, not intellectual" (Bailyn, 2001). And we know that this contrast between history and memory matters when our highest political leaders do not even comprehend the meaning of the term "revisionism" when they use it to deride or condemn critics of their policies?

There can be no doubt that the "history/memory puzzle" has caught on with remarkable traction in the past two decades or so. And over the past century, the Western world has experienced at least two major memory booms. The first took place roughly during 1890–1920, leading up to and transformed by World War I and its staggering losses. That boom was rooted in the collapse of empires, the origins of new nation-states, a nostalgia for vanishing worlds and cultures, in industrial and urban alienation, in newly invented traditions and widespread monument building, in celebration days on national calendars, and in a host of major intellectuals who probed memory in their work (including Henry Bergson, Sigmund Freud, Marcel Proust, Virginia Wolf, Maurice Halbwachs, and others). In America, two memory booms also occurred during approximately the same periods. Let me suggest my own list of reasons for the current phenomenon of a memory boom from a historian's perspective. This list is hardly exhaustive, it is not in any particular order of priority, and meant only to be suggestive.

THE SHEER SCALE OF VIOLENCE IN THE TWENTIETH CENTURY

The mixture of nationalism, imperialism, and technology in war in the twentieth century made it the most violent in human history. Perhaps this has created a new paradigm in which all human societies have to measure their values, institutions, and prospects (or we wish they would). If the nineteenth century was the century of "progress," as so many have claimed, the twentieth century, in spite of all its marvels of scientific development and imagination (its enormous strides in medicine, in women's rights, and in life expectancy), has left a most indelible mark on our comprehension of human evil. In his 1994 book *The Age of Extremes: A History of the World,*

1914–1991, Eric Hobsbawm makes this point. Among the twelve eminent thinkers he asked to comment on the ultimate meaning of the twentieth century at the outset of the book is the Spanish anthropologist Julio Carlos Baroja, who captures the incongruence between individual survival and comfort and the horrific violence of our age. "There's a great contradiction," says Baroja, "between one's own life experience – childhood, youth, and old age passed quietly and without major adventures – and the facts of the twentieth century … the terrible events through which humanity has lived through" (Hobsbaum, 1994). Because our species has been so violent in the past four to five generations, perhaps social memory has reached a new scale of potency and visibility. War and genocide in the past century (and in our current post–9/11 world as well) has challenged us with uncounted numbers of victims and witnesses whose stories must be known. In the twentieth century, it was the victims of wars, not merely those who fought, who became the subject along with their testimony. As never before, the witness to or the victim of great violence is the new and most determining engine of memory – legally and morally, whether in war crimes trials, truth commissions, autobiographies, films, or other mediums.

THE HOLOCAUST

Perhaps it is obvious, but just how, and how much, Jews and other Americans, as well as citizens of all other countries, ought (or were able) to develop a sense of the past in relation to the Nazi Holocaust during World War II became the central symbol of historical memory consciousness in the last quarter of the twentieth century. Peter Novick's recent book, *The Holocaust in American Life*, which argued that Americans had become obsessed and stultified by Holocaust remembrance, touched many nerves, and reminded us of the dangers of a surfeit of memory. But it only added fuel to the fire of memory study and entered an argument without end. Daniel Goldhagen's 1996 book, *Hitler's Willing Executioners: Ordinary Germans and the Holocaust*, served as a lesson in just how vexing the meaning of the Holocaust is for developing any sense of a normal past for the middle of the twentieth century in Germany. And a decade before that, the famous Historikerstreit in Germany (the "historians' controversy"), succeeded by a "limits of representation" debate in the 1990s, exposed the agony of "debating" the Holocaust at all. The Historikerstreit was an extended exchange between opposing sides respresented by the historian Ernst Nolte and the philosopher Jurgen Habermas. Nolte argued that the Holocaust should not be treated as a unique event but as part of and compared to other atrocities in history that were just as evil (Stalin's mass murders for example). Habermas charged Nolte and his defenders of trying to "normalize" (Goldhagen, 1996; Maier, 1988; Novick, 1999) Nazism in a new, conservative narrative of German nationalism, to integrate Auschwitz into a longer view of German development. As a subject in historiography and of public history in many parts of the world (museums in Germany, memorials in cities all over the West, and in the National Holocaust Museum in Washington, DC), Holocaust studies and commemorations continue unabated.

ANNIVERSARY CONSCIOUSNESS

Beginning with the American Bicentennial in 1975–1976, but especially taking hold in the 1980s and 1990s with the bicentennial of the French Revolution, the centennial of the Statue of Liberty, a host of World War II commemorations, and then the Columbus quincentennial, the world has witnessed a preoccupation with civic remembrance as perhaps never before. This is in part media-driven and politically driven, but it also reflects something deeper in our cultural need for therapeutic remembrance and absolution at the end of the twentieth and beginning of the twenty-first centuries. For Americans, the coming flood of books, conferences, films, and commemorations surrounding the two-hundredth anniversary of the birth of Abraham Lincoln in 2009 and the Civil War sesquicentennial to follow will be hard to avoid.

THE END OF THE COLD WAR

Perhaps nothing politicized and proliferated expressions of identity and memory as the great changes of 1989–1991. After 1989, with startling suddenness, the struggle over public, collective memories became a burgeoning international controversy. This has led to new nations, new secessions, new wars and genocides, all of which are enacted at least in part in the name of memory. The Cold War, it seems, contained for a long time a certain urge in the world to kill for memory. On the positive side, democracies have also emerged in the name of memory. Unfortunately, the urge to kill for memory is both ancient and new every day and every generation in the world.

THE EXPLOSION OF NEW HISTORIES

The multiplication of knowledge, the creation of whole new fields of study, especially the phenomenon of "area studies" in the humanities, and the advent of the variety of persuasions and theories that travel under the label, postmodernism, have brought a new and powerful challenge to the idea of objective knowledge in historical studies. Relativism is nothing new to historians, but this challenge has caused greater attention to be placed on questions of group memories, even the notion of racial memory and gendered ways of knowing. All the new subjectivity has also brought increased interest in competing versions of the past and in the illusive problem of "authenticity" in language, behavior, and cultural expression.

MULTICULTURALISM AND MUSEUM CONTROVERSIES

In America, our growing pluralism and diversity, coupled with a post–Cold War turning inward of national concerns, fomented a series of "culture wars" over racial, ethnic, and interest group memories and identities. This has led to numerous disputes over national history standards for curriculum, and over museum exhibits of all kinds, struggles over who owns cultural artifacts, bones, sites, their names and interpretations. We do not tend to call such disputes multiculturalism as much as we used to, but it has fostered an often valuable debate over whether we can ever again achieve a unified national narrative of American history – in schooling or in the political culture. The pursuit of the whole from its parts, the story of the one and the many, has been a troubled but rewarding journey down the memory road. The public museum has become the site of much of our contention over who owns the past and how it ought to be represented. Whose stories will be told in the public arena (in the spaces of our civil religion, on the Mall in Washington, DC)? The debacle over the Enola Gay exhibit at the National Air and Space Museum is only the most famous example of many such controversies. Ed Linenthal and Tom Englehardt's book *History Wars* (1996) examined this dispute and others. And Linenthal, in a marvelous book on the Oklahoma City bombing, *The Unfinished Bombing*, demonstrated poignantly the growing rift between the "commemorative voice" and the "historical voice" in public history discourse (Linenthal, 2001; Linenthal & Engelhardt, 1996).

HERITAGE TOURISM AND THE COMMODIFICATION OF MEMORY

State-sponsored, highly commercial tourism to historical and cultural sites has become one of the largest growth industries in the world. Such heritage pilgrimages and consciousness is, no doubt, having a profound impact on public tastes for history; journeys into realms of nostalgia and exoticism are available for anyone who can afford to travel. The market for such tourism has stimulated an even greater obsession with the illusive idea of "authenticity" in objects, sites and material culture. Affluence and demographic change have shaped this phenomenon in recent decades; far more people are in higher education than ever before in Western developed countries and they have leisure time and disposable income for "culture" as never before. The bibliography that the Gilder Lehrman Center for the Study of Slavery and Abolition compiles and publishes each year on "Slavery and Abolition" across the globe, shows no less than 50 entries for 2004 on the field of public history and heritage tourism alone (Lowenthal, 1996).

THE GROWING DISTANCE BETWEEN PROFESSIONAL HISTORY AND PUBLIC MEMORY

The popularity of film, novels, and popular histories, and an apparent distrust out in the mass culture for "academic" history, demonstrates a serious gulf between elite knowledge and the huge public interest in the past. The "loss of audience," the power of the visual mediums, the struggle to establish a new paradigm of what academic authority even means in this age of mass culture are all concerns for those of us who study memory in modern societies. At least among some historians, I think we became intrigued with the Memory Boom because we want to reach wider audiences and fear irrelevance.

AN AGE OF DIMINISHED EXPECTATIONS

Perhaps we are living in a time of an extended fin-de-siècle melancholia, an era of the decline or exhaustion of civic culture. If since the end of the clarity – the unities and certainties – of the Cold War (or since the great upheavals of the 1960s), we have experienced a breakdown in agreed-upon institutions, values, languages, or methods of cohesion, then this too may account, in part, for a growing social preoccupation with memory and identity. Perhaps many people for two and three decades now have been looking backward or inward, or for escapes into nostalgia and heritage they can possess, when looking ahead is no longer a source of confidence. Finding a memory community is much better than "bowling alone" (Putnam, 2000).

THE URGE TO REPAIR, OR RAGE FOR RESTITUTION

All over the world at the beginning of the twenty-first century, nations and cultures are struggling to heal from, memorialize, adjudicate, or at least understand and explain traumatic pasts. Untold scars have been left on individuals and whole societies awaiting some kind of airing, confrontation, or justice. In the past two decades, no less than some 20 truth or reconciliation commissions of one kind and another have been attempted in nearly as many countries. In the 1990s, it is as if the sepulcher of the past was opened, the power of "victim" groups rose markedly, and stories of past oppression by armies, dictatorships, prison systems, apartheids, and even democratic governments like the United States in the case of the Japanese internment, came rushing out. And many anguished questions flowed out of that sepulcher as well: What does the present owe the past? Who or what decides the nature of "repair" for past wrongs? (Brooks, 2004; Thompson, 2002; Torpey, 2006). Where do the moral and the practical meet in remembering and debating crimes or social evils that evolved in centuries long past? What is collective, intergenerational responsibility for the past? For slavery? What is it about modernity in the past century, much less the recent decades, that has allowed, or compelled the creation of spaces where these questions have become so pressing and contested in the marketplace of ideas? What would reparations for something like New World slavery look like in our time? Should we try to see it through a tort lens, a legal class action claim on society by descendants of slaves? Or should we only hope for any real repair through a lens of atonement, of apology and all manner of symbolic action that might lead to social policy? This is, of course, a rich, controversial debate with a long shelf life.

On September 9, 2001, 2 days before the attacks on New York and Washington, the United Nations conference of racism and retrospective justice in Durban, South Africa, boycotted by the Bush administration, issued several resolutions. The first is so simple it almost reads like a middle school lesson of the day. But its words may say it all about why we are reaping this memory harvest, with all its lessons and its blood. "We are conscious," said the U.N. Declaration, "of the fact that the history of humanity is replete with major atrocities as a result of the gross violation of human rights and believe that lessons can be learned through remembering history to avert future tragedies." "Never forget" has become such a cliché in our times. But it lies deep at the root of the memory boom and always will. When faced, understanding the worst aspects of the past can lead us to knowledge and light, if not redemption. Thus could Avishai Margalit conclude that "even the project of remembering the gloomiest of memories is a hopeful project. Probing the genuine tragedy in the past, those stories that fit no progressive narrative and crash into dead ends, says Margalit, "rejects the pessimist thought that all will be forgotten ..." "Why ought humanity remember moral nightmares rather than moments of human triumph – moments in which human beings behaved nobly," he asks? Because, Margalit contends, "the issue for us to sort out is what humanity ought to remember rather than what is good for humanity to remember" (Margalit, 2001).

There are, of course, risks as historians alter their gaze on to matters of social and public memory. We could become servants of the very "culture wars" that have given rise to so many struggles over memory in our time. Memory is usually invoked in the name of nation, ethnicity, race, religion, or someone's felt need for peoplehood and victimhood. It often thrives on grievance; its lifeblood is mythos and telos. Like our subjects, we can risk thinking with memory rather than about it. The world is riven with too much memory; its obsessions can paralyze whole peoples and stifle democratizing and universalizing principles. But it is precisely because of this dilemma that we should study historical memory. We should know its uses and perils, its values and dark tendencies. People will develop a sense of history by one means or another. The greatest risk, writes the essayist Cynthia Ozick, is that they will derive that sense of the past only from the "fresh-hatched inspiration" of their "Delphic priests." History is often weak in the face of the mythic power of memory and its many oracles. But we run the greatest risk in ignoring that weakness, wishing that the public would adopt a more critical, interpretive sense of the past. "Cut off from the uses of history, experience, and memory," cautions Ozick, the "inspirations" alone of any culture's Delphic priests "are helpless to make a future" (Ozick, 1991). As historians, we are bound by our craft and by our humanity to study the problem of memory, and thereby help make a future.

We must respect the poets and priests, honoring them by studying and learning from them. We should study and understand the power of the myths that define societies and cultures. But then, standing at the confluence of the two stream (history and memory), we should write the history of memory, observing and explaining the turbulence we find. In "To a Historian," Walt Whitman invited us to mingle our best skills with his own in this exciting task:

> You who celebrate bygones,
> Who have explored the outward, the surfaces of the races, the life that
>   has exhibited itself,
> Who have treated of man as the creature of politics, aggregates, rulers
>   and priests,
> I, habitan of the Alleghanies, treating of him as he is in himself in his
>   own rights,
> Pressing the pulse of the life that has seldom exhibited itself, (the great
>   pride of man in himself)

Chanter of Personality, outlining what is yet to be,
I project the history of the future (Whitman, 1926).

Whitman says the poet can see further ahead by seeing deeper into the
human condition than the scholar who is restricted to researching surfaces.
Perhaps. But we should take his challenge. Neither poets nor historians can
stand alone in using and explaining the past. Because all memory is in some
way prelude, we have to chant together.

REFERENCES

Augustine ([398]1996). *Confessions*. (E. B. Pussy, Trans.) New York: Book of the Month Club.

Bailyn, B. (2001). Considering the slave trade: History and memory. *William and Mary Quarterly*, *58*(1), 245–252.

Barthes, R. (1957). *Mythologies*. London: Jonathan Cape.

Boym, S. (2001). *The future of Nostalgia*. New York: Basic Books.

Brooks, R. L. (2004). *Atonement and forgiveness: A new model for black reparations*. Berkley: University of California Press.

Douglass, F. ([1845]2003). *Narrative of the life of Frederick Douglass, Written by Himself*. Boston: Bedford Books.

Faulkner, W. (1931). *The Hamlet: A novel of the Snopes family*. New York: Random House.

Goldhagen, D. J. (1996). *Hitler's willing executioners: Ordinary Germans and the Holocaust*. New York: Knopf.

Halbwachs, M. (1950). *The collective memory*. New York: Harper and Row.

Hobsbaum, E. (1994). *The age of extremes: A history of the world, 1914–1991*. New York: Pantheom.

Hutton, P. H. (1993). *History as an art of memory*. Hanover, NH: University Press of New England.

   (2005). Quickening memory and the diversification of historical narrative. *Historical Reflections/reflexions Historiques*, *31*(2), 201–216.

Klein, K. L. (2000). On the emergence of memory in historical discourse. *Representations*, *69*, 127–150.

Linenthal, E. T. (2001). *The unfinished bombing: Oklahoma city in American memory*. New York: Oxford University Press.

Linenthal, E. T., & Engelhardt, T. (Eds.). (1996). *History wars: The Enola Gay and other battles for the American past*. New York: Metropolitan Books.

Lowenthal, D. (1996). *Possessed by the past: The heritage crusade and the spoils of history*. New York: Free Press.

Lukacs, J. (1968). *Historical consciousness or the remembered past*. New York: Schocken Books.

Maier C. (1988). *The unmasterable past: History, holocaust, and German national identity*. Cambridge: Harvard University Press.

Margalit, A. (2001, September 9). Ethics of memory. *New York Times*, pp. 83–84.

   (2004). *The ethics of memory*. Cambridge: Harvard University Press.

Nora, P. (1989). Between memory and history: Les Lieux de Memoire. *Representations, 26*, 7–25.

Novick, P. (1999). *The holocaust in American life*. Boston: Houghton Mifflin.

Ozick, C. (1991). *Metaphor and memory: Essays* (p. 281). New York: Vintage International.

Putnam, R. (2000). *Bowling alone: The collapse and revival of American community*. New York: Simon and Schuster.

Rasmussen, R. K. (1995). *Mark Twain A to Z: The essential reference to his life and writings*. New York: Facts on File.

Thompson, J. (2002). *Taking responsibility for the past: Reparation and historical justice*. Cambridge, UK: Polity.

Torpey, J. (2006). *Making whole what has been smashed*. Cambridge: Harvard University Press.

Weimar Claims its Past, Including the Horrors. (2007, May 15). *New York Times*.

Whitman, W. (1926). To a historian. In E. Holloway (Ed.), *Leaves of Grass* (p. 3). Garden City, NY: Doubleday.

Winter, J. (2006). *Remembering war: The Great War between memory and history in the twentieth century*. New Haven: Yale University Press. www.twainquotes.com.

Young, J. E. (1993). *The texture of memory: Holocaust memorials and meaning*. New Haven: Yale University Press.

11

Historians and Sites of Memory

JAY WINTER

Historians are interested in sites of memory, understood as places where groups of people engage in public activity through which they express "a collective shared knowledge ... of the past, on which a group's sense of unity and individuality is based" (Assmann, 1995). The group that goes to such sites inherits earlier meanings attached to the event, as well as adding new meanings. Their activity is crucial to the presentation and preservation of commemorative sites. When such groups disperse or disappear, sites of memory lose their initial force, and may fade away entirely. Thus, historians are more interested in remembrance as a cultural practice than in memory as an individual's capacity to recall or reconfigure the past.

The term, sites of memory, abumbrated in a seven-volume study edited by Pierre Nora (n.d.) has been extended to many different texts, from legends, to stories, to concepts. In this brief essay, I define the term more narrowly to mean physical sites where commemorative acts take place. In the twentieth century, most such sites marked the loss of life in war. It is these sites that have attracted the attention of entire battalions of historians in the past twenty-five years.

What makes such sites of memory attractive for historical research is their character as topoi with a life history. They have an initial, creative phase, when they are constructed or adapted to particular commemorative purposes. Then follows a period of institutionalization and routinization of their use. Such markings of the calendar, indicating moments of remembrance at particular places, can last for decades, or they can be abruptly halted. In most instances, the significance of sites of memory fades away with the passing of the social groups which initiated the practice. There are entire libraries of historical accounts of this trajectory on the local, national, and transnational level.

What lies behind this literature are archives. Sites of memory operate on many levels of aggregation and touches many facets of associative life. Although such sites were familiar in the ancient and medieval period, they have proliferated in more recent times. Consequently, the subject has attracted much academic and popular discussion. We therefore concentrate here on sites of memory in the epoch of the nation state, primarily in the nineteenth and twentieth centuries. States leave behind mountains of documents, and these sources – written or visual – have given flesh and blood to the work of scholars all over the world.

A second feature of this subject accounts for its recent interest throughout the historical profession. The Weberian model of secularization has been coming under increasingly caustic criticism. Historians have found many ways to trace the presence of the sacred in modern life. To a great degree, the sacred has moved outside the churches and into secular space. Commemorative sites, alongside museums and exhibitions, are now repositories of the sacred; they are the churches and cathedrals of modernity. They have their own calendars, parallel to but distinct from the liturgical one. In the modern period, most sites of memory were imbedded in events marked distinctively and separately from the religious calendar. However, there has been some overlap. Visiting a commemorative site on Armistice Day, November 11, in countries remembering the end of the 1914–1918 war, is close enough to the Catholic feast of All Saints on November 2; in some countries with a large Catholic population, the two days occupy a semisacred space of public commemoration. First comes the visit to the cemetery; then the visit to the war memorial or other site. The day marking the end of World War II in Europe, May 8, is also the saint's day of Joan of Arc. Those engaging in commemorative acts on that day may be addressing the secular celebration or the Catholic one; some celebrate the two together. Usually the site chosen to mark the day differs.

Here, too, we can see why historians flock to this subject. It is a lightning rod to catch the energy imbedded in moral discourse in modern society. Commemoration at sites of memory is an act arising out of a conviction, shared by a broad community, that the moment recalled is both significant and informed by a moral message. Sites of memory materialize that message. Moments of national humiliation are rarely commemorated or marked in material form, although here, too, there are exceptions of a hortatory kind. "Never again" is the hallmark of public commemoration on the Israeli Day of Remembrance for victims of the Nazi persecution of the Jews. The shell of public buildings in Hiroshima remind everyone of the moment the city was incinerated in the first atomic attack. Where moral doubts persist about a war or public policy, commemorative sites are either hard to fix or places of contestation. That is why there is no date or place for those who want to commemorate the end of the Algerian War in France, or the end of the Vietnam War in the United States. There was no moral consensus about the nature of the conflict; hence, there was no moral consensus about what was being remembered in public, and when and where were the appropriate time and place to remember it (Prost, 1999).

When the Japanese prime minister visits a shrine to war dead, he is honoring war criminals as well as ordinary soldiers. The same was true when President Ronald Reagan visited the German cemetery at Bitburg, where lie the remains of SS men alongside the graves of those not implicated in war crimes. And yet both places were sites of memory; contested memory; embittered memory, but memory nonetheless.

The critical point about sites of memory is that they are there as points of reference not only for those who survived traumatic events but also for those born long after them. The word "memory" becomes a metaphor for the fashioning of narratives about the past when those with direct experience of events die off. Sites of memory inevitably become sites of second-order memory, or postmemory, that is, they are places where people remember the memories of others, those who survived the events marked there. Historians have made this theme a matter of considerable scholarly work in recent years.

HISTORICAL REMEMBRANCE AND SITES OF MEMORY

One important philosophical matter has drawn the critical gaze of historians. It is to object to a stylized and unpersuasive analytical distinction between history on one side as documented narratives and memory on the other as free-floating tales that may or may not be true. Historians think otherwise, and work to bring the two closer together. Increasingly, over the twentieth century and beyond, the space between history and memory has been reconfigured. In between is a varied set of cultural practices that may be described as forms of "historical remembrance." Many such practices emerge when people confront sites of memory. In doing so, such people engage in a practice that I term "historical remembrance." The term is an alloy, a compound, which we need because the two defining concepts we normally use, history and memory, are insufficient guides to this field. Commemoration requires reference to history, but then the contestation begins. Whose history, written for whose benefit, and on which records? The contemporary memory boom is about history, to be sure, but historians are not its sole or even its central proprietors. Witnesses demand the right to be heard, whatever historians say. When the Enola Gay exhibition at the

Smithsonian Institution in Washington, "The Last Act: The Atomic Bomb and the End of World War II," was constructed painstakingly as history in 1995, it was attacked and rejected by people – ex-servicemen – who had their own history. And the "witnesses" won. The exhibition was reorganized. This was no simple tale of sordid political pressure. Here was a real collision between "history" and "memory," a collision arising out of the different subject positions of those involved in the exhibition. The outcome was a kind of "historical remembrance" which made space for the claims both of historians and of those whose lives as soldiers they were describing.

If "history" has difficulty in withstanding the challenges of "memory," the opposite case can be just as problematic. Witnesses forget, or reconstruct their narratives as a kind of collage, or merge what they saw with what they read. Memory alone renders history, a documented account of the past, impossible. Furthermore, "memory" is a category with its own history, and its own mysteries. Cognitive psychologists and neuroscientists have taken huge strides in understanding how individuals remember, but leaders in the field admit that there is a vast amount of fundamental work still to be done. How much harder is it to construct a model or set of pathways to describe how groups of people remember together?

And yet these traces are all around us. "Historical remembrance" is a discursive field, extending from ritual to cultural work of many different kinds. It differs from family remembrance by its capacity to unite people who have no other bonds drawing them together. It is distinctive from liturgical remembrance in being freed from a preordained religious calendar and sanctified ritual forms. And yet historical remembrance has something of the familial and something of the sacred in it. When all three are fused, as in some powerful war memorials – Maya Lin's Vietnam memorial in Washington, DC, comes to mind – historical remembrance is a phenomenon of enduring power.

Adopting the term "historical remembrance" has other advantages as well. Using it helps us avoid the pitfalls of referring to memory as some vague cloud that exists without agency, and to history as an objective story that exists outside of the people whose lives it describes. Historians have memories, too, and their choice of subject is rarely accidental. They are part of the memory boom, although not its leading part. When they join other men and women who come together in public to remember the past – their past – they construct a narrative that is not just "history" and not just "memory," but a story that partakes of them both. Historical remembrance is what they do, and how they contribute to a memory boom that extends well beyond the historical profession. Sites of memory are places where historical remembrance happens. The traces of these practices are at the heart of many historical accounts in all parts of the world.

This approach to the subject provides a solution to some of the controversies surrounding the topic of sites of memory. Three in particular stand out. Some critics claim that commemorative practices sacralize war and the political order that governs it (Klein, 2000). But this objection misses the point that pacifists have used sites of memory for precisely the opposite purpose. Languages of mourning have sacred elements in them, but they are never alone. Historical remembrance subsumes these cadences as it admits the power of family rhetoric to shape the language people use when they come to sites of mourning.

A second objection is that sites of memory proliferate because memory has ceased to exist within our lives, and therefore needs to be created in artificial forms. Thus, Pierre Nora spoke of concocted *lieux de mémoire* occupying the space of vanished and authentic *milieux de mémoire* (Nora, 1992). This argument betrays an ingrained Eurocentrism. Anyone who even glances at the power of living sites of memory in Latin America or India, for example, will realize that the distinction cannot hold. *Milieux de mémoire* are alive and well, and so are oral and written traditions of remembrance which inform them.

A third objection is that sites of memory are places where people escape from politics. We remember because we cannot see an achievable future; thus, the efflorescence of interest in sites of memory coincides with the period of disillusionment following the 1960s when Marxism collapsed as a theory of history and a theory of society. Memory, from this angle, is a "fix" for those who fear the future, and who have given up their conviction that they can master it (Maier, 1993, 2001). This argument is incomplete at best. In some cases, the quest for memory does offer an alternative to a plan for the future. But among Guatemalan Indians or Palestinians or Vietnamese people, the construction of narratives about a past recently disfigured by massive violence is not alternative to politics but, rather, its direct expression. Sites of memory are places where local politics happens. The men and women who come to such places arrive with a mixture of motives and hopes; to claim that they are there to flee politics is absurd.

On one point, however, the critical conversation about sites of memory has not gone far enough. All the critics cited here base their arguments on a clear separation of history and memory. This position cannot be sustained. It makes no sense to juxtapose history and memory as adversarial and separate concepts. As I have already noted, they overlap in too many ways to be considered as pure categories, each living in majestic isolation on its separate peak. Historical remembrance is an analytical category of use here, in that it enables us to understand more fully both the field of force between history and memory and the people who fashion, appropriate, and pass on to us sites of memory.

COMMEMORATION AND POLITICAL POWER

Much of the historical debate about sites of memory concerns the extent to which they are instruments of the dominant political elements in a society. One school of opinion emphasizes the usefulness to political elites of public events at such sites establishing the legitimacy of their rule (Nora, n.d.). Some such events are observed by whoever is in power – witness Bastille Day in Paris or Independence Day in Philadelphia or elsewhere in the United States. But other events are closely tied to the establishment of a new regime and the overthrow of an older one: November 7 was the date in the calendar marking the Bolshevik Revolution and establishing the communist regime in power in Russia. That date symbolized the new order and its challenge to its worldwide enemies. The march past of soldiers and weapons deployed by the Soviet army in Moscow was a moment of commemoration as well as of muscular pride, demonstrating outside the Kremlin their place in Russian and world history.

This top-down approach proclaims the significance of sites of memory as a materialization of national, imperial or political identity. Anzac Day, April 25, is celebrated as the moment when the Australian nation was born. It commemorates the landing of Australian and New Zealand troops as part of the British-led expeditionary force sent to Turkey in 1915. The fact that the landing was a failure does not diminish the iconic character of the date to Australians. It is the day, they hold, when their nation came of age (Inglis, 1992). There are many sites of memory where this day is marked. First, people come to war memorials throughout Australia. Second, there is a state event at the Australian War Memorial in Canberra, an edifice built in the shape of Hajia Sofia in Istanbul. On the walls of this building are inscribed the names of all Australian soldiers who died in the war. Third, there is an annual pilgrimage, still robustly attended in the twenty-first century, to the shores of Gallipoli itself. There, Australians mark the Gallipoli landings on the beaches where they took place.

By no means are all commemorative activities or sites of memory associated with warfare. The birthdates of monarchs or deceased presidents are marked in similar ways. Queen Victoria's birthday, May 24, was Empire Day in Britain; now (1999) it is celebrated as Commonwealth Day. The creation of such commemorative dates was part of a wider movement of what some scholars have termed "the invention of tradition." That is, at the end of the nineteenth century, new nation states and preeminent imperial powers deepened the repertoire of their ceremonial activity. Such flourishes of the majesty of power were then immediately sanctified by a spurious pedigree. To display ceremonies with a supposed link to ancient habits or forms located in a foggy and distant past created an effective cover for political innovation, instability, or insecurity (MacKenzie, 1986; Ranger & Hobsbawm, 1986). Interestingly for our purposes, such traditions have only a tenuous attachment to a site, thereby increasing the flexibility of choices available to those who want to invent traditions.

This functionalist interpretation of the history of commemoration has been challenged. A second school of scholarship emphasizes the ways that sites of memory and the public commemorations surrounding them show how dominated groups contest their subordinate status in public. However much political leaders or their agents try to choreograph commemorative activity, there is much space for subversion or creative interpretation of the official commemorative script. Armistice Day, November 11, was, for different groups, a moment when different groups came to war memorials, some for the celebration and others for the denigration of military values. Pacifists announced their message of "Never again" through their presence at such sites of memory; military men and their supporters used these moments and the aura of these sites to glorify the profession of arms, and to demonstrate the duty of citizens, if necessary, to give their lives for their country in a future war. The contradictions in these forms of expression on the same day and in the same places have never been resolved (Gregory, 1994; Winter, 1999).

This alternative interpretation of the political meaning of sites of memory emphasizes the multivocal character of remembrance and the potential for new groups with new causes to appropriate older sites of memory. From this point of view, there is always a chorus of voices in commemorations; some are louder than others, but they never sound alone. Decentering the history of commemoration ensures that we recognize the regional, local, and idiosyncratic character of such activities and the way a top-down approach must be supplemented by a bottom-up approach to the performance of scripts about the past at commemorative sites in villages, small towns, and provincial cities, as well as in the centers of political power.

Very occasionally, these dissonant voices come together, and a national moment of remembrance emerges. However, on such occasions, there is no one single site of memory at which this braiding together of leaders and led takes place. One example of this diffusion of remembrance is the two-minute silence, observed in Britain between 1919 and 1938 at 11 AM on November 11. Telephonists pulled the plugs on all conversations. Traffic stopped. The normal flow of life was arrested. Then the World War II intervened, and such disruption to war production was not in the national interest. Thereafter, the two-minute silence was moved to the Sunday nearest to November 11. But in the two decades between the wars, it was a moment of national reflection, located everywhere. Mass Observation, a pioneering social survey organization, asked hundreds of ordinary people in Britain what they thought about during the silence. The answer was that they thought not of the nation or of victory or of armies but of the men who weren't there. This silence was a meditation about absence. As such, it moved away from political orchestration into the realm of family history. To be sure, families commemorated their own within a wider social and political framework. But the richest texture of remembrance was always within family life. This intersection of the public and the private, the macro-historical and the micro-historical, is what has given commemoration in the twentieth century its power and its rich repertoire of forms. But the very complexity of these processes means that sites of memory are not always the foci of acts of remembrance.

In addition, some buildings have been converted into sites of memory unofficially. A cinema where workers organized a strike, a home where women created a midwifery or child care centre, a school where people made homeless by a natural disaster can all be turned into sites of memory by those who lived important moments there (Hayden, 1992). Official certification is not necessary when groups of people act on their own.

THE BUSINESS OF REMEMBERING

Unofficial sites of memory must be preserved through the time and cash of groups of people. That is a crucial defining feature of sites of memory: they cost money and time to construct or preserve. They require specialists' services – landscapers, cleaners, masons, carpenters, plumbers, and so on; they need funding and, over time, refunding. There are two kinds of expenditure we can trace in the history of sites of memory. The first is capital expenditure; the second is recurrent expenditure.

The land for such sites must be purchased; and an appropriate symbolic form must be designed and then constructed to focus remembrance activities. The first step may require substantial sums of public money. Private land, especially in urban areas, comes at a premium. Then there are the costs of architects' fees, especially when a public competitive tender is offered inviting proposals from professionals. Finally, once the symbolic form is chosen, it must be constructed out of selected materials and finished according to the architect's or artist's designs.

When these projects are national in character, the process of production is in the public eye. National art schools and bodies of "experts" have to have their say. Standards of "taste" and "decorum" are proclaimed. Professional interests and conflicts come into play. Much of this professional infighting is confined to national commemorative projects, but the same complex stepwise procedure occurs on the local level, too, this time without the same level of attendant publicity. Local authorities usually take charge of these projects, and local notables can deflect plans toward their own particular visions, whatever public opinion may think about the subject.

Most of the time, public funding covers only part of the costs of commemorative objects. Public subscriptions are critical, especially in Protestant countries where the concept of utilitarian memorials is dominant. In Catholic countries, the notion of a "useful" memorial is a contradiction in terms; symbolic language and utilitarian language are deemed mutually exclusive. But the Protestant voluntary tradition has it otherwise. In Protestant countries, commemorative projects took many forms, from the sacred to the mundane: in Britain there are memorial wards in hospitals, memorial scholarships in schools and universities, alongside memorial cricket pitches and memorial water troughs for horses. In the United States and in Australia, there are memorial highways. The rule of thumb is that private citizens pick up most of the tab for these memorial forms. The state provides subsidies and occasional matching grants, but the money comes out of the pockets of ordinary people. The same is true in Britain with respect to a very widely shared form of public commemoration: the purchase of paper poppies, the symbol of the Lost Generation of World War I. These poppies are worn on the lapel, and the proceeds of the sale go to aid disabled veterans and their families.

Recurrent expenditure for sites of memory is almost always paid for by taxpayers. War cemeteries require masons and gardeners. The Imperial (now Commonwealth) War Graves Commission looks after hundreds of such cemeteries all over the world. The cost of their maintenance is a public charge. Private charities, in particular Christian groups, maintain German war cemeteries. Once constructed, memorial statues, cemeteries, or highways also become public property, and require public support to prevent them from decomposing. They are preserved as sites of commemorative activity, and leave all kinds of records which historians have used with alacrity.

Much of this commemorative activity is directed toward inviting the public to remember in public. This means directing the public toward particular sites of remembrance. Some of them are nearby their homes. In Britain and France, there are war memorials in every city, in every town, and in every village; it is there that Armistice Day ceremonies are held annually. Churches throughout Europe of all denominations have memorial plaques to those who died in war. Special prayers were added to the Jewish prayer book to commemorate the victims of the Nazis in World War II, and later, those who died on active service in the Israeli army.

Remembrance in local houses of worship or at war memorials required that the public travel a short distance from their homes to sites of remembrance. But given the scale of losses in the two world wars, and the widely dispersed cemeteries around the world in which lie the remains of millions of such men and women, the business of remembrance also entails international travel. Such voyages start as pilgrimage; many are mixed with tourism (Lloyd, 1992). But, in either case, there are train and boat journeys to take; hotel rooms to reserve; guides to hire; flowers to lay at graves; trinkets and mementos to purchase. In some places, museums have arisen to tell more of the story the pilgrims have come to hear and to share. There, too, money is exchanged along with the narratives and the symbols of remembrance.

This mixture of the sacred and the profane is hardly an innovation. It is merely a secular form of the kind of pilgrimage, for example, that made San Juan de Compostela in Spain the destination of millions of men and women in the Middle Ages who came to honor the conventionally designated resting place of the remains of one of the original Apostles. Pilgrimage to war cemeteries is public commemoration over long – sometimes very long – distances. Where does pilgrimage stop and tourism take over? It is impossible to say, but, in all cases, the business of remembrance remains just that – a business. And this business, like all others, has a history.

AESTHETIC REDEMPTION

The life history of sites of memory is described by more than political gestures and material tasks. Frequently, a site is also an art form, the art of creating, arranging, and interpreting signifying practices. This field of action can be analysed on two different levels: the first is aesthetic; the second is semiotic. The two are intimately related, and both have been the subject of increasing interests among historians.

Some national commemorative forms are distinctive. Others are shared by populations in many countries. The figure of Marianne as the national symbol affixed to thousands of town halls throughout France could not be used in Germany or Britain. The German Iron Cross, on commemorative plaques, denotes the location and the tradition in which commemoration is expressed. Germany's heroes' forests or fortresses are also imbricated in Teutonic history.

At times, the repertoire of one country's symbols overlap with that of others, even when they were adversaries. After World War I, the first industrialized war fought among fully industrialized nations, many commemorative forms adopted medieval notation. Throughout Europe, the revolutionary character of warfare was marked by a notation of a backward-looking kind. Medieval images of heroic and saintly warriors recaptured a time when combat was between individuals, rather than the impersonal and unbalanced duel between artillery and human flesh. The war in the air took on the form and romance of chivalry. On the losing and the winning sides, medievalism flourished. We can see these traces clearly in stained glass windows in many churches, where the site of memory for the two world wars takes on a meaning by virtue of its proximity to older religious images and objects. Twentieth-century warfare thus takes on a sacred coloration when its sites of memory are located within a sacred grammar and a sacred building. All of these signifying practices have a history.

There is an equally active historical interest in which forms artists and their patrons choose to represent an event or an era. Until very late in the twentieth century, on war memorials the human form survived. In some instances, classical images of male beauty were chosen to mark the "lost generation"; others adopted more stoical and emphatically un-triumphalist poses of men in uniform. In most cases, victory was either partially or totally eclipsed by a sense of overwhelming loss. Within this aesthetic landscape, traditional Christian motifs were commonplace. The form of the grieving mother – Stabat Mater – brought women into the local and national constellation of grief.

There is a sectarian history here, too. In Protestant countries, the aesthetic debate took on a quasi-religious character. War memorials with crosses on them offended some Protestants, who believed that the Reformation of the sixteenth century precluded such "Catholic" notation. Obelisks were preferable, and relatively inexpensive, too. In France, war memorials were by law restricted to public and not church grounds, although many local groups found a way around this proscription. In schools and universities, the location of such memorials touched on such issues. Some were placed in sacred space – in chapels – semisacred space – around chapels – or in secular space. Public thoroughfares and train stations also housed such lists of men who had died in war. Placement signified meaning.

Twentieth-century warfare democratized bereavement. Previously armies were composed of mercenaries, volunteers and professionals. After 1914, Everyman went to war. The social incidence of war losses was thereby transformed. In Britain, France, and Germany, virtually every household had lost someone – a father, a son, a brother, a cousin, a friend. Given the nature of static warfare on the Western front, many – perhaps half – of those killed had no known grave. Consequently, commemorative forms highlighted names above all. The names of the dead were all that remained of them, and chiseled in stone or etched on plaques, these names were the foci of public commemoration both on the local and the national scale.

Sites of memory preserved the names of those who were gone. In some rare cases – Australia is one of them – war memorials listed the names of all those who served. This notation was a constant rebuke to those who passed the site knowing full well that their names were not inscribed on the memorial. Most of the time, however, the dead were the names that mattered, so much so, that alphabetical order replaced social order. The overwhelming majority of war memorials list those who died in this way. A small minority listed men by rank, and some listed men by the date or year of death. But sites of memory were built for the survivors, for the families of those who were not there, and these people needed easy access to the sole signifier left to them – the name of the dead person.

This essential practice of naming has inspired a host of historical studies. It set the pattern for commemorative forms after the World War II and beyond. After 1945, names were simply added to Great War memorials. This was partly in recognition of the links between the two twentieth-century conflicts; partly it was a matter of economy. After the Vietnam War, naming still mattered, and World War I forms inspired memorials, most notably Maya Lin's Vietnam Veterans' Memorial in Washington. Her work clearly drew on Sir Edwin Lutyens's Memorial to the missing on the River Somme at Thiepval, inaugurated in 1932.

By the latter decades of the twentieth century, artistic opinion and aesthetic tastes had changed sufficiently to make abstraction the key language of commemorative expression. Statues and installations thereby escaped from specific national notation and moved away from the earlier emphasis upon the human figure. The exception to the rule is Soviet commemorative art, which resolutely stuck to the path of heroic romanticism in marking out the meaning of what they called the Great Patriotic War. In many instances in Western Europe, but by no means all, forms that suggested absence or nothingness replaced classical, religious, or romantic notions in commemorative art.

This shift was noticeable in Holocaust remembrance, which today constitutes an entire field of historical research. Holocaust sites of memory – concentration and extermination camps, in particular, but also places where Jews had lived before the Shoah – could not be treated in the same way as sites commemorating the dead of the two world wars. The first difficulty was the need to avoid Christian notation to represent a Jewish catastrophe. The second was the allergy of observant Jews to representational art, either forbidden or resisted within Orthodox Jewish tradition. The third was the absence of any sense of uplift, of meaning, of purpose in the deaths of the victims. Those who died in the Holocaust may have affirmed their faith thereby, but what is the meaning in the murder of one million children? To a degree, their deaths meant nothing, and therefore the Holocaust meant nothing.

Representing nothing became a challenge met in particular ways. Some artists provided installation art which literally vanished through the presence of visitors. Others projected photographs of the vanished world onto the facades of still erect buildings, occupied by non-Jews. Others adopted postmodern forms to suggest disorientation, void, emptiness. Daniel Liebeskind's Jewish annex to the Berlin Historical Museum is one such site. It has been likened to a Jewish star taken apart, or a lightning bolt in stone and glass. Whatever metaphor one chooses, it is a disturbing, tilted, nonlinear representation of the unrepresentable.

Since the 1970s, commemoration of the World War II has become braided together with commemoration of the Holocaust. This presented aesthetic as well as social and political challenges, all documented by many historians. Great War commemorative forms had sought out some meaning, some significance in the enormous loss of life attending that conflict. There was an implicit warning in many of these monuments. "Never again" was there ultimate meaning. But "never" had lasted a bare twenty years. Thus after the World War II, the search for meaning became infinitely more complex. And the fact that more civilians died than soldiers in the World War II made matters even more difficult to configure in art.

Finally, the extreme character of the World War II challenged the capacity of art – any art – to express a sense of loss when it is linked to genocidal murder or thermonuclear destruction. We have mentioned how Auschwitz defied conventional notations of "meaning," though some individuals continue to try to rescue redemptive elements from it. The same is true for the atomic destruction of Hiroshima and Nagasaki. Sites of memory are places where people affirm their faith that history has a meaning. What kind of site is appropriate where the majority of people see no meaning at all in the events being marked in time and in space? Ignoring Auschwitz or Hiroshima is impossible, but locating them within earlier commemorative structures or gestures is either problematic or absurd or both. Thus historians entered and to a degree dominate the discussion of the Holocaust as that set of events that set a limit to what can be represented in scholarship of any kind.

RITUAL

Under the influence of many different forms of anthropology and cultural studies, especially those related to the work of Michel de Certeau and Louis Morin in France, historians have been more and more attentive to the words and gestures of those who come together at sites of memory to recall particular aspects of the past, their past. Such moments are rarely the simple reflection of a fixed text, a script rigidly prepared by political leaders determined to fortify their position of power. Inevitably, commemoration overlaps with political conflicts, but it can never be reduced to a direct function of power relationships. Here we are in the sphere of meanings, not meaning.

Historians have focused on at least three stages in the history of rituals surrounding public commemoration. The first we have already dealt with: the construction of a commemorative form. But there are two other levels in the life history of monuments which need attention. The second is the grounding of ritual action in the calendar, and the routinization of such activities; the third is their transformation or their disappearance as active sites of memory.

One case in point may illustrate this trajectory. The date July 1, 1916, is not a national holiday in Britain; but it marks the date of the opening of the British offensive on the river Somme, an offensive that symbolized the terrible character of industrial warfare. On that day, the British army suffered the highest casualty totals in its history; on that day, a volunteer army, and the society that had created it, were introduced to the full terrors of twentieth-century warfare. To this day, groups of people come to the Somme battlefields to mark this day, without national legislation to enable them to do so. Theirs are locally defined rituals. A party of Northumberland men and women bring their bagpipes and mark the moment when the Battle of the Somme began at a gigantic crater they purchased to ensure it would not be ploughed over and forgotten. Others from Newfoundland go to the still extant trench system at Beaumont Hamel where their ancestors were slaughtered on July 1, 1916. There is a bronze caribou at the site to link this place to the landscape from which the men of Newfoundland – then a British colony – came as volunteers to fight for King and Country. In France, November 11 is a national holiday, but it is not in Britain. Legislation codifies activities the origins and force of which lie on the local level. After 1939, remembrance of the Great War dead was located on the closest Sunday to November 11. What mattered most about this is that churches became the sites where remembrance occurred. The ritual of Protestant churches domesticated war remembrance and blunted its appeal. There is still today (2006) a movement to return war remembrance to where it belongs, in the midst of life, on whatever day November 11 happens to fall.

Public commemoration flourishes within the orbit of civil society, and these associations leave records that historians have exploited in many sophisticated ways. This is less true among historians of countries where dictatorships rule; Stalinist Russia smashed civil society to a point that it could not sustain commemorative activity independent of the party and the state (Merridale, 1999). But, elsewhere, local associations matter. And so do families. Commemorative ritual survives when it is inscribed within the rhythms of community and in particular, family life. Public commemoration lasts when it draws its power from the overlap between national history and family history, and family history is a burgeoning field of historical research. Most of those who take the time to engage in the rituals of remembrance bring with them memories of family members touched by these vast events. This is what enables people born long after wars and revolutions to commemorate them as essential parts of their own lives. For example, children born in the aftermath of World War I told the story of their family upbringing to grandchildren born sixty or seventy years later. This transmission of childhood memories over two or sometimes three generations gives family stories a power that is translated at times into activity – the activity of remembrance (Winter & Sivan, 1999). That activity has a history, and a rich one at that.

There are occasions when the household itself becomes a site of memory. The great German sculptor and artist Käthe Kollwitz kept the room of her dead son as a kind of shrine, just as it was when he volunteered for war in 1914. In Paris, there is a public housing project in a working-class neighborhood, where above every apartment door is listed the name of a soldier who had died in the Great War. This is their home, too, the metaphoric residence of those who were denied the chance the rest of us have of living and dying one at a time.

This framework of family transmission of narratives about the past is an essential part of public commemoration. It also helps us understand why some commemorative forms are changed or simply fade away. When the link between family life and public commemoration is broken, a powerful prop of remembrance is removed. Then, in a short time, remembrance atrophies and fades away. Public reinforcements may help keep alive the ritual and practice of commemoration. But the event becomes hollow when removed from the myriad small-scale social units that breathed life into it in the first place. The difference between the small-scale and large-scale settings of commemoration has preoccupied historians of Africa, South and Southeast Asia, and South America in particular. What they have shown are the ways commemorative sites and practices have been revived and reappropriated. The site of a massacre in Mexico City in 1968 was the altar of human sacrifice, Tlatelolco, among the Aztecs. No one was ignorant of this fact at the time. The same sites used for one purpose can be used for another. But most of the time, sites of memory live through their life cycle, and, like the rest of us, inevitably fade away.

This natural process of dissolution closes the circle on the history of sites of memory and the public commemoration which occurs around them – and rightly so, because they arise out of the needs of groups of people to link their lives with salient events in the past. When that need vanishes, so, too, does the glue that holds together the social practice of commemoration. Then collective memories fade away, and sites of memory decompose, or simply fade into the landscape. Let me offer two instances of this phenomenon. For decades, the national war memorial in Dublin, designed by Sir Edwin Lutyens, was completely overgrown with grass. No one could tell what it was, and this was no accident. That 100,000 Irishmen died for Britain's King and Country was not an easy matter to interpolate in Irish history after 1918. But with the waning of sectarian violence in the latter decades of the twentieth century, the grass was cut and the monument reappeared, as if out of thin air. Sites of memory vanish, to be sure, but they can be conjured up again when people decide once again to mark the moment they commemorate. At other times, resurrection is more difficult. For years, I asked my students at Cambridge what did they see at the first intersection into town from the railway station. Most answered that they saw nothing at all. What they did not see was the town war memorial, a victorious soldier striding back home, right at the first traffic light into town. They did not see it because it had no meaning to them. It was simply white noise in stone. For them to see it, someone had to point it out, and others had to organize acts of remembrance around it. Without such an effort, sites of memory vanish into thin air and stay there.

We have reached, therefore, a quixotic conclusion. The historical record shows in myriad ways that public commemoration is both irresistible and unsustainable. Constructing sites of memory is a universal social act, and yet these very sites are as transitory as are the groups of people who create and sustain them. Time and again people have come together at particular places, in front of particular sites of memory, to seek meaning in vast events in the past and try to relate them to their own smaller networks of social life. These associations are bound to dissolve, to be replaced by other forms, with other needs, and other histories. At that point, the characteristic trajectory of sites of memory, bounded by their creation, institutionalization, and decomposition, comes to an end.

REFERENCES

Assmann, J. (1995). Collective memory and cultural identity. *New German Critique,* *65,* 125–134.
Gregory, A. (1994). *The silence of memory.* Leamington Spa: Berg.
Hayden, D. (1992). *The power of place.* Cambridge, MA: MIT Press.
Inglis, K. (1992). World War One memorial in Australia. *Guerres mondiales et confits contemporains, 167,* 51–58.
Klein, K. L. (2000). On the emergence of memory in historical discourse. *Representations, 69,* 127.
Lloyd, D. (1992). *Battlefield tourism: Pilgrimage and the commemoration of the Great War in the United Kingdom, Canada and Australia.* Oxford: Berg Press.
MacKenzie, J. (Ed.). (1986). *Imperialism and popular culture.* Manchester: Manchester University Press.
Maier, C. S. (1993). A Surfeit of memory? Reflections on history, melancholy and denial. *History & memory, 5,* 136–151.
   (2001). *Hot Memory ... Cold Memory: On the Political Half-Life of Fascist and Communist Memory.* Paper presented at the conference on *The Memory of the Century,* Institut für die Wissenschaften vom Menschen, Vienna, March 2001.
Merridale, C. (1999). War, death and remembrance in Soviet Russia. In J. Winter & E. Sivan (Eds.), *War and remembrance in the twentieth century* (pp. 61–83). Cambridge: Cambridge University Press.
Nora, P. (1992). *The era of commemoration. Realms of memory, iii, Symbols* (p. 618). Paris: Gallimard.
Nora, P. (Ed.). (n.d.). *Les lieux de mémoire* (Vols. 1–7). Paris: Gallimard.
Prost, A. (1999). The Algerian War in French collective memory. In J. Winter & E. Sivan (Eds.), *War and remembrance in the twentieth century* (pp. 161–176). Cambridge: Cambridge University Press.
Ranger T., & Hobsbawm E. (Eds.). (1986). *The Invention of tradition.* Cambridge: Cambridge University Press.
Winter, J. (1999). *Sites of memory, sites of mourning: The Great War in European cultural history.* Cambridge: Cambridge University Press.
Winter J., & Sivan E. (1999). *Setting the framework. War and remembrance in the twentieth century* (pp. 1–40). Cambridge: Cambridge University Press.

PART V

HOW DOES MEMORY SHAPE
CULTURE?

Culture is no explanation – that much is (or should be) obvious to all social scientists. Saying that people do this or believe that "because that's their culture" is at most a descriptive statement – telling us that the behavior or belief in question is widespread in the particular group we are considering – but it begs the question: Why are those behaviors or beliefs common in that group?

Surprisingly, this is a rather new interest in the social sciences. Chiefly responsible for this odd lack of interest was the perennial reluctance of many social scientists to consider micro-processes and their aggregation – that is, the way that individual processes and behaviors create large-scale social phenomena (Schelling, 1978). However, in the last twenty years, a new anthropology and psychology of cultural transmission has emerged, founded on the systematic study of micro-processes – the field has its theoretical foundations (Boyd & Richerson, 1985; Sperber, 1985; Tooby & Cosmides, 1992), its mathematical formalisms (McElreath & Boyd, 2007), and droves of empirical studies (see e.g., Atran, 1990; Boyer, 1994; Hirschfeld, 1996 and many others). The main thrust in most of these studies is the study of particular cognitive dispositions and their consequences for cultural transmission, a domain that Pascal Boyer surveys in the final chapter of this book.

One of the ancestors of this field is Milman Parry, who as a young classicist in the 1930s proposed an original (and to many scholars scandalous) explanation of Homeric formulae, these recurrent pairs of nouns and epithets ("rose-fingered Dawn," "fleet-footed Achilles," "heifer-eyed Aphrodite," "Apollo, rouser of armies," etc.) that crop up in so many verses of *The Iliad* and *The Odyssey*. Parry's hypotheses were that the Homeric text was a compilation of songs previously transmitted in oral forms; that those were sung by illiterate poets who did not learn them by heart but composed

them on the go, on the basis of conventional themes and plots; and, crucially, that oral composition of this nature would make such demands on
memory that the poet would use a set of ready-made formulae, to make
their sentences fit the hexameters' frame (Parry & Parry, 1971). The thesis
was not exactly well received, assuming as it did that the *Ur-Text* of Western
civilization originated in the folklore of illiterate peasants. Parry set out to
make his case by taking the rash and unprecedented step (among classi-
cists) of doing ethnography. The idea was to study modern poets who used
oral composition – to provide a live example, as it were, of how the process
led to the proliferation of formulae – which he did demonstrate in his studies of traditional Serbian bards (Lord, 1960).

Parry's demonstration ushered in a renewed interest in the question of
classical literacy (Havelock, 1986) but also, more directly relevant to the
present theme, to a new anthropological interest in the psychology of oral
transmission, as well as the contrast between orality and literacy (Goody,
1968, 1977; Ong, 1982). These do not just differ as means of transmission –
they differ in the demands they make on human memory, and consequently
on the kinds of concepts and norms that they typically support. In this volume, this theme is taken up by David Rubin, a specialist on autobiographical
memory (Rubin, 1986) but also on traditional Southern U.S. ballads (Rubin,
1995) and the cognitive neuroscience of recollection (Rubin, 2006). Rubin
starts from apparently the humblest of memory achievements, the counting
rhyme, to illustrate a variety of features and processes that apply to memory
in general. There may seem to be a long way from *eenie meenie miney moe*
to the neural correlates of autobiographical memory, but Rubin shows how
a sound theory of memory could link these two memory phenomena (and
most others) in an empirically sound psychology of memory and culture –
the overarching theme of this volume.

REFERENCES

Atran, S. A. (1990). *Cognitive foundations of natural history. Towards an anthropol-
ogy of science.* Cambridge: Cambridge University Press.
Boyd, R., & Richerson, P. J. (1985). *Culture and the evolutionary process.* Chicago:
University of Chicago Press.
Boyer, P. (1994). *The naturalness of religious ideas: A cognitive theory of religion.*
Berkeley, CA: University of California Press.
Goody, J. (1968). *Literacy in traditional societies.* Cambridge: Cambridge University
Press.
Goody, J. (1977). *The domestication of the savage mind.* Cambridge: Cambridge
University Press.

Havelock, E. A. (1986). *The muse learns to write: Reflections on orality and literacy from antiquity to the present*. New Haven: Yale University Press.

Hirschfeld, L. A. (1996). *Race in the making: Cognition, culture and the child's construction of human kinds*. Cambridge, MA: The M.I.T. Press.

Lord, A. B. (1960). *The singer of tales*. Cambridge: Harvard University Press.

McElreath, R., & Boyd, R. (2007). *Mathematical models of social evolution: A guide for the perplexed*. Chicago. London: University of Chicago Press.

Ong, W. J. (1982). *Orality and literacy: The technologizing of the word*. London; New York: Methuen.

Parry, M., & Parry, A. (1971). *The making of Homeric verse: The collected papers of Milman Parry*. Oxford: Clarendon Press.

Rubin, D. C. (1995). *Memory in oral traditions: The cognitive psychology of epic, ballads, and counting-out rhymes*. New York: Oxford University Press.

Rubin, D. C. (2006). The basic-systems model of episodic memory. *Perspectives on Psychological Science, 1*(4), 277–311.

Rubin, D. C. (Ed.). (1986). *Autobiographical memory*. New York: Cambridge University Press.

Schelling, T. C. (1978). *Micromotives and macrobehavior* (1st ed.). New York: Norton.

Sperber, D. (1985). Anthropology and psychology. *Towards an epidemiology of representations. Man, 20*, 73–89.

Tooby, J., & Cosmides, L. (1992). The psychological foundations of culture. In J. H. Barkow, L. Cosmides & et al. (Eds.), *The adapted mind: Evolutionary psychology and the generation of culture* (pp. 19–136). New York, NY: Oxford University Press.

12

Oral Traditions as Collective Memories: Implications for a General Theory of Individual and Collective Memory

DAVID C. RUBIN

This chapter is about the cultural memory and transmission of oral traditions, especially those that use poetics and music. The latter include many of the best studied and most stable forms of oral traditions, including children rhymes, ballads, songs, and epic poetry. Oral traditions are of interest because, unlike written traditions, they depend primarily on memory for their survival. Thus, by examining the products of long periods of oral transmission, we can learn something about the processes of memory used. Working in the other direction, by using our knowledge of memory, we can better understand how the products came into being and what their likely limitations are. Although they are often viewed only as art forms in current times, oral traditions did, and often still do, transmit valuable practical and moral information and in many forms, such as the epics sung in the Balkans, give insight into major conflicts (Foley, 1991; Havelock, 1978; Lord, 1960; Ong, 1982).

In large part, this chapter is drawn from my earlier work on oral traditions (e.g., Rubin, 1995), but here I intend to show how it provides a more general view of memory as used in the cultural transmission of information. My goal is to show that current theories of memory need to be expanded in principled and theoretically well-supported ways if they are going to be maximally useful in helping us understand individual and collective memory. This is hard to show in single chapter in an abstract way, so I will start with two genres of oral traditions and then, after presenting data on these, I will expand to memory in general.

Examples from Children's Counting-Out Rhymes and Ballads

I begin with a few examples to make the topic less abstract. After all, oral traditions themselves are not abstract in content but always illustrate the abstract through use of the concrete (Havelock, 1978). The most commonly known piece for most readers from an oral tradition is probably the following:

> Eenie, meenie, miney, mo
> Catch a tiger by the toe.
> If he hollers, let him go.
> Eenie, meenie, miney, mo.

This may seem like a cute little scrap of nonsense, but it has remained stable, popular, and widespread across the English-speaking world for over a century. The poetics are subtle and exhaustive. Most of the words contain a repeated sound pattern, usually word repetition, rhyme, or alliteration, and all the words not involved in the meaning are involved in one of these poetic devices.

Consider the first line. *Eenie* is part of *meenie*. *Meenie, miney,* and *mo* alliterate. *Eenie, meenie,* and *miney* rhyme, as do *mo, toe,* and *go*. In terms or articulation, the initial vowel in *meenie, miney, mo* (i.e., *e, i, o*) is a front-to-back progression as in *fee, fi, fo, fum, I smell the blood of an Englishman* or in *Old McDonald had a farm, ee eye, ee eye, oh*. Thus, *meenie, miney, mo* sounds better than *miney, meenie, mo,* and the order is unlikely to change. The remaining sound, /n/, repeats in the same location in three words. The whole line repeats as the last line, where the one single-syllable word, *mo,* coincides with the person who is chosen. This change from the two-syllable pattern (which would be *monie*) adds closure, and because the line is trochaic (i.e., it has feet consisting or a stressed syllable followed by an unstressed syllable), it emphasizes the end-rhyme scheme by putting a stress on the final, rhyming syllable. In summary, there is not a phoneme or even a distinctive feature in the first line that can change without breaking some pattern. The middle two lines offer more flexibility and so do change over time and over retellings, where that flexibility allows or where social forces require, but the changes always maintain the rhythmic, poetic, and other forms of organization of the piece and genre (Rubin, 1995).

Eenie Meenie is the most frequent rhyme in Abrahams and Rankin's (1980) compilation of counting-out rhymes, and we could find 82 versions of it dating back to the 1880s. In oral traditions, there is no correct version, but using the version listed earlier as a standard, the changes among the rhymes vary where they can without disrupting the basic poetic, rhythmic, imagery, and meaning organization. The first and last line varied before 1910, mostly outside the United States, including *Eena meena mina mo* and *Eena deena dina do*. Note that the whole line had to change to preserve the rhyme and alliteration patterns. The middle two lines also changed, although rarely. These, like the changes in the first line, maintained the organization by providing completely new lines. My favorite, in which a beatnik is caught, is *If he hollers daddy-o, Play it cool and let him go.*

Other changes occurred in single words. The word *hollers* was American, not English, and in Great Britain and New Zealand, and only in these countries, it often changed to *squeals*, although now *hollers* has become worldwide. Other versions had *cries, chatters, quarrels, roars,* and *screams,* but these were rarer. *Hollers,* which alliterates with the *he* of *If he hollers,* remains the most common. Other single-word changes occur in words that do not have any poetic links and have synonyms with the same number of syllables. These are usually in unstressed words and include *his* for *the, when* for *if,* and *the* for *a.* Before the 1940s, the term for what was caught was a racial slur. This changed steadily over time until now *tiger* is the only word widely used. However, while the replacement was ongoing, a host of mostly two-syllable words was considered by the community using the rhyme, including *baby, beatnik, beggar, feller, lamb, lion, lizard, monkey, neighbor, pig, robber,* and *rooster. Tiger* alliterates with *toe,* and it is a two-syllable trochaic word making it arguably the best word in the language for its location in the rhyme. Thus, the forms of organization remain stable even when the individual words change. What is transmitted through those who use the genre is not the rote memorization of exact words but solutions that fit the genre. In cognitive psychology, the word used to describe such genre organization is Bartlett's (1932) term, "schema." Here the schemata are for rhythm, poetics, imagery, and meaning, not just for meaning.

Similar counting-out rhymes occur in many cultures where they determine in a relatively peaceful manner the child who will play an often unpleasant role in a game. Romanian shares the Romance-language roots of English, but it is surrounded linguistically by Hungarian, Slavic, and Turkish languages. Thus, the rhymes have similar properties that are not, a product of easy borrowing from the English rhymes and so provide a test of the ideas developed on English rhymes (Rubin, Ciobanu, & Langston, 1997). The rhyme we collected most was the following:

> Din Oceanul Pacific, (From the Pacific Ocean)
> A iesit un peste mic. (A little fish came out)
> Si pe coada lui scria (And on its tail is written)
> Iesi afara dumneata. (Out goes you.)

We collected 63 versions of this rhyme. Of these, 49 were the variant shown. The remaining 14 versions all varied from it in the last two lines.

One was *Iu, iu, iu / Iesi afară tu (You, you, you / Out goes you)*. Another was *A B C / Iesi afară dumneata (A B C / Out goes you)*. The remain 12 variants came only from girls and were *Te iubesc / nu mă uita (I love you / don't forget me)*. The rhyme seems like it could fit into the English genre (and stereo-typed cultural sex roles), and in general the rhymes we collected share with the English genre many properties including having four lines with four beat per line, line internal and end rhyme, alliteration, and allowing many repeating and nonsense words.

Preliterate children may use oral traditions for memory because they cannot rely on writing. However, even adults make use of song and poetry to aid memory. I choose a recent ballad as an example because it is an event for which we have eyewitness and newspaper accounts and because the ballad was involved in a copyright dispute, which adds additional information about variants and how they changed over time. Thus, one can examine how accurately information is transmitted and what biases are caused by the genre of ballads and of newspaper reporting (see A. Cohen, 1973, for more on this issue).

On December 27, 1903, Number 97, a fast mail train, reached Monroe, Virginia, behind schedule. The engineer taking charge at Monroe tried to make up the time, but he was new to the Southern Railway and unfamiliar with the treacherous points in the route. Just north of Danville, Virginia, the tracks round a curve, descend, and cross a trestle about 90 feet above a creek (see N. Cohen 1981; Lyle, 1991; Wallace, & Rubin, 1988 for more details). Here are the two verses that carry most of the story line. It comes from the Appeals Court record of the copyright case (White, 1952, p. 513):

> It's a mighty rough road from Lynchburg to Danville
> And a line on a three mile grade.
> It was on this grade when he lost his air-brakes
> And you see what a jump he made.
>
> He was going down grade making ninety miles an hour
> When his whistle began to scream,
> He was found in the wreck with his hand on the throttle
> And was scalded to death by the steam.

The story was fit into a ballad tradition, in which there were many other ballads about train or shipwrecks. As part of this tradition, it included stan-zas of four lines with four beats per line and with the last beat of lines two and four often being filled with a rest or held note. The last words of line two and line four rhyme. There is high imagery and action-filled meaning structured so that each stanza is a self-contained unit of meaning and imagery. The genre is complex, well studied, and dates back to the Middle Ages, so much is known about it (for more details, see Rubin, 1995; Wallace, & Rubin, 1991).

As with the counting-out rhymes, the changes that occur over time and in singing the ballad multiple times tend not to violate the organization of the genre. There are several ways to demonstrate this using *The Wreck of the Old 97* as an example. We tested traditional ballad singers in North Carolina, that is, people who knew ballads most of which they learned from listening to another singer (Wallace & Rubin, 1988). The five who knew *The Wreck of the Old 97* sang it twice separated by a period of about six months. All of these singers played a stringed instrument, even if they did not when singing the versions we collected. The quarter notes are the notes that they would have played on that instrument. This adds both musical and motor forms of organization that can be grouped as "finger memory" to these notes of the ballad.

Each singing by each singer was unique, there was much more stability within singers than across singers, and the melody seemed more stable than the words. The variability that did occur tended to be within the regularities of the genre. End rhyme, the number of beats per line, and lines per verse remained relatively constant, as did the gist of verses, sequence of lines within a verse, and sequence of verses. Singers added or deleted verses that embellished the story. Melodic changes were also limited by the constraints of the particular type of scale used, the time signature, and the basic melodic line of the quarter notes. The words and music are integrated. Singers often need to play or hum a stanza before they can recall the words. The words have a metrical pattern, which must correspond to the rhythmical pattern, the beat structure, and the time signature of the music further limiting the kind of changes that could occur.

In addition to this more observational approach, to test our ideas, we undertook experiments with 27 undergraduates who had not heard the ballad before and were not experts in the tradition. To show that the organization made a difference, the undergraduates listened to the ballad sung 10 times, waited 10 minutes and recalled the ballad as close to verbatim as possible. We found that lines that were higher in visual imagery were recalled better ($r = .49$) but not lines rated as being important to understanding the meaning of the ballad ($r = .06$). However, lines that carried the meaning by being causally connected to other lines were recalled better ($r = .44$), as were lines in which the music better fit the words ($r = .44$).

We then tested another 27 undergraduates using the same procedure but changed 24 words so that they were no longer poetically linked. For instance, *saying Steve* became *telling Steve* and *mighty rough road* became *mighty tough road*. This dropped the overall recall of the ballad only slightly from 60 percent to 55 percent. However, the 24 words that were poetically linked were recalled 51 percent of the time and their non-poetically linked words were recalled only 24 percent of the time. More telling was the kind of errors made. *Saying Steve* was recalled correctly by nine people, omitted by three, and changed to something else by the rest. In the version that we changed to *telling Steve,* no one recalled *telling Steve* correctly; 13 people omitted it and 2 people changed it back to the original version, which they had not heard. That is, they corrected our change to the more poetically linked original of *saying Steve.* Similarly, *mighty rough road* was recalled correctly by 13 people and omitted by 4. *Mighty tough road* was recalled correctly by no one, omitted by five people, and changed back to *mighty rough road* by one person (Wallace & Rubin, 1988).

In another experiment, we recorded the ballad either (a) spoken with normal intonation and rhythm, (b) spoken to capture the rhythm of the ballad, or (c) spoken to capture the rhythm of the ballad with the rhythm also marked by tapping. Otherwise, the procedure did not vary from what was just described. There was no significant difference among these groups on amount recalled (57%, 56%, and 64%), but there was an interaction between which lines were best recalled and the three listening conditions. To probe why some lines were remembered better in different listening condition, we asked how the percentage recall of each line correlated with our metrical agreement measure. In the rhythmical-voice condition and in the rhythmical-voice-plus-beat condition, there were significant correlations ($r = .52$ and $r = .57$, respectively). However, in the normal-voice condition, metrical agreement did not significantly correlate with percentage recalled ($r = .38$). Thus, when the rhythm was stressed, lines with good fit to the rhythm were better recalled (Wallace & Rubin, 1988).

In order to investigate how difficult it would be to learn such a complex and interrelated set of organizations, we had undergraduates learn ballads (Rubin, Wallace, & Houston, 1993). The learning process for each ballad consisted of hearing each ballad once, recalling it, hearing it four more times, and recalling it again. This was repeated for a different ballad each week for five weeks. The ballads were each 10 verses long and analyzed to document the various forms of organization in them, including 30 easy-to-identify properties that we could look for in the recalls. Over the course of learning five ballads, the undergraduates' ability to learn after hearing a ballad sung once increased dramatically. There was one and a half times as many words recalled, twice as many rhyming words, and three times as much line structure in their recall of the fifth ballad than their recall of the first ballad.

After all recalls were completed, we asked the undergraduates to spend 20 minutes composing a new ballad that would fit with the ones they heard and then to list all the rules they followed. The composed ballads were about two-thirds as long as the ones heard. They had about half of the 30 characteristics that we had identified and about one quarter of the characteristics were stated as explicit rules. Moreover, there was no relationship between the rules stated and the rules followed. For instance, as is common in ballads, there was no setting in any of the five ballads learned, very few words were more than two syllables long, the nouns were concrete and easy to image rather than being abstract, and the main character always died. All 14 of our undergraduates omitted having a setting, 11 used few words longer than two syllables, 12 used mostly concrete nouns, but none of the 14 undergraduates stated any of these as an explicit rule. In contrast, 13 of the 14 undergraduates stated the rule that the main character dies, but only 11 followed it. Thus, the undergraduates began to master a complex genre in part by observing some regularities in it consciously and in part by learning to mimic the style without being able to verbalize how they did it.

Thus, our ideas were confirmed based on a textual analysis of ballads, on observations of changes in traditional singers, and with experiments in the laboratory. By mixing the various strengths of these forms of inquiry, we could become more certain of our ideas than we could by using any one alone. Like counting-out rhymes, ballads are not learned in a fixed rote manner, even by undergraduates who were not expert in the genre. We found that the forms of organization that help structure memory seem to be any forms of organization present that is appreciated, and that with expertise, the appreciation of structure in the to-be-remembered material is increased. Of course, someone not well trained in cognitive psychology might wonder if people would ever remember anything without making use of all the forms of organization that would help them, but, in fact, most psychological and psycholinguistic theories claimed that we used only the abstract meaning of a text as an aid to memory.

WHAT DOES STANDARD MEMORY THEORY TELL US?

Cognitive psychology tells us a great deal about how oral traditions are maintained. It makes a real contribution to the study of oral traditions by making clear the division between implicit and explicit memory, the role of organization and schemata, the idea of cuing and of matching the cues at recall to the cues that were present at encoding, transfer, interference, spaced practice, overlearning, and numerous other heavily studied and well-understood concepts and phenomena. This contribution is easy to expand to the study of collective memory in general.

However, most of the ideas from cognitive psychology were developed in tasks more restricted than the varied conditions of transmission of oral traditions, and so there a few ideas that do not generalize well. Even these are informative to the study of oral traditions, and because they show failures or limitations of theories in psychology, they are of special interest to the study of memory in general. For instance, depth of processing fails because shallow rhyme processing is extremely powerful. Similarly, the standard rumor paradigm used in cognitive and social psychology predicts a rapid change (Allport & Postman, 1947; Bartlett, 1932) that does not occur in oral traditions, whereas models of transmission proposed by folklorists do much better (see Rubin, 1995 for details of why). More serious is the tendency in memory research to reify memories, that is, to make them single things that tend to be located in a single place and stored as a single unit as opposed to a process (Kolers & Roediger, 1984). Moving from this to a view that can account for data and observations in oral traditions and other real-world memory requires a reanalysis of how memory functions.

Consider the recall of the oral traditions just reviewed. In laboratory terms, it is classic serial recall. The words must be recalled in order. Therefore, we know a great deal about some of the mechanisms involved from laboratory research for lists of unrelated words and the verbatim learning of prose and poetry. The study of oral traditions shows the nature of that serial recall more clearly than earlier work. People cannot summarize the overall meaning of a piece from an oral tradition that uses poetics or music until they recall the whole piece with the goal of summarizing in mind. They cannot tell you what happens in the middle or how it ends in any detail without recalling from the beginning to that part. Similarly, they cannot tell you the end-rhyme scheme or visual image or spatial location used in a part of the piece until they get to it. They need a "running start." Why is this the case? Why is it that the information is not "content addressable," to use the computer term? Each word recalled provides cues for the next word. The cues involve all of the forms of organization that might be involved in recalling the next word. Thus, part way into a ballad the next word to be recalled is being cued by schema, or forms of organization, that involve meaning, imagery, spatial layout, rhyme, alliteration, assonance, rhythm, and motor movements accompanying the verbal output and melody.

Providing a cue in only one of these systems at a time, as in asking for the overall meaning of the piece, or a particular part of it, is just not enough. But singing through to that part activates cues in all relevant systems (see Rubin, 1995, 2006 for details). Such cuing can be extremely powerful. Please consider the following nine cues and answer them in order. Please think of a word that: (a) is a building material, (b) is a mythical being, (c) is a unit of time, (d) rhymes with eel, (e) rhymes with post, (f) rhymes with beer, (g) is a building material that rhymes with eel, (h) is a mythical being that rhymes with post, and (i) is a unit of time that rhymes with beer. I have in mind three target words. So that you will not see them when thinking of your answer, I have put these target words at the end of the next paragraph. They are the only common answers to (g), (h), and (i), and I would bet that they were your answers to these cues. However, I doubt that more that one of these three target words was your answer to any of the first six cues, and, for most people, based on our studies, none would be listed. Thus, combining the single cues leads to a much higher hit rate on my three targets than can be expected from their individual strengths (see Rubin & Wallace, 1989, for details and mathematical derivations). In terms of oral traditions, if one has sung far enough to know what the meaning and rhyme scheme of the next line has to be then the last word of the rhyme does not have to be remembered – it is known. In terms of memory, such cuing can reduce the memory load to zero, once a running start is obtained. This and the previous paragraph are a summary of a theory of serial recall in oral traditions described in more detail in Rubin (1995).

AN EXPANDED THEORY FOR INDIVIDUAL AND COLLECTIVE MEMORY

We want to expand from situations in which memory is for only one modality and for only one form or organization at a time to the typically more complex situations, which are normally of interest in collective memory. Therefore, a model of memory more complex than the one developed for simple situations needs to be considered but one that is not restricted to the serial recall of many oral traditions (Cabeza et al., 2004; Greenberg & Rubin, 2003; Rubin, 2005, 2006). By the way, the target words were steel, ghost, and year.

Consider a real-world situation that would become part of your autobiographical memory and life story if you were there, and that might become part of an oral tradition ballad. Imagine that you were one of the two children under the trestle who survived when the *Old 97* jumped the tracks and crashed down just beyond the area where you were playing. It was a hot day at the end of September. A continuous loud steam whistle announces a train out of control. Then there is a crashing sound as the engine and several mail cars leave the track and crash into the creek. After a silence, the final mail car, which was hanging on the tracks, lands on top of the others. Steam and dust are followed by smoke from the fires started. A hundred or more bright yellow canaries that were being carried as freight escape and fly around the scene of destruction. Then you can hear the cries of the injured and, within a half hour, help arrives. Immediately people ask you what had happened and how you are. The next year, as part of a commemoration, a newspaper reporter collects your autobiographical memory for his story. What would you need as a memory theorist to describe that decade old memory?

I would claim that, at a minimum, you would need information stored and processed in at least the following semiautonomous systems. You would need a good spatial system to describe the layout and to place objects and actions within it. This is separate from a visual system; you would know the general layout from sound and touch even if there were so much steam, dust, and smoke that you could not see it. You would need a visual system to identify to objects, and note the steam and the flock of yellow canaries; an auditory system to decode the sounds; an olfactory system for the smells; and so forth for each sense.

Why keep the senses separate as opposed to having a single abstract memory system for the processing and storage of all kinds of sensory information? There are many reasons. First, each system has its own schemata that are unique to it, and that can be changed by experience. What one knows about the visual organization of the world does not apply easily to odors. Second, each system is functionally different. It handles different kinds of input and that input is typically used for different things. For instance, olfaction typically provides hedonistically important information in a very rapid fashion, but it does not indicate the location of the source of the odor. Third, each system is biologically different, which has implications for the mechanisms it has to offer for the memory. The need for and properties of sensory information store, working memory buffers, and long-term memory are not the same for all senses. Some of this is because of the stimuli to be handled, the primary functions of the sensory system outside of memory, and other functions of the areas of the brain used by the sense. Thus, visual stimuli can change more rapidly than tastes and smells, and tastes and smells result from chemicals entering the body that can serve as their own sensory information store.

Sensory systems with a spatial system to integrate them are not enough. There would be language heard and language used to code nonlinguistic inputs. There would also be narrative to structure the story of the episode into understandable, causally related, individual events. Narrative is not the same as language. One can have coherent narratives in mime, in silent film, in comics, and even is a single painting or picture without having any words. Moreover, as with the individual senses, narrative and language (defined as structure at the level of the sentence or below) occupy different brain areas and suffer under different neurological insult (see Rubin & Greenberg, 2003, for a review). In addition to all of this cold cognition, emotions would be needed for any kind of an adequate description of how you felt and what you experienced at the time. Emotions have two major roles to play. The first is as a modulator of the memory, increasing the level of encoding as a function of arousal. The second is more like the role of the senses, language, and narrative. You would experience particular emotional reactions, which would depend not only on your biology and personality dispositions but also on your experiences up to that time.

Finally, to integrate the information in these various systems, you would need a system, or more likely two systems, that would provide an integrated, unitary memory. The first system is the standard medial temporal, hippocampus-based memory system usually studied in case of amnesia (Nadel & Moscovitch, 1997; Squire 1987; Squire, Stark, & Clark, 2004). It binds information stored in the other systems just mentioned in an automatic and fairly stupid way, with some modulation from the emotion system. Second is a frontal-lobe search-and-retrieval system that searches for previously stored information in a more intelligent way and is associated with inhibitive processing and a host of nonmnemonic process. Its role in assembling memories is a newer addition to memory theory and is mainly a result of neuroimaging studies.

In the spirit of this chapter, I have kept the arguments for different systems focused on the role they would have to play in an autobiographical memory, like the hypothetical one I propose for experiencing the wreck of the *Old 97* or for the ballad that resulted from it. The autobiographical memory would be richer, more subject to change, and less musical. The ballad would be more restricted and stable as a result of the added schemata of the ballad genre and the subgenre of train- and shipwreck ballads (i.e., in literary terms, to genre convergence). However, the evidence for separate systems, each with their own forms of organization, or schemata, which would affect recall, goes way beyond this form of analysis. Evidence for the separate systems comes from neuroanatomy, neuropsychology, neuroimaging, cognitive-experimental psychology, and individual differences research. Each system, except for the medial-temporal explicit-memory system, is used for tasks other than memory and thus there is considerable knowledge about each system from its nonmnemonic functions that informs its role in memory (see Rubin, 2006 for a detailed review).

The neurological damage and early neuroimaging provide strong evidence for physical separation of these systems and neuroimaging is beginning to show their temporal separation as well, revealing the order of the processes involved. For instance, in autobiographical memory, the frontal and medial-temporal memory systems are active before the visual system (Daselaar et al. in press), and in the serial recall of oral traditions we would expect rhythmic entrainment of many of the systems outlined as the piece is sung. For instance, when the end of line 2 of a stanza of *The Wreck of the Old 97* is reached, brain regions involved in rhyme should become active in the search for the last word of line 4 of that stanza. Similarly, one would expect visual and spatial areas to become more active during the course of the singing of a stanza and to reduce their activity at the end of the stanza.

EXPANDED METHODS FOR COLLECTIVE MEMORY

The approach that I am going to recommend is an ethological one. It is perhaps best described in Tinbergen's (1960) *The Herring Gull's World.* One example of its application to the contents of autobiographical memory can be found in Linton (1986). Newell (1973, p. 303) provides an excellent description of a related approach from cognitive science in which he argues that one should try to have a theory of "a genuine slab of human behavior"; Brown writes about the success of such an approach in social psychology (1989); and a similar approach is favored by Neisser (1982). At a methodological level, I have written about my attempts at using an ethological approach for various areas of memory research (Rubin, 1989). The most direct contrast to it is theory-driven or hypothesis-testing research in which a strong theory about the nature of the world leads one to set up ideal conditions to falsify the theory. This approach is certainly the most elegant and useful when it can be applied but, in the area of individual and collective memory, I do not find much worthy of that kind of effort yet. Within current cognitive psychological theories, the opposition I am referring to parallels the opposition between top-down and bottom-up processing within an individual faced with understanding some stimulus.

The first step is to observe the kind of individual or collective memory that you want to understand. Describe the important features of it and if possible quantify that description. The quantification need not be a simple more or less comparisons; relations among variables can be more stable and more important. Once you have observed and described, you can theorize. Here it is very important not to be too attached to the way that you initially described the phenomena under study and especially to your theory of it. As we know from studies of problem solving and creativity, the representation you use to describe the object of study is crucial. The description and theory will interact and change each other. The next step is to design experiments to test your hunches, ideas, or theory (depending on your level of formalism and arrogance). Here, Tinbergen's experiments of providing adult gulls with a variety of different size, color, and shapes of eggs to try to hatch, or baby chicks with different shaped bills to peck at are forceful examples. The theory may then need to be revised. If you use a more ethological approach this is great and seems to be a natural progression. Revising a theory is also optimal for theory-driven, top-down research; if you always reject the null hypothesis and thereby support your theory, you certainly are not being an efficient experimenter. There was really no need to keep testing your theory if it was so good or your tests were so easy; you should have been doing something else. However, in practice, theory-driven researchers seem unhappy about changing their theories in public.

I started this chapter with examples of two genres of oral traditions and a limited number of pieces from those traditions. The actual research started with a great deal of description. In fact, the genres we studied were selected because so much of the description had been done for us already by folklore scholars. Then we did experiments where possible. For the children's rhymes, experiments in the usual sense were more difficult because the users of the tradition are harder to question than are adults. If we were child psychologists, we might have done such experiments, or we might have changed to jump-rope rhymes, which are sung by older children and that use some of the same rhymes. Instead, we compared changes in rhymes over time and we asked if the conclusions that we drew on one corpus of rhymes would hold for a new corpus to which we did not have access when we described the first. For the ballads, we did experiments of the same kind that people had been doing for decades in psychological laboratories. The only change was in the material to be learned. In this process, we formulated the theory of serial recall with multiple cuing and suggested tests for this theory.

If, as suggested, one is starting with a phenomenon, such as explaining what is stable and what changes in oral traditions, and not a theory, two hints are in order. First, be ready to find something you cannot explain. A good description of a highly replicable finding is not a guarantee that you will know why it occurred. Second, use any help that you can get. If you do not start by setting out to test one theory, you will probably have to read many different theories. If you are interested in a real-world phenomenon and not a laboratory task, you will need a collection of methods and, if you get far enough, a collection of laboratory tasks. At least you will not be accused of having too narrow a focus. You will have to decide for yourself whether you are a scholar or a dilettante.

ACKNOWLEGEMENT

Funding while writing this chapter came from the National Institute of Aging Grant Number R01 AG023123. Correspondence can be addressed to david.rubin@duke.edu.

REFERENCES

Abrahams, R. D., & Rankin, L. (Eds.). (1980). *Counting-out rhymes: A dictionary.* Austin: University of Texas Press.

Allport, G. W., & Postman, L. (1947). *The psychology of rumor.* New York: Henry Holt.

Brown, R. (1989). Roger Brown. In G. Lindzey (Ed.), *A history of psychology in auto-biography* (Vol. 8, pp. 36–60). Stanford, CA: Stanford University Press.

Bartlett, F. C. (1932). *Remembering: A study in experimental and social psychology.* London: Cambridge University Press.

Cabeza, R., Prince, S. E., Daselaar, S. M., Greenberg, D. L., Budde, M., Dolcos, F., et al. (2004). Brain activity during episodic retrieval of autobiographical and laboratory events: An fMRI study using a novel photo paradigm. *Journal of Cognitive Neuroscience, 16,* 1583–1594.

Cohen, A. B. (1973). *Poor Pearl, poor girl!: The murdered-girl stereotype in ballad and newspaper.* Austin: University of Texas Press.

Cohen, N. (1981). *The long steel rail: The railroad in American folksong.* Urbana, IL: University of Illinois Press.

Daselaar, S. M., Rice, H. J., Greenberg, D. L., Cabeza, R. LaBar, K. S., & Rubin, D. C. (2008). The spatiotemporal dynamics of autobiographical memory: Neural correlates of recall, emotional intensity, and reliving. *Cerebral Cortex, 18,* 217–229.

Foley, J. M. (1991). *Immanent art: From structure to meaning in traditional oral epic.* Bloomington: Indiana University Press.

Greenberg, D. L., & Rubin, D. C. (2003). The neuropsychology of autobiographical memory. *Cortex, 39,* 687–728.

Havelock, E. A. (1978). *The Greek concept of justice: From its shadow in Homer to its substance in Plato.* Cambridge, MA: Harvard University Press.

Kolers, P. A., & Roediger, H. L. III (1984). Procedures of mind. *Journal of verbal learning and verbal behavior, 23,* 425–449.

Ong, W. J. (1982). *Orality and literacy: The technologizing of the word.* London: Methuen.

Lord, A. B. (1960). *The singer of tales.* Cambridge, MA: Harvard University Press.

Linton, M. (1986). Ways of searching and the contents of memory. In D. C. Rubin (Ed.), *Autobiographical memory* (pp. 50–67). Cambridge: Cambridge University Press.

Lyle, K. L. (1991). *Scalded to death by the steam.* Chapel Hill, NC: Algonquin Books.

Nadel, L., & Moscovitch, M. (1997). Memory consolidation, retrograde amnesia and the hippocampal complex. *Current Opinion in Neurobiology, 7,* 217–227.

Neisser, U. (1982). *Memory observed.* San Francisco: W. H. Freeman.

Newell, A. (1973). You can't play 20 questions with nature and win: Projective comments on the papers of this symposium. In W. G. Chase (Ed.), *Visual information processing* (pp. 283–308). New York: Academic Press.

Rubin, D. C. (1989). Issues of regularity and control: Confessions of a regularity freak. In L. W. Poon, D. C. Rubin, & B. A. Wilson (Eds.), *Everyday cognition in adult and later life* (pp. 84–103) Cambridge: Cambridge University Press.

(1995). *Memory in oral traditions: The cognitive psychology of epic, ballads, and counting-out rhymes.* New York: Oxford University Press.

(2005). A basic-systems approach to autobiographical memory. *Current Directions in Psychological Science, 14,* 79–83.

(2006). The basic-systems model of episodic memory. *Perspectives on Psychological Science, 1,* 277–311.

Rubin, D. C., Ciobanu, V., & Langston, W. (1997). Children's memory for counting-out rhymes: A cross-language comparison. *Psychonomic Bullletin & Review, 4,* 421–424.

Rubin, D. C., & Greenberg, D. L. (2003). The role of narrative in recollection: A view from cognitive and neuropsychology. In G. Fireman, T McVay, & O. Flanagan (Eds.), *Narrative and consciousness: Literature, psychology, and the brain* (pp. 53–85). New York: Oxford University Press.

Rubin, D. C., & Wallace, W. T. (1989). Rhyme and reason: Analyses of dual cues. *Journal of Experimental Psychology: Learning, Memory, and Cognition, 15,* 698–709.

Rubin, D. C., Wallace, W. T., & Houston, B. C. (1993). The beginnings of expertise for ballads. *Cognitive Science, 17,* 435–462.

Squire, L. R. (1987). *Memory and brain.* New York: Oxford University Press.

Squire, L. R., Stark, C. E., & Clark, R. E. (2004). The medial temporal lobe. *Annual Review of Neuroscience, 27,* 279–306.

Tinbergen, N. (1960). *The Herring Gull's World.* New York: Basic Books.

Wallace, W. T., & Rubin, D. C. (1988). "The Wreck of the Old 97": A real event remembered in song. In U. Neisser & E. Winograd (Eds.), *Remembering reconsidered: Ecological and traditional approaches to the study of memory* (pp. 283–310). Cambridge: Cambridge University Press.

(1991). Characteristics and constraints in ballads and their effects on memory. *Discourse Processes, 14,* 181–202.

White, N. I. (Ed). (1952). *The Frank C. Brown collection of North Carolina folklore. (Vol. II).* Durham, NC: Duke University Press.

13

Cognitive Predispositions and Cultural Transmission

PASCAL BOYER

We call those concepts and norms that seem to be shared within a group and differ from those of other groups "cultural." We call concepts and norms "cultural" if people have them *because* other people in their group have them or had them before. This suggests that transmission of concepts and norms is at the heart of what constitutes human cultures.

To what extent does cultural transmission require memory? The answer of modern cognitive anthropology is slightly surprising. If we understand "memory" in the ordinary sense of information about past situations that we can access and consider explicitly, the answer is that cultural transmission does not actually require as much of *that* kind of memory as we would generally assume. Indeed, a great deal of cultural transmission takes place outside of explicit memories, as I explain here. But memory, for psychologists, includes more than just explicit memories (Roediger, Wheeler, & Rajaram, 1993). It comprises systematic information about the social and natural environment, what is called "semantic memory," as well as the many skills and habits known as "procedural memory." Once we understand memory, as psychologists do, as including all these processes beyond conscious inspection (Roediger, 1990), then memory really is the crux of cultural transmission. In the pages that follow, I will justify these statements on the basis of a few examples of cultural domains where the work of memory (in the wider sense) has been extensively studied.

WHAT IS CULTURAL TRANSMISSION?

Let me start with a few examples of the kind of transmission phenomena anthropologists study. In two different domains, I will provide both a familiar and an "exotic" illustration, as a first indication of the range of variation:

Religious concepts. [a] Some people in the United States and European nations seem to take it for granted that an invisible agent (God) is aware of their actions and *cares* about them, about the moral aspects of their behavior. [b] Many people in the Solomon Islands have frequent interaction with their dead forebears, to whom they occasionally sacrifice a pig – a goodwill gesture that keeps the ancestors happy.

Ethnic categorization. [a] Most people in the United States know which of a small number of "ethnic" categories they belong to. Although these categories are sometimes defined in terms of a particular phenotype (skin tone, or other physical features), some members of a group do not look at all like the stereotype of the group. What matters is descent more than external appearance. [b] Many people in West Africa consider that craftsmen (blacksmiths, potters, weavers) are intrinsically impure, so that one should not share food, let alone have sex, with them. Even the members of such groups who do not practice the craft are impure. What matters is descent more than actual occupation.

Ritual behavior. [a] People in religious congregations, for example, at a service in a synagogue or church, engage in a variety of scripted, rigidly prescribed rituals supposed to produce real though unobservable effects. [b] Turkana people in Kenya organize a ritual in which people are enjoined to walk in a procession toward a bull, rub their bodies against the animal's head, kill it, and then carefully tread on its carcass.

How do we understand and explain the fact that these particular concepts and norms, about gods and ancestors and social categories and specific ritual actions, seem to be successfully transmitted, such that they are (at least roughly) shared among most people of a particular group, and often similar to what could be observed several years or generations before? We are often tempted to think that people have the same concepts and norms as other members of their group because they just "observed" and "absorbed" what was "in the air" as they grew up. This, obviously, is less than satisfactory, to say the least, although this type of answer until recently was more or less all that cultural anthropology had to say about cultural transmission. In the last twenty years or so, however, there has been considerable development in research about the evolutionary and cognitive background to the acquisition of culture (Sperber & Hirschfeld, 2004), to which this chapter can serve as an introduction.

CULTURE AS MENTAL EPIDEMICS

Culture is the aggregation of many episodes of individual transmission. Anthropological models of cultural evolution start from the assumption that what we observe as cultural representations and practices are variants of cultural traits found in roughly similar forms in a particular place or group, because they have resisted change and distortion through innumerable processes of acquisition, storage, inference, and communication (Boyd & Richerson, 1985; Sperber, 1996). In this way, the spread of specific variants of cultural representations (such as a particular belief or concept represented by a human mind) is formally analogous to the spread of alleles in a gene-pool. In particular, the tools of population genetics can be applied to the spread of cultural traits and allow us to predict their spread, given such parameters as the initial prevalence of a trait, the likelihood of transmission and various biases (Boyd & Richerson, 1985). Also, such models allow a formal description of the different possible connections between genetic evolution and cultural transmission (Durham, 1991).

The biologist Richard Dawkins summarized all this by describing culture as a population of *memes* which, like genes, are just "copy-me programs" (Dawkins, 1976). Genes produce organisms that behave in such a way that the genes are replicated – otherwise the genes in question would not be around. Memes are units of culture: notions, values, stories, and so on that get people to speak or act in certain ways that make other people store a replicated version of these mental units. A joke or a popular tune are simple illustrations of such copy-me programs.

To make sense of the transmission of memes, Sperber and colleagues put together an *epidemiological* framework to describe the mechanisms of cultural transmission (Atran, 1990; Boyer, 1994a; Hirschfeld, 1994; Sperber, 1985). An epidemic occurs when a group of individuals display similar symptoms. To explain what happened, you must understand the particular ways in which the human body reacts to the presence of this particular agent. Human minds are inhabited by a large population of mental representations. Most of them are found only in one individual, but some are present in roughly similar forms in various members of a group. To account for this is to explain the statistical fact that a similar condition affects a number of organisms, as, for example, in epidemics.

MEMORY, CULTURAL ENTROPY, AND COGNITIVE PREDISPOSITIONS

Before we proceed, let me underscore what is (as anthropological experience suggests) the wrong way to approach the transmission process. For a long time, cultural anthropologists have followed the recommendations of Emile Durkheim and other founders of modern sociology, that is, to ignore human psychology altogether and treat cultural facts, for example, American race-concepts or Solomon Island religion, only at the level of the group (see, for instance, Durkheim, 1947; Hertz, 1960). In other words, the relative success of cultural transmission should be considered as given, and the actual processes that support it could be left aside. (To be fair, this position made great sense at a time when our understanding of cognitive development, memory and other neurocognitive processes was extremely rudimentary, and would not have explained much of human cultures.)

More recent models of cultural transmission aimed to replace mythical notions like "collective memory" and "absorbing what's in the air" with a concrete, measurable process of transmission. People communicate with other people, they meet individuals with similar or different notions or values, they change or maintain or discard their ways of thinking because of these encounters, and so forth. What we call their "culture" is the outcome of all these particular encounters.

This, however, also raises a problem. No two minds are alike. When people receive and handle some information, they produce inferences that make sense of that information by bringing to bear all manners of available information from memory, most of which is highly idiosyncratic. This suggests that cultural "memes" undergo mutation, recombination and selection inside the individual mind every bit as much and as often (in fact probably more and more often) than during transmission between minds. We do not just transmit the information we received. We process it and use it to create new information, some of which we do communicate to other people. So how come there is similarity at all, if representations come from so many sources and undergo so many changes? To rephrase this, cultural transmission though individual events of communication should in principle lead to extreme cultural entropy, in which people in a group all entertain very different norms and concepts. What is the source of negative entropy or additional order?

Recent cognitive anthropology has suggested that the answer lay in the wealth of findings and models from experimental and developmental psychology, linguistics, neuropsychology, and the neurosciences. All of these converge to show that all normal human minds share a number of *cognitive predispositions* that make certain kinds of concepts and inferences particularly likely to occur. Even though the contents of memory are different in each individual, some common principles, most of which are not available to conscious inspection, complement and organize incoming information. So some kinds of inferences tend to go in particular directions, no matter where you start from. They constitute statistical "attractors" for cultural transmission (Claidière & Sperber, 2007). In the following sections, I will document the effects of such predispositions in various domains of human cultures. Cognitive predispositions are not just general *constraints*, for example, on the amount of material that can be acquired, on the capacity of attention and memory. Cognitive predispositions also consist in specific *domain-specific expectations* about the kinds of objects and agents to be found in the world. Human expertise about the natural and social environment, including what is often called "semantic knowledge," is best construed as consisting of different *domains* of competence. Each of these corresponds to recurrent evolutionary problems, is organized along specific principles, is the outcome of a specific developmental pathway and is based on specific neural processes. This domain-specific view of cognition informed by different principles was first popularized by developmental psychologists (Gelman, 1978; Gelman & Baillargeon, 1983) who proposed distinctions among physical-mechanical, biological, social, and numerical competencies as based on different learning principles (Hirschfeld & Gelman, 1994). This way of slicing up semantic knowledge has received considerable support from both developmental psychology and the study of highly specific cognitive impairment (Caramazza, 1998). Neuroimaging and cognitive neuroscience are now adding to the picture of a federation of evolved competencies that has grown out of laboratory work with children and adults.

If cognitive dispositions are domain-specific, this suggests that their effects on cultural transmission will be specific, too. For instance, from an early age, we have particular expectations about how sounds combine to produce speech. This is why children pay attention to some properties of verbal input more than others. In the same way, we seem to have specific expectations about the difference between inert objects and intentional agents, and these guide the way we pay attention to specific information about animals, plants and other natural objects. The notion of domain-specific predispositions explains the very familiar phenomenon, that cultural acquisition in different domains takes different routes. For instance, acquiring language or notions of kinship relations, friendship, or love is effortless and largely implicit; we do not realize that we are learning anything at all. Acquiring table manners or social hierarchies is not difficult either, but it is largely explicit; we know that we are learning something. We also know that what we learn is special to a particular group or society. Finally, acquiring the principles of algebra or theology is both explicit and effortful. All of this signals that different cognitive predispositions are involved and make the transmission of cultural material more or less transparent and more or less difficult.

RELIGIOUS CONCEPTS

Do people know what their religious concepts are? This may seem a rather odd question, but it is in fact an important one, and the true answer is probably in the negative. In most domains of mental activity, only a small part of what goes on in our brains is accessible to conscious inspection. For instance, we constantly produce grammatical sentences in our native tongue with impeccable pronunciation, often without any idea how this is done. Or we perceive the world around us as made up of three-dimensional objects, but we are certainly not aware of the ways in which our visual cortex transforms two retinal images into this rich impression of solid objects out there. The same goes for all our concepts and norms. We have some notion of what they are, but we certainly do not have full access to the way our minds create and sustain them.

In the same way, most of the mental machinery that sustains religious concepts is not consciously accessible. Indeed, experimental tests show that people's actual religious concepts often diverge from what they believe they believe (Barrett, 1998; Barrett & Keil, 1996). This is why theologies, explicit dogmas, scholarly interpretations of religion cannot be taken as a reliable description of either the contents or the causes of people's beliefs. For instance, the psychologist Justin Barrett showed that Christians' concept of God was much more complex than the believers themselves assumed. Most Christians would describe their notion of God in terms of transcendence and extraordinary physical and mental characteristics. God is everywhere, attends to everything at the same time. However, subtle experimental tasks reveal that, when they are not reflecting upon their own beliefs, these same people use another concept of God, as a human-like agent with a particular viewpoint, a particular position and serial attention. God considers one problem and then another. Now, that concept is mostly tacit. It drives people's thoughts about particular events, episodes of interaction with God, but it is not accessible to people as their "belief" (Barrett, 2002; Barrett & Keil, 1996).

To illustrate this and some further arguments about concepts of gods and spirits, let me make use of the anthropologist Roger Keesing's account of the Kwaio religion (Keesing, 1982), see more extensive discussion in Boyer (2001). The Kwaio live in the Solomon Islands; most of their religious activities, as described by Keesing, involve interacting with ancestors, especially the spirits of deceased members of their own clans, as well as more dangerous wild spirits. Interaction with these *adalo* (the term denotes both wild spirits and ancestors) is a constant feature of Kwaio life. People frequently pray to the dead or give them sacrifices of pigs or simply talk to them. Also, people "meet" the ancestors in dreams. Most people are particularly familiar with and fond of one particular *adalo*, generally the spirit of a close relative, and maintain frequent contact with that spirit. Now, Kwaio people need not be told that spirits can perceive what happens, or that they can make a difference between their wishes and reality. People are just told that, for instance, "the spirits are unhappy because we failed to sacrifice a pig for them."

A systematic investigation reveals that such notions of religious agency, despite important cultural differences, are highly similar the world over. There is a small repertoire of possible types of supernatural characters, many of whom are found in folktales and other minor cultural domains, although some of them belong to the important gods or spirits or ancestors of religion (Boyer, 1994b, 2000a). All these concepts are informed by very general assumptions from broad categories such as person, living thing, or man-made object. A spirit is a special kind of person, a magic wand a special kind of artifact, a talking tree a special kind of plant. Such notions combine (a) specific features that violate some default expectations for the domain with (b) expectations held by default as true of the entire domain. For example, the familiar concept of a ghost combines (a) socially transmitted information about a physically counterintuitive person (disembodied, can go through walls, etc.), and (b) spontaneous inferences afforded by the general person concept (the ghost perceives what happens, recalls what he or she perceived, forms beliefs on the basis of such perceptions, and intentions on the basis of beliefs).

These combinations of explicit violation and tacit inferences are culturally widespread and may constitute a memory optimum. Associations of this type are recalled better than more standard associations but also better than oddities that do not include domain-concept violations (Boyer & Ramble, 2001). The effect obtains regardless of exposure to a particular kind of supernatural beliefs, and it has been replicated in different cultures in Africa and Asia (Barrett, 1998; Barrett & Keil, 1996; Boyer & Ramble, 2001).

This situation, in which a certain cultural assumption (a) includes counterintuitive aspects and (b) activates an intuitive background, can be conceived as a cognitive optimum for cultural transmission, in that the assumption has both the initial salience and the inferential potential that contribute to its acquisition and use (Boyer, 1994a). This, obviously, applies to the fundamental principles underlying religious representations, not to the specific set of "surface" features that accompany them. For instance, the principle of intentional agents with counterintuitive physical properties is widespread the world over; but in each cultural environment it is accompanied with detailed, and highly variable explicit notions about the characteristics and behavior of those agents.

To sum up, we can explain human sensitivity to particular kinds of supernatural concepts as a by-product of the way human minds operate in ordinary, nonreligious contexts. Because our assumptions about fundamental categories such as person, artifact, animal, and so on are so entrenched, violations of these assumptions create salient and memorable concepts.

GODS AND MORALITY

The effect of intuitive expectations goes further. Most information about religious matters is about supernatural *agents,* who are described as "interested parties" in our moral choices (Boyer, 2000b). This means that the gods or the ancestors are not indifferent to what we do, and this is why we must act in particular ways or refrain from certain courses of action. As far as anthropologists know, people in most places conceive of some supernatural agents as having some interest in their decisions. This can take different forms. Christians, for instance, consider that God expects some particular kinds of behavior and will react to departures from the norm. People who interact with their ancestors, like the Kwaio, have a much less precise description of what the ancestors want, but it is part of their everyday concerns that the adalo are watching them.

Why are supernatural agents involved in our moral understandings? Some clues can be found in the development of moral understandings, which seem to appear very early in childhood. Indeed, Eliot Turiel has shown that even preschoolers have a good intuitive understanding of the difference between social conventions and moral prescriptions (so that beating up people is wrong even if no one told you so, while being noisy is wrong only if there was an injunction to keep quiet) (Turiel, 1983, 1998). Also, children make a difference between moral principles and prudential rules (do not leave your notebook near the fireplace). They justify both in terms of their consequences, but assume that social consequences are specific to moral violations. So experimental studies show that there is an early developed specific inference system, a specialized moral sense underlying moral intuitions. Notions of morality provide an initial basis on which children can understand adult moral views. This capacity for entertaining abstract intuitions about the moral nature of courses of action (without, of course, being able to explicate them) was found also in children with various amounts of experience with other children, in different cultures, and even in children with exceptional experiences of abuse or neglect.

Supernatural agents are usually represented as having full access to morally relevant information. That is, people represent a given situation, and represent some information about it that is relevant to social interaction, and they assume that the supernatural agent also has that information. Obviously, all this consists in tacit assumptions. After representing a particular behavior as wrong, and feeling guilty, it seems quite natural to assume that some other agent with full access also feels the behavior was wrong.

To recapitulate, both the notions of supernatural agency and that of religious morality are grounded in intuitive expectations that are not specific to religion. The successful cultural transmission of these norms and concepts requires that cultural information be of a specific format, that triggers activation of intuitive expectations about agency (some of which are violated, most of which are confirmed by religious notions) and about morality (most of which are enriched by the religious tradition). In an important way, the transmission of religion does not reduce to concepts and norms being "downloaded" from cultural elders to novices, and "memorized" by the latter. Memory effects are more specific. Information about religious agents and their moral interests is preserved to the extent that it triggers spontaneous inferences from cultural novices. These inferences are based on semantic, generally implicit memory structures that are similar in all normal minds, leading to the recurrent religious notions observed in human cultures.

ESSENTIALIZED SOCIAL CATEGORIES

People the world over *categorize* their social environment. That is, they do not just think they interact with individuals, but tend to see them as members of more general classes like families, social class, ethnic group, caste, race, lineage, or gender (Hirschfeld, 1988). People often categorize social groups by assuming that there are *natural* differences between them (Haslam, Rothschild, & Ernst, 2000).

Assumptions that groups have a common "nature" are particularly salient in the case of racial ideologies. Although "race" concepts have no actual foundation in genotypic similarities (Marks, 1995), they are universally understood as based on some natural principle, on undefined properties transmitted through biological descent rather than tradition or accident (Hirschfeld, 1996). In contrast to their alleged basis in immutable natural differences, these understandings are clearly influenced by power relations between groups (Stoler, 1991), which explains, for instance, why Jews in the United States, a dominated minority originally considered as biologically different, only recently became "white" in most Americans' understanding of the term (Brodkin, 1998).

In many different places, members of arbitrary social categories are maintained in a low social (and generally economic) status. These may be members of culturally specific groups (Ainu in Japan, tribal people in India) or technical specialists (undertakers or blacksmiths or potters in Africa and Asia). The latter case is particularly interesting in that many members of such groups do not practice or know anything about the trades in question. Most African blacksmiths and potters are still considered such even though no-one in their groups ever makes pots or smelts iron. In such caste systems, people of different groups are said to carry very different "natures," which supposedly explains why they should not intermarry or even come into close contact (Daniel, 1984; Quigley, 1993).

Why are these ideas so "natural" that they are found the world over and seem so intuitively obvious to most people? This is a complex issue, because several different cognitive predispositions are involved, and each coin to the successful transmission of tribute different aspects of "social essentialism."

To begin with, several authors have suggested that social groups may be construed in terms of *biological essentialism*, that is, as analogous to animal species (Atran, 1990; Boyer, 1990; Gil-White, 2001; Rothbart & Taylor, 1990). Essentialist intuitions are very robust and explicit in representations of the natural world. Animal species are intuitively construed in terms of species-specific "causal essences" (Atran, 1998). That is, their typical features and behavior are interpreted as consequences of possession of an undefined, yet causally relevant quality particular to each identified species. A cat is a cat, not by virtue of having this or that external features – even though that is how we recognize it – but because it possesses some intrinsic and undefined quality that one only acquires by being born of cats. This assumption appears early in development (Keil, 1994) so that preschoolers consider the "insides" a crucial feature of identity for animals even though they of course only use the "outside" for identification criteria (Gelman & Coley, 1991).

For this essentialist mode of understanding social categories, input conditions include the following: (a) some living things are presented as having common external features – a prototype; (b) they are all born of other members of the same category; and (c) there is no reproduction outside the category (Atran, 1998). So humans may process ethnic groups and some other social categories as if they were "species" because (a) category-based endogamy and (b) descent-based membership make them partly similar to living species (Gil-White, 2001).

In this interpretation, the understanding of the social world seems to be parasitic on intuitive biology. Indeed, members of the target group are often said to carry a particular "something" that is (a) undefined, (b) inherited, (c) unchangeable, and (d) causally efficacious. Racist ideology in the United States assumes that black people have "something" that is common to all of them and makes them different from whites, that this something is inherited rather than transmitted by tradition or education or a product of specific circumstances; but the ideology stops at explicating what that "something" actually consists of. Even though modern racial ideology mentions genes, no one *needs* such explicitation to hold the essentialist assumptions. In many places in Africa and Asia castes of craftsmen are explicitly construed as based on natural qualities: the people in question are thought to be essentially different from the rest by virtue of some inherited, internal quality. Blacksmiths in West Africa are supposedly different, they are all descended from blacksmiths – you cannot become a blacksmith, you are born a blacksmith.

Biological understandings, however, are not sufficient to explain other features of essentialised social categories, such as the notion that contact with some groups is potentially dangerous (Kurzban & Leary, 2001). Consider the notion of "miscegenation," a truly exotic concept for non-Americans, which denotes the possibility of adulterating white "essence" by mixing it with black. Various forms of the "one-drop rule" in antebellum United States or apartheid South Africa meant that any trace of black ancestry made one person black – although the reverse was never the case. Indeed, it is always the subordinate group that "trumps" other biological descent. Although people may derive pride or status from, for example alliances with or some distant ancestry from royalty or the upper class, this never makes them full-fledged members of these high-status groups. But having one low-caste ancestor, in caste or "race" ideologies, is enough for membership. Also, in many situations of "essentialized" social categories, people have the intuitions (a) that members of the subordinate group carry some dangerous, invisible substance, (b) that any contact with them can transmit that substance, and (c) that the amount or frequency of contact is irrelevant. In caste systems the world over we find the common assumption that contact of any kind (through sex, food-sharing, in some cases even conversation) can transmit some undefined, dangerous substance that is characteristic of a group.

These principles are very similar to those produced by the *contagion-contamination system*, a set of cognitive predispositions that produces strong feelings of aversion to (even very remote) contact with likely sources

of pathogens (decayed corpses, dirt, excrement, etc.). As Rozin and colleagues have shown, easy acquisition of such disgust reactions is vital to gen-
eralists like rats and humans (Nemeroff, 1995; Rozin, Haidt, & McCauley,
1993). More generally, pathogen avoidance is made very efficient by three
intuitions: (1) that pathogen presence is usually invisible, (2) that contagion
accompanies all sorts of different modes of contact, and (3) that the amount
or frequency of contact is irrelevant (Siegal, 1988). Note that these three features exactly match the underlying principles of magic: (1) the medium of
magical influence is usually invisible, (2) it can produce its effects in different
ways, and (3) there is no "dose effect" in magic.

This would explain the intuitive, easy acquisition and strong cultural
transmission of such notions. No one needs to be provided with an explicit
account of what makes some people dangerous or of why any form of contact is dangerous. These expectations come for free, as it were, in human
minds. All that cultural transmission does in this case is transfer them to
social categories instead of kinds of animals, plants, and substances.

Finally, the fact that some social categories are essentialised may also activate dispositions for *coalitional thinking*. One of the most solid and famous
results of social psychology is that it is remarkably easy to create strong feelings
of group-membership and solidarity between arbitrarily chosen groups (Tajfel,
1970). These well-known results demonstrate the extraordinary strength of the
human propensity towards group solidarity, what Matt Ridley called "groupishness" (Ridley, 1996). Humans are extremely good at using coalitional affiliation to carry out collaborative endeavors by efficiently allocating trust among
cooperators (Kurzban, 2001; Levine & Kurzban, 2006). People will spontaneously form groups where a certain degree of trust ensures co-operation and
mutual benefits. Coalitional solidarity presupposes an activity in which join-
ing is (presumably) voluntary, defection is possible, benefits can be accrued
by cooperation and there is a notable cost in being a cooperator when others
defect. There is now ample psychological evidence for a coalitional psychology, a specific kind of inferences that apply to these trust-based groups but not
to other forms of social interaction (Levine & Kurzban, 2006).

In a series of striking experiments, Kurzban and colleagues showed that
this coalitional psychology is probably involved in representations of "race"
by Americans (Kurzban, Tooby, & Cosmides, 2001). For many years, social
psychology experiments had shown that "race" was automatically encoded.
No matter what explicit instructions are given, no matter how irrelevant
race is, no matter how much extra cognitive work has to be done, participants always seem to recall the racial identity of the faces they saw during an experiment. On evolutionary grounds, Kurzban et al. reasoned that
"race" was automatically encoded because it was a proxy for coalitional

affiliation. Indeed, when subjects were required to encode coalitional links, their memory of racial identity was considerably confused.

This coalitional interpretation is also suggested by a more general *social dominance* framework (Sidanius & Pratto, 1999). In this model, ostracism and dominance behaviors result not just from the desire to stay with one's group or to favor one's clan, but also in a more insidious way to favor one's group in a way that maintains the other group's lower-status position. That is, what drives people's behavior is a coalitional structure in which it is actually advantageous to try and keep members of other groups in a lower-status position, with distinctly worse outcomes. This has important consequences. In classical "stereotyping" models, all members of the target group would be equally discriminated against. In the dominance model, males would be the prime targets for prejudice, as they constitute a more salient threat to one's coalitional advantages. This indeed seems to be the case (Sidanius & Pratto, 1999).

To sum up, then, the notion that people belong to a particular "race" or "caste" by virtue of descent, together with its implications for social interaction, seems to recruit various forms of cognitive dispositions, to do with biological essentialism, with contamination and with coalitional affiliation.

RITUALIZED BEHAVIOR IN GROUPS AND INDIVIDUALS

In all human groups one finds some form of ritualized activity. Here is an example from the Turkana of Kenya (Lienard, 2003) of the ritual sacrifice of an ox. The animal must be of a specific color and shine. The animal should ideally be sacrificed by a left-handed twin. In the sequence preceding the sacrifice, ritual participants circumambulate the ritual scene three more times and then gather in a semicircle, facing East. The animal is made to go around the dancers three times counterclockwise. At some point in the ritual, the members of the clan offering the ox approach one at a time the sacrificial ox and carefully rub their body from forehead to loin on the animal's forehead, in a gentle upward thrust, an operation made difficult by the animal's attempts to get loose and to shake its head violently. The ritual officer cuts the animal lengthwise at the level of the diaphragm/upper abdomen. The body is then spread at the center of the ritual scene. During the next phase of the ritual, clans regroup and people line up to cross finally the ritual field from west to east walking right through the ox's split body, being careful to tread on a puddle of chyme – taken from the animal's stomach – in which has been placed the axe used to give the ultimate death blow. Among the crowd of each clan, elders and men are first to pass, followed by adolescent girls and girls in age of marriage, then the mothers with children and finally the young unmarried men. The sacrificer and his assistants make sure that everyone passing through the carcass steps on the axe placed in the chyme before proceeding.

Why do people perform such behaviors? Naturally, there are all sorts of reasons why one should perform a particular ritual in a particular instance. What I mean here is more general. Ritualized behavior can be defined as by *compulsion* (one must perform the particular sequence), *rigidity* (it must be performed the right way), *redundancy* (the same actions are often repeated inside the ritual) and *goal-demotion* (the actions are divorced from their usual goals) (Bloch, 1974; Humphrey & Laidlaw, 1993; Rappaport, 1999). So what are the effects of ritualized behavior, such that individuals find collective rituals attention-grabbing and participation in such ceremonies compelling? Some general features or effects of this kind of scripted, rigid, and so on, behavior should explain why, all else being equal, it appears with such frequency in human cultures.

To explain this, we must take into account that ritualized behavior can be observed in other circumstances, in particular:

Children's rituals. Most children engage in ritualistic behaviors at a particular stage of development, starting at two, peaking at five and subsiding around seven. The behaviors include perfectionism, attachment to favorite objects, concerns about dirt and cleanliness, preoccupation with just-right ordering of objects, preferred household routines (Evanset al., 1997; Zohar & Felz, 2001).

Obsessive-compulsive disorder. In some people, intrusive thoughts and compulsions can evolve into full-blown obsessive-compulsive disorder, with stereotyped and repetitive activities with no rational justification (American Psychiatric Association, 1995). In most patients, the rituals are a spontaneous response to obsessive thoughts about potential danger, notably contamination and contagion (fear to catch other people's germs, to ingest contaminated substances, to pass on diseases to one's children or others), possible harm to others or to oneself (e.g., handling kitchen utensils and wounding people), as well as social ostracism following shameful or aggressive acts (thoughts about assaulting others, shouting obscenities, exhibitionism, etc.).

In these different contexts, of them we seem to find, not just the same organization of behavior but also a number of *recurrent themes*. Many rituals seem to focus around such themes as: pollution and purification, danger and protection, the possible danger of intrusion from other people, the required use of particular colors or specific numbers, the need to construct an ordered environment (Dulaney & Fiske, 1994). A ritual space or instruments are described as "pure" or "safe" (or on the contrary as the locus of concentrated "pollution") or the point of the ritual is to "purify" people or objects, to "cleanse" mind or body, and so on. These particular features are by no means universally associated with ritualized behavior, but they are so frequent that their recurrence deserves a special explanation.

On the basis of anthropological and neuropsychological evidence, we proposed a synthetic model of ritualized behavior (Boyer & Lienard, 2006) that focused on the following points:

1. *The Hazard-Precaution Repertoire: potential danger.* Human cognitive structures include a specific "Safety Motivation System" (Szechtman & Woody, 2004) for dealing with *potential* danger, with neural structures distinct from fear-systems responding to *actual* danger (LeDoux, 2003). This system is specifically focused on recurrent hazards such as predation, intrusion by strangers, contamination, contagion, social offence and harm to offspring. The system does not seem to respond in the same way to more recent potential dangers such as tobacco or cars (Mathews, Jang, Hami, & Stein, 2004). We call this system "Hazard-Precaution" system because it also includes some rudimentary descriptions of possible precautions, including avoidance (of other people), contact avoidance and disgust (against contamination), attention to traces and indirect signals (against intrusion and predation), hyper-vigilance and heightened anxiety.

2. *Complex ritual rules and working memory.* Many ritual prescriptions turn usually automatic behavior (speaking, washing, getting dressed etc.) into highly controlled behavior that requires sustained attention. An example is having to tie one's shoe-laces *three* times with the right hand and *four* times with the left hand. In patients' compulsive rituals, this results in "swamping" of working memory, so that the person cannot attend to stimuli and situations outside the ritualized action (Ursu, Stenger, Shear, Jones, & Carter, 2003; Zalla, Verlut, Franck, Puzenat, & Sirigu, 2004). We have argued that the same is true of collective ritualized behavior. The frequent combination of a positive prescription ("do *x* ...") and a negative one ("... while avoiding to do *y*") would seem to engage working memory and executive control in a way that is not usually present in everyday action flow.

3. *Working memory and intrusive thoughts.* Many patients state that performing the ritual is one way of inhibiting or repressing unwanted

thoughts (Salkovskis, 1985). In our view the "swamping" of working memory may constitute a spontaneous and moderately efficient form of *thought-suppression*, with some similarities to the suppression processes studied experimentally by Wegner and colleagues (Wegner & Erskine, 2003; Wegner & Schneider, 2003). So patients with complicated compulsions spontaneously design a kind of activity so demanding in cognitive control that intrusive thoughts can be, at least for a while, pushed away from consciousness.

This would explain the organization and contents of most individual ritualized behaviors, pathological or not. But how does that translate to features of collective rituals? Freud had suggested that these were a form of collective obsessive neurosis (Freud, 1906[1948]), but that is hardly a satisfactory explanation. A more parsimonious model would suggest that the existence of a Hazard Precaution system makes certain kinds of cultural recipes particularly attention-grabbing and compelling (Lienard & Boyer, 2006).

Consider, again, the question in terms of cultural acquisition and transmission. When a ritual such as the Turkana ceremony, described earlier, is organized, cultural novices receive all sorts of information, most of which implicit, about the sequence of actions prescribed. Occasions for ritual are often described in ways that overlap with the Hazard-Precaution Repertoire, for example threats to fitness such as famine or illness, invisible germs or miasma, dangerous invisible pollution present in newborn infants, dead bodies, and menstruating women (Bloch & Parry, 1982; Metcalf & Huntington, 1991). Also, as I said earlier, most collective rituals include such operations as washing and cleaning, checking and rechecking that a particular state of affairs really obtains, as well as creating a symmetrical or otherwise orderly environment (Dulaney & Fiske, 1994; Fiske & Haslam, 1997). All of these items of communicated information should result in some activation of the Hazard-Precaution system, probably less intense than in situations in which people directly encounter clues for potential danger.

Many aspects of collective rituals activate the Hazard-Precaution system by including typical clues for relevant potential dangers. In other words, witnessing or performing the prescribed actions should result in activation of the Hazard-Precaution system. This does not mean that participants in a collective ritual deliberately use the ceremony to express Hazard-Precaution themes, or that participation in such rituals has the anxiety-reducing effects observed in individual ritualized behavior. Collective rituals are culturally successful, that is transmitted from generation to generation, because they enjoy some transmission advantage over other variants. In our model, one important factor is that cultural ceremonies include various cues that activate the Hazard-Precaution system. Mention of Hazard-Precaution themes (e.g., there is an invisible danger about, there is "pollution," we need to "cleanse" a particular space, etc.) makes these kinds of collective action more attention-grabbing and compelling than possible variants that do not include such themes.

EXTERNAL STORAGE AS A MEMORY AID

So far, we have considered the effect of largely implicit, semantic memory structures, in the form of intuitive expectations, on the acquisition and elaboration of socially transmitted information. People receive some cultural "input" in the form of other people's utterances, gestures, or in the form of various artifacts. Because this input triggers activation of highly similar inferential processes in different people, they result in highly recurrent features of human cultures.

Now these transmission processes are made much more complicated by the development of external information storage. We are used to thinking of this as a feature of modern or at least complex state-based societies, with literacy, specialized scholars and complex teaching institutions. But it may be of help to begin with an example from a simpler form of social organization, to highlight the contribution of cognitive dispositions to this form of external memory.

Before literacy appeared in a few state societies, many groups had developed sophisticated ways of storing information outside individual minds. Familiar examples include the *qipu* of Peru, long strings along which knots would represent particular events and amounts of objects. The system was used almost exclusively for accounting purposes (Ascher & Ascher, 1981). In a more complex manner, various pictographic systems were developed in many different societies, to record particular events or provide an aid to the recitation of myths and the performance of rituals. These systems often comprised hundreds of distinct stylized symbols. They have often been considered as precursors to writing, as a form of "proto-writing" (see for instance Evans, 1908; Gelb, 1963).

As writing, these systems are obviously extremely limited. Each sign stands for a complex concept, but there is no expressive power beyond the limited list of signs (a few hundred at the most) and there is no combinatorial power at all. Juxtaposition is the only way of combining signs, and it is intrinsically ambiguous. Indeed, the only known way to express complex thoughts in writing is to encode *speech* rather than *concepts* (DeFrancis, 1989), and this is precisely something pictographic systems cannot do. However, the perspective may be misleading, and founded on hindsight (knowing how literacy developed) rather than a proper understanding of the functions of pictographic systems (Severi, 1987). The latter were generally used, not as expressive communication devices, but as efficient memory aids.

Consider, for instance, the sets of pictographic plates used by Cuna shamans (in Panama). Among the Cuna, each of a set of identified conditions is treated by a specific song, chanted by a specialist, a shaman, according to a supposedly rigid ritual sequence (Haya, Holmer, & Wassén, 1947; Reverte, 1968; Severi, 1987). Now, Cuna shamans have long used a highly elaborate system of pictography to provide convenient transcriptions of these chants. Each song corresponds to a series of plates that include dozens or hundreds of specific signs. The plates are not generally used during the rituals themselves but serve as memory-aids in the training of new shamans. This is made all the more indispensable as the long and complex songs are couched in an archaic or esoteric language specific to shamans. Consider, for instance, the *akualel*, a song for restoring departed souls to the body (Nordenskiöld, 1938, p. 557ff.). The song describes evil spirits who made off with the soul of the patient, causing various symptoms and misfortune. The shaman is supposed to send his own tutelary spirits to fight the thieves, bring back the soul and restore it to the patient's body (see Figure 13.1).Each of the signs stands for a verse or fragment of the song, for example:

1	Downstream by the river banks
2	God
3	placed near your houses, for your well-being
4	[the stones called] Nelenusakele
5	Akualele
6	Kunakalele – this I am advising you
7	I am talking about medicines
8	A good medicine I am telling you about …

Note some important characteristics of this use of pictographs as memory aids. First, there is no evidence that Cuna shamans established a common, unambiguous system of signs with standardized forms and conventional reference. Rather, ethnographers such as Nordenskiöld found a whole variety of idiosyncratic systems transmitted along lineages of shamans and apprentices. Second, even in each shaman's plate of drawings, each sign does not stand for a stable set of utterances but rather cues memory to the relevant utterance – one sign may trigger an ingle word in one context and a whole

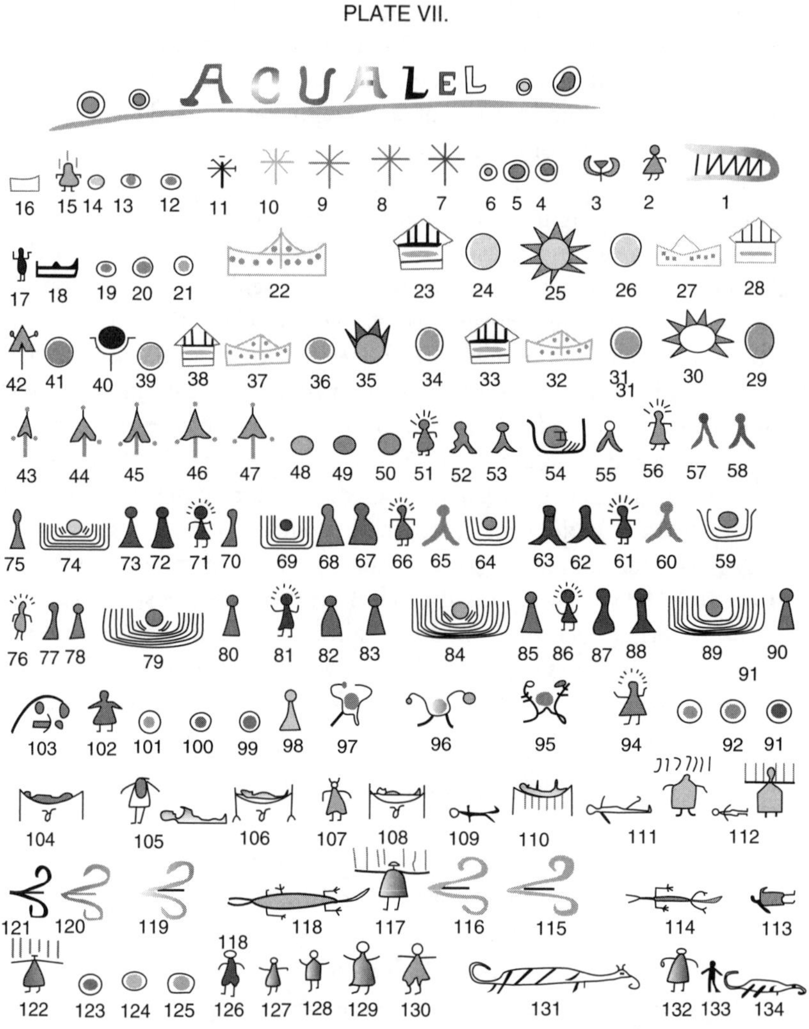

PLATE VII.

FIGURE 13.1 Pictographs to accompany recitation of the *akualel* song by Cuna shamans. This only shows the first part of the song. Numbers added by the editors. (From Nordenskiöld, 1938 Plate VII).

sentence in another. Third, the pictographs are only used in this ritual context, and the sentences they cue make no sense outside that particular situation (Severi, 2002). The songs themselves are predominantly reflexive, that is, they describe what the healer does as he is doing it, a common feature of shamanistic ceremonies.

The signs in such pictographic systems are used, not as repository of stable meanings, but as memory aids. Now it makes little sense to think of particular information as "stored in" or "expressed by" memory aids. These are powerful and efficient only to the extent that they reliably trigger specific inferences in the minds of their users. A particular mental event reliably occurs when a particular user is confronted with the physical object used as memory aid. This is true of "stickie" notes and knotted handkerchiefs, and applies in the same way to sets of pictographs.

There is a long tradition of such memory aids and techniques of memory, from Classical Antiquity to the Renaissance and modern mnemotechnics. Classical texts such as Cicero's *Ad Herennium* (Cicero & Caplan, 1964) mention such techniques as the famous method of *loci* – associating each item to be recalled with a specific stop on a familiar journey. In Classical culture, the arts of memory were a crucial part of the rhetorical training essential to the civilized life. In the Renaissance, a new development of the arts of memory combined with a mystical view of the many "signs" and "signatures" to be found in the external world – a system of correspondences between all observable aspects of Nature (Spence, 1984; Yates, 1966), see also Carruthers and Ziolkowski (2002) for original documents. Note that these "arts of memory" never assumed that information can be stored without elaboration or transformation. On the contrary, an essential goal was to find ways of combining, ordering and imagining information such that retrieval would be easier. In other words, Classical and Renaissance specialists accepted that memory works by *inferences* triggered by specific cues. Without the inferential system, the cue and the store are useless.

There is a lesson here, not just for the study of these sign-systems but more generally for our views about external storage of information, including in its modern, literate and digital forms. We often assume that external storage is just that, a form of "storage" in which information that may otherwise be in our minds can be downloaded, then retrieved in a similar form as need dictates. In the meantime, some external medium (words in books, pictographs in the Cuna drawings, digital sequences in a computer) "contains" the relevant information. However, information is not a static property of the strings of symbols, but a property of the processes they trigger in the interpretation device – which could be a human agent in the case of writing or a computer program in the case of digital memory. The words are only ink-patterns, the digital sequences are only streams of noughts and ones. To emphasize a trite but important point, it is only through interpretation that they refer to anything at all.

In other words, stored information works as what psychologists call a "cue" to a specific inferential process. The efficiency of the storage system is a function of how predictable these inferential processes are. Now, this is where some properties of literacy (and subsequent techniques) may be misleading. Because the physical symbols (words and pictures) are relatively stable, it seems to us that the interpretative work that gives them meaning is highly predictable and not too complicated. Both assumptions are false, as most students of literacy have noted. The physical stability of manuscripts and books never guaranteed the corresponding stability of the works (Maybin, 1994), as books convey meaning only against a background of mostly tacit, often historically specific assumptions.

LITERACY AND MEMORY IN RELIGION

For some time now, anthropologists have emphasized the specific aspects of literate cultures and the contrast with oral transmission, based on face-to-face contact between (generally) personally known interlocutors (Ong, 1977, 1982). Literacy seems to introduce an entirely new way of communicating and organizing information, first by allowing commmunication between distant individuals, also by making communication impersonal, and finally by introducing forms of representations (lists, tables, graphs) that are just not available to oral communication (Goody, 1968, 1977).

How does that interact with the kind of cognitive predispositions described in the previous sections? This would be the subject of a whole treatise, so I will only mention a single domain, that of religious thought and practices. Literate religion generally occurs in the context of large polities with a fair measure of social stratification, such as kingdoms or city-states (Maryanski & Turner, 1992). Such polities, kingdoms, and city-states, gradually provided specific economic niches for individuals and groups specialised in the provision of specific services, such as lineages or castes of specialized craftsmen, servants, functionaries, and scribes (Greif, 2006) but also religious specialists (Goody, 1986). A religious guild is a group that derives its livelihood, influence, and power from the fact that it provides particular services, in particular the performance of rituals (Boyer, 2001).

Services provided by such institutionalized groups differ from those of informal, generally orally based religious groups centered on shamans or mediums. The literate version generally constitutes a specific *brand*, that is, a kind of goods and services that is (a) clearly distinct from what others could provide, (b) similar regardless of which member of the guild provides it, and (c) exclusively provided by one organization. A Catholic priest offers rituals that are quite different from the ancestor-based rituals his African congregation were used to; but Catholic rituals are also quite stable from one priest to another; some observable features make it easy for most observers to distinguish between say a Catholic mass and what is offered by rival churches. The fact that literate religious institutions develop such brandlike identification is probably an optimal way for such groups to compete with the informal, more shamanistic version of religion. The latter always survives even when institutionalized religion dominates. The alternative is always available and often tempting as apparently more dramatic and efficacious than priest-based religion (Whitehouse, 2000).

In this competition, literacy is particularly important, as a technique that supports the kind of surface uniformity and stability that is necessary to developing and identifying a brand. By using a standard text (a scripture) and training literate specialists (priests), religious groups can survive because they offer predictable and distinctive services. In this sense, the presence of literacy does change the contents and organization of cultural concepts and norms (Goody, 1977). It supports, for instance, religious ontologies that include universally relevant, highly abstract gods or a god rather than locally bound ancestors and spirits. It also supports the notion that ritual specialists are replaceable technicians rather than medium-like persons with exceptional qualities.

IS THERE A CAPACITY FOR CULTURE?

Humans receive vast amounts of information from cultural elders and peers. They use that information to build conceptual structures, some aspects of which are group-specific and form the basis of what we usually call "cultures." It is convenient to date the appearance of modern-type cultures at the symbolic "explosion" that occurred some time between 100,000 and 50,000 years BP, with an abrupt change in the number and quality of artifacts produced by modern humans, with a great variety of new objects, some of which of no practical utility, the use of ochre, the first cave-paintings, elaborate burial practices, etc. An important difference with earlier cultural manifestations lies in the diversity of objects and representations, which may indicate the emergence of those group-level similarities and between-group differences that are typical of human cultures.

It is tempting to think of modern humanization as some kind of cognitive breakthrough that made human minds became more flexible, more capable of novelty, in a word more open. For some scholars, the crucial event is the appearance of complex verbal communication with a recursive syntax

(Bickerton, 1990) – but note that we do not know much about the date of this putative transition between early pidginlike idioms and modern language. Other scholars see cultural explosion as the effect of a new capacity for symbolic reference and a newly acquired flexibility in "off-line" mental representations (Donald, 1991), although again this is difficult to gauge from the archaeological record. Finally, the appearance of episodic memory in the form of "mental time-travel" has been hailed as the major development that allowed modern social and cultural phenomena (Tulving, 2001).

To go further than speculative proposals, one should think of this question in a properly evolutionary-psychological framework. First, we should describe the appearance of modern human cultures in terms of the specific neurocognitive capacities involved in cultural transmission – as documented by experimental evidence in the domain. As we saw earlier, people do not have a capacity for "absorbing what's in the air" – acquiring cultures is a complicated, domain-specific process. Second, we should consider neurocognitive systems that were and are plausibly affected by small, incremental genetic changes. Natural selection most likely did not result in a massive leap from "nonsymbolic" to "symbolic" minds but only in slow changes towards the modern form. Third, we must have some strong evidence that these gradual changes would have incrementally positive consequences for the organisms' fitness. It is not at all self-evident in what sense a more "cultural" organism is more fit than another – the advantages of this type of information transmission must be documented rather than taken for granted. We are still very far from such an evolutionary picture of early cultural evolution.

Some proposals however do make sense in terms of both the archaeological record and the experimental psychology evidence. Steven Mithen offers for instance a cognitive interpretation of the cultural explosion of the Upper Paleolithic (Mithen, 1996). Evolution resulted in the accretion and complexification of a large number of pan-specific cognitive capacities geared to task-specific problem solving. These "Darwinian algorithms" have clear input conditions, that is, they only attend to and handle information in a particular domain, such as intuitive physics, "theory of mind," but also more limited domains such as cues for parental investment, mate-choice, coalition-building, living-kind categorization, and so on (Tooby & Cosmides, 1992). Mithen argues that cultural explosion is the effect of significant changes in cognitive architecture, in particular of multiple information exchanges between modular capacities. The difference between early and modern Humans is not so much in the operation of each specialized capacity (intuitive biology, theory of mind, tool-making, intuitive physics) but in the possibility to use information from one domain in the course of activities monitored by another domain. So artifacts are used as body-ornaments, serving social purposes; biological knowledge is used in visual symbols; tool-making develops local traditions and makes efficient use of local resources, tapping information from "natural history intelligence." Most strikingly, this is the period when visual symbols take a "religious" appearance.

This makes good sense of the archaeological record – and in particular of the successes and limitations of early humans – it leaves open the question of what drives and more importantly what limits "cognitive fluidity" and the exchange of information between specialized systems. Indeed, a mind with such features runs the risk of belief-promiscuity, that is, the creation of a wealth of irrelevant or harmful associations and conceptual combinations (Cosmides & Tooby, 2000). An important contribution to cultural evolution may lie, precisely, in the capacity to limit fluidity, to select conceptual associations on the basis of relevance.

This is why Michael Tomasello and colleagues have argued that other aspects of human cognition are required for the evolution of cultures (Tomasello, Carpenter, Call, Behne, & Moll, 2005). Cultural transmission requires intuitive psychology (or "theory of mind") abilities. For instance, human tool-making requires sophisticated perspective-taking capacities that are beyond the abilities demonstrated in apes (Tomasello, 2000; Tomasello, Kruger, & Ratner, 1993) and this applies *a fortiori* to the transmission of complex norms and concepts. This, however, may be insufficient. As Tomasello and colleagues have demonstrated, some rudiments of this understanding of goals is present in other apes (Warneken & Tomasello, 2006). So a crucial component that is distinctly human may be a particular *motivation* to engage in coordinated action by monitoring other agents' goals and trying to adjust one's own behavior to these goals. This motivation, which appears very early is normal human infants, is strikingly absent in experimental and observational studies of non-human apes. It may also underlie the specific social and cultural deficits of autistic children (Tomasello et al., 2005).

Finally, and most important, successful cultural transmission requires successful human communication. The inferential processes described in this chapter reflect a general property of human communication, namely the ostensive-inferential transfer of information. Human communication does not work by downloading information (as a code system, e.g., honey bee dancing) but by demonstrating communicative intentions (Grice, 1975; Sperber & Wilson, 1995). That is, even banal conversations require that listeners construct by inference an optimally relevant interpretation of utterances, which cannot be directly decoded from what is said.

This feature is so fundamental to communication in humans that some authors see it as the most important stone on the road to modern culture (Sperber, 2006a, 2006b). Ostensive-inferential communication is necessary for language to acquire its expressive power but may have predated sophisticated, syntax-based language in human evolution. Organisms with some rudiments of relevance-based inferential communication can easily create stable communicative idioms (Hurford & Kirby, 1995) although the converse is less plausible. This view receives some support from developmental evidence of the very early development of relevance-driven, inferential communication in infants (Csibra, 2007; Gergely, Egyed, & Király, 2007).

To sum up, we now have at least a tentative list of those specific capacities that made cultural evolution possible, although it is probably sterile to look for the "magic bullet" that triggered the transition from other-animal cultures and traditions (Avital & Jablonka, 2000) into full-blown cumulative human cultures (Boyd & Richerson, 1996). Humans differ from other apes in many of their capacities, and most of them are involved in the appearance and transmission of cultures.

EPILOGUE: TWO ROLES FOR MEMORY

In the different domains surveyed here, cultural transmission involves a variety of memory processes, beyond what we generally call "memories," that is, explicitly represented information about past scenes. Indeed, I have mostly focused on memory processes that do not belong to the familiar domain of explicit, episodic memory, what is commonly called "memory." I emphasized a variety of processes that are, by their very nature, outside conscious inspection, yet prove to be crucial in the selection and organization of cultural material.

Naturally, this is only half the story, as far as memory in culture is concerned. I said that people produce spontaneous inferences on the basis of particular gestures and utterances – but that requires that people first attend to and then remember the utterances and gestures in question. For instance, I described the fact that people infer a straightforward "psychology of ancestors" as intentional agents, from the facts that people sacrifice to the ancestors and apparently talk to them. But to do that people have to recall what happened during those rituals. More generally, the material that triggers most relevant utterances is material that has been transmitted and recalled.

So there are two important roles for memory in cultural transmission:

a. Given particular input, people also recall the *surface features* of that input – the particular gestures and words used, the specific shapes of the visual patterns used, etc. This recall is obviously strongly constrained by the operating principles of episodic memory, a topic that I did not consider here (but see a thorough survey in Rubin, this volume);

b. Given particular cultural input, people build group-specific norms and concepts by inference – these inferences are strongly constrained by what I called cognitive dispositions, in other words stable features of semantic memory.

In the domains described here, there is a constant interplay between the workings of explicit episodic memory and the largely implicit processes that govern knowledge acquisition and belief fixation. For instance, in most religious traditions people explicitly transmit a variety of statements about supernatural agents; but the tacit counterpart of these statements, the fact for example, that agents have perceptions and memories, is supplied by our intuitive, largely tacit psychological assumptions. The same goes for morality, or for concepts of ethnic groups as based on essential qualities. In all these domains, I tried to suggest that we can replace the traditional assumption of "cultural downloading" with a more precise cognitive model. We can construe the various physical objects and events that people experience as so many *cues* that trigger specific *inferences*. As inferential processes are substantially similar in different minds, human groups can maintain a (rough) similarity in concepts and norms among a particular social group, what we call a culture.

REFERENCES

American Psychiatric Association. (1995). *Diagnostic and statistical manual of mental disorders* (4th ed.). Washington, DC: American Psychiatric Publishing, Inc.

Ascher, M., & Ascher, R. (1981). *Code of the quipu: A study in media, mathematics, and culture.* Ann Arbor: University of Michigan Press.

Atran, S. A. (1990). *Cognitive foundations of natural history. Towards an anthropology of science.* Cambridge: Cambridge University Press.

(1998). Folk biology and the anthropology of science: Cognitive universals and cultural particulars. *Behavioral & Brain Sciences, 21*(4), 547–609.

Avital, E., & Jablonka, E. (2000). *Animal traditions: Behavioural inheritance in evolution.* Cambridge, UK; New York: Cambridge University Press.

Barrett, J. L. (1998). Cognitive constraints on Hindu concepts of the divine. *Journal for the Scientific Study of Religion, 37,* 608–619.

(2002). Smart Gods, dumb Gods, and the role of social cognition in structuring ritual intuitions. *Journal of Cognition and Culture, 2*(3), 183–193.

Barrett, J. L., & Keil, F. C. (1996). Conceptualizing a nonnatural entity: Anthropomorphism in God concepts. *Cognitive Psychology, 31*(3), 219–247.

Bickerton, D. (1990). *Language & species.* Chicago: University of Chicago Press.

Bloch, M. (1974). Symbols, song, dance, and features of articulation: Is religion an extreme form of traditional authority? *European Journal of Sociology, 15,* 55–81.

Bloch, M., & Parry, J. (Eds.). (1982). *Death and the regeneration of life.* Cambridge: Cambridge University Press.

Boyd, R., & Richerson, P. J. (1985). *Culture and the evolutionary process.* Chicago: University of Chicago Press.

(1996). Why culture is common, but cultural evolution is rare. In W. G. Runciman, J. M. Smith & R. I. M. Dunbar (Eds.), *Evolution of social behaviour patterns in primates and man* (pp. 77–93). Oxford, England: Oxford University Press.

Boyer, P. (1990). *Tradition as truth and communication: A cognitive description of traditional discourse.* Cambridge: Cambridge University Press.

(1994a). Cognitive constraints on cultural representations: Natural ontologies and religious ideas. In L. A. Hirschfeld & S. Gelman (Eds.), *Mapping the mind: Domain-specificity in culture and cognition* (pp. 391–411). New York: Cambridge University Press.

(1994b). *The naturalness of religious ideas: A cognitive theory of religion.* Berkeley, CA: University of California Press.

(2000a). Cultural inheritance tracks and cognitive predispositions: The example of religious concepts. In H. Whitehouse (Ed.), *Mind, evolution and cultural transmission* (pp. 57–89). Oxford: Berg Publishers.

(2000b). Functional origins of religious concepts: Conceptual and strategic selection in evolved minds [Malinowski Lecture 1999]. *Journal of the Royal Anthropological Institute, 6,* 195–214.

(2001). *Religion explained. Evolutionary origins of religious thought.* New York: Basic Books.

Boyer, P., & Lienard, P. (2006). Why ritualized behavior in humans? Precaution systems and action-parsing in developmental, pathological and cultural rituals. *Behavioral & Brain Sciences, 29,* 1–56.

Boyer, P., & Ramble, C. (2001). Cognitive templates for religious concepts: Cross-cultural evidence for recall of counter-intuitive representations. *Cognitive Science, 25,* 535–564.

Brodkin, K. (1998). *How Jews became white folks and what that says about race in America.* New Brunswick, NJ: Rutgers University Press.

Caramazza, A. (1998). The interpretation of semantic category-specific deficits: What do they reveal about the organization of conceptual knowledge in the brain? *Neurocase: Case Studies in Neuropsychology, Neuropsychiatry, & Behavioural Neurology, 4*(4–5), 265–272.

Carruthers, M. J., & Ziolkowski, J. M. (2002). *The medieval craft of memory: An anthology of texts and pictures.* Philadelphia, PA.: University of Pennsylvania Press.

Cicero, M. T., & Caplan, H. (1964). *Ad C. Herennium de ratione dicendi (Rhetorica ad Herennium)*. London, Cambridge, MA: W. Heinemann; Harvard University Press.

Claidière, N., & Sperber, D. (2007). The role of attraction in cultural evolution. *Journal of Cognition and Culture, 7*(1–2), 89–111.

Cosmides, L., & Tooby, J. (2000). Consider the source: The evolution of adaptations for decoupling and metarepresentation. In D. Sperber (Ed.), *Metarepresentations: A multidisciplinary perspective* (pp. 53–115). New York: Oxford University Press.

Csibra, G. (2007). Teachers in the wild. *Trends in Cognitive Sciences, 11*(3), 95–96.

Daniel, E. V. (1984). *Fluid signs: Being a person the Tamil way*. Berkeley: University of California Press.

Dawkins, R. (1976). *The selfish gene*. New York: Oxford University Press.

DeFrancis, J. (1989). *Visible speech. The diverse oneness of writing systems*. Honolulu: University of Hawaii Press.

Donald, M. (1991). *Origins of the modern mind*. Cambridge, MA: Harvard University Press.

Dulaney, S., & Fiske, A. P. (1994). Cultural rituals and obsessive-compulsive disorder: Is there a common psychological mechanism? *Ethos, 22*(3), 243–283.

Durham, W. H. (1991). *Coevolution. Genes, cultures and human diversity*. Stanford: Stanford University Press.

Durkheim, E. (1947). *The elementary forms of the religious life*. New York: Collier Books.

Evans, A. (1908). *The european diffusion of pictography and its bearings on the origin of script*. Oxford: At the Clarendon Press.

Evans, D. W., Leckman, J. F., Carter, A., Reznick, J. S., Henshaw, D., & Pauls, D. L. (1997). Ritual, habit, and perfectionism: The prevalence and development of compulsive-like behavior in normal young children. *Child Development, 68*(1), 58–68.

Fiske, A. P., & Haslam, N. (1997). Is obsessive-compulsive disorder a pathology of the human disposition to perform socially meaningful rituals? Evidence of similar content. *Journal of Nervous & Mental Disease, 185*(4), 211–222.

Freud, S. (1906[1948]). Zwangsbehandlungen und Religionsübungen. In A. E. A. Freud (Ed.), *Gesammelte Werke von Sigmund Freud, chronologisch geordnet* (Vol. 7, pp. 107–116). London: Imago Publishing.

Gelb, I. J. (1963). *A study of writing*. 2nd ed. Chicago: University of Chicago Press.

Gelman, R., & Baillargeon, R. (1983). A revision of some Piagetian concepts. In J. H. Flavell & E. M. Markman (Eds.), *Handbook of Child Psychology, vol. 3: Cognitive Development* (pp. 121–143). New York: Wiley & Sons.

Gelman, S., & Coley, J. (1991). Language and categorisation: The acquisition of natural kind terms. In S. Gelman & J. P. Byrnes (Eds.), *Perspectives on language and thought: Interrealtions in development*. Cambridge: Cambridge University Press.

Gergely, G., Egyed, K., & Király, I. (2007). On pedagogy. *Developmental Science, 10*(1), 139–146.

Gil-White, F. (2001). Are ethnic groups 'species' to the human brain? Essentialism in our cognition of some social categories. *Current Anthropology, 42*, 515–554.

Goody, J. (1968). *Literacy in traditional societies.* Cambridge: Cambridge University Press.

(1977). *The domestication of the savage mind.* Cambridge: Cambridge University Press.

(1986). *The logic of writing and the organization of society.* Cambridge: Cambridge University Press.

Greif, A. (2006). *Institutions and the path to the modern economy: lessons from medieval trade.* Cambridge; New York: Cambridge University Press.

Grice, H. P. (1975). *Logic and conversation.* In P. Cole & J. L. Morgan (Eds.), *Speech acts* (pp. 41–58). New York: Academic Press.

Haslam, N., Rothschild, L., & Ernst, D. (2000). Essentialist beliefs about social categories. *British Journal of Social Psychology, 39*(1), 113–127.

Haya, G., Holmer, N. M., & Wassén, H. (1947). *Mu-Igala, or the way of Muu; a medicine song from the Cuna Indians of Panama.* Göteborg: Elanders boktryckeri aktiebolag.

Hertz, R. (1960). *A contribution to the study of the collective representation of death.* London: Cohen & West.

Hirschfeld, L. A. (1988). On acquiring social categories. Cognitive development and anthropological wisdom. *Man, 23,* 611–638.

(1994). The acquisition of social categories. In L. A. Hirschfeld & S. A. Gelman (Ed.), *Mapping the mind: Domain-specificity in culture and cognition.* New York: Cambridge University Press.

(1996). *Race in the making: Cognition, culture and the child's construction of human kinds.* Cambridge, MA: The M.I.T. Press.

Humphrey, C., & Laidlaw, J. (1993). *Archetypal actions. A theory of ritual as a mode of action and the case of the Jain puja.* Oxford: Clarendon Press.

Hurford, J. R., & Kirby, S. (1995). Neural preconditions for proto-language. *The Behavioral and brain sciences, 18*(1), 1.

Hutchins, E. (1995). How a cockpit remembers its speeds. *Cognitive Science, 19*(3), 265–288.

Keesing, R. (1982). *Kwaio religion. The living and the dead in a Solomon Island society.* New York: Columbia University Press.

Keil, F. C. (1994). The birth and nurturance of concepts by domains: The origins of concepts of living things. In L. A. Hirschfeld & S. A. Gelman (Eds.), *Mapping the mind: Domain specificity in cognition and culture* (pp. 234–254). New York: Cambridge University Press.

Kurzban, R. (2001). The social psychophysics of cooperation: Nonverbal communication in a public goods game. *Journal of Nonverbal Behavior, 25*(4), 241–259.

Kurzban, R., & Leary, M. R. (2001). Evolutionary origins of stigmatization: The functions of social exclusion. *Psychological Bulletin, 127*(2), 187–208.

Kurzban, R., Tooby, J., & Cosmides, L. (2001). Can race be erased? Coalitional computation and social categorization. *Proceedings of the National Academy of Sciences of the United States of America, 98*(26), 15387–15392.

LeDoux, J. (2003). The emotional brain, fear, and the amygdala. *Cell Molecular Neurobiology, 23*(4–5), 727–738.

Levine, S. S., & Kurzban, R. (2006). Explaining clustering in social networks: Towards an evolutionary theory of cascading benefits. *Managerial & Decision Economics, 27*(2–3), 173–187.

Lienard, P. (2003). *Le comportement rituel: Communication, cognition et action. Générations, âges et territoire: contribution à l'ethnographie de deux populations du Cercle Karimojong (Les Turkana du Kenya et les Nyangatom d'Ethiopie).* Université Libre de Bruxelles, Bruxelles.

Lienard, P., & Boyer, P. (2006). Why cultural rituals? A cultural selection model of ritualized behaviour. *American Anthropologist, 108*(4), 814–827.

Marks, J. (1995). *Human biodiversity: Genes, race, and history.* New York: Aldine de Gruyter.

Maryanski, A., & Turner, J. H. (1992). *The social cage. Human nature and the evolution of society.* Stanford: Stanford University Press.

Mathews, C. A., Jang, K. L., Hami, S., & Stein, M. B. (2004). The structure of obsessionality among young adults. *Depression & Anxiety, 20*(2), 77–85.

Maybin, J. (1994). *Language and literacy in social practice: A reader.* Clevedon, Avon, England; Philadelphia: Multingual Matters Ltd. in association with the Open University.

Metcalf, P., & Huntington, R. (1991). *Celebrations of death. The anthropology of mortuary ritual (2nd ed.).* Cambridge: Cambridge University Press.

Mithen, S. J. (1996). *The prehistory of the mind.* London: Thames & Hudson.

Nemeroff, C. J. (1995). Magical thinking about illness virulence conceptions of germs from "Safe" versus "Dangerous" others. *Health Psychology, 14*(2), 147–151.

Nordenskiöld, E. (1938). *An historical and ethnological survey of the Cuna Indians [arranged and edited by Henry Wassén].* Göteborg: Göteborgs Museum, Etnografiska Advelningen.

Ong, W. J. (1977). *Interfaces of the word: Studies in the evolution of consciousness and culture.* Ithaca, NY: Cornell University Press.

——— (1982). *Orality and literacy: The technologizing of the word.* London; New York: Methuen.

Quigley, D. (1993). *The interpretation of caste.* Oxford; New York: Clarendon Press; Oxford University Press.

Rappaport, R. A. (1999). *Ritual and religion in the making of humanity.* Cambridge, UK; New York: Cambridge University Press.

Reverte, J. M. (1968). *Literatura Oral de los Indios Cuna.* Panama.

Ridley, M. (1996). *The origins of virtue* (1st ed.). London; New York: Viking.

Roediger, H. L., III. (1990). Implicit memory: Retention without remembering. *American Psychologist, 45*(9), 1043–1056.

Roediger, H. L., III, Wheeler, M. A., & Rajaram, S. (1993). Remembering, knowing, and reconstructing the past. In L. M. Douglas (Ed.), *The psychology of learning and motivation. Advances in research and theory,* (Vol. 30, pp. 97–134): Academic Press, Inc, San Diego, CA.

Rothbart, M., & Taylor, M. (1990). Category labels and social reality: Do we view social categories as natural kinds? In K. F. G. Semin (Ed.), *Language and social cognition.* London: Sage Publications.

Rozin, P., Haidt, J., & McCauley, C. R. (1993). Disgust. In M. Lewis & J. M. Haviland (Eds.), *Handbook of emotions* (pp. 575–595). New York: The Guildford Press.

Salkovskis, P. M. (1985). Obsessional-compulsive problems: A cognitive-behavioural analysis. *Behav Res Ther*, 23(5), 571–583.

Severi, C. (1987). The invisible path. Ritual representation of suffering in cuna traditional thought. *Res. Anthropology and Aesthetics*, 14, 66–85.

(2002). Memory, reflexivity and belief reflections on the ritual use of language. *Social Anthropology*, 10(1), 18.

Sidanius, J., & Pratto, F. (1999). *Social dominance. An intergroup theory of social oppression and hierarchy*. Cambridge: Cambridge University Press.

Siegal, M. (1988). Children's knowledge of contagion and contamination as causes of illness. *Child Development*, 59, 1353–1359.

Spence, J. D. (1984). *The memory palace of Matteo Ricci*. New York: Viking Penguin.

Sperber, D. (1985). Anthropology and psychology. Towards an epidemiology of representations. *Man*, 20, 73–89.

(1996). *Explaining culture: A naturalistic approach*. Oxford: Blackwell.

(2006a). Conceptual tools for a naturalistic approach to cultural evolution. In S. C. Levinson & J. Pierre (Eds.), *Evolution and culture: A Fyssen foundation symposium*. Cambridge, MA: MIT Press.

Sperber, D. (Ed.). (2006b). *An evolutionary perspective on testimony and argumentation*. Mahwah, NJ: Lawrence Erlbaum Associates Publishers.

Sperber, D., & Hirschfeld, L. A. (2004). The cognitive foundations of cultural stability and diversity. *Trends in Cognitive Sciences*, 8(1), 40–46.

Sperber, D., & Wilson, D. (1995). *Relevance. Communication and cognition* (2nd ed.]. Oxford: Blackwell.

Stoler, A. L. (1991). *Sexual affronts and racial frontiers: National identity, 'mixed bloods' and the cultural genealogies of Europeans in colonial Southeast Asia*. Ann Arbor: University of Michigan.

Szechtman, H., & Woody, E. (2004). Obsessive-compulsive disorder as a disturbance of security motivation. *Psychological Review*, 111(1), 111–127.

Tajfel, H. (1970). Experiments in inter-group discrimination. *Scientific American*, 223, 96–102.

Tomasello, M. (2000). *The cultural origins of human cognition*. Cambridge, MA: Harvard University Press.

Tomasello, M., Carpenter, M., Call, J., Behne, T., & Moll, H. (2005). Understanding and sharing intentions: The origins of cultural cognition. *Behavioral and Brain Sciences*, 28(5), 17.

Tomasello, M., Kruger, A. C., & Ratner, H. H. (1993). Cultural learning. *Behavioral and Brain Sciences*, 16, 495–510.

Tooby, J., & Cosmides, L. (1992). The psychological foundations of culture. In J. H. Barkow, L. Cosmides & et al. (Eds.), *The adapted mind: Evolutionary psychology and the generation of culture*. (pp. 19–136). New York, NY, USA: Oxford University Press.

Tulving, E. (2001). Origin of autonoesis in episodic memory. In H. L. I. Roediger & J. Nairne (Eds.), *The nature of remembering: Essays in honor of Robert G. Crowder* (pp. 17–34). Washington, DC: American Psychological Association.

Turiel, E. (1983). *The development of social knowledge. Morality and convention*. Cambridge: Cambridge University Press.

(1998). The development of morality. In W. Damon (Ed.), *Handbook of child psychology* (5th ed., Vol. 3, pp. 863–932). New York: Wiley.

Ursu, S., Stenger, V. A., Shear, M. K., Jones, M. R., & Carter, C. S. (2003). Overactive action monitoring in obsessive-compulsive disorder: Evidence from functional magnetic resonance imaging. *Psychological Sciences, 14*(4), 347–353.

Warneken, F., & Tomasello, M. (2006). Altruistic helping in human infants and young chimpanzees. *Science, 311*(5765), 1301–1303.

Wegner, D. M., & Erskine, J. A. K. (2003). Voluntary involuntariness: Thought suppression and the regulation of the experience of will. *Consciousness & Cognition: An International Journal, 12*(4), 684–694.

Wegner, D. M., & Schneider, D. J. (2003). The white bear story. *Psychological Inquiry, 14*(3–4), 326–329.

Whitehouse, H. (2000). *Arguments and icons. Divergent modes of religiosity.* Oxford: Oxford University Press.

Yates, F. A. (1966). *The art of memory.* Chicago: University of Chicago Press.

Zalla, T., Verlut, I., Franck, N., Puzenat, D., & Sirigu, A. (2004). Perception of dynamic action in patients with schizophrenia. *Psychiatry Research, 128*(1), 39–51.

Zohar, A. H., & Felz, L. (2001). Ritualistic behavior in young children. *Journal of Abnormal Child Psychology, 29*(2), 121–128.

INDEX